A Basic Grammar of the Ugaritic Language

A BASIC GRAMMAR OF THE UGARITIC LANGUAGE

WITH SELECTED TEXTS AND GLOSSARY

BY

STANISLAV SEGERT

University of California Press
Berkeley Los Angeles London

UNIVERSITY OF CALIFORNIA PRESS
Berkeley and Los Angeles, California

UNIVERSITY OF CALIFORNIA PRESS, LTD.
London, England

Library of Congress Cataloging in Publication Data

Segert, S. (Stanislav)
A basic grammar of the Ugaritic language.

Bibliography: p. xviii
Includes index.
1. Ugaritic language—Grammar.
I. Title.
PJ4150.S39 1984 492'.6 83-18055
ISBN 0-520-03999-8

PRINTED IN THE UNITED STATES OF AMERICA

3 4 5 6 7 8 9

In memoriam

Claude François-Armand Schaeffer-Forrer

Table of Contents

Acknowledgments . . . viii
How to Use This Book . . . x
Abbreviations . . . xv
Bibliography . . . xviii

1–7. Basic Grammar
Analytical table of contents of parts 1–7 . . . 3
1. Introduction . . . 13
2. Writing . . . 19
3. Phonology . . . 27
4. Word Formation . . . 39
5. Morphology . . . 47
6. Function of Words in the Sentence . . . 83
7. Sentence Structure . . . 107

8. Selected Texts . . . 123
List of texts . . . 125
81. *Texts containing only nominal forms* . . . 129
82. *Texts containing verbal forms* . . . 131
83. *Texts containing a variety of sentence types* . . . 133
84. *Non-literary texts in autograph and transliteration* . . . 135
85. *Literary texts in autograph and transliteration* . . . 141
86. *Non-literary texts* . . . 148
87. *Poetic texts: Recurrent passages* . . . 157
88. *Poetic texts: Selected passages* . . . 159
89. *List and concordance of major texts* . . . 168

9. Glossary . . . 175
91. *Arrangement* . . . 177
92. *Words and meanings* . . . 177
93. *Glossary to selected texts in section 8* . . . 178

10. Paradigms and Surveys . . . 207
101. *Paradigms of pronouns, nouns, and verbs* . . . 209
101.1. *Personal pronouns* . . . 209
101.2. *Nouns* . . . 209
101.3. *Verbs: simple active pattern (G)* . . . 210
101.4. *Verbs: derived patterns* . . . 210
102. *Survey of nominal and verbal forms and markers* . . . 211
102.1. *Sequence of markers in verbal patterns and forms* . . . 211
102.2. *Homographic nominal and verbal forms* . . . 211

Acknowledgments

This grammar of the Ugaritic language is dedicated to the memory of Claude François-Armand Schaeffer, who devoted the greater part of his life to the excavation of Ugarit, an ancient city buried under a hill called Ras Shamra. During the twenty-sixth excavation season, in 1963, Professor Schaeffer invited the author to participate in the excavations, enabling him to form a priceless direct acquaintance with the site which provided virtually all the material for this grammar. Professor Schaeffer's help and encouragement were unflagging and are remembered with deep gratitude.

The author of the grammar of any recently deciphered language must draw on the pioneering works of decipherers, editors, commentators, and other scholars. The author of this grammar is especially indebted to Cyrus H. Gordon, whose Ugaritic grammars gave him the opportunity to learn the language and provided him with many suggestions for further research.

Both this brief grammar and the forthcoming longer version have benefited from criticism by many scholars, including (in alphabetic order): John A. Emerton (Cambridge), Paul W. Gaebelein (Pasadena, California), Harold L. Ginsberg (New York), Lester L. Grabbe (Kingston-on-Hull, England), Michael Heltzer (Haifa), William J. Horwitz (Norman, Oklahoma), Alan S. Kaye (Fullerton, California), Samuel E. Loewenstamm (Jerusalem), David Marcus (New York), Dennis Pardee (Chicago), Marvin H. Pope (New Haven, Connecticut), Jaan Puhvel (Los Angeles), and Matitiahu Tsevat (Cincinnati, Ohio).

At the meeting of the Ugaritic Study Group of the Society of Biblical Literature held on December 19, 1981, in San Francisco, carefully prepared by Conrad L'Heureux (Dayton, Ohio) and chaired by Bruce Zuckerman (Los Angeles), Barry Bandstra (Beaver Falls, Pennsylvania), Robert M. Good (Wilmington, Delaware), Simon Parker (Boston), and David Wortman (Madison, Connecticut) provided helpful comments on the brief grammar, while the late, well-remembered Mitchell Dahood presented useful parallels to Ugaritic from the ancient Semitic language of Ebla.

The author is grateful to the many scholars who have sent him their publications through the years of his work on this grammar. For information on the latest archeological finds outside Ugarit, he is particularly grateful to Pierre Bordreuil (Paris and Beirut) and to Helmer Ringgren (Uppsala).

Thanks are also due to the author's students in Ugaritic courses given in 1955–1956 at the Charles University in Prague, in 1968–1969 at the Johns Hopkins University in Baltimore, and from 1969 on at the University of California, Los Angeles. Their keen interest and searching comments have contributed much.

In Summer, 1983, while doing research as a Fulbright Scholar at the University of Münster, the author had the opportunity to use a copy of the KTU with up-to-date corrections. Thanks are due to Professors Oswald Loretz and Manfried Dietrich, Directors of Ugarit-Forschung, for their kind permission to use the improved KTU readings in this grammar.

For the editing of this work, the author thanks Douglas M. Nelson (Powell, Wyoming) and John R. Miles (University of California Press). During the author's 1983 stay in Europe, the final copyediting was done by Michael Patrick O'Connor (Ann Arbor, Michigan). The author gladly acknowledges Dr. O'Connor's efforts to make the style of the grammar more accessible to American students.

Cyndy Miller and David Zapf, who performed the difficult task of typesetting the work at Eisenbrauns (Winona Lake, Indiana), and Dave Baker, who did the pasteup, deserve best thanks for their understanding and care.

For help in the proof-reading, the author thanks his graduate students: James Platt, who checked the references to texts; Karen Masterson and Stanley Soderberg, who tested the suitability of the grammar for self-teaching.

Finally, the author must express his gratitude to his children, Eva and Jan, for their help in typing and in the revision of his English style; and to his wife Jarmila, who has typed and retyped the manuscript over the years.

These and others who have kindly and efficiently helped the author in his work on the grammar will share in any positive evaluation that may be accorded it. The traces of long and sometimes complicated work on a grammar can be recognized by discerning users. Any proposals for improvement will be gratefully accepted by the author.

Stanislav Segert
University of California, Los Angeles
May, 1984

How to Use This Book

In 1929, the first cuneiform tablet, inscribed with previously unknown signs, was found during archeological excavations at Ras Shamra (ancient Ugarit) in northern Syria. Since then a special discipline, sometimes called Ugaritology, has arisen. The impact of the Ugaritic language and of the many texts written in it has been felt in the study of Semitic languages and literatures, in the history of the ancient Near East, and especially in research devoted to the Hebrew Bible. In fact, knowledge of Ugaritic has become a standard prerequisite for the scientific study of the Old Testament.

The Ugaritic texts, written in the fourteenth and thirteenth centuries B.C., represent the oldest complex of connected texts in any West Semitic language now available (1984). Their language is of critical importance for comparative Semitic linguistics and is uniquely important to the critical study of Biblical Hebrew. Ugaritic, which was spoken in a northwestern corner of the larger Canaanite linguistic area, cannot be considered a direct ancestor of Biblical Hebrew, but its conservative character can help in the reconstruction of the older stages of Hebrew phonology, word formation, and inflection. These systems were later—that is, during the period in which the biblical texts were actually written—complicated by phonological and other changes.

The Ugaritic texts are remarkable, however, for more than just their antiquity and their linguistic witness. They present a remarkably vigorous and mature literature, one containing both epic cycles and shorter poems. The poetic structure of Ugaritic is noteworthy, among other reasons, for its use of the "parallelism of members" that also characterizes such ancient and archaizing poems in the Hebrew Bible as the Song of Deborah (in Judges 5), the Song of the Sea (in Exodus 15), Psalms 29, 68, and 82, and Habakkuk 3.

Textual sources and their rendering

The basic source for the study of Ugaritic is a corpus of texts written in an alphabetic cuneiform script unknown before 1929; this script represents consonants fully and exactly but gives only limited and equivocal indication of vowels. Our knowledge of the Ugaritic language is supplemented by evidence from Akkadian texts found at Ugarit and containing many Ugaritic words, especially names written in the syllabic cuneiform script. Scholars reconstructing the lost language of Ugarit draw, finally, on a wide variety of comparative linguistic data, data from texts not found at Ugarit, as well as from living languages. Evidence from Phoenician, Hebrew, Amorite, Aramaic, Arabic, Akkadian, Ethiopic, and recently also Eblaitic, can be applied to good effect.

For the student, as well as for the research scholar, it is important that the various sources of Ugaritic be distinguished in modern transliteration or transcription. Since many of the texts found at Ugarit are fragmentary or physically damaged, it is well for students to be clear about what portion of a text that they are reading actually survives and what portion is a modern attempt to fill in the blanks. While the selected texts in section **8** reflect the state of preservation in detail, in the other sections of the grammar standardized forms are presented, based on all available evidence.

Suggestions for the study of Ugaritic

Since the study of Ugaritic is becoming part of standard equipment for serious students of the Hebrew Bible, it was thought necessary to produce a basic grammar suitable for both elementary classroom instruction and for study without a teacher.

The presentation of the Ugaritic grammatical system in this book is basically recognitive and analytic. Direct evidence from the Ugaritic texts is clearly distinguished from supplemental data from other sources and languages. The reconstructions proposed may be improved in the future, as more data and the results of further study become available. In spite of the efforts of more than a generation of scholars, the interpretation of many Ugaritic linguistic phenomena and of many passages in the Ugaritic texts remains uncertain and controversial.

It would be difficult to undertake the study of Ugaritic without knowledge of a related Semitic language. Since so many students of Ugaritic are interested in this language because of its relation to the language and literature of the Hebrew Bible, this grammar is addressed largely to them; a fair knowledge of Biblical Hebrew may be considered a prerequisite for effective use of this grammar. Students who know Akkadian will be able to put their knowledge to good use, as will those who know Classical or Modern Standard Arabic. Most of the linguistic phenomena in Ugaritic for which no exact parallel can be found in Biblical Hebrew do find a parallel in one of these tongues, e.g., Arabic has the postvelar and interdental consonants, the three basic qualities of the vowel, and the case endings.

For more detailed study of Ugaritic language, literature and culture, knowledge of French is necessary, since nearly all first editions of the texts and archeological reports were provided by French scholars.

Suggestions for self-instruction

Since the Ugaritic signs can be rendered exactly and unequivocally in transliteration, the beginning student is not required to start—as is usual in learning a Semitic language—with the writing system. Rather, he should acquaint himself first with the inventory and the conventional pronunciation of the Ugaritic consonants and vowels (**32**, **33**). In order to read and interpret correctly the Ugaritic words quoted in the grammar, he ought to have read the basic information on the Ugaritic writing system (**22.3**), but the actual shapes of the Ugaritic cuneiform letters may be learned later.

The student should next turn his attention to morphology (**5**): pronouns, nouns, numerals, strong verbs, prepositions, and conjunctions (**51–53**; **54.1–2**; **56–57**). While studying basic morphology, the student may read the introductory readings (**81** and **82**).

Syntax will be learned from the sample sentences (**83**) and from the syntactic sections of the grammar (**6** and **7**). The further reading of samples from non-literary (**84**) and literary (**85**) texts should be accompanied by detailed study of the grammar.

Finally, the student will proceed to the selection of both non-literary and literary texts (**86–88**) offered without commentary. Special attention should be devoted to passages which depict recurring situations and actions (**87**). The words used in the selections in **8** are contained in the glossary (**9**). It is recommended, however, that the student have worked through the entire grammar before reading **86–88**.

The paradigms of basic pronominal, nominal and verbal forms (**10.1**) are meant both as a guide to morphology and as an aid for reading the texts. For this purpose, the list of schematic written forms and their various reconstructions and functions (**10.2**) may be found useful.

Presentation of the texts

In this grammar two systems of quotation are used, one for alphabetic and the other for syllabic texts. The alphabetic texts are quoted according to the system used in KTU. In this convenient system the first digit of a text number indicates the type of text; the following number is the serial number of the text, according to the sequence in which it was found (with exception of 1.1–1.25, for which the numbering follows CTA). Roman numerals indicate column numbers, and the last number(s) refer to the line(s) of the tablet or inscription.

There are eight categories of texts according to KTU:

1. Literary and religious texts: 1.1–1.161
2. Letters: 2.1–2.72
3. Contracts: 3.1–3.9
4. Lists and economic documents: 4.1–4.767
5. Alphabets and school exercises: 5.1–5.22
6. Inscriptions on seals, labels, ivories and other objects: 6.1–6.63
7. Not classified: 7.1–7.217
8. Illegible: 8.1–8.30

The syllabic texts from Ugarit are quoted according to the editions in the volumes of the series Mission de Ras Shamra (P:III; P:IV; P:VI; U:V; U:VI; U:VII) and in the journals Syria and Revue d'Assyriologie. See also below, section **89**, List and Concordance of Major Texts.

Transliteration and transcription

1. *Alphabetic texts.*

Ugaritic alphabetic texts are presented and quoted in this grammar according to the edition of M. Dietrich, O. Loretz, and J. Sanmartín, Die keilalphabetischen Texte aus Ugarit. Teil 1 Transkription, abbreviated KTU; cf. B 42:1. The editors kindly supplied material for several corrections. Minor differences in presentation are listed at f. here below.

Ugaritic signs are transliterated, in a one-to-one correspondence, by letters of the Latin alphabet in lower-case italic type with certain diacritical marks, e.g., *rb khnm, arṣ, yšu, il, yrḫ*. The complete Ugaritic alphabet in transliteration is given in **21.3.**

Note also the following features:

a. Ugaritic signs which cannot be read with certainty are transliterated by Latin letters in lower-case roman type, e.g., ḫrṣ, *lušḫ*r ḫlmẓ.

b. Letters that may be the result of scribal error in the original are indicated by an exclamation point after the affected letter, e.g., *lw*!*m*. Letters emended by a modern editor are indicated in the same way, but transliterated in lower-case roman type, e.g., *l*k!*m* (emended from the alleged scribal error *lw*!*m*).

c. Letters, words, or signs which have been restored where a text is damaged or incomplete are indicated by Latin letters in lower-case roman type in brackets, e.g., *i*[lm], *aṯr*[t.y]m.

d. Letters, words, or signs to be omitted from the text on the basis of editorial emendation are indicated by Latin letters in lower-case roman type in angle brackets, e.g., *aṯ<t>rt*, *wšm<.>mn*.

e. Letters or words added to the text by editorial emendation are indicated by Latin letters in lower-case roman type within parentheses, e.g., *tštn.y*(n), *km.*(mhry.)*nḥšm*.

f. The transliteration system used here differs from that of KTU in the following details: the last letter of the Ugaritic alphabet is transliterated s̀ (the sign ś, used in KTU, may lead to confusion with Hebrew śīn); fully preserved cuneiform letters are given here in italic type (KTU uses roman type), those damaged in roman type (in KTU, roman type, followed by an asterisk); traces of letters are indicated by – (KTU uses x); scribal errors and emendations are marked by ! (KTU adds emended words in round brackets); erased letters are omitted here (in KTU they are given with the indication "Rasur").

2. *Syllabic texts*

There exists no one-to-one correspondence between syllabic cuneiform signs and individual Latin letters. Moreover, no simple list of syllabic transcriptions can be given—the number of signs to be transcribed is large.

The transcription of the syllabic signs employs the letters of the Latin alphabet in lower-case italic type. The signs used in writing a word are connected by dashes, e.g., *a-ši-ru-ma*.

In this as in other features of the syllabic transcription, we follow the system employed in the original editions of these texts by C. Virolleaud, E. Dhorme, J. Nougayrol and others in the journal Syria and the volumes of the series Mission de Ras Shamra. (This system differs in some respects from general current Assyriological practice.)

Note also these features of the transcription:

a. The colon preceding a transcribed word represents a "gloss wedge," a sign in the original Akkadian indicating that the following word is foreign, e.g., *:nap-ki-ma*; generally this marks a native (Ugaritic) word in an Akkadian context.

b. Logograms or word-signs in Akkadian cuneiform syllabic writing are rendered by Latin letters in lower-case roman type, e.g., ilu-milku, ili-*mu-lik*.

c. The so-called determinatives of the syllabic script, which were not pronounced, are given in round brackets; e.g., (āl) for "city" and (d) or (il) for "god."

d. Restored words, letters, or signs are given in square brackets, as in the system for alphabetic transliteration; e.g., *ḫu-r*[a-ṣu].

e. Sumerian logograms of uncertain or disputed reading are rendered by Latin letters in upper-case roman type, e.g., IM.

f. Uncertain readings or reconstructions are indicated by a question mark in round brackets after the affected reading or reconstruction, e.g., *ba-ta-qú*(?) U:V:137:38′; *ša-d*[u-ú(?)] U:V:131:11′.

3. *Phonological reconstructions*

Phonological reconstruction of the elements of the Ugaritic language is made possible by supplementing the Ugaritic evidence with data from related Semitic languages. The similarity and the consistency of both consonantal and vocalic systems in these languages provide a relatively high probability for these reconstructions, though further finds and continuing research may bring improvement.

Note these devices used to represent phonological reconstructions:

a. Latin letters in lower-case roman type within slash brackets indicate phonological reconstructions, e.g., /rabbu/, /ᶜāširūma/, /yiššaᵓu/.

b. The asterisk indicates a hypothetical form or phoneme, e.g., *yinšaᵓu.

c. The wedge indicates phonological evolution; it is placed between an original form and a later form of a word, e.g., *yinšaᵓu > /yiššaᵓu/.

4. *Words from other languages*

Words from languages other than Ugaritic are given in Latin letters in lower-case roman type with a preceding indication of the names of the language. Note these abbreviations especially: Akkad(ian), Arab(ic, Classical), Aram(aic), Gr(eek), H(ebrew), Ph(oenician). E.g., Aram. dāliq, Akkad. ayyābu, Gr. chrysos.

Abbreviations

1. *General*

abs., absol.	absolute
acc.	accusative
act.	active
C	consonant
cf.	compare
coll.	collective
constr.	construct
dem.	demonstrative
det.	determinative *or* determined (state)
DN	divine name
du.	dual
f., fem.	feminine
gen.	genitive
gen.-acc.	genitive-accusative
GN	geographical name
imperf.	imperfect
imper.	imperative
inf.	infinitive
juss.	jussive
Kt.	Ketib
m., masc.	masculine
part.	participle
pass.	passive
perf.	perfect
pl., plur.	plural
PN	personal name
pref.	prefix
pron.	pronoun
refl.	reflexive
rel.	relative
S	semivowel
sing.	singular
subj.	subjunctive
suff.	suffix(ed pronoun)
V	vowel or short vowel
V̄	long vowel
w. suff.	with suffixed pronoun

2. *Verbal patterns*

UGARITIC

G	simple active (G = ground)
Gp	simple passive
Gt	simple reflexive
N	reciprocal/passive (pref. /n-/)
D	factitive active (D = doubled)
tD	factitive reflexive
Dp	factitive passive
L	factitive active (L = lengthened [vowel after first root consonant])
tL	factitive reflexive
R	factitive active (R = repeated [consonants of root])
Š	causative active (pref. /š-/)
Šp	causative passive
Št	causative reflexive
C	internal causative active

ARAMAIC, SYRIAC

Pe.	Pə^{c}al cf. G
Pa.	Pa^{c}ēl cf. D
Ap.	$^{\supset}$Ap^{c}ēl cf. Š
Ha.	Hap^{c}ēl cf. Š
Etp.	Etpə^{c}ēl cf. Gt
Etpa.	Etpa^{cc}al cf. tD

HEBREW

Q.	Qal cf. G
N.	Nip^{c}al cf. N
Pi.	Pi^{c}ēl cf. D
Hi.	Hip^{c}īl cf. Š
Hitpa.	Hitpa^{c}ēl cf. tD

ARABIC

I	cf. G & Gp
II	cf. D & Dp
III	cf. L
IV	cf. Š & Šp
V	cf. tD
VI	cf. tL
VII	cf. N
VIII	cf. Gt
X	cf. Št

3. *Signs*

>	becomes
<	developed from
|	line division
//	parallel to
*	reconstructed form for an older stage
ʹ	stress
/ /	phonemic reconstruction
< >	ancient scribal errors to be deleted from the text
+ +	ancient additions to the text
°	a text given in **8** in full
( )	additions to the text proposed by modern scholars
!	error (after a letter in italics); its emendation (after a letter in roman characters)

4. *Languages*

Akkad.	Akkadian
Amor.	Amorite
Anc.-Aram.	Ancient Aramaic
Arab.	Arabic
Aram.	Aramaic
Bibl.-Aram.	Biblical Aramaic
EA	El-Amarna texts
Egypt.	Middle Egyptian
Eng.	English
ESA	Epigraphic South Arabian
Eth.	Ethiopic
Gr.	Greek
H., Hebr.	Biblical Hebrew
Imp.-Aram.	Imperial Aramaic
Nabat.-Aram.	Nabatean Aramaic
Old-Canaan.	Old Canaanite
Palm.-Aram.	Palmyrene Aramaic
Phoen.	Phoenician
Postbibl.-H.	Postbiblical Hebrew
Pun.	Punic
Sumer.	Sumerian
Syr.	Syriac
Yaudi-Aram.	Yaudi Aramaic

5. *Books*

B	Bibliography, pp. xviii and following, below.
BGUL	A Basic Grammar of the Ugaritic Language (this volume)
Cowley	A. E. Cowley, Aramaic Papyri of the Fifth Century B.C. Oxford 1923.
CRAIBL	Comptes-rendus de l'Académie des Inscriptions et Belles-Lettres, B 82:3
CTA	Corpus des tablettes en cunéiformes alphabétiques. . . , B 41:1
KAI	H. Donner – W. Röllig, Kanaanäische und aramäische Inschriften. I. Wiesbaden 1966.
Kraeling	E. G. Kraeling, The Brooklyn Museum Aramaic Papyri. New Haven 1953.
KTU	Die keilalphabetischen Texte aus Ugarit, B 42:1
P	Palais royal d'Ugarit. . . , B 44:1–3
RA	Revue d'Assyriologie, B 82:6
U	Ugaritica. . . , B 21:1
UT	C. H. Gordon, Ugaritic Textbook, B 21:1

Bibliography

Abbreviations in the Bibliography:

AnOr	Analecta Orientalia. Roma: Pontificium Institutum Biblicum.
AOAT	Alter Orient und Altes Testament. Kevelaer: Butzon & Bercker/Neukirchen-Vluyn: Neukirchener Verlag
BSAW	Berichte über die Verhandlungen der Sächsischen Akademie der Wissenschaften zu Leipzig. Philologisch-historische Klasse. Berlin: Akademie-Verlag.
MRS	Mission de Ras Shamra. Paris: Imprimerie Nationale et al.
PIB	Pontificium Institutum Biblicum, Roma.
UF	Ugarit-Forschungen, see B 81:1.
RSP	Ras Shamra Parallels, see B 71:7.

Only relatively recent publications of immediate interest for the student of the Ugaritic language are listed. Additional bibliographical information can be found in publications listed here in section B 1.

Short characterizations of the publications, especially as concerns their usefulness for the study of the Ugaritic language in beginning and intermediate stages, are provided.

B 1. Bibliographical Tools.

B 11. Bibliographies on Ugarit.

B 11:1. M. Dietrich – O. Loretz – P.-R. Berger – J. Sanmartín, Ugarit-Bibliographie 1928–1966 (AOAT 20/1–4). 1973. [Complete bibliographical data, with indexes of titles, authors, bibliography, series and periodicals. A further volume on 1967–1971 data was prepared for printing in 1983.]

B 12. Bibliographical sections in books.

B 12:1. J. P. Lettinga, Ugaritic. 129–145. J. H. Hospers, ed., A Basic Bibliography for the Study of the Semitic Languages, vol. I. Leiden: Brill, 1973. [General Interest Works; Philology; Literature; History and Civilization; Religion.]

B 12:2 Corpus des tablettes. . . , see B 41:1. [General bibliography; bibliographical data on individual texts.]

B 12:3. Ras Shamra, see B 63:3. [Detailed bibliography, arranged according to the subjects.]

B 12:4. Craigie, see B 71:6. [A guide for further study and reading, 102–110.]

B 12:5. Del Olmo Lete, see B 42:4. [Cf. Abbreviaturas bibliographicas, 649–662.]

B 13. Running bibliographies.

As both newly discovered texts and new studies are appearing at a fast pace, bibliographies in printed books have to be supplemented by data from periodically issued bibliographies.

B 13:1. Newsletter for Ugaritic Studies, see B 81:2. [Listing of books, articles in books and journals, book reviews.]

B 13:2. Keilschriftbibliographie, in the journal Orientalia (Roma). [E.g. in 51 (1982):1*–135*; Ugaritisch, 54*–60*; Ug. Schrift, 22*; word index, 129*130*.]

B 13:3. Elenchus Bibliographicus Biblicus (Roma). [E.g. in 61 (1980): index, 1269; North-West Semitic, 655–657; Religio canaanea, 825–832; Archaeologia: Ugarit (+ Mari) 1010–1011.]

B 13:4. Internationale Zeitschriftenschau für Bibelwissenschaft und Grenzgebiete (Düsseldorf). [E.g. in 28 (1981/82): Ugarit, 282–288; Ugaritisch, 300–301.]

B 14. Special bibliographies.

B 14:1. E. R. Martinez, Hebrew-Ugaritic Index to the Writings of Mitchell J. Dahood: A Bibliography with Indices of Scriptural Passages, Hebrew and Ugaritic Words and Grammatical Observations. Rome: PIB 1967.

B 14:2. E. R. Martinez, Hebrew-Ugaritic Index II with an Eblaite Index to the Writings of Mitchell J. Dahood. A Bibliography with Indices of Scriptural Passages, Hebrew, Ugaritic and Eblaite Words and Grammatical Observations, Critical Reviews, Doctoral Dissertations and Related Writings. Rome: Biblical Institute Press 1981.

B 2. Grammar and related studies.

B 21. Grammars.

B 21:1. Cyrus H. Gordon, Ugaritic Textbook; Grammar, Texts in Transliteration, Cuneiform Selections, Glossary, Indices (AnOr 38) 1965. Supplement to the Ugaritic Textbook (pp. 549–556). 1967. [Grammar, 1–158; Texts in Transliteration, 159–256, 1*–31* (+257–296); Cuneiform Selections, 297–346; Glossary, 347–507, 549–556; Indices, 507–537. The pioneering work appeared in 1940 and was since then carefully re-worked and updated. Covers all Ugaritic texts available at the time of publication.]

B 21:2. H. Cazelles, Précis de grammaire ugaritique. Bibbia e Oriente 21 (1979):253–265.

B 22. Studies.

B 22:1. Mitchell Dahood, Ugaritic-Hebrew Philology: Marginal Notes on Recent Publications. Rome: PIB 1965. [An extended review of B 21:1; with additional material.]

B 22:2. J. Aistleitner, Untersuchungen zur Grammatik des Ugaritischen (BSAW 100/6). 1954. [Orthography; formation and inflection of nouns: verbal forms: complete listing 78–147.]

B 22:3. Kj. Aartun, Die Partikeln des Ugaritischen (AOAT 21/1–2). 1974, 1978. [Detailed study of adverbs, particles of negation and affirmation, vol. 1: prepositions and conjunctions, vol 2: indexes, bibliography.]

B 22:4. P. Fronzaroli, Ugaritic Phonetics (trans. A. S. Kaye). Fullerton: California State University 1973. [Trans. of La Fonetica Ugaritica, Roma 1955.]

B 3. Lexical tools.

B 31. Concordances.

B 31:1. Richard E. Whitaker, A Concordance to the Ugaritic Literature. Cambridge, Massachusetts: Harvard University Press 1972. [Contains words with context. References to CTA (B 41:1) and UT (B 42:2). A new edition is being prepared since 1981.]

B 32. Dictionaries and glossaries with English equivalents.

B 32:1. Glossary in Gordon, Ugaritic Textbook (B 21:1), 347–507, 549–556. [Covers all texts; items often provided with references to texts and with comparative material.]

B 32:2. Glossary in Gibson, Canaanite Myths and Legends (B 42:3), 141–160. [Covers major poetic texts; selected references to texts, occasionally to related Semitic languages.]

B 33. Dictionaries and glossaries with equivalents in other languages.

B 33:1. Joseph Aistleitner, Wörterbuch der ugaritischen Sprache (BSAW 106/3). Dritte Auflage. 1967. [First edition of 1963 was edited, after the death of author in 1960, by O. Eissfeldt. Covers all texts available then, quotations according to Virolleaud-Eissfeldt system. Complete listing of basic and derived forms with references to texts, frequent quotations of context, ample comparative material.]

B 33:2. Cf. Del Olmo Lete, Mitos y leyendas de Canaan (B 42:4). [Glosario, 503–645. Covers literary texts KTU 1.1–25. Derived forms listed; comparative material; many references to lexical studies.]

B 33:3. Cf. Caquot – Sznycer – Herdner, Textes ougaritiques (10.52:1). [Vocabulaire, 585–600; Noms propres, 600–602. References to the translated texts and lexical comments to them.]

B 34. Proper names.

B 34:1. F. Gröndahl, Die Personennamen der Texte aus Ugarit. (Studia Pohl 1). Roma: Pontificium Institutum Biblicum 1967. [Names from alphabetic and syllabic texts, Semitic, Hurrian, Anatolian and other.]

B 34:2. A. Cooper – M. H. Pope, Divine Names and Epithets in the Ugaritic Texts. 333–469. RSP III (B 71:7). [32 Ug. names (and 10 epithets) with parallels in the Old Testament.]

B 34:3. M. C. Astour – D. E. Smith, Place Names. 249–369, RSP II (B 71:7). [115 alphabetic and 85 syllabic names with parallels in the Old Testament.]

B 4. Editions of texts.
Only major collections are listed here.

B 41. Ugaritic texts in transliterations with autographs.

B 41:1. A. Herdner, Corpus des tablettes en cuneiforme alphabétiques découvertes à Ras Shamra-Ugarit de 1929 à 1939 (MRS X). 1963. [Vol. I] (Texte), [Vol. II] (Figures et planches). [219 texts (literary texts nos. 1–28) in transliteration, variant readings, description of tablets, bibliography of individual texts, 1–291. Bibliographie générale, 293–339. Autographs, fig. 1–306. Photographs, pl. I–LXXXVIII.]

B 41:2. Ch. Virolleaud, Le Palais royal d'Ugarit, II. Textes en cunéiformes alphabétiques des Archives Est, Ouest et Centrales. (MRS VII). 1957. [189 texts, transliterations accompanied by autographs, French translation and commentary; indexes; some photographs, pl. I–XXVI.]

B 41.3. Ch. Virolleaud, Le Palais royal d'Ugarit, V. Textes en cunéiformes alphabétiques des Archives Sud, Sud-Ouest et du Petit-Palais. (MRS XI). 1965. [172 texts; cf. to B 41:2, but no photographs.]

B 41:4. Ch. Virolleaud, Les nouveaux textes mythologiques et liturgiques de Ras Shamra. 545–606. Ugaritica V (cf. B 62:4), 1968. [11 texts found in 1961; cf. to B 41:3.]

B 41:5. M. Dahood – P. D. Miller. 31–54. L. R. Fisher, ed., The Claremont Ras Shamra Tablets. (AnOr 48). 1971. [Ed. of KTU 4.709 and 3.9; transliteration, English translation and commentary, autographs and photographs.]

B 41:6. W. Herrmann, Yariḫ und Nikkal und der Preis der Kuṯarāt-Göttinnen: Ein kultisch-magischer Text aus Ras Schamra. (Beihefte zur Zeitschrift für die alttestamentliche Wissenschaft, 106). Berlin: Töpelmann 1968. [Text KTU 1.24. with German translation and detailed commentary.]

B 42. Ugaritic texts in transliteration only.

B 42:1. M. Dietrich – O. Loretz – J. Sanmartín, Die keilalphabetischen Texte aus Ugarit einschliesslich der keilalphabetischen Texte ausserhalb Ugarits. (AOAT 24) Teil 1: Transkription. 1976. [1341 texts available up to 1971; indexes pointing to original publications. The autographs and photographs will be published in vol. 2.]

B 42:2. Gordon, Ugaritic Textbook, B 21:1. [Texts corresponding to CTA, PRU II and V, Ugaritica V.]

B 42:3. J. C. L. Gibson, Canaanite Myths and Legends. Edinburgh: Clark 1978. [Major literary texts (cf. KTU 1.2–6, 14–19, 23–24), arranged according to poetic cola, with English translation, notes and introductions; also poetic minor texts, but without translation. Glossary, bibliography xiii–xx, 167.]

B 42:4. G. Del Olmo Lete, Mitos y leyendas de Canaan segun la tradición de Ugarit. Madrid: Cristiandad 1981. [Literary texts KTU 1.1–25, arranged according to poetic cola and verses with variant readings, accompanied with Spanish translation and references to differing translations; general introduction and introductions to poems, with emphasis on literary features; glossary; ample bibliographical references in footnotes; indexes.]

B 42:5. P. Xella, I testi rituali di Ugarit. I. Testi. Roma: Consiglio Nazionale delle Ricerche. 1981. [77 texts from KTU, 6 texts from Ras Ibn Hani; with Italian translation and commentary; Ug. glossary, 391–395.]

B 42:6. Gray, The Legacy of Canaan, see B 71:1. [Selected passages, cf. index 330–332, with English transl. and commentary.]

B 42:7. J. Gray, The Krt Text in the Literature of Ras Shamra. Leiden: Brill (1955), second edition 1964. [English translation, detailed commentary and introduction.]

B 42:8. U. Cassuto, The Goddess Anath: Canaanite Epics of the Patriarchal Age. (Transl. from the original Hebrew of 1951 by I. Abrahams.) Jerusalem: Magnes Press 1971. [Translations into Hebrew and English, detailed introduction and commentary.]

B 43. Texts found outside of Ugarit.

B 43:1. Cf. KTU (B 42:1), 507. [5 texts, references to publications.]

B 43:2. J. L. Cunchillos, Bibliographie des textes de Ras Ibn Hani. UF 14 (1983): 27–32.

B 44. Texts from Ugarit in other writing systems and languages.
Only major collections are listed.

B 44:1. J. Nougayol, Le Palais royal d'Ugarit, III. Textes accadiens et hourrites des Archives Est, Ouest et Centrales (MRS VI). 1955. [Lists of proper names, 238–268.]

B 44:2. J. Nougayrol, Le Palais royal d'Ugarit, IV. Textes accadiens des Archives Sud (Archives internationales). (MRS IX). 1956. [Lists of proper names, 244–258.]

B 44:3. J. Nougayrol, Le Palais royal d'Ugarit, VI. Textes en cunéiformes babyloniens des Archives du Grand Palais et du Palais Sud d'Ugarit. (MRS XII). 1970. [Proper names, 137–149.]

B 44:4. J. Nougayrol, Textes suméro-accadiens des archives et bibliothèques privées d'Ugarit. 1–446. Ugaritica V, see 10.62:4. [Texts no. 1–173 (vocabularies containing Ugaritic words in syllabic writing: 130–131, 137–138); list of Ugaritic words, 351–352; proper names, 325–339.]

B 44:5. E. Laroche, Documents en langue hourrite provenant de Ras Shamra. 447–544. Ugaritica V, see 10.62:4.

B 5. Translations of Ugaritic texts.

B 51. Into English:

B 51:1. C. H. Gordon. Ugaritic Literature. Rome: PIB 1949 [Literary and non-literary texts.]

B 51:2. H. L. Ginsberg, Ugaritic Myths, Epics and Legends. 129–155. J. B. Pritchard, ed. Ancient Near Eastern Texts Relating to the Old Testament. Princeton: Princeton University Press. 1950. Third edition, 1969. [Baal and Anath, Keret, Aqhat; notes, bibliographies.]

B 51:3. Th. H. Gaster, Thespis: Ritual, Myth and Drama in the Ancient Near East. (1950). New York: Harper & Row 1966. [Index of Ug. texts: 110–111; Baal (1.1–6, 10), Gracious Gods (1.23), Aqhat (1.17–19). Introductions and comments with ample comparative anthropological material.]

B 51:4. Gray, The Legacy of Canaan, see B 71:1.

B 51:5. C. H. Gordon, Poetic Legends and Myths from Ugarit. Berytus 25 (1977):5–135.

B 51:6. Gibson, Canaanite Myths and Legends, see B 42:3.

B 51:7. M. D. Coogan, Stories from Ancient Canaan. Philadelphia: Westminster Press 1978. [Major poetic texts; no indication of original lines and columns.]

B 51:8. U. Cassuto, The Goddess Anath, see B 42:8.

B 51:9. Gray, The Krt Text. . . , see B 42:7.

B 52. Into other languages.

B 52:1. André Caquot, Maurice Sznycer, et Andrée Herdner, Textes ougaritiques. Tome I: Mythes et légendes. Paris: Les Editions du Cerf 1974. [French translation of major epic texts (1.1–6, 10, 12, 23, 24, 17–19, 20–22, 14–16), with ample notes, introductions (gods of Ugarit, 49–100), indices and glossary, 587–602.]

B 52:2. J. Aistleitner, Die mythologischen und kultischen Texte aus Ras Schamra. Budapest: Akadémiai kiadó. (1958) Zweite Auflage 1964. [German translation with short introductions.]

B 52:3. A. Jirku, Kanaanäische Mythen und Epen aus Ras Schamra-Ugarit. Gütersloh: Mohn 1962. [German translation with notes.]

B 52:4. Del Olmo Lete, see B 42:4. [Spanish translation with many notes and detailed introductions.]

B 6. General information about Ugarit.

B 61. Books.

B 61:1. G. Saadé, Ougarit: Métropole Cananéenne. Lattaquié: author 1979. [Geography, history, archeology-with many plans and photographs-, documents.]

B 61:2. J. Gray, The Canaanites (Ancient Peoples and Places). London: Thames and Hudson, 1964. [Survey of Ugarit's culture, with many pictures.]

B 61:3. C. H. Gordon, The Common Background of Greek and Hebrew Civilizations. (1962). New York: Norton 1965.

B 61:4. M. Liverani, Storia di Ugarit nell' età degli archivi politici. (Studi Semitici, 6). Roma: Centro di Studi Semitici 1962. [History of Ugarit in 14th–13th cent. B.C.; contacts with other countries.]

B 61:5. M. Heltzer, The Rural Community in Ancient Ugarit. Wiesbaden: Reichert 1976.

B 61:6. A. Caquot – M. Sznycer, Ugaritic Religion (Iconography of Religions, XV/8). Leiden: Brill 1980. [Pictures, plates I–XXIX; introduction, bibliography.]

B 61:7. J.-M. de Tarragon, Le culte à Ugarit d'après les textes de la pratique en cunéiformes alphabétiques. Paris: Gabalda 1980.

B 62. Collections of studies.

B 62:1. Cl. F.-A. Schaeffer, Ugaritica I. Études relatives aux découvertes de Ras Shamra (MRS III). 1939.

B 62:2. Cl. F.-A. Schaeffer et al., Ugaritica II. Nouvelles études relatives aux découvertes de Ras Shamra. (MRS V). 1949.

B 62:3. Cl. F.-A. Schaeffer et al., Ugaritica III. (MRS VIII). 1956.

B 62:4. Cl. F.-A. Schaeffer et al., Ugaritica, V. (MRS XVI). 1968. [Cl. F.-A. Schaeffer, Commentaires sur les letters et documents trouvés dans les bibliothèques privées d'Ugarit, 607–768, pl. I–VIII.]

B 62:5. Ugaritica VI, publié à l'occasion de la XXXe campagne de fouilles à Ras Shamra (1968) sous la direction de Claude F.-A. Schaeffer. [39 articles; texts, 165–179, 319–332, 375–378; Ugaritic philology, 181–186, 461–477.]

B 62:6. Ugaritica VII. (MRS XVIII). 1978. Paris: Geuthner/Leiden: Brill. [Text editions and commentaries; studies.]

B 62:7. Festschrift für Claude F.-A. Schaeffer zum 80. Geburtstag am 6. März 1979. = UF 11 (1979). [84 articles; indexes.]

B 62:8. G. D. Young, ed., Ugarit in Retrospect: Fifty Years of Ugarit and Ugaritic. Winona Lake, Indiana: Eisenbrauns 1981. [13 articles: history and archaeology, 3–78; language and literature, 81–179; retrospect and prospect, 183–200; bibliography, indexes.]

B 62:9. La Syrie au Bronze Récent: Cinquantenaire d'Ougarit–Ras Shamra (Extraits de la XXVIIe Paris 1980.) R(encontre) A(ssyriologique) I(nternationale) (= Protohistoire du Levant, Mémoire no. 15). Paris: Recherches sur les civilisations 1982. [Articles sur Ras Shamra, Ras Ibn Hani, etc.]

B 63. Articles in encyclopedias.

B 63:1. A. S. Kapelrud, Ugarit. IV:724b–732a. The Interpreter's Dictionary of the Bible. Nashville: Abingdon 1962. [Short survey with 11 pictures and bibliography.]

B 63:2. J. C. de Moor, Ugarit. 928a–931b. Cf. to B 63:1, Supplementary Volume, 1976. [Updating of B 63:1; bibliography.]

B 63:3. Ras Shamra (Ugarit our Ougarit). 1124–1466. Supplément au Dictionnaire de la Bible, eds. H. Cazelles – A. Feuillet, fasc. 52, 53. Paris: Letouzey & Ané 1979. [J.-C. Courtois, Archaeology, 1126–1295, 25 fig., 1439–1442; M. Liverani, History, 1295–1348; A. Caquot, Ugaritic literature, 1361–1417; M. Sznycer, Administrative and economic documents, 1417–1425; E. Jacob – H. Cazelles, Ugarit and the Old Testament, 1425–1439; J. L. Cunchillos, Equivalences for KTU/UT, 1443–1466. Bibliography: 1287–1295, and ample references throughout.]

B 7. Ugarit and the Hebrew Bible.

B 71. Publications in English.

B 71:1. J. Gray, The Legacy of Canaan: The Ras Shamra Texts and Their Relevance to the Old Testament. (Supplements to Vetus Testamentum, V), Leiden: Brill (1957). Second ed. 1965. [Ugaritic literary texts and forms, religion, social structure; many passages from texts (cf. B 42:6); bibliography, 312–325.]

B 71:2. W. F. Albright, Yahweh and the Gods of Canaan: A Historical Analysis of Two Conflicting Faiths. Garden City, New York: Doubleday 1968. [Canaanite poetry and religion.]

B 71:3. F. M. Cross, Canaanite Myth and Hebrew Epic: Essays in the History of the Religion of Israel. Cambridge, Massachusetts: Harvard University Press 1973. [Religion, Cultus, Yahweh and Ba^{c}l.]

B 71:4. A. S. Kapelrud, The Ras Shamra Discoveries and the Old Testament. Oxford: Blackwell 1963 (and reprints).

B 71:5. Ch. F. Pfeiffer, Ras Shamra and the Bible. Grand Rapids, Michigan: Baker 1962. (1970).

B 71:6. P. C. Craigie, Ugarit and the Old Testament. Grand Rapids, Michigan: Eerdmans 1982. [Archaeology, life, language and literature; perspectives. A Guide for further study and reading, 102–110.]

B 71:7. Ras Shamra Parallels: The Texts from Ugarit and the Hebrew Bible. (AnOr 49–51).

Vol. I. 1972. L. R. Fisher, ed. [A. Schoors, Literary Phrases, 1–90; M. Dahood, Ugaritic Hebrew Parallel Pairs, 71–382; also in vol. II:1–39; vol. III:1–206; J. M. Sasson, Flora, Fauna and Minerals, 383–452.]

Vol. II. 1975. L. R. Fisher, ed. [Professions, institutions, politics, 41–129; L. R. Fisher, Literary Genres in the Ugaritic Texts, 131–152.]

Vol. III. 1981. S. Rummel, ed. [R. E. Whitaker, Ugaritic Formulae, 207–219; S. Rummel, Narrative Structures in the Ugaritic Texts, 221–332.]

B 72. Books in other languages.

B 72:1. R. de Langhe, Les Textes de Ras Shamra-Ugarit et leur Rapports avec le Milieu Biblique de l'Ancien Testament. I–II. Gembloux: Duculot . . . 1945. [Detailed study of Ugaritic archaeology, texts, writings, language, religion.]

B 72:2. D. Kinet, Ugarit—Geschichte und Kultur einer Stadt in der Umwelt des Alten Testaments. Stuttgart: Katholisches Bibelwerk 1981.

B 8. Periodicals.

B 81. Devoted primarily to Ugaritic studies.

B 81:1. Ugarit-Forschungen: Internationales Jahrbuch für die Altertumskunde Syrien-Palästinas. K. Bergerhof – M. Dietrich – O. Loretz, eds. Kevelaer: Butzon & Bercker/Neukirchen-Vluyn: Neukirchener Verlag. [Appears as an annual, 1 (1968) –; most recent issue 15 (1983). Articles in German, English, French; book reviews; indexes.]

B 81:2. Newsletter for Ugaritic Studies. P. C. Craigie, ed. Canadian Society of Biblical Studies – Society of Biblical Literature, Calgary, Alberta, Canada. [Appears about 3 times a year, 1 (April 1972) –; most recent issue 31 (April 1984). Listing of articles, books and book reviews on Ugarit and related topics, with short abstracts; reports on new texts, congresses, courses, etc.]

Reprints under the title Ugaritic Studies. 1/1972–10/1976; (II) 1976–1979; (III), 1980–1983. [With indexes.]

B 82. Presenting primary material.

B 82:1. Syria (Paris).
B 82:2. Annales archéologiques de Syrie, 1–15 (1951–1965); Annales archéologiques arabes syriennes, 16– (1966–) (Damascus).
B 82:3. Comptes-rendus de l'Académie des Inscriptions et Belles-Lettres (Paris).
B 82:4. Semitica (Paris).
B 82:5. L'Annuaire du Collège de France (Paris).
B 82:6. Revue d'Assyriologie (Paris).

B 83. Orientalist periodicals.

Archiv für Orientforschung (Wien)
Bulletin of the American Schools of Oriental Research (Philadelphia)
Journal of the American Oriental Society (New Haven, Connecticut)
Journal of Near Eastern Studies (Chicago)
Journal of Semitic Studies (Manchester)
Maarav (Santa Monica, California)
Oriens Antiquus (Roma)
Orientalia (Roma)
Rivista di Studi Fenici (Roma)
Die Welt des Orients (Göttingen)

B 84. Periodicals primarily devoted to biblical studies

Bibbia e Oriente (Milano)
Biblica (Roma)
Biblical Archaeologist (Philadelphia)
Catholic Biblical Quarterly (Washington)
Journal of Biblical Literature (Chico, California)
Revue Biblique (Jerusalem/Paris)
Vetus Testamentum (Leiden)
Zeitschrift für die alttestamentliche Wissenschaft (Berlin)

B 85. Review periodicals, abstracts, book lists.

Bibliotheca Orientalis (Leiden)
Orientalische Literaturzeitung (Leipzig)
Old Testament Abstracts (Washington)
Elenchus Bibliographicus Biblicus (Roma)
The Society for Old Testament Study: Book List (London)

Parts 1–7

Basic Grammar

Analytical Table of Contents to Parts 1–7

1. Introduction 13

11. *The Ugaritic Language* 13
11.1. Name 13
11.2. City and kingdom of Ugarit 13
11.3. Date 13
12. *The position of Ugaritic among the Semitic languages* 13
12.1. Classification of the Semitic languages 14
12.2. The Canaanite languages 14
12.3. Conservative features of the Ugaritic language 14
12.4. Ugaritic and the other ancient languages of Syria-Palestine 14
13. *Stages and styles of the Ugaritic language* 15
13.1. Stages 15
13.2. The poetic language 15
13.3. The language of documents and letters 15
13.4. The informal language 15
14. *Sources for the Ugaritic language* 16
14.1. Non-literary texts 16
14.2. Literary texts 16
14.3. Texts and words in syllabic cuneiform writing 16
15. *Discovery and publication of Ugaritic texts* 16

2. Writing 19

21. *The Ugaritic cuneiform alphabet* 19
21.1. Origins 19
21.2. Shapes of the signs 19
21.3. The consonantal signs 22
21.31. Violations of the alphabetic principles 22
21.4. The signs for vowels 22
21.5. The order of the signs 23
21.6. Sign values and transliteration 23
21.7. Other graphical features 24
21.8. Use for other languages 24

22. *The cuneiform syllabary* 24
22.1. Origins and principles 25
22.2. Ugaritic phonemes and segments of cuneiform syllabic signs 25
22.3. Denotation of Ugaritic words in Akkadian syllabic cuneiform texts 26

3. Phonology 27

31. *Terminology and methods* 27
31.1. Sounds and signs 27
31.2. The grapheme 27
31.3. The phoneme 27
31.4. Phonetics 27
32. *Reconstruction of Ugaritic phonemes* 28
32.1. Sources and presuppositions 28
32.2. Use of living and traditional Semitic languages 28
32.3. Use of Ugaritic alphabetic and syllabic evidence 28
33. *The phonological system of Ugaritic* 28
33.1. Segments and suprasegmental features 28
33.2. Consonantal and vocalic phonemes 28
33.3. Vowel length 29
33.4. Consonant doubling 29
33.5. Syllable structure 29
34. *The consonantal system of Standard Ugaritic* 29
34.1. Place and manner of articulation 29
34.2. Phonological and phonetic identification of consonants 30
34.21. Laryngeals 30
34.22. Postvelars 31
34.23. Velars 31
34.24. Palato-alveolars 31
34.25. Alveolars 31
34.26. Dentals 31
34.27. Interdentals 32
34.28. Bilabials 32
35. *The vowels of Standard Ugaritic* 32
35.1. Evidence for the vowels 32
35.2. Short and long vowels 32
35.3. Phonetic characteristics of vowels 33
36. *Ugaritic phonemes and their Semitic correspondences* 33
36.1. Atypical correspondences 33
37. *Some non-standard features* 33
37.1. Archaic features 33
37.2. Innovative features 35
38. *Phonetic and phonological changes* 35
38.1. Kinds of change 35
38.2. Changes involving consonants 35

38.21. Assimilation 35
38.22. Loss 36
38.23. New consonants 36
38.3. Changes involving the semivowels /w/ and /y/ 36
38.31. Initial *w- > /y-/ 36
38.32. Monophthongization 36
38.4. Changes involving the vowels 36
38.41. Assimilation 36
38.42. Dissimilation 37

4. Word Formation 39

41. *The word* 39
41.1. Delimitation 39
41.2. Categories of words 39
42. *The structure of words* 39
42.1. System and periphery 39
42.2. Patterns 40
42.3. Roots 40
43. *The formation of nouns (including numerals)* 40
43.1. Patterns with fewer than three root consonants 41
43.2. Patterns with three root consonants 41
43.21. Monosyllabic bases 41
43.22. Bisyllabic bases with short vowels 41
43.23. Bisyllabic bases with long vowels 41
43.24. Patterns with doubled consonants 42
43.25. Patterns with root consonants repeated 42
43.26. Patterns with prefixes 42
43.27. Patterns with afformatives 43
43.28. Patterns with infixes 43
43.29. Other patterns 43
43.3. Nouns with more than three root consonants 44
43.4. Compound nouns 44
44. *The formation of pronouns* 44
45. *The formation of particles* 45
46. *The formation of verbs* 45
46.1. Roots 45
46.2. Verbal classes 45
46.3. Characteristic vowels 45
47. *Words of foreign origin* 46
48. *Names* 46
48.1. Personal names (PN) 46
48.2. Divine names (DN) 46
48.3. Geographical names (GN) 46

5. Morphology 47

51. *Pronouns* 47
51.1. Personal pronouns, independent and suffixed 47
51.11. Forms of personal pronouns 47
51.12. Independent forms 48
51.13. Suffixed forms 48
51.2. Interrogative pronouns 48
51.3. The determinative/relative pronoun 49
51.4. Demonstrative pronouns 49
52. *Nouns* 49
52.1. Categories 49
52.2. Gender 49
52.3. Number 49
52.31. Singular 50
52.32. Dual 50
52.33. Plural 50
52.4. Case 50
52.41. Diptotic names 50
52.5. State 51
52.6. Determination and indetermination 51
52.7. The system of nominal inflection 51
53. *Numerals* 51
53.1. Kinds of numerals 51
53.2. Forms of numerals 53
53.3. Cardinal numerals 53
53.4. Ordinal numerals 54
53.5. Fractions 54
53.6. Multiplicative numerals 54
53.7. Quantitative expressions outside the system of numerals 54
54. *Verbs* 54
54.1. Lexical and inflectional categories 54
54.11. System of characteristic vowels 55
54.12. System of verbal patterns 55
54.13. Aspects/tenses: perfect and imperfect 56
54.14. Moods: jussive and other volitive moods, imperative 56
54.15. Finite verbal forms: person, number, gender 57
54.16. Verbal nouns (infinitives and participles) 57
54.17. Verbal classes (strong and weak) 57
54.18. Verbal forms with suffixed personal pronouns 57
54.2. Simple active pattern (G): 58
54.21. Perfect 58
54.22. Imperfect 59
54.23. Volitive moods 62
54.24. Imperative 62

54.25. Absolute infinitive 63
54.26. Construct infinitive 64
54.27. Active participle 65
54.28. Passive participle 65
54.3. Simple patterns: passive, reflexive, and reciprocal/passive 65
54.31. Simple passive pattern (Gp) 65
54.32. Simple reflexive pattern (Gt) 66
54.33. Reciprocal/passive pattern (N) 66
54.4. Derived verbal patterns 66
54.41. Factitive active pattern (D) 67
54.42. Factitive reflexive pattern (tD) 67
54.43. Factitive passive pattern (Dp) 67
54.44. Š-Causative active pattern (Š) 68
54.45. Š-Causative reflexive pattern (Št) 68
54.46. Š-Causative passive pattern (Šp) 68
54.47. Internal causative pattern (C) 68
54.5. Verbal classes 69
54.51. Identification of forms 69
54.52. Strong and weak verbs 69
54.53. Verbs I /n/ and /l-q-ḥ/ 70
54.54. Verbs I /y/ 70
54.55. Verbs II /w/ and /y/ 71
54.56. Verbs II = III ($C_1C_3C_3$) 72
54.57. Verbs III /y/ and /w/ 73
54.58. Verbs with four root consonants 75
54.6. Forms with suffixed pronouns 75
54.61. Finite forms 75
54.62. Verbal nouns 75
55. *Adverbs* 75
55.1. Adverbs and other particles: forms and functions 75
55.2. Nouns with adverbial markers 76
55.3. Demonstrative adverbs 76
55.4. Temporal adverbs 76
55.5. Interrogative adverbs 76
55.6. Expressions of negation and affirmation 77
55.7. Expressions of existence and its modifications 77
56. *Prepositions* 77
56.1. General remarks 77
56.2. One-consonant prepositions 78
56.21. Preposition *b-* 78
56.22. Preposition *l-* 78
56.23. Preposition *k-* 78
56.3. Biconsonantal prepositions 78
56.4. Triconsonantal prepositions 78
56.5. Prepositions in *-ay /-ē/ 78
56.6. Forms with suffixed pronouns 79

57. *Conjunctions* 79
57.1. Forms and functions 79
57.2. Coordinating conjunctions 79
57.21. Conjunction *w-* 79
57.22. Other coordinating conjunctions 79
57.23. Disjunctive conjunctions 80
57.3. Subordinating conjunctions 80
57.4. Particles introducing clauses 80
58. *Interjections* 80
58.1. Interjections introducing a clause 81
58.2. Postpositive elements 81

6. Function of Words in the Sentence 83

61. *Function of pronouns* 83
61.1. Independent personal pronouns 83
61.2. Suffixed personal pronouns 83
61.3. Interrogative pronouns 84
61.4. Determinative/relative pronouns 84
61.5. Demonstrative pronouns 84
62. *Function of nouns* 84
62.1. Substantive and adjective nouns 84
62.2. Gender 85
62.3. Number 85
62.4. Case 86
62.5. State 86
62.6. Indetermination 86
63. *Function of numerals* 87
63.1. Cardinal numerals, simple and compound 87
63.2. Numerals and counted objects 87
63.3. Other numerals 87
63.4. The quantitative expression *kl* "all" 88
64. *Function of verbal forms* 88
64.1. Finite verbal forms: person, number, gender 88
64.2. Finite verbal forms: aspects/tenses 88
64.21. Perfect and imperfect 88
64.22. The perfect in poetry 89
64.23. The imperfect in poetry 89
64.24. The perfect in prose 89
64.25. The imperfect in prose 90
64.26. Special functions of the aspects/tenses 90
64.3. Moods 90
64.31. Indicative and volitive moods 90
64.32. Jussive 90
64.33. Subjunctive 91

64.34. Energic 91
64.35. Imperative 91
64.4. Verbal nouns 92
64.41. In general 92
64.42. The absolute infinitive 92
64.43. The construct infinitive 93
64.5. Participles 93
64.51. Adjective verbal nouns 93
64.52. Active participles 94
64.53. Passive participles 95
64.6. Manners of action 95
64.61. Verbal patterns: manner of action and voice 95
64.62. Kinds of manners of action 95
64.63. Simple manner of action (G, Gp, Gt; N) 95
64.64. The system of characteristic vowels 96
64.65. Factitive manner of action (D, Dp, tD; L; R) 96
64.66. Causative manner of action (Š, Šp, Št; C) 97
64.67. Reciprocal manner of action (N) 97
64.7. Voice 97
64.71. Kinds of voice 97
64.72. Active voice 97
64.73. Passive voice (internal; with prefix /n-/) 98
64.74. Reflexive voice 98
65. *Function of adverbs* 99
65.1. Kinds 99
65.11. In verbal clauses 99
65.12. With prepositions 99
65.13. With nouns 99
65.2. Negative and affirmative particles 99
65.21. Static negation *l-* 99
65.22. Dynamic negation *al* 100
65.23. The negative particle *bl* 100
65.24. Affirmative particles 100
65.3. Expressions of being and non-being 101
66. *Function of prepositions* 101
66.1. Prepositional constructions 101
66.2. Function depending on the context 101
66.3. Various functions of prepositions 102
66.4. Compound prepositions 102
67. *Function of conjunctions* 102
67.1. Kinds 102
67.2 Coordinating conjunctions 103
67.21. Conjunction *w-* 103
67.22. Other coordinating conjunctions 103
67.23. Disjunctive conjunctions 103
67.3. Subordinating conjunctions 103

67.31. Conjunction *d-* 104
67.32. Conjunction *hm* 104
67.33. Conjunction *k-* 104
67.34. Deictic temporal conjunctions 104
68. *Function of interjections* 104

7. Sentence Structure 107

71. *Approaches* 107
71.1. Methods of syntactic analysis 107
71.2. Prose texts 107
71.21. Formulas in prose texts 107
71.3. Poetry 108
71.31. Principles 108
71.32. Colon and verse 108
71.33. Bicolon 109
71.34. Tricolon 109
72. *Sentences and their parts* 110
72.1. Definitions and terms 110
72.2. Parts of clause 110
72.21. Constituents 110
72.22. Components 110
72.3. Kinds of clauses and sentences 110
72.31. Kinds of clauses 110
72.32. Kinds of sentences 111
73. *Clause constituents* 111
73.1. Subject 111
73.11. Subject expressed 111
73.12. Subject not expressed 112
73.13. Vocative 112
73.2. Predicate 112
73.21. Nominal predicate 112
73.22. Verbal predicate 113
73.23. Predicate not expressed 113
74. *Adverbial components* 113
74.1. Object 113
74.2. Complement to the object 114
74.3. Adverbial modifier 114
75. *Adnominal components* 114
75.1. Complement to the subject 115
75.2. Apposition 115
75.3. Adjectival attribute 115
75.4. Genitival attribute 116
75.5. Adnominal adjunct 116

76. *Clauses* 116
76.1. Kinds 116
76.2. Declarative clauses 117
76.3. Interrogative clauses 117
76.4. Volitive clauses 117
76.5. Some relations between parts of clause 118
76.51. Coordinate components and constituents 118
76.52. Agreement 118
77. *Sentences* 118
77.1. Kinds 118
77.2. Coordinate sentences 118
77.3. Subordinate sentences with relative clauses 119
77.4. Subordinate sentences with object clauses 119
77.5. Subordinate sentences with adverbial clauses 120
77.51. Comparative sentences 120
77.52. Temporal sentences 120
77.53. Causal sentences 120
77.6. Conditional sentences 120
77.7. Some relations between clauses in the sentences 121
77.71. Clause order 121
77.72. Ellipses 121
78. *Some combinations of sentences* 121
78.1. Direct speech 121
78.2. Parallel passages 121

1. Introduction

11. *The Ugaritic language*

11.1. Name

The name of the Ugaritic language is derived from the ancient name of the city of Ugarit, preserved in the alphabetic texts as *ugrt* /ˀugarīt-/ (1.40:10, 35, 36 etc.) and in the cuneiform syllabary most frequently as *u-ga-ri-it* (P:III:16.140:3 (p. 45), etc.).

11.2. City and kingdom of Ugarit

The city of Ugarit was discovered under a mound called in Arabic Ras (esh-)Shamra ("Fennel Cape"). The mound is located about one kilometer from the Mediterranean Sea and is about ten kilometers north of the city of Lādiqīye (French Lattaquié, ancient Greek Laodikeia) in north Syria. Nearly all the remains of the Ugaritic language have been discovered during excavations carried out at this site since 1929. A small number of Ugaritic texts have been found at Ras Ibn Hani, five kilometers south of Ras Shamra, where excavations began in 1977. A few texts, all short, using the Ugaritic alphabet have been found elsewhere in the western Mediterranean area: on Cyprus (Hala Sultan Tekke, near Larnaca), in Syria (Tell Sukas; Kadesh), Lebanon (Kamid el-Loz; Sarepta), and Palestine (Mount Tabor; Taanach; Beth Shemesh).

It may be supposed that Ugaritic was spoken at least in the territory of the kingdom of Ugarit, an area about sixty square kilometers. The boundaries of the kingdom extended in the north to the area around Mount Ṣapān (classical Mons Casius, modern Žebel ˀAqraᶜ, at the modern Turkish border), and in the east to the Orontes River Valley. In the south, the small states of Siannu and Ušnatu were attached to the kingdom of Ugarit at various times.

11.3. Date

According to archeological criteria, the extant Ugaritic texts were written in the fourteenth and thirteenth centuries B.C., in the Late Bronze Age. Most of them were found between a level showing traces of an earthquake and fire which ravaged the city about 1365 B.C. and the levels evidencing the final destruction of Ugarit, around 1200 B.C.

12. *The position of Ugaritic among the Semitic languages*

The Ugaritic language belongs to the Northwest group of Semitic languages, but full consensus about its position within this group has yet to be reached.

12.1. Classification of the Semitic languages

The Semitic languages are usually divided into three large groups according to linguistic criteria which coincide with geographical distribution: (1) the East (or Northeast) group, to which only Akkadian belongs; (2) the Northwest (or North) group, whose representatives are usually divided into two subgroups, Canaanite and Aramaic; and (3) the Southwest (or South) group, which consists of two branches, the northern, represented by Arabic, and the southern, including the Ethiopic languages and the Epigraphic South Arabian.

12.2. The Canaanite languages

The term "Canaanite" is used in modern Semitic linguistics for a cluster of languages comprising Phoenician, Hebrew and some less-well documented languages. This usage does not reflect exactly the usual ancient meaning of the geographical name Canaan (*kn^{c}n*). This ancient word (cf. the derived adjective *kn^{c}ny* 4.96:7 and syllabic cuneiform (māt) *ki-na-ḫi* U:V:36:B:6′ "(the land of) purple") denotes mostly what was known as Phoenicia in the first millennium B.C. Ugarit, situated to the north, was not considered part of Canaan in this narrow sense of the term.

Features of the Canaanite languages attested in the Ugaritic language include (1) the change of Proto-Semitic *ḏ (d^1) to /ṣ/; (2) the change, in later texts, of Proto-Semitic and Standard Ugaritic /ṯ/ to /š/; (3) the monophthongizations *aw > /ō/ and *ay > /ē/; (4) the assimilation of /n/ to an immediately following consonant; and (5) dual and plural endings of nouns with /-m-/. Many lexical correspondences link Ugaritic with the other Canaanite languages, notably with Biblical Hebrew.

12.3. Conservative features of the Ugaritic language

At least some of the conservative features of the Ugaritic language may be explained by its relative antiquity and by the location of Ugarit on the northern periphery of the Canaanite linguistic area. Of these conservative features the following can be mentioned: (1) the preservation of a rich inventory of consonants; (2) the use of special forms for the genitive-accusative of third-person pronouns; (3) the use of the /š-/ prefix in the causative pattern of the verb; and (4) the lack of the definite article. These features are sometimes adduced as arguments against the Canaanite character of the Ugaritic language. The Ugaritic language may be characterized as an ancient North Canaanite dialect.

12.4. Ugaritic and the other ancient languages of Syria-Palestine

Some features of Ugaritic are similar to those of Northwest Semitic languages contemporary or even older in attestation.

Old Canaanite dialects are reflected in glosses, names and Canaanitisms in the Amarna letters, written in Akkadian to the rulers of Egypt in the first half of the fourteenth century B.C. from Syria-Palestine; among the cities represented are Qatna, Byblos, Sidon, Hazor, and Jerusalem. Most of the texts were found in 1887 at Akhenaten's court city, Tell el-Amarna.

The Amorite language is preserved in thousands of personal names contained in cuneiform syllabic documents from Syria (Mari and Alalakh, early to mid-2nd millennium B.C.) and Mesopotamia (Ur, late 3rd millennium B.C.).

Eblaitic, a Semitic language of the city of Ebla in central Syria in the late 3rd millennium B.C., has been known only since 1975. Even though its character has not yet been adequately determined, some features similar to those of Ugaritic can be observed in it.

13. *Stages and styles of the Ugaritic language*

13.1. Stages

Since the sources for the Ugaritic language are limited with a few exceptions to one place, no differentiation of dialects on a regional basis may be expected. During the two centuries in which the extant Ugaritic texts were written, some observable language development took place, probably over a longer interval of time than 1400–1200 B.C.: the oldest documents preserve still older stages of the language, transmitted by oral tradition. The latest texts, written before the destruction of the city of Ugarit, reflect the more developed language of everyday use. Some of these late texts were written immediately before the destruction, and the unbaked clay tablets on which they were inscribed were found in the kiln where they had been placed for baking more than three thousand years ago.

13.2. The poetic language

The longest extant Ugaritic texts are the poems. These display a highly formulaic poetic language, apparently formed through many centuries of oral tradition. The language of Ugaritic poetry is based on the common Canaanite poetic dialect which later served also as the basis for ancient Hebrew poetic language. Some linguistic features, such as the postpositive element *-m*, the aspectual function of the perfect and imperfect, and lack or rarity of the article, are characteristic of both Ugaritic poetry and the archaic and archaizing poems in the Hebrew Bible. Also common to both are some stylistic or literary features, such as the use of pairs of synonyms (the so-called A- and B-words) in parallel cola and the parallelistic construction of verses.

13.3. The language of documents and letters

Among the extant Ugaritic texts written in prose, the royal documents (often official) and the letters exchanged among kings and high officials are especially close to the literary texts; the style is refined and the orthography precise. The language differs, however, from the language of poetry, most notably in that it employs the perfect and imperfect not to denote aspects but to denote tenses, past and non-past.

13.4. The informal language

A few late texts offer hints about the everyday language of Ugarit. Some texts written by uneducated persons or perhaps foreigners reveal features of actual pronunciation otherwise concealed by the standardized orthography. Cf. **86.5**.

14. *Sources for the Ugaritic language*

14.1. Non-literary texts

The majority of the 1341 Ugaritic alphabetic cuneiform tablets which are collected in KTU are non-literary; included are diverse documents, lists, contracts, and diplomatic and private letters. Some letters are interesting because of their style, including the use of certain literary formulas and expressions. In the letters and contracts fixed formulas are consistently used; many of the formulas are based on Akkadian models. Many lists and economic documents (KTU 4) contain few or no sentences; the same is true for many writing exercises (KTU 5) and short inscriptions (KTU 6).

Among the religious and ritual texts, there are lists, with few or no syntactic connections, of deities and offerings. Other texts contain instructions for ritual acts to be performed on certain days, usually of a specified month. Texts related to various kinds of divination are also preserved. Religious texts of these types are rather formulaic, and the interpretation of them is difficult. Since some rituals contain passages also found in literary texts, the dividing line between these two categories is hard to draw; for this reason literary and religious texts are grouped together in KTU 1.

14.2. Literary texts

The number of Ugaritic literary texts published up to 1976, KTU's date of publication, does not exceed fifty; many of the tablets are, however, large, with three or even four columns on each side, and relatively well preserved.

14.3. Texts and words in syllabic cuneiform writing

During excavations at Ras Shamra about 1500 tablets and fragments inscribed in syllabic cuneiform writing have been found; about 800 texts had been published as of 1980. Only three of these texts are in the Ugaritic language. Sumerian and Hittite are represented by a few texts, Hurrian by about thirty texts. The other texts are Akkadian, with Ugaritic names and glosses used occasionally. Ugaritic words are also contained in quadrilingual vocabularies, with equivalents in Sumerian, Akkadian, and Hurrian.

15. *Discovery and publication of Ugaritic texts*

Nearly all the Ugaritic texts were found during the French archeological excavations at Ras Shamra; these were directed from 1929 until 1969 by Claude F.-A. Schaeffer. The work was interrupted by World War II and crises in the Near East. Reports and texts have been promptly published, most in the journal Syria and in the series Mission de Ras Shamra. During later excavations, conducted at Ras Shamra since 1971, relatively few texts were unearthed. Since 1977 about 100 Ugaritic tablets were discovered by Syrian-French archeological teams at Ras Ibn Hani, south of Ras Shamra.

Books and articles dealing with various aspects of Ugaritic studies are listed in various bibliographies, see **B8**, above. There are two periodicals devoted to Ugaritic matters: the annual Ugarit-Forschungen (Neukirchen-Vluyn/Kevelaer, Germany) and Ugaritic Newsletter (Calgary, Alberta, Canada).

2. Writing

Ugarit was a cosmopolitan city in which various languages were spoken and several writing systems were in use. For the Ugaritic language a cuneiform alphabetic writing was used. Occasionally isolated Ugaritic words, especially personal and geographical names, are given in cuneiform syllabic texts. Only three fragmentary tablets present connected texts of Ugaritic written in syllabic signs (e.g., U:V:153).

21. *The Ugaritic cuneiform alphabet*

21.1. Origins

The Ugaritic alphabet is apparently a combination of the principle of consonantal alphabetic writing with the technique of cuneiform writing imported from Mesopotamia where it was used for the syllabic writing of Akkadian texts. The alphabetic principle was probably taken over from Byblos or some other place south of Ugarit. The Ugaritic letters are similar in appearance to the simpler signs of the Mesopotamian syllabary. The cuneiform signs were written with a kind of stylus on clay tablets, which were usually then baked in an oven. The system of Ugaritic alphabetic writing corresponds—with the exception of the secondary signs indicating three vocalic values—to the system of the West Semitic linear alphabet, known from Bronze Age Canaanite inscriptions from Byblos, various sites in Palestine, and the Sinai, and represented later by Phoenician writing. According to this system, every sign corresponds to a consonantal phoneme.

21.2. Shapes of the signs

The forms of the Ugaritic letters can be characterized as simple combinations of the various types of wedges used in cuneiform syllabic signs. The basic elements are the vertical wedge , the horizontal wedge , the wedge in oblique position  (rather rare), and the angle wedge (German "Winkelhaken") . The simple wedges can be repeated in either horizontal  or vertical  fashion; they can also be connected at right angles  or in a triangle . Both vertical and horizontal wedges can also be combined on one axis, i.e., , . In the accompanying table, the Ugaritic letters are arranged according to their forms, beginning with the simple ones and continuing to the more complicated combinations.

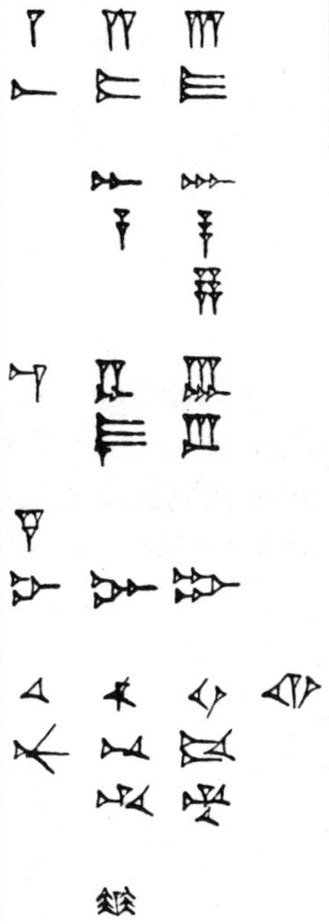

Simple wedges				
vertical	*g*	*ṣ*	*l*	
horizontal	*t*	*p*	*h*	
Combined wedges				
horizontal		*a*	*n*	
vertical		*z*	*ḫ*	
			y	
Wedges at right angles	*m*	*b*	*d*	
		i	*u*	
Wedges in triangle(s)	*s*			
	k	*w*	*r*	
Angle wedge(s)	ʿ	*ṯ*	*d̠*	*š*
	ǵ	*q*	*ẓ*	
		ṭ	*ḥ*	
Imitation of a linear letter		*s̀*		

Graphical variants.
Instead of three wedges or wedge-combinations four are used:

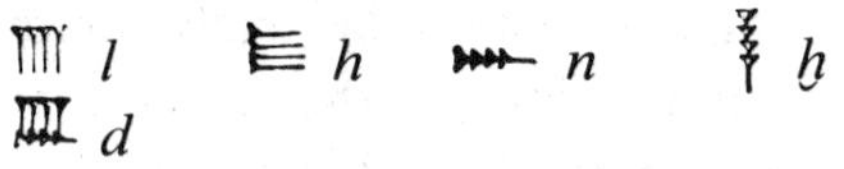

Variant of *r* with added wedges:

Some signs offer variants written with the same (or nearly the same) number of wedges as the main form; they are listed on the right side of the transliteration sign while the standard forms appear on the left side:

Reduced alphabet variants

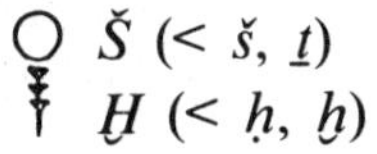

Hebrew	no.	sign	translit-eration	sound	english equivalent	other equivalent	syllabic cuneiform equivalent
אַ	1	𐎀	*a*	/ʾa/, /ʾā/	(ʾā) "he (ʾ) asked"		*a*
אִ	2	𐎛	*i*	/ʾi/, /ʾī/, /ʾē/	(ʾi) "do (ʾ)it"		*i*
אֻ	3	𐎜	*u*	/ʾu/, /ʾū/, /ʾō/	(ʾū) "the ooze"		*u*
ב	4	𐎁	*b*	/b/	b		*be*
ג	5	𐎂	*g*	/g/	g		*ga*
ד	6	𐎄	*d*	/d/	d		*di*
(ד̄)	7	𐎏	*ḏ*	/ḏ/, /ž/	th "this"; cf. s in "measure"		
ה	8	𐎅	*h*	/h/	h "head"		*ú*
ו	9	𐎆	*w*	/w/	w		*wa*
ז	10	𐎇	*z*	/z/	z		*zi*
ח	11	𐎈	*ḥ*	/ḥ/		Arabic ḥ(ā)*	*ku*(!)
(כ̄)	12	𐎃	*ḫ*	/ḫ/		German ch "Bach"	*ḫa*
ט	13	𐎉	*ṭ*	/ṭ/		Arabic ṭ(ā)**	*ṭí*
	14	𐎑	*ẓ*	/ẓ/ (= ṯ̣)		Arabic ẓ(ā̤)**	
י	15	𐎊	*y*	/y/	y		
כ	16	𐎋	*k*	/k/	k		
ל	17	𐎍	*l*	/l/	l		
מ	18	𐎎	*m*	/m/	m		
נ	19	𐎐	*n*	/n/	n		
ס	20	𐎒	*s*	/s/	s		
	21	𐎝	*s̀*	/s+u/	su "Susanna"		*zu/sú*
ע	22	𐎓	*ᶜ*	/ᶜ/		Arabic ᶜ(ain)*	
(ג̄)	23	𐎙	*ǵ*	/ǵ/		Dutch g "gracht"	*ḫa*
פ	24	𐎔	*p*	/p/	p		[p]*u*
צ	25	𐎕	*ṣ*	/ṣ/		Arabic ṣ(ād)**	*ṣa*
ק	26	𐎖	*q*	/q/		Arabic q(āf)**	*qu*
ר	27	𐎗	*r*	/r/	r "rib"		*ra*
שׁ	28	𐎌	*š*	/š/	sh "she"		
ת	29	𐎚	*t*	/t/	t		*tu*
(ת̄)	30	𐎘	*ṯ*	/ṯ/	th "thin"		*ša*

* pronounced with constriction of the pharynx, slight: /ḥ/, strong: /ᶜ/

** emphatic consonants, /q/, /ṣ/, /ẓ/, /ṭ/, may be pronounced like /k/, /s/, /ṯ/, /t/, but with the root of the tongue pressed up toward the velum.

For graphic variants see p. 20.

The syllabic cuneiform equivalents are from KTU 5:14 (P:II:189), only partially preserved.

21.3 The consonantal signs

Like West Semitic linear alphabetic writing, Ugaritic cuneiform alphabetic writing is based on a one-to-one relationship: one letter expresses only one consonantal phoneme; one consonantal phoneme is expressed by only one letter. In principle the vocalic phonemes are not expressed in this type of writing; they were known to both scribes and readers familiar with the spoken language and especially with its systems of word formation and inflection. In the Ugaritic language—as in the other ancient West Semitic languages—every syllable begins with a consonantal phoneme (C + V, or C + V + C). After a consonant closing a syllable no vowel was pronounced (CVC).

21.31 Violations of the alphabetic principles

The principle of indicating one phoneme by one sign was violated by the introduction of three signs expressing combinations of two phonemes, of a glottal stop (phonetically a zero) followed—or preceded—by a vowel: *a* /ʾ+a/, *i* /ʾ+i/, *u* /ʾ+u/. By this device the principle of expressing only consonants was also violated. The signs *i* and *u* were added to the alphabet as nos. 28 and 29.

A sign for the combination /s+u/ was added as no. 30: *ś*. It was used rarely, only in some non-literary texts.

21.4. The signs for vowels

The strictly consonantal system of the West Semitic alphabet is supplemented in Ugaritic writing by three signs whose vocalic element is relevant. These three signs indicate the vowels /a/, /i/, /u/ in combination with the glottal stop (expressed in the other West Semitic alphabets by the letter ʾalep). In most instances the three "ʾalep" signs express the sequence glottal stop + vowel, but they are sometimes used for the sequence vowel + glottal stop. If there is no vowel after the glottal stop, the *i* sign is used. The distinctive element of these three signs is the vowel, while the glottal stop (ʾalep) is common to all of them; therefore they are transliterated by simple *a*, *i*, *u*. These three signs do not distinguish vocalic phonemes exactly enough; they indicate both short and long vowels, and even related vowels resulting from contraction of an original diphthong.

sign	glottal stop + short vowel	glottal stop + long vowel	glottal stop + long vowel (< *diphthong)	short vowel + glottal stop
a	/ʾa/	/ʾā/		/aʾ/
u	/ʾu/	/ʾū/	/ʾō/ < *ʾaw	/uʾ/
i	/ʾi/	/ʾī/	/ʾē/ < *ʾay	/iʾ/, /uʾ/, /aʾ/

/ʾa/: *alp* /ʾalp-/ 1.24:20 = **88.1** "1000"; *ksa* /kussiʾa/ (acc.) 1.100:7 = **86.73** "throne, seat"
/ʾā/: *aklm* /ʾākilūma/ 1.12:I:26 "devourers"; *ša* /šaʾā/ (du.) 1.4:VIII:5 "lift up!"
/ʾu/: *um* /ʾumm-/ 1.19:III:29 = **88.65** "mother"
/ʾū/: *rpum* /rapiʾūma/ (nom.) 1.22:I:21 "netherworld shades"
/ʾō/: *u* /ʾō/ 1.23:63 "or"

/ˀi/: *il* /ˀil-/ 1.10:III:8 "god"

/ˀī/: *rpim* /rapiˀīma/ (gen.-acc.) 1.22:II:19 "netherworld shades" (Rarely, in some late texts, *-y* was used for /ī/; cf. *ky* /kī/ **57.3.**)

/ˀē/: *in* /ˀēn-/ 1.19:III:11 "there is not"

no vowel after /ˀ/: *mit* /miˀt-/ 3.1:27 = **86.31** "hundred"; *ǵmit* /ǵamiˀti/ 1.4:IV:34 = **85.2** "you have been thirsty"; *ṣin* /ṣaˀn-/ 1.4:VI:41 "small cattle"; *mid* /muˀd-/(?) 1.14:I:23 "multitude"(?); *mud* /muˀd-/(?) 1.5:III:23 "multitude"

21.5. The order of the signs

The traditional sequence of the 30 cuneiform signs of Ugaritic is presented on several tablets (5.6, 5.12, 5.13, 5.17, 5.19, 5.20, 5.21). It is given with equivalents in syllabic cuneiform on the fragmentary tablet 5.14. The alphabet tablet 5.6 (P:II:184) is depicted here.

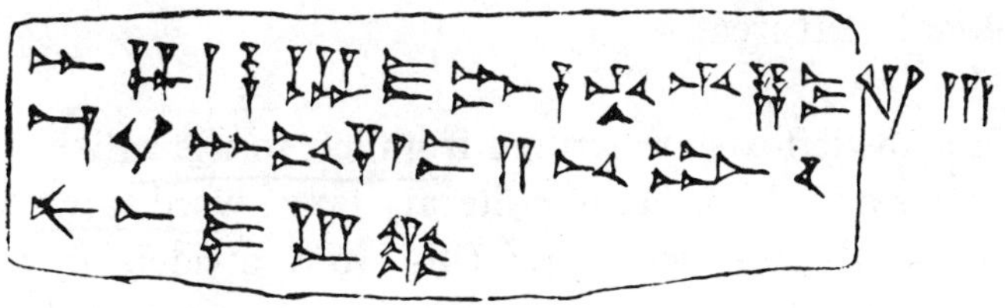

a	*b*	*g*	*ḫ*	*d*	*h*	*w*	*z*	*ḥ*	*ṭ*	*y*	*k*	*š*	*l*
m	*ḏ*	*n*	*ẓ*	*s*	ᶜ	*p*	*ṣ*	*q*	*r*	*ṯ*			
ǵ	*t*	*i*	*u*	*s̀*									

The order of the signs on the Ugaritic alphabet tablets indicates an original alphabet which consisted of 27 consonantal signs, to which were added the last sign, *s̀*, and the second and third to last, the signs denoting /i/ and /u/ in combination with the glottal stop.

Since the alphabet tablets were found only after many Ugaritic word lists and vocabularies had already been published, this traditional order is not used by modern scholars. In most modern lexical publications, the sequence of 22 Hebrew letters is used as a basis and the other Ugaritic letters are added after the Hebrew letters to which they are most closely related.

In the following list, line 2 gives the Hebrew alphabet; lines 1 and 2 read together give the order of the Ugaritic alphabet tablets, while lines 2 and 3 read together give the order used in modern publications.

1					*ḫ*												*š*			*ḏ*		*ẓ*									*ṯ ǵ*			*i u s̀*
2	*a*		*b*	*g*		*d*		*h*	*w*	*z*	*ḥ*		*ṭ*		*y*	*k*		*l*	*m*		*n*		*s*		ᶜ		*p*	*ṣ*	*q*	*r*	[š]	*t*		
3		*i u*					*ḏ*					*ḫ*		*ẓ*										*s̀*		*ǵ*							*ṯ*	

21.6. Sign values and transliteration

The Ugaritic alphabet was created especially for the Ugaritic language, in which (as in other West Semitic languages), the consonantal phonemes were considered more relevant than the vocalic phonemes. Word structure in the language is basically determined by the consonantal phonemes, which are fully and exactly represented, while the vocalic phonemes are, for the most part, not expressed. The phonological values of the consonantal letters have been determined by comparison with the consonant systems of other Semitic languages, especially Hebrew and Arabic. See table on p. 21.

In Ugaritic writing, the vowels are indicated only if associated with a glottal stop. Neither the vowel quantity (long/short) nor the peculiar quality of monophthongized vowels (ē < *ay, ō < *aw) is exactly expressed.

Latin letters in italic type, some with diacritical marks, are used to transliterate Ugaritic cuneiform letters, e.g., *b*, *a*, *ḥ*, *š*. Latin letters in roman type between slashes are used for phonemic reconstruction of sounds and words, e.g., /b/, /a/, /ā/, /š/. The transliteration system proposed by C. H. Gordon and accepted by most scholars, including the editors of KTU, is used here. Its main advantage is the consistent application of phonological criteria, which can be established with more certainty than hypothetical phonetic realizations. Its practical advantages are its simplicity and widespread use.

21.7. Other graphical features

Nearly all Ugaritic alphabetic texts are written from left to right (like syllabic cuneiform texts). In nearly all literary texts and in formal non-literary texts, words are divided by a small vertical wedge 𒀸 (similar to the Ugaritic letter *g*). This word divider or dividing wedge (German "Trennungskeil") is rendered by a period in transliteration, e.g., *arbᶜ.aṯt* 4.349:2 = **81.4** "four women."

21.8. Use for other languages

In the city of Ugarit, the Ugaritic cuneiform alphabet was used also for Hurrian (e.g. 1.42; 1.111:3–6, 8–12) and for Akkadian (1.67; 1.69; 1.70; 1.73). The short alphabetic cuneiform texts found in Lebanon and Palestine (cf. above **11.2**) apparently rendered words of local Canaanite dialects.

22. *The cuneiform syllabary*

Since Ugaritic words written in cuneiform syllabic signs provide substantial data about vowels and word formation, even beginning students of Ugaritic need basic information about the syllabic writing system. The data are taken from Akkadian texts found at Ugarit in which Ugaritic sounds, names, and words are given in cuneiform syllabic writing. The syllabic phonetic signs are transcribed in italics, the Akkadian values for logograms in roman type, and the original Sumerian values for logograms in upper case roman type. A variety of signs used for the same word or syllable can be distinguished in transcription by accents and subscripts: (1) the value called primary (more or less arbitrarily) bears no accent; (2) the second value bears an acute accent, e.g., *ú* (read *u* two) U:V:137:II:29′; (3) the third value bears a grave accent, e.g., *kàs* (read *kas* three) U:V:137:II:2′; (4 and further) all higher values bear index numbers, e.g., de_4 P:III:16.343:9 (p. 129).

In general, the transcription used by French scholars (Virolleaud, Dhorme, Nougayrol) is retained.

22.1. Origins and principles

The cuneiform syllabic writing, which was brought to Ugarit from Mesopotamia, was invented for the non-Semitic Sumerian language and then was adapted for the East Semitic Akkadian language. At Ugarit, the cuneiform syllabary of the Middle Babylonian type was used.

The system of syllabic cuneiform writing consists of phonetic syllabic signs, logograms, and determinatives (semantic and morphological indicators). A logogram (the less suitable term "ideogram" is also used) is a sign which expresses a word. It carries a phonetic value derived from Sumerian, while the relevant meaning is that of the Middle Babylonian dialect of Akkadian. Most of the signs used in the syllabic cuneiform texts from Ugarit are syllabic signs, which express various types of syllables: vowel (V); consonant + vowel (CV); vowel + consonant (VC); and consonant + vowel + consonant (CVC). These signs can be employed to represent the phonemes of the Ugaritic language and their combinations.

22.2. Ugaritic phonemes and segments of cuneiform syllabic signs

Reconstructed Ugaritic consonantal phonemes can correspond to consonantal elements of the cuneiform syllabic signs used in Ugarit. Some Ugaritic phonemes correspond closely to Akkadian phonemes. Others, which do not have exact equivalents in Akkadian, are rendered by consonantal elements used for phonologically similar Akkadian consonants. Unvoiced, voiced and emphatic consonants are not sufficiently distinguished in the syllabic cuneiform writing. As there were no laryngeals in Middle Babylonian Akkadian language and writing, the syllabic cuneiform signs render Ugaritic laryngeals rather occasionally and indirectly.

In principle cuneiform syllabic writing expresses all vowels; even the length of vowels is often indicated by repeating the vocalic element. The Ugaritic vocalic qualities /a/, /i/, and /u/ and also /ē/ were expressed by the corresponding vocalic elements in the syllabary. Since there is no vowel o in Akkadian, the Ugaritic /ō/ is indicated by u, the closest vowel in the Akkadian system. See tables on p. 26.

22.3. Denotation of Ugaritic words in Akkadian syllabic cuneiform texts

In most instances the Ugaritic character of a personal, divine or geographical name is not indicated. In some cuneiform syllabic texts, however, Ugaritic names are marked as Ugaritic by the so-called "Glossenkeil," expressed in transcription by a colon, e.g. nār:*ra-aḫ-ba-n*[*a*] P:VI:56:rev.:2′ "(river) Raḫban." The Glossenkeil is also prefixed to Ugaritic words in some Akkadian texts, e.g., *:ma-aq-qa-du* P:III:16.153:12 (p. 147) "right of pasture," *:nap-ki-ma* (gen. pl.) P:VI:56:rev.:5′ "(of) the springs." Some Ugaritic words are written in the syllabic texts without this special sign, e.g., *tap-de*$_4$*-tum* P:III:16.131:19 (p. 139) "counterpart"; *na-ḫa-li* (gen.) P:III:16.251:7 (p. 109) "heritage." The Ugaritic words in the quadrilingual vocabulary lists written in cuneiform syllabary are indicated as such by their position in the last column, after the columns devoted to Sumerian, Akkadian, and Hurrian.

The elements of cuneiform syllabic signs used for rendering Ugaritic phonemes are listed below according to system used in the Akkadian glossaries of P:III, IV, VI, U:V, etc.

segment of syllabic sign	Ugaritic phoneme	segment of syllabic sign	Ugaritic phoneme
a	/a/, /ā/	*r*	/r/
e	/ē/, /i/, /a/	*s*	/s/
ḫ	/ḫ/, /ġ/; /ḥ/, /ᶜ/	*ṣ*	/ṣ/
i	/i/, /ī/	*š*	/š/, /ṯ/; /ž/–*ḏ*
k/g/q	/k/–/g/–/q/	*t/d/ṭ*	/t/–/d/–/ṭ/
l	/l/	*u*	/u/, /ū/, /ō/; /w/
m	/m/	*y*	/y/
n	/n/	*z*	/z/, /ẓ/; /ḏ/
p/b	/p/–/b/		

Cf. also:

∅	cf. /ʾ/, /h/, /ᶜ/, /ḥ/
ʾ	/ʾ/; /h/, /ᶜ/

Ugaritic phonemes as rendered in the cuneiform syllabic writing are arranged below according to phonological criteria.

Ugaritic consonant	segment of syllabic sign
/ʾ/	∅ (rarely ʾ)
/h/	∅
/ᶜ/	∅ (rarely *ḫ*-, -*ḫ*), – ʾ
/ḥ/	*ḫ*
/ġ/	*ḫ*
/ḫ/	*ḫ*
/q/, /g/, /k/	*q–g–k*
/š/	*š*
/ž/–*ḏ*	*š* (in foreign words)
/ṣ/, /z/, /s/	*ṣ–z–s*
/ẓ/	*z*
/ḏ/	*z* (in Ugaritic words)
/ṯ/	*š*
/ṭ/, /d/, /t/	*ṭ–d–t*
/b/, /p/	*b–p*
/l/, /r/; /n/; /m/	*l*; *r*; *n*; *m*
/y/	*y* (*i̯*)
/w/	*w*, *u*

Ugaritic vowel	segment of syllabic sign
/a/, /i/, /u/	*a*, *i*, *u*
/ā/, /ī/, /ū/	*a*, *i*, *u*; *a–a*, *i–i*, *u–u*
/ē/	*e*, *e–e*
/ō/	*u*, *u–u*

3. Phonology

31. *Terminology and methods*

31.1. Sounds and signs

In language sound is primary; the written form of a language is only a secondary, derived, and never perfect rendering of the sounds. Since the only direct sources for the Ugaritic language are written documents, the relationship of the signs of the writing system to the sounds of the language has to be considered.

31.2. The grapheme

The grapheme is the basic unit of a graphic system. In Ugaritic alphabetic writing nearly all graphemes are consonant letters. The Ugaritic signs *a*, *i*, *u* indicate combinations of sounds, a vowel preceded or followed by a glottal stop. Signs of the cuneiform syllabic writing indicate syllables which can be divided into segments, which correspond to Ugaritic sounds with varying degrees of precision.

31.3. The phoneme

The phoneme is the sound unit in the phonological system of a language, determined by opposition to other phonemes. Phonology can be defined as the study of the system of sounds as they function in a language. The sounds of the Ugaritic language are here treated as phonemes forming a system.

31.4. Phonetics

Phonetics is the study of real speech sounds. For a language known only from written records, phonetic approaches can be used only indirectly, insofar as living languages can be consulted for help in reconstructing phonemes. Reference to phonetic reality has some practical advantages; it will help the student in learning to distinguish Ugaritic phonemes. Some of these distinctions go beyond those usually known to the student of Hebrew, e.g., in Ugaritic it is necessary to distinguish pharyngeal /ḥ/ from postvelar /ḫ/.

32. *Reconstruction of Ugaritic phonemes*

32.1. Sources and presuppositions

As there are no phonetic records of the Ugaritic language, the written documents have to be utilized for the reconstruction of the sounds; sounds directly observable in related Semitic languages may be referred to. One of the presuppositions of the reconstruction of Ugaritic is the one-to-one relationship of Ugaritic grapheme to phoneme. Another presupposition is the affinity of the Ugaritic language with other Semitic languages with similar phonological systems which have either been spoken without interruption since antiquity, such as Arabic, or preserved by a continuous tradition, such as Biblical Hebrew and Syriac.

32.2. Use of living and traditional Semitic languages

Both the Ugaritic system of consonants and the Ugaritic system of vowels are close to those of Classical Arabic in its modern standard pronunciation. It is also possible to consider the phonetic values of the sounds of contemporary Arabic dialects for the phonetic characterization of Ugaritic phonemes. To some extent the traditional pronunciation of Biblical Hebrew—in its most reliable form, the Sephardic tradition—can also be used. In addition, some features of the traditional pronunciation of Syriac, especially in its older, Eastern tradition, can be helpful.

32.3. Use of Ugaritic alphabetic and syllabic evidence

Ugaritic alphabetic writing distinguishes consonantal phonemes with great precision, but the rendering of vocalic phonemes is incomplete and inexact. Ugaritic words written in syllabic cuneiform signs provide ample, if not always consistent, data about the vowels, while the consonants are often indicated with some ambiguity. The critical use and combination of these two kinds of source material provide a reliable basis for the reconstruction of most inflectional morphemes and for many word patterns.

33. *The phonological system of Ugaritic*

33.1 Segments and suprasegmental features

Though the sounds used in words and sentences can largely be segmented into phonemes, there are some features used in utterances which cannot be accommodated in a linear, segmentable sequence. These suprasegmentals of stress and intonation may be related to individual phonemes or to higher units—syllables, words and sentences. The suprasegmental features cannot be directly observed in Ugaritic sources. (In reconstructed forms and in words from related Semitic languages, word stress is indicated by ´, e.g., /šā́t|tu/.)

33.2. Consonantal and vocalic phonemes

Consonants and vowels are distinguished by phonetic characteristics. The different distribution and function of consonants and vowels can be observed even in Ugaritic. A vowel can occur only as the second component of a syllable, while a consonant must occur as the first component of the syllable and may occur as the third component. The consonants in Ugaritic (as in the other Semitic languages) serve mostly to express roots, while the vowels serve to form patterns and actual forms.

33.3. Vowel length

Vowel length is a distinctive feature in Ugaritic; it is appropriate to consider long vowels as phonemes different from short vowels, not as variants of them. Length can serve as a marker of the plural: /malkātu/, with long /ā/, means "queens," against the singular, with short /a/, /malkatu/ "queen." No signs indicate vowel length in Ugaritic alphabetic writing. Indications of long vowels by repeating vocalic segments in syllabic writing are not used consistently. Vowel length must usually be determined by comparison with related forms in other languages, especially Arabic and Hebrew. In reconstructions, long vowels are marked by a macron (a short horizontal line above the letter): /ā/, /ī/, /ū/, /ē/, /ō/. The secondary vowels /ō/ and /ē/ (from *aw and *ay) occur only long.

33.4. Consonant doubling

The term "long" should not be applied to consonants; the appropriate term is doubled or geminate consonant. The first of the two consonants occurs always at the end of a syllable (which is thus closed), and the second at the beginning of the following syllable: -VC|CV-. There is no sign for consonant doubling in Ugaritic alphabetic writing. In a few instances the doubled consonants may be indicated by repetition of the appropriate sign. The doubling of consonants in syllabic cuneiform writing is neither consistent nor reliable.

33.5. Syllable structure

The vowels of Ugaritic words can be reconstructed to the extent that patterns of syllable structure can be established. There are two kinds of syllables: open syllables, consisting of a consonant and a vowel (CV), and closed syllables, consisting of an opening consonant, a vowel and a closing consonant (CVC). The vowel in an open syllable can be either short or long: CV: /la|ba|nu/, /ᵓa|ti|nu/; CV̄: /dū/, /bā|ᵓū/. Closed syllables can have a short vowel: CVC: /mal|ku/, /baᶜ|lu/, /ᵓil|ᵓa|ku/, /ᵓat|ta/. It is not clear whether closed syllables can have a long vowel; if such structures are possible, they are rare; e.g., /šā́t|tu/ (?).

34. *The consonantal system of Standard Ugaritic*

34.1. Place and manner of articulation

The consonants of Ugaritic can be classified into groups according to the place of articulation. Going from the glottis to the lips, there are laryngeals (including glottals and pharyngeals), postvelars, velars, palato-alveolars, alveolars, dentals, interdentals, and bilabials.

The Ugaritic consonants can also be divided into groups based on manner of articulation. These are stops (occlusives, plosives): /ʾ/ — /q/, /g/, /k/ — /ṭ/, /d/, /t/ — /b/, /p/; fricatives (spirants): /ʿ/, /ḥ/ — /ḫ/, /ǵ/ — /š/ — /ṣ/, /z/, /s/ — /ẓ/, /ḏ/, /ṯ/; and sonants, a group including the liquids, /l/ and /r/, the nasals /n/ and /m/, and the semivowels /y/ and /w/.

	stops and fricatives			sonants		
	unvoiced	voiced	emphatic	nasals	liquids	semivowels
glottals	/ʾ/	/h/				
pharyngeals	/ḥ/	/ʿ/				
postvelars	/ḫ/	/ǵ/				
velars	/k/	/g/	/q/			
palato-alveolars	/š/	/ž/ ?				/y/
alveolars	/s/	/z/	/ṣ/		/l/	
interdentals	/ṯ/	/ḏ/	/ẓ/			
dentals	/t/	/d/	/ṭ/	/n/	/r/	
bilabials	/p/	/b/		/m/		/w/

34.2. Phonological and phonetic identification of consonants

The consonant groups are discussed in order of place of articulation, moving from the glottis to the lips. The individual consonants are listed in the corresponding order: emphatic, voiced, voiceless.

The characteristics of their pronunciation are meant primarily as practical help which will give opportunity to read aloud Ugaritic texts, especially poetry. As attempts to reconstruct the ancient pronunciation, these characteristics have to be considered tentative and approximate.

34.21. Laryngeals

The laryngeals include both glottals and pharyngeals. The cover term laryngeal for both groups is useful, since all four consonants share the tendency to change neighboring vowels into /a/.

The glottal stop /ʾ/, from the phonetic point of view, is no sound but only an interruption in the airstream. From the phonological point of view, however, it is a phoneme. In the Indo-European languages the glottal stop is usually not a phoneme; it is sometimes pronounced to mark the juncture between two vowels, e.g., in Eng. "Jaffa (ʾ)orange," "sea (ʾ)eagle." In Ugaritic writing there is no sign for /ʾ/ alone; the glottal stop is indicated only in combination with vowels, in the signs *a*, *i*, *u*.

The voiced glottal /h/ is pronounced as Eng. h in "head," "have," "rehearse."

The voiceless pharyngeal fricative /ḥ/ is articulated with minimal constriction of the pharynx; it corresponds to Arab. ḥ. It is produced by narrowing but not blocking the airstream.

The voiced pharyngeal fricative /ʿ/ is pronounced with constriction of the pharynx and voicing; it corresponds to Arab. ʿ.

34.22. Postvelars

The postvelar consonants are articulated in the area directly behind the velum (soft palate).

The voiced postvelar fricative /ǵ/, the voiced counterpart of /ḫ/, occurs in Sephardic Hebrew pronunciation as the spirantized counterpart of g (i.e., gimel without dageš); cf. also Dutch g in "gracht," North German g in "Tage."

The voiceless postvelar fricative /ḫ/, which corresponds to Arab. ḫ, is pronounced like ch in Scottish "loch," and the so-called ach-laut of German "acht," "Bach."

34.23. Velars

The emphatic velar stop /q/ corresponds to Arab. q.

The voiced velar stop /g/ is pronounced like Eng. g in "give."

The voiceless velar stop /k/ is pronounced like Eng. k in "king."

34.24. Palato-alveolars

The palato-alveolars are pronounced with the tongue near the hard palate.

The voiced palato-alveolar fricative /ž/, counterpart of /š/, occurs as a late variant of the voiced interdental /ḏ/. It is like the sibilant sounds in Eng. "measure" and French "je."

The voiceless palato-alveolar fricative /š/ is comparable to Arab. and H. š and to Eng. sh in "ship."

The palato-alveolar semivowel /y/ is articulated at the same place as the vowel /i/. It is pronounced like Eng. y in "yoke."

34.25. Alveolars

The alveolars /s/, /z/, and /ṣ/, together with /š/ and /ž/, are called also sibilants.

The emphatic alveolar /ṣ/ is pronounced like Arab. ṣ, with the root of the tongue pressed up.

The voiced alveolar fricative /z/ is pronounced like Eng. z in "zero."

The voiceless alveolar fricative /s/ is pronounced like Eng. s in "simple."

The last letter of the Ugaritic alphabet, *ś*, indicates mostly /s/ + /u/.

The alveolar lateral /l/ is articulated with the tongue held so that the airstream moves around both sides. It is pronounced like Eng. l in "leaf."

34.26. Dentals

The dental consonants are pronounced with the tongue near the upper teeth.

The dental liquid /r/ is articulated with the tip of the tongue; it is presented like Scottish r in "burn," Italian r in "Roma," Czech r.

The dental nasal /n/ is pronounced like Eng. n in "nap."

The emphatic dental stop /ṭ/ is pronounced like Arab. ṭ, with the root of the tongue pressed up.

The voiced dental stop /d/ is pronounced like Eng. d in "daddy."

The voiceless dental stop /t/ is pronounced like Eng. t in "tip."

34.27. Interdentals

The interdental fricatives are articulated with the tongue-tip poised between the upper and lower teeth.

The emphatic interdental is transliterated /ẓ/, but this is somewhat misleading as the consonant is voiceless (as the other emphatics are); a more appropriate transliteration would be ṯ̣, indicating the close relation to the interdental /ṯ/. The interdental articulation of the cognate Arabic sound is preserved in conservative Bedouin dialects; the standard pronunciation in modern Arabic is secondary, perhaps influenced by non-Semitic languages.

The voiced interdental /ḏ/ is like Arab. ḏ or Eng. th in "this," "father."

The voiceless interdental /ṯ/ is like Arab. ṯ or Eng. th in "thin," "path."

34.28. Bilabials

The bilabials are articulated with both lips.

The voiced bilabial stop /b/ is like Eng. b in "bit."

The voiceless bilabial stop /p/ is like Eng. p in "path."

The bilabial nasal /m/ is like Eng. m in "more."

The bilabial semivowel /w/ is articulated in a way similar to that of the vowel /u/. It corresponds to Arab. w and to Eng. bilabial w in "win," "awake."

35. *The vowels of Standard Ugaritic*

35.1. Evidence for the vowels

The Ugaritic signs *a*, *i*, *u* indicate—in combination with the glottal stop—the three basic vowel qualities, though they do not indicate vowel quantity. Syllabic cuneiform writing can be used to indicate the secondary vowel /ē/ and to mark vowel quantity, but it is not consistent in indicating length. The length of vowels in Ugaritic must be reconstructed largely by comparison with other Semitic languages.

35.2. Short and long vowels

The three basic short vowels are /a/, /i/, /u/. The three basic long vowels, /ā/, /ī/, /ū/, correspond to the three basic short vowels. The two additional long vowels are secondary, the result of monophthongization of diphthongs: /ē/ < *ay and /ō/ < *aw.

The Ugaritic vocalic phonemes can be represented in the form of two vowel triangles.

35.3. Phonetic characteristics of vowels

The basic values of the Ugaritic system, a relatively simple one, can be related to certain values of the more complicated vowel system of English.

The low vowels, /a/ and /ā/, are articulated at the velum; /a/ is like the vowel of Eng. "cup," /ā/ is like the first vowel of Eng. "father."

The high front vowels, /i/ and /ī/, are articulated at the palate; /i/ is like the vowel of Eng. "pin," /ī/ is like the vowel of Eng. "sheep."

The high back vowels, /u/ and /ū/, are articulated at the velum with the help of rounded lips; /u/ is similar to Eng. "put," /ū/ to Eng. "rude," "doom."

The mid-front vowel, /ē/, is articulated at the palate, cf. Eng. "there."

The mid-back vowel, /ō/, is articulated at the velum; cf. Eng. "port," "door."

36. *Ugaritic phonemes and their Semitic correspondences*

The chart on p. 34 presents the Ugaritic phonemes arranged according to their phonetic characteristics, as they are expressed in the alphabetic and syllabic writing systems, in relationship to the phonemes of several other Semitic languages and their hypothetical common ancestor so-called Proto-Semitic.

These correspondences are helpful in comparing Ugaritic words and forms with those of the other languages.

segment of syllabic sign	Ugaritic sign	Ugaritic phoneme	Arabic	Hebrew	Aramaic / Syriac	Akkadian	Proto-Semitic
∅, -ʾ-	(*a*, *i*, *u*)	/ʾ/	ʾ	ʾ	ʾ	ʾ/∅	*ʾ
∅	*h*	/h/	h	h	h	∅	*h
-*ḫ*-	*ḥ*	/ḥ/	ḥ	ḥ	ḥ	∅	*ḥ
∅, -ʿ-, -*ḫ*-	ʿ	/ʿ/	ʿ	ʿ	ʿ	∅	*ʿ
-*ḫ*-	*ḫ*	/ḫ/	ḫ	ḥ	ḥ	ḫ	*ḫ
-*ḫ*-	*ġ*	/ġ/	ġ	ʿ	ʿ	∅	*ġ
-*q*-, -*g*-, -*k*-	*k*	/k/	k	k	k	k	*k
	g	/g/	ǧ	g	g	g	*g
	q	/q/	q	q	q	q	*q
-*š*-	*d̠*	/ž/ (?)					
-*š*-	*š*	/š/	s	š	š	š	*š
			š	ś	ś/s	š	*ś (s^1)
-*ṣ*-, -*z*-, -*s*-	*s*	/s/	š	s	s	s	*s
	z	/z/	z	z	z	z	*z
	ṣ	/ṣ/	ḍ	ṣ	(q)/ʿ	ṣ	*ḍ (d^1)
			ṣ	ṣ	ṣ	ṣ	*ṣ
-*z*-	*ẓ*	/ẓ/(ṯ̣)	ẓ	ṣ	ṭ	ṣ	*ẓ (ṯ̣)
-*z*-	*d̠*	/d̠/	d̠	z	d	z	*d̠
-*š*-	*ṯ*	/ṯ/	ṯ	š	t	š	*ṯ
-*ṭ*-, -*d*-, -*t*-	*t*	/t/	t	t	t	t	*t
	d	/d/	d	d	d	d	*d
	ṭ	/ṭ/	ṭ	ṭ	ṭ	ṭ	*ṭ
-*b*-, -*p*-	*p*	/p/	f	p	p	p	*p
	b	/b/	b	b	b	b	*b
-*n*-	*n*	/n/	n	n	n	n	*n
-*m*-	*m*	/m/	m	m	m	m	*m
-*l*-	*l*	/l/	l	l	l	l	*l
-*r*-	*r*	/r/	r	r	r	r	*r
-*y*-, -*i*-	*y*	/y/	y	y	y	y/∅	*y
-*w*-, -*u*-	*w*	/w/	w	w	w	w/∅	*w
-*i*-	*i* /ʾi/	/i/	i	i/e	i	i	*i
-*i*-, -*i*-*i*-	*i* /ʾī/	/ī/	ī	ī	ī	ī	*ī
-*e*-, -*e*-*e*-	*i* /ʾē/	/ē/	ay	ē	ay	ī	*ay
-*a*-	*a* /ʾa/	/a/	a	a	a	a/e	*a
-*a*-, -*a*-*a*-	*a* /ʾā/	/ā/	ā	ā/ō	ā	ā	*ā
-*u*-, -*u*-*u*-	*u* /ʾō/	/ō/	aw	ō	aw	ū	*aw
-*u*-	*u* /ʾu/	/u/	u	u/o	u	u	*u
-*u*-, -*u*-*u*-	*u* /ʾū/	/ū/	ū	ū	ū	ū	*ū

36.1. Atypical correspondences

There are some important atypical correspondences. One of them involves Ugaritic /ǵ/, which may correspond to Proto-Semitic and Arab. ẓ, H. and Akkad. ṣ, and Aram. ṭ. Note, for example, /n-ǵ-r/ "to guard" (Arab. naẓara, H. and Akkad. n-ṣ-r, Aram. n-ṭ-r), /ǵ-m-ʾ/ "to be thirsty" (Arab. ẓamiʾa, H. ṣāmēʾ, Akkad. ṣamū); /y-q-ǵ/ "to awake" (Arab. yaqiẓa, H. y-q-ṣ).

37. *Some non-standard features*

37.1. Archaic features

In the archaic texts 1.12 and 1.24, the interdental *ḏ* is preserved in words which elsewhere are written with *d*, e.g., *ḏ* 1.24:45 "that of"; *aḫḏ* 1.12:II:32 "he took." In these texts, too, *ẓ* appears where *ṭ* is used elsewhere in Ugaritic, e.g., *lẓpn* 1.24:44 "kind" (cf. *lṭpn* 1.15:II:13 = **87.2**); cf. also *ḫlmẓ* 1.115:2 = **82.5** "dragon" (Akkad. ḫulmiṭṭu; cf. H. ḥomæṭ "lizard").

37.2. Innovative features

In some late, informal texts, a reduced inventory of phonemes is used. The original /ṯ/ merges with /š/; the result of the merger is transliterated *Š̌* (the Ugaritic sign is a circle); cf. 4.31:2 = **86.53** *bŠ̌Š̌ ʿŠ̌r* "for 16" (cf. *ṯṯ* 4.630:6 = **82.2**). Pharyngeal /ḥ/ is supplanted by /ḫ/; the result is written with the /ḫ/ sign (sometimes transliterated *Ḫ*); cf. *ypḫ* 4.31:9 "witness" (cf. *ypḥ* 3.9:18 = **84.2**).

The letter *ḏ* was probably used to indicate /ž/ in foreign words: *aḏdd* /ʾaždād-/(?) 4.709:2 GN (H. ʾAšdōd).

In some late texts, isolated instances of the change /ā́/ > /ō/ (common in Canaanite languages) can be observed, e.g., *ṯut* /ṯaʾōti/ gen.-acc. pl. 1.80:3 = **86.51** "sheep" (instead of /-āt-/); cf. also *a-du-nu* /ʾadōnu/ P:VI:139:2 (instead of /ʾadānu/), cf. *a-da-nu* U:V:130:II:9′ "father."

38. *Phonetic and phonological changes*

38.1. Kinds of changes

Unconditioned changes affect phonemes in all positions. Conditioned changes are motivated by the particular position of a phoneme in a word (beginning, end), or by contact—immediate or not—with other phonemes. These changes, called combinatory changes, can be regressive, caused by a following phoneme, or progressive, through the impact of a preceding phoneme. Combinatory changes may involve immediately adjoining phonemes or non-adjacent phonemes. Such changes may be total, as in the assimilation $C_1C_2 > C_1C_1$, or partial, as in the assimilation $C_1C_2 > C_3C_2$, where C_1 is voiceless but both C_2 and C_3 are voiced phonemes.

38.2. Changes involving consonants

38.21. Assimilation

Progressive assimilation takes place in immediate contact.

*-dt- > /-tt/ : *ylt* /yalattā/ < -*dt- 1.23:53 "they (du. fem.) bore"
*-lq- > /-qq-/ : *iqḥ* /ʾiqqaḥu/ < -*lq- 1.14:IV:41 = **88.72** "I shall take"
*-nC- > /-CC-/ : *at* /ʾattā/ < *-nt- 1.2:IV:11; *at-ta* U:V:130:II:4 "you"; *ytt* /yatattī/ < *-nt- 1.100:75 = **86.73** "I gave"; *ap* /ʾappu/ < *-np- 1.18:IV:26 = **88.64**; *ap-pu* U:V:137:II:19′ "nose"

Regressive assimilation occurs also at distance.

*š-ṯ > /ṯ-ṯ-/: *ṯṯb* /ṯaṯib/ < *šaṯib 2.14:18 "return!"

38.22. Loss of consonants

Loss of /ʾ/ may occur before another laryngeal: *ʾaʿdubu- > *ʿdbk* 1.18:IV:22 = **88.64** "I shall direct you"; it may also occur after another laryngeal: compare *šbʿid* /-ʿʾ-/ 2.12:9 and *šbʿd* /-ʿ-/ 2.12:8 "seven times."

Loss of /h/ occurs in suffixed pronouns: *aštn* < *-nh- 1.19:III:34 = **88.65** "I shall put him." Cf. also *bbtw* /bi-bētiwu/(?) 3.9:4 = **84.2** "in his house" < *-bētiu < *-bētihu; perhaps also *lwm* /lēwum(u)/ 3.9:6 = **84.2** "to them" < *lēhum-(?).

38.23. New consonants

New consonants may appear to ease pronunciation. Cf. perhaps /n/ before suffixed pronouns: *ʿmnk* 2.71:11 "with/at you"; *aqbrnh* 1.19:III:34 = **88.65** "I shall bury him" (or energicus?).

A new consonant may replace the original one: *-m- > *-mp- > /-p-/ in *špš* /šapš-/ 6.24:2 = **81.2**; *ša-ap-šu* U:V:138:3′ "sun" (cf. H. šæmæš < *šamš-; H. šimšōn but Gr. Sampsōn).

Cf. also perhaps new /w/ before /u/, replacing *h, **38.22.**

38.3. Changes involving the semivowels /w/ and /y/

38.31. Initial *w- > /y-/

The change of *w- > /y-/ is characteristic of the Northwest Semitic languages. Cf. *yʿl-* /yaʿil-/ 1.17:VI:22 "mountain goat" but Arab. waʿ(i)l; *yrḫ* /yarḫ-/ 1.105:1 = **81.3** "month" but Akkad. warḫu. The exceptions are the conjunction *w-* /wa/ "and," some forms from the roots /w-l-d/ "to bear" and /w-p-ṯ/ "to spit," and a few personal names.

38.32. Monophthongization

A diphthong (short vowel + semivowel) is changed to a single long vowel.

*-uw- > /-ū-/: *ybl* /yūbalu/ < *yuwb- 1.23:52 = **88.2** "it is/was brought"
*-iy- > /-ī-/: *ḥmt* /ḥāmīt-/ < *-iyt- 1.14:IV:4; *:ḫa-mì-ti* P:III:16.86:4 (p. 138) "wall" (pl. *ḥmyt* /ḥāmiyāt-/ 1.119:27 = **86.75**)
*-aw- > /-ō-/: *u* /ʾō/ < *ʾaw 1.23:64 "or" (H. ʾō, Arab. ʾaw)
*-ay- > /-ē-/: *in* /ʾēn/ 1.19:III:11 "there is not" (H. ʾayin, ʾēn)

Double semivowel /-ww-/ or /-yy-/ remains unchanged.

ayl /ʾayyal-/ 1.6:I:24 "deer"
ʿwrt /ʿawwart-/ 1.19:IV:5 = **87.4** "blindness"

38.4. Changes involving the vowels

38.41. Assimilation

Vowels may assimilate to a preceding or following consonant.
After or before a labial, V > /u/.

šm /šum-/ 1.1:IV:14; *šu-um-* P:III:15.139:9 (p. 167) "name" (cf. H. šēm < *šim)
bn /bun-/(?) 4.350:1 "son" (cf. *bu-nu-šu* U:V:137:II:31 "son of man(kind)") (cf. H. bēn < *bin)

After or before a laryngeal, V > /a/.

išal /ʾišʾal-/ < *-šʾul- 2.34:28 "I shall ask"
išlḥ /ʾišlaḥ-/ < *-šluḥ- 1.24:21 = **88.1** "I shall send"

Vowels may also assimilate to following semivowels; before /y/, V > /i/, and before /w/, V > /u/.

iy /ʾiy(y)a/(?) < *ʾayy- (cf. H. ʾayya, ʾē) 1.6:IV:4 "where?"; *iyṯr* 4.153:5 PN ("where is Bull?"); cf. *ayaḫ* 4.338:8 PN ("where is (my) brother?")

Vowels may regressively assimilate to other vowels.

ulp /ʾullūp/ < *ʾallūp- "leader" 1.40:20–21; *ul-lu-pí* (gen.) P:III:11.787:11 (p. 194) PN (cf. H. ʾallūp)

Vowel assimilation may, in later texts, be motivated by case endings.

uḫy /ʾuḫuya/ < *ʾaḫu- (nom.) 2.41:20 = **83.3** "my brother"; *iḫy* /ʾiḫiya/ < *ʾaḫi- (gen.) 2.41:18 = **83.3** "of my brother"

Progressive vowel assimilation also occurs in compound nouns.

ilib /ʾilʾib-/ < *-ʾab- 1.109:12=**86.71** "ancestral god"

38.42. Dissimilation

The vowel of a verbal prefix is dissimilated from the characteristic vowel of the imperfect (so-called Barth-Ginsberg Law.)

prefix vowel	characteristic vowel	
/-i-/	/-a-/	*ilak* /ʾilʾaku/ 1.4:VII:45 "I shall send"
/-a-/	/-u-/	*amlk* /ʾamluk-/ 1.6:I:62 "I shall reign"
	/-i-/	*atn* /ʾatinu/ 1.24:22=**88.1** "I shall give"
/-u-/	/-ā-/	*uba* /ʾubāʾa/(?) 1.100:72=**86.73** "may I enter" (?)

4. Word Formation

41. *The word*

41.1. Delimitation

While there are various definitions of the word in modern linguistics, for the purposes of this grammar it is sufficient to adopt the concept the native Ugaritians used in their writing system. Ugaritian scribes separated words in the majority of texts by dividing wedges, rendered by periods (.) in transliteration. The one-consonant particles are usually written together with the following word (as in Hebrew); in some, mostly non-literary texts, they are separated by a dividing wedge. (In KTU all words, including the one-consonant particles, are separated by spaces.) Since all syllables begin with a consonant, all words begin with a consonant as well. A word can end with either a vowel or a consonant.

41.2. Categories of words

As in the other Semitic languages, Ugaritic words can be divided into three large groups: nouns, verbs, and particles.

The nouns include, beside substantive and adjective nouns, numerals and pronouns.

The verbs exhibit more uniformity than the other categories of words, in both finite forms and verbal nouns.

The particles can be divided into adverbs, prepositions, conjunctions, and interjections, according to functional and distributional criteria.

42. *The structure of words*

42.1. System and periphery

The majority of Ugaritic words are formed according to a system characterized by two elements: the root, generally consisting of three consonants, and the pattern, which always includes vowels and frequently includes consonants as well. Both root and pattern are discontinuous morphemes.

Certain genuine Semitic words do not fit the system; their bases can have either a smaller (one or two) or a larger (four or more) number of consonants. Some special groups of these words can be singled out, such as (a) basic nouns, (b) particles, (c) onomatopoeic words (those which imitate sounds), (d) compound nouns, and (e) names. Words of foreign origin are generally adapted to the Ugaritic system of word formation. The foreign origin of a word can be recognized if it exhibits more than three root consonants or presents an unusual combination of sounds, even if the foreign model is not known.

42.2. Patterns

The pattern can be defined as a non-contiguous morpheme. In combination with root it is used to form words, especially nouns and verbs.

Nominal patterns are used to form different types of nouns. In certain patterns semantic characteristics can be observed, e.g., the pattern qattāl- is used to indicate the agent by whom the action is regularly performed.

Verbal patterns are used in combination with roots to create sets of verbal forms which express manner of action and voice.

The elements of nominal and verbal patterns can be characterized according to (a) whether they are vocalic or consonantal and (b) their position in relation to the root consonants. Between the root consonants are vowels: short, long or a zero vowel, as in the patterns of the type qVtl: qatl-, qitl-, etc. Some patterns involve doubling or repeating elements of the root.

The additional morphemes are distinguished according to their position: (a) prefix (preformative), before the first root consonant; (b) infix, between root consonants; (c) afformative, after the last root consonant. (The apparent asymmetry in this terminology is due to the use of "affix" as a linguistic term covering all three kinds listed here. In this grammar, the term "suffix" is reserved for words attached to nominal and verbal forms, such as suffixed personal pronouns.)

Prefixes, infixes, afformatives, and vowels used to form basic patterns of nouns and verbs are to be carefully distinguished from prefixes, infixes, afformatives, and vocalic changes that occur in the inflection of nouns and verbs.

42.3. Roots

The root can be defined as a discontinuous morpheme usually consisting of three consonants. It appears in nominal and verbal forms, combined with the vocalic and consonantal elements of the patterns. The discontinuity of the root does not affect its real character.

The traditional notion that the triconsonantal root indicates the basic meaning of a word may be retained as a working hypothesis.

43. *The formation of nouns (including numerals)*

Nouns, both basic and those generated from a verbal root, exhibit a relatively large number of forms. Nominal patterns can be classified according to (a) the number and distribution of root consonants and (b) the formative morphemes: vowels between root consonants, doubling and repeating of certain root consonants, prefixes, afformatives and infixes; not all of these morphemes are visible in the consonantal writing. Basic nouns tend to have fewer than three consonants.

Pattern	Reconstructed form	Written form alphabetic	Written form syllabic	Meaning	Corresponding (and related) forms

43.1. Patterns with fewer than three consonants

Pattern	Reconstructed form	Written form alphabetic	Written form syllabic	Meaning	Corresponding (and related) forms
	C_1-				
q-	/p-/	*p*	*pí-*	"mouth"	H. pǣ, Arab. fū, fī, fā
C_1VC_3					
qal-	/ʾab-/	*ab*	*a-bi*	"father"	H. ʾāb, Arab. ʾab(ū)
f.	/ʾamat-/	*amt*		"maidservant"	H. ʾāmā, Arab. ʾamat
qil-	/ʾil-/	*il*	ilum(*lum*)	"god"	H. ʾēl
f.	/ʾišat-/	*išt*	*i-ša-ti*	"fire"	(H. ʾēš), Akkad. išātu
qul-	/šum-/	*šm*	*šu-mu-*	"name"	H. (šēm < *šim), Arab. (ism),

43.2. Patterns with three root consonants

43.21. Monosyllabic bases

Pattern	Reconstructed form	Written form alphabetic	Written form syllabic	Meaning	Corresponding (and related) forms
$C_1VC_2C_3$-					
qatl-	/ʾarṣ-/	*arṣ*	*ar-ṣum*	"earth"	H. ʾǽræṣ < *ʾarṣ-, Arab. ʾarḍ
	/raʾš-/	*riš*	*ra-a-ša*	"head"	H. rō(ʾ)š < *raʾš-, Arab. raʾs
	/malk-/	*mlk*	*ma-al-ku*	"king"	H. mǽlæk < *malk-
f.	/malkat-/	*mlkt*		"queen"	H. malkā
II /y/	*bayt- > /bēt-/	*bt*	*be-ti-*	"house"	H. (báyit), bēt, Arab. (bayt)
II=III	/ᶜamm-/	*ᶜm*	*am-mu-*	"uncle"	H. ᶜAmmī- (in PN), Arab. ᶜamm
qitl-	/rigl-/		*ri-ig-lu*	"foot"	H. (rǽgæl < *ragl-), Arab. riǧl
qutl-	/ʾudn-/	*udn*		"ear"	H. ʾózæn < ʾuḏn, Arab. ʾuḏn

43.22. Bisyllabic bases with short vowels

Pattern	Reconstructed form	Written form alphabetic	Written form syllabic	Meaning	Corresponding (and related) forms
$C_1VC_2VC_3$-					
qatal-	/dakar-/	*dkr*	*da-ka-rum*	"male"	H. zākār < *zakar, Arab. ḏakar
qutal-	/kunap-/	*knp*	*ku-na-p(i)*	"wing"	H. (kānāp), Arab. (kanaf)
qatil-	/yariḫ-/	*yrḫ*	*ya-ri-ḫi-*	"moon," "month"	H. yārē(a)ḥ < *yariḥ-
f.	/qadišt-/	*qdšt*	*qa-diš-ti*	"hierodule"	H. qədēšā < *qadišat-
qitil-	/ᶜiḏir-/		*i-zi-ir*	"help"	H. (ᶜḗzær < *ᶜizr-)
qatul-	/qaṭun-/	*qṭn*	*qà-tu-na*	"small"	H. qāṭōn < *qaṭun-
qutul-	/ḥudur-/	*ḥdr*	[ḫ]*u-du-rum*	"room"	H. (ḥǽdær), Arab. (ḥidr)

43.23. Bisyllabic bases with long vowels

Pattern	Reconstructed form	Written form alphabetic	Written form syllabic	Meaning	Corresponding (and related) forms
$C_1\bar{V}C_2VC_3$-					
qātal-	/ʾāpan-/	*apn-*		"wheel"	H. ʾōpān < *ʾāpan-
qātil-	/yāṣir-/	*yṣr*	*ya-ṣí-ru-ma* (pl.)	"potter"	H. yōṣer < *yāṣir-
	/lāʾiy-/	*liy*	*la-i-ya*	"victorious"	
f.	/ḥāmīt-/ < *iyt-	*ḥmt*	*ḫa-mì-ti*	"wall"	H. ḥōmā < *ḥām(iy)ā
$C_1VC_2\bar{V}C_3$-					
qatāl-	/ṯalāṯ-/	*ṯlṯ*		"three"	H. šālōš < ṯalāṯ-, Arab. ṯalāṯ

Pattern	Reconstructed form	Written form alphabetic	Written form syllabic	Meaning	Corresponding (and related) forms
qatāl- f.	/tahāmat-/	thmt	ta-a-ma-tum	"ocean"	H. (təhōm), Arab. (tihāmat), Akkad. (tiāmtu)
qutāl-	/ḫurāṣ-/	ḫrṣ	ḫu-r[a-ṣu]	"gold"	Akkad. ḫurāṣu
qatīl-	/ḫarīm-/		ḫa-ri-mu	"split"	
	/ḥarīm-/		ḥa-ri-mu	"separated"	H. ḥārīm (PN)
C_1VwC_2VC- *qawtal- >					
qōtal-	/kōṯar/	kṯr	ku-šar-ru	DN	Arab. kawṯar, Phoen. khousōr
f.	/kōṯarat-/	kṯrt		DN	H. kōšārōt (pl.)

43.24. Patterns with doubled consonants

$C_1VC_2C_2VC_3$-

| qattal- | /ʾayyal-/ | ayl | a-ya-li | "deer" | H. ʾayyāl, Arab. ʾayyal |

$C_1VC_2C_2\bar{V}C_3$-

qattāl-	/qarrād-/	qrd	qa-ra-di	"warrior"	Akkad. qarrādu
qittīl-	/ʾibbir/ < *ʾa-	ibr		"buffalo"	H. (ʾabbīr)
qattūl-	/ʾaddūr-/	adr	a-du-rum	"noble"	H. (ʾaddīr)
quttūl-	/ʾullūp-/	ulp	ul-lu-pí	"leader"	H. (ʾallūp), Arab. (ʾalūf, ʾullāf)

$C_1VC_2VC_3C_3$-

| qutull- | /mulukk-/ | mlk | mu-lu-uk-ku | GN | |
| f. | /ʾurubbat-/ | urbt | | "opening" | H. (ʾărubbā) |

43.25. Patterns with root consonants otherwise repeated

C_1-C_2-C_3VC_3-

| qatlal- (?) | | ṣḥrr | | "scorched" | (cf. H. ṣəḥōr-), (cf. Arab. ṣaḥrāʾ) |

C_1-C_2-C_3-C_2-C_3

| qataltal- (?) | | ysmsm | | "beautiful" | |

$C_1VC_3C_1VC_3$

| qalqal- | | ʿrʿr | | "tamarisk" | H. ʿarʿār < *-ʿar, Arab. ʿarʿar |

43.26. Patterns with prefixes

Prefix ʾ- (also used for indicating an auxiliary vowel, ʾVC|C-)

ʾi-	/ʾirbiy-/(?)	irby		"locusts" (coll.)	H. ʾarbǣ, Akkad. erbū, erbiu
ʾu-	/ʾuṣbaʿ-/	uṣbʿ		"finger"	H. (ʾæṣbaʿ < *ʾi-), Arab. (ʾiṣbaʿ)
ʾa-	/ʾaqhat-/	aqht		PN	H. (qəhāt, PN)
	/ʾarbaʿ-/	arbʿ		"four"	H. ʾarbaʿ, Arab. ʾarbaʿ
	/ʾalʾiy-/	aliy		"very strong"	

Prefix ʿ-

| ʿa- | /ʿaqšar-/ | ʿqšr | | "scaly" | |

Pattern	Reconstructed form	Written form alphabetic	syllabic	Meaning	Corresponding (and related) forms
Prefix y-					
ya-	/yašpuṭ-/		*ya-aš-pu-ṭì*	PN	H. (yišpoṭ)
Prefix š-					
ša-	/šamrar-/	*šmrr*		"poisoning"	
Prefix t-					
ta-	/tarbāṣ-/	*trbṣ*	*ta-ar-ba-ṣi*	"stable"	Akkad. tarbāṣu
f.	/talʾiyat-/	*tliyt*		"victory"	
Prefix m-					
mu-	/munaḫḫim-/	*mnḫm*	*mu-na-ḫi-mu*	PN ("comforter")	H. Mənaḥem (PN)
maqtal-	/magdal-/	*mgdl*	*ma-ag-da-la*	"tower"	H. migdāl < *magdal, Syr. magdlā
	/malʾak-/	*mlak*		"messenger"	H. malʾāk, Arab. malʾak
f.	/markabt-/	*mrkbt*	*mar-kab-te*	"chariot"	H. mærkābā, mirkǽbæt
maqtil-	/marziḥ-/	*mrzḥ*	*mar-zi-ḫi*	"cultic feast"	H. marzēaḥ
f.	/maṣṣibat-/ < *-nṣ-	*mṣbt*	*ma-ṣi-bat*	GN	H. maṣṣēbā < *-ib-
Prefix n-					
na-	/naḥbal-/	*nḥbl*	*na-ʾa-ba-li*	GN	

43.27. Patterns with afformatives

(The patterns with feminine afformatives /-(a)t-/ are listed—marked with f.—after the corresponding masculine forms (unmarked) in the preceding paragraphs.)

Afformative -ūt					
-ūt-	/ʾadrūt-/		*ad-ru-ti*	"nobility"(?)	(cf. H. -ūt-)
Afformative -y					
-ay(a)	/ṭallaya/	*ṭly*	*ṭa-la-ya*	DN f.	(cf. H. Śāray PN)
-īy-	/gazarīy-/	*gzry*	*ga-za-ri-ya*	Gazarian (GN)	(cf. H. -ī, Arab. -īy-)
Afformative -n					
-ān-	/ᶜurubān-/	*ᶜrbn*	*ú-ru-ba-nu*	"guarantee"	H. (ᶜērābōn)
-īn-	/ᶜabdīn-/	*ᶜbdn*	*ab-di-na*	PN	
Afformative -l					
	/šimʾāl-/	*šmal*		"left"	H. śəmō(ʾ)l, Arab. (šimāl)

43.28. Patterns with infixes

Infix -t-	/ṯitmanēt-/(?)	*ṯtmnt*		PN f.	(cf. H. šəmīnī, Arab. ṯamāniya)

43.29. Other patterns

Two afformatives					
-īy- + -ān-	/ʾuṯrīyān-/	*uṯryn*	*uš-r*[i-ya]*-ni*	"successor"	
-t- + -ān-	/ᶜaqalatān-/(?)	*ᶜqltn*		"crooked"	H. ᶜăqallātōn

Pattern	Reconstructed form	Written form alphabetic	syllabic	Meaning	Corresponding (and related) forms
Prefix and afformative					
ˀa- -ān-	/ˀalˀiyān-/	*aliyn*		"victorious"	
m- -ān-		*mmskn*		"mixing bowl"	(cf. H. mimsāk)
Prefix and infix					
(ˀ)i- -t-		*ištmᶜ*	*-iš-ta-mi*	GN ("listening")	H. (ˀæštəmōaᶜ)

43.3. Nouns with more than three root consonants

Four-consonant nouns often have a liquid as a second root consonant.

krśu (nom.) 4.225:16; *krsi* (gen.) 4.225:17 "chair" (cf. the more frequent *ksu* 1.4:VIII:12)
ḫnzr- cf. *ḫnzrk* 1.5:V:9 "your swine"
fem. *almnt* 1.16:VI:50 = **85.1** "widow" (cf. H. ˀalmānā, Aram. ˀarməlā)
ṯmn /ṯamānī/(?) < *-iy 1.15:II:24 "8"; cf. *ṯmnym* 1.4:VII:11 "80"

Five-consonant nouns are extremely rare.

algbṯ 4.158:15 "(a precious stone)," perhaps a word of foreign origin

43.4. Compound nouns

General compound nouns (other than proper names) are very rare.

bl + *mt* "no" + "death" : *blmt* 1.17:VI:27 = **88.63** "immortality"
il + *ˀab- "god" + "father" : *ilib* 1.109:12 = **86.71** "ancestral god"
bn + *ˀ-n-š : *bnš*, pl. *bnšm* 3.5:16 = **86.33**, *bu-nu-šu* U:V:131:7′ "son of man(kind), man"

Many personal names are compounds:

Nouns containing a substantival (genitival) attribute; they are often treated as an inflectional unit.

ᶜmlbu (nom.) 4.165:7; *ᶜmlbi* (gen.) 4.344:6 PN ("Uncle of Lion")
abdi-*an-ti* (nom.) P:VI:82:2 PN ("Servant of ᶜAnat")
ᶜbdrpu (nom.) 4.609:33 PN ("servant of Rapiˀu")

Sentence names, with nominal or verbal predicate.

ršpab 4.141:I:16, rašap-*a-bu* U:V:5:17 PN ("Rašap (is) father")
bᶜlytn 4.628:2 PN ("Baal gave")
ybnil 4.141:I:8, *ya-ab-ni*-ilu P:VI:107:1 PN ("may Il build/create")

44. *The formation of pronouns*

The pronouns are generally formed from morphemes which contain one or two consonants. The vowels are often distinctive—e.g., /-ta/ masc. and /-ti/(?) fem. in the second person singular pronouns—but they are difficult to determine as they are not indicated in the alphabetic writing. In pronouns of demonstrative character, various deictic elements are represented: /d/ (< *ḏ), /h/, /ʾ/, /k/, /l/, /m/, /n/, /y/.

45. *The formation of particles*

The basic particles are formed from short elements usually containing one consonant only. There are many particles whose nominal origin can be clearly seen, while there are few particles of verbal origin. In deictic particles, deictic elements similar to those found in the pronouns occur.

46. *The formation of verbs*

46.1. Roots

Verb forms are generated from roots. Some roots are attested only in verbal forms, while others are also used in nominal forms. Most verbal roots consist of three root consonants. Some classes of "weak" verbs go back to bases consisting of two consonants only. There are only a few verbs with four consonants; probably all of them can be considered variants of bases with three consonants.

46.2. Verbal classes

Verbs with three consonants include all strong verbs, and some classes of weak verbs, those with one or more phonetically weak root consonants which are assimilated or eliminated in some forms. The remains of two-consonant bases can be observed in other classes of weak verbs, and also in some sets of forms in verbs which are otherwise adapted to the triconsonantal system. Only a few verbs with more than three root consonants are attested, as noted above.

46.3. Characteristic vowels

In the simple active pattern, the vowels between the second and third root consonant of the finite forms indicate the character of the verb, i.e., whether it is a verb of action, a verb expressing a changeable state, or a verb indicating a permanent state. This feature is of a semantic order and is not basically changed by the inflection.

The characteristic vowels in the forms of the perfect are in principle opposite to those in the forms of imperfect (and imperative); a kind of polarity may be observed.

	perfect	imperfect
verbs of action	/-a-/	/-u-/
stative verbs, temporary quality	/-i-/	/-a-/
stative verbs, permanent quality	/-u-/	/-a-/

This system is affected by phonetic changes, e.g., a laryngeal in the second or third position of the root changes the characteristic vowel toward /a/, and in many forms of verbs III /w/ and

/y/, the characteristic vowel is contracted. In alphabetic writing, direct evidence for the characteristic vowels is limited to forms of verbs with glottal stop in the second position of the root (II /ʾ/) and some forms of verbs with glottal stop in the third position of the root (III /ʾ/) since only vowels associated with a glottal stop are indicated. Additional evidence can be obtained from forms in syllabic writing, mostly components of proper names. Indirect information is provided by the polarity between the characteristic vowel and the prefix vowel of the imperfect.

47. *Words of foreign origin*

Words taken over from other Semitic languages—many of them from Akkadian—are mostly adapted to Ugaritic patterns. Cultural words of Sumerian origin entered Ugaritic vocabulary mostly through Akkadian. Ugaritic texts also contain words of Hurrian, Old Anatolian, Indo-European, and Egyptian origin.

48. *Names*

Most names attested at Ugarit are composed of Ugaritic elements. The proportion of foreign words among all types of names is considerable.

48.1. Personal names (PN)

In addition to simple names, basic and derived (e.g., with the afformative /-ān-/), there are many compound names of different types, such as nouns with genitival attributes and sentence names.

48.2. Divine names (DN)

Names of gods are often provided by an epithet. There are double names for one deity (e.g., *nkl wib* 1.24:1 = **88.1** "Nikkal-Ibb"). Two names connected with a coordinating conjunction usually denote two gods, appearing often together (e.g., *gpn.wugr* 1.3:III:36 "Gupan and Ugar").

48.3. Geographical names (GN)

Names of places, countries, mountains, rivers, etc. appear mostly as substantive nouns. There are also many adjectives derived from geographical names, e.g., *ugrty* 4.33:8 "Ugaritian."

5. Morphology

This section deals with the inflection of nouns, including pronouns and numerals, and verbs. The particles are not inflected, though some take suffixed pronouns.

51. *Pronouns*

There are various classes of pronouns: personal pronouns, independent (or separate) and suffixed, the determinative/relative pronoun, and the interrogative pronouns. Indefinite and demonstrative pronouns were not yet fully developed.

51.1. Personal pronouns, independent and suffixed

51.11. Forms of personal pronouns

		independent	suffixed (gen. or acc.)
			to nouns
sing.	1.	*ank a-na-ku* /ʾanāku/ "I"	in nom. ∅ /-ī/ "my"
		an /ʾanā/(?)	in gen., acc. *-y* /-ya/
			to verbs *-n* /-nī/ "me"
	2.m.	*at at-ta* /ʾatta/(?) "you"	*-k* /-ka/(?) "your"
	2.f.	*at* /ʾatti/(?) "you"	*-k* /-ki/(?) "your"
	3.m. nom.	*hw* /huwa/ "he"	*-h* /-hu/ "his"
	3.m. gen.-acc.	*hwt* /huwat-/ "his/him"	
	3.f. nom.	*hy* /hiya/ "she"	*-h* /-ha/ "hers"
	3.f. gen.-acc.	*hyt* /hiyat-/ "her(s)"	
du.	1.		*-ny* /-nayā/(??) "our"
	2.		*-km* /-kumā/(?) "your"
	3. nom.	*hm* /humā/(?) "they"	*-hm* /-humā/(?) "their"
	3. gen.-acc.	*hmt* "their/them"	
pl.	1.		*-n* /-na/(?), /-nu/(?) "our"
	2.m.	*atm* /ʾattum-/(?) "you"	*-km* /-kum-/(?) "your"
	2.f.		*-kn* /-kin(n)a/(?) "your"
	3.m. nom.	*hm* /hum-/(?) "they"	*-hm* /-hum-/(?) "their"
	3.m. gen.-acc.	*hmt* /humat-/(?) "their/them"	
	3.f.		*-hn* /-hin(n)a/(?) "their"

51.12. Independent forms

The first element in the first person singular and in all second person forms is *ʾan-. The forms of the second person contain personal markers beginning with /-t-/; these correspond to the afformatives of the perfect. The forms of the third person contain the deictic element /h-/.

The pronoun of the first person singular occurs in two forms, *ank* /ʾanāku/, in syllabic writing *a-na-ku*, and *an* /ʾanā/(?). There is no difference in function. The shorter form is limited to literary texts, while the longer form appears in all types of texts; in some texts both forms are attested.

In the third persons two different sets of forms are attested. The shorter forms are used for the nominative. The other set, extended by /-t-/, is used for the genitive-accusative case: 3. sing. m. *hwt*, /huwatu/(?), 3. sing. f. *hyt* /hiyati/(?), 3. plur. m. *hmt* /humat-/, 3. du. *hmt* /humāt-/(??).

51.13. Suffixed forms

Personal pronouns suffixed to nouns are all virtually in the genitive case; they express for the most part the possessive relation. The personal pronouns suffixed to finite verb forms are in the accusative case; they indicate the direct object.

The forms in both these functions are identical except in the first person singular, in which the object suffix contains /-n-/: *-n* /-nī/, while the possessive suffix is /-ī/ or /-ya/.

The personal markers of the second person forms correspond to those of the independent pronouns and of the perfect.

The suffixed pronouns of the third person developed from the simple forms of the independent pronouns, and indeed the plural suffix *hm* is often written as a separate word, e.g., *ašṣi.hm* 1.2:IV:2 "I will cause them to go out."

A first-person dual pronoun is attested, written *-ny*, e.g., *bʿlny* 2.70:1 "our lord"; *adtny* 2.11:1 "the lady of the two of us."

The possessive pronoun of the first person singular is indicated in the written forms either by *-y* or by zero. The distribution of these forms depends on the case, number, and gender of the noun: *-y* is indicated in the genitive and accusative of the singular, in the genitive-accusative of the feminine plural, and in both cases of the dual and of the masculine plural. In these nominal forms ending in /-i/ (masc. sing. gen., fem. pl. gen.-acc.), /-ī/ (masc. pl. gen.-acc.), /-a/ (masc. sing. acc.), /-ā/ du. nom.), /-ē/ du. gen.-acc.), as well as /-ū/ (masc. pl. nom.), the suffixed pronoun is apparently /-ya/. The pronoun suffixed to forms ending with short /-u/, in the nominative singular of both genders and the nominative plural of feminines, is not indicated in writing in literary texts. This form of the suffixed pronoun is apparently /-ī/ (< *-uya). In some non-literary texts this pronoun is indicated by *-y*, e.g., *umy* /ʾummī/ 2.16:6 = **84.1** "my mother."

In some forms of suffixed pronouns attached to prepositions or verb forms, the consonant /n/ appears before the consonant of the pronoun; in some cases the /n/ appears and the expected /h-/ of the pronoun is omitted.

51.2. Interrogative pronouns

personal *my* /miya/ "who?"
impersonal *mh* /mah/(?), /mā/(?) "what?"

adjectival *mn* "which?, what?";
the form with generalizing *-m*, *mnm* "whatever, whoever," (cf. Akkad. mīnu(mmē))

51.3. The determinative/relative pronoun

The determinative/relative pronoun, "that of/which," has forms differentiated according to gender and number, and perhaps also case (cf. Arab. sing. nom. ḏū, gen. ḏī, acc. ḏā). Like the Arabic cognate, the older Ugaritic form is *ḏ* 1.24:45, but Standard Ugaritic uses forms in *d*.

sing. m. *d du-ú* /dū/	f. *dt* /dāt-/(?)
pl. m. *dt* /dūt-/(?)	f. *dt* /dāt-/(?)

51.4. Demonstrative pronouns

The system of demonstrative pronouns is not fully developed in the Ugaritic language; the pronouns occur chiefly in the late prose texts. The basic form of the adjectival demonstrative pronoun *hnd* "this" is used for sing. m., 3.4:1 = **86.32**; sing. f., 2.33:35 = **86.42**; pl. m., 2.33:32 = **86.42**. The form with the feminine marker *hndt* appears in function corresponding to that of a substantive noun, a subject, "this one," 2.38:12 = **86.41**.

52. *Nouns*

52.1. Categories

Substantive nouns and adjective nouns are not formally differentiated; they differ only in syntactic function. Certain morphological types are more frequent with the adjective nouns.

The following inflectional categories can be observed in nouns: gender (masculine and feminine), number (singular, dual, and plural), case (nominative, genitive and accusative) and state (absolute and construct).

The category of indetermination is occasionally indicated in nominal predicates, cf. **52.6**.

52.2. Gender

Nouns which have no gender marker are for the most part masculine, though some feminine nouns do not have feminine marker. Many of these denote feminine beings, such as *um* /ʾummu/ 1.23:33 "mother," but some denote objects like *ḥrb* /ḥarbu/ 1.4:VI:57 = **87.7** "sword, knife." The marker of the feminine gender contains the consonant /t/. This /-t/ in some cases is directly attached to the base of the noun; in others there is a vowel /a/ before /-t/. The two types of feminine marker, /-t/ and /-at/, can be distinguished in written forms only in some instances.

52.3. Number

Beside the singular, which has no marker, and plural, which shows external endings, Ugaritic also possessed a dual, also marked externally. The dual is used more frequently in Ugaritic than in any other Semitic language.

52.31. Singular

The singular has no marker. Some nouns in the singular have collective meaning.

52.32. Dual

The dual is used not only for parts of the body and for objects which come in "natural" pairs, but also for any two objects or persons, e.g., *kdm yn* 4.279:4 = **86.24** "two jars (of) wine." The marker of the dual in the absolute state appears in the writing as *-m*. The vocalization may be reconstructed as /-āmi/ in nominative and /-ēmi/ < *-aymi in the genitive-accusative. The endings in the construct state are /-ā/ and /-ē/.

52.33. Plural

The (external) plural is formed by adding plural afformatives. (No internal or broken plurals, formed by vowel changes between the root consonants, are attested.) The afformatives of the absolute state of the masculine plural are /-ūma/ in the nominative and /-īma/ in the genitive-accusative; in the construct state they are /-ū/ and /-ī/. The feminine plural afformative is a modification of the feminine marker; it has a long /ā/ before the /-t/, with case markers probably following the /-t/, /-ātu/ for the nominative and /-āti/ for the genitive-accusative, in both absolute and construct state.

52.4. Case

Thanks to the three signs which represent the glottal stop with a vowel, it is possible to recognize the case endings of the nouns with final root consonant /ʾ/ (glottal stop). This evidence can be supplemented by Ugaritic names with case endings attested in Akkadian syllabic cuneiform texts.

In the singular there are three cases: nominative, ending in /-u/, genitive, in /-i/, and accusative, in /-a/. The endings are directly attested for the masculine.

The dual endings are reconstructed as /-ā(mi)/ for the nominative and /-ē(mi)/ < *-ay(mi) for the genitive-accusative (cf. Arab. -ā(ni) and -ay(ni)).

In the masculine plural, as in the dual, there are only two different forms, /-ū(ma)/ for the nominative and /-ī(ma)/ for the genitive-accusative. Case differentiation in the feminine plural was probably indicated by short vowels after the feminine plural marker. These vowels would correspond partly to the case endings of the singular: nominative /-ātu/, like singular /-(a)tu/, genitive-accusative /-āti/, cf. singular /-(a)ti/ for genitive only (cf. Arab. and Akkad. -ātu and -āti).

This case system is triptotic (with three case forms) in the singular of both genders, and diptotic (with two case forms) in the dual and plural.

52.41. Diptotic names

Certain types of personal and geographic names have (though not consistently) diptotic inflection even in singular: nom. /-u/, gen.-acc. /-a/: masculine personal names with afformative

/-ān-/, e.g., nom. *rap-a-nu* /rapʾānu/ U:V:88:19′, gen.-acc. (ana) *rap-a-na* /rapʾāna/ U:V:54:2; cf. perhaps also GN fem. in gen. *u-ga-ri-ta* RS 6.198.5 (Syria 16:189). (Cf. Arabic diptotic forms, e.g., ᶜimrānu—ᶜimrāna PN; Makkatu—Makkata GN "Mekka.")

52.5. State

In Ugaritic, as in the other West Semitic languages, nouns occur in the absolute state, if the noun is not immediately followed by a genitival attribute, or in the construct state, if the noun is immediately followed by a genitival attribute, usually a noun or a suffixed pronoun.

There is no observable difference between the absolute and construct forms in the masculine singular, the feminine singular, or the feminine plural. The differentiation of absolute and construct states can be observed in the dual, both masculine and feminine, and in masculine plural. Construct forms end in a long vowel, while absolute forms have, after a long vowel, a morpheme consisting of a nasal consonant and a short vowel.

52.6. Determination and indetermination

The morpheme indicated by *-m* on a noun used as a predicate in a nominal clause may be considered a marker of indetermination, e.g., *nḥtm* 1.23:47 = **88.2** "(is) going down." There is no definite article in Ugaritic.

52.7. The system of nominal inflection

	masculine endings			feminine endings		
sing. abs. and constr.	Ug.	(Arab.)	(Akkad.)	Ug.	(Arab.)	(Akkad.)
nom.	/-u/	-u	-u(m)	/-(a)tu/	-atu	-(a)tu(m)
gen.	/-i/	-i	-i(m)	/-(a)ti/	-ati	-(a)ti(m)
acc.	/-a/	-a	-a(m)	/-(a)ta/	-ata	-(a)ta(m)
du. abs. nom.	/-āmi/	-āni	-ān	/-(a)tāmi/	-atāni	-(a)tān
gen.-acc.	/-ēmi/	-ayni	-ēn/-īn	/-(a)tēmi/	-atayni	-(a)tēn
du. constr. nom.	/-ā/	-ā	-ā	/-(a)tā/	-atā	
gen.-acc.	/-ē/	-ay	-ī	/-(a)tē/	-atay	
pl. abs. nom.	/-ūma/	-ūna	-ū	/-ātu/	-ātu	-ātu(m)
gen.-acc.	/-īma/	-īna	-ī	/-āti/	-āti	-āti(m)
pl. constr. nom.	/-ū/	-ū	-ū	/-ātu/	-ātu	-āt
gen.-acc.	/-ī/	-ī	-ī	/-āti/	-āti	-āt

(Cf. also H. du. m. abs. -ay(i)m, constr. -ē; f. abs. -tay(i)m, constr. -tā; pl. m. abs. -īm; pl. f. abs. and constr. -ōt; Yaʾudi-Aram. pl. m. nom. -w for -ū, gen.-acc. -y for -ī.)

	masculine forms	feminine forms
sing. abs. and constr.		
nom.	*ksu* /kussiʾu/, *kàs-pu*	*mit* /miʾtu/, *pat* /piʾatu/
gen.	*ksi* /kussiʾi/	*mit* /miʾti/, *a-na-ti*
acc.	*ksa* /kussiʾa/	*šnt* /šanata/
du. abs. nom.	*qrnm* /qarnāmi/	*mitm* /miʾtāmi/
gen.-acc.	*qrnm* /qarnēmi/	*mitm* /miʾtēmi/
du. constr. nom.	*kp* /kappā/	*ṯt* /ṯit(t)ā/
gen.-acc.	*diy* /dāʾiyē/	*ṯt* /ṯit(t)ē/
pl. abs. nom.	*mrum* /murʾūma/ *ba-a-lu-ma*	*mat* /miʾātu/
gen.-acc.	*mrim* /marīʾīma/ *la-ab-ni-ma*	*mat* /miʾāti/
pl. constr. nom.	*mru* /murʾū/ *mur-ú*	*mat* /miʾātu/
gen.-acc.	*mri* /murʾī/ *mur-i*	*mat* /miʾāti/

ksu "throne"
ksp, *kàs-pu* "silver"
mit, pl. *mat* "100"
pat "edge"
ʿnt, *a-na-tum*, gen. *a-na-ti* DN ʿAnat
šnt "year"
qrn "horn"
kp ("palm" >) "tray, pan"
diy "wing"
mru, gen. *mri*, pl. constr. *mur-ú* "commander"
mri (gen.) /marīʾ-/(?) "fatling"
la-ab-nu-ma (nom. pl.), *la-ab-ni-ma* (gen. pl.) GN Labnuma

53. *Numerals*

53.1. Kinds of numerals

The cardinal numerals (one, two, three, etc.) are basic. They are substantive nouns; the numeral for "1" is an exception—it is treated as an adjective.

The ordinal numerals (first, second, third), insofar as they are used, are derived from the cardinal numerals according to certain patterns. It is not improbable that some of the forms attested are actually those of cardinal numerals used as ordinals.

The fractions are formed according to certain nominal patterns, some without a prefix, others with a prefix *m*-. The multiplicative numerals are formed with the morpheme /-(ʾ)id-/.

Some functionally related expressions for quantity may also be mentioned here, such as *kl* "all, every."

53.2. Forms of numerals

		cardinal				ordinal		
		masc.		fem.				
"1"		*aḥd*	*aḥt*			"1st"	*prᶜ* (?)	
		/ᵓaḥad-/	ᵓaḥatt-/					
		nom.	gen.-acc.	nom.	gen.-acc.			
"2"	abs.	*ṯnm*	*ṯnm*	*ṯtm* (?)	*ṯtm*	"2nd"	*ṯn*	/ṯānī/ (?)
		/ṯināmi/	/ṯinēmi/		/ṯit(t)ēmi/			
	constr.	*ṯn*	*ṯn*	*ṯt*	*ṯt*			
		/ṯinā/	/ṯinē/	/ṯit(t)ā/	/ṯit(t)ē/			

	digits			tens					
	masc.	fem.							
				"20"	*ᶜšrm*				
					/ᶜišrūma/(?)				
"3"	*ṯlṯ*	*ṯlṯt*	/ṯalāṯ(at)-/	"30"	*ṯlṯm*	/-ūma/	"3rd"	*ṯlṯ*	/ṯāliṯ-/(?)
"4"	*arbᶜ*	*arbᶜt*	/ᵓarbaᶜ(at)-/	"40"	*arbᶜm*		"4th"	*rbᶜ*	/rābiᶜ-/
"5"	*ḫmš*	*ḫmšt*	/ḫam(i)š(a)(t)-/	"50"	*ḫmšm*		"5th"	*ḫmš*	/ḫāmiš-/
"6"	*ṯṯ*	*ṯṯt*	/ṯiṯṯ(at)-/	"60"	*ṯṯm*		"6th"	*ṯdṯ*	/ṯādiṯ-/
"7"	*šbᶜ*	*šbᶜt*	/šabᶜ(at)-/	"70"	*šbᶜm*		"7th"	*šbᶜ*	/šābiᶜ-/
"8"	*ṯmn*	*ṯmnt*	/ṯamānī(t)-/(?)	"80"	*ṯmnym*	/-iyūma/	"8th"	*ṯmnt*	/ṯāminīt-/(?) (fem.)
"9"	*tšᶜ*	*tšᶜt*	/tišᶜ(at)-/	"90"	*tšᶜm*				
"10"	*ᶜšr*	*ᶜšrt*	/ᶜaš(a)r(a)(t)-/						

	sing.	du.	pl.
"100"	*mit* /miᵓt-/	*mit* nom. /miᵓtāmi/ gen.-acc. /-ēmi/	*mat* /miᵓāt-/
"1,000"	*alp* /ᵓalp-/	*alpm* nom. /ᵓalpāmi/	*alpm* /ᵓal(a)pūma/, constr. *alp*
"10,000"	*rbt*	*rbtm*	*rbt*, *rbbt*

53.3. Cardinal numerals

The numeral "1" /ᵓaḥad-/ is an adjective noun which agrees with its substantive noun in gender. In the feminine form the last root consonant, /d/, is assimilated to the immediately following feminine marker /-t-/: *ᵓaḥadt- > /ᵓaḥatt-/.

The numeral for "2" is a noun in the dual number.

The cardinal numbers from "3" through "10" occur in two forms: a morphologically "masculine" form, i.e., without a feminine marker, and a morphologically "feminine" form, with the marker /-(a)t-/.

Various nominal patterns are used for the numerals: "3" /ṯalāṯ-/ (cf. Arab. ṯalāṯ-, H. šālōš); "5" /ḫam(i)š-/ (cf. H. ḥāmēš, Arab. ḫams); "7" /šabᶜ-/ (cf. Arab. sabᶜ, H. šæbaᶜ < *šabᶜ); "9" /tišᶜ-/ (cf. Arab. tisᶜ, H. tēšaᶜ < *tišᶜ-); "10" /ᶜašar-/ or /ᶜašr-/ (cf. H. ᶜāśār < *ᶜaśar- and ᶜǽśær < *ᶜaśr-; Arab. ᶜašr- and ᶜašarat-). The root of the numeral "8" consists of four consonants: /ṯ-m-n-y/.

The numerals for tens are marked by endings in *-m-* corresponding to the endings of the plural: /-ūma/ in the nominative and /-īma/ in the genitive-accusative (cf. Arab. -ūna, -īna).

The numeral "100" occurs in the singular for "100," and in the dual for "200"; in the plural it is used with the appropriate digit for "300" and above. The singular form written *mit* was probably pronounced /miʾt-/, with the feminine marker /-t-/ (against the bisyllabic forms, Arab. miʾat- and H. mēʾā < *miʾat). The dual *mitm* was apparently pronounced /miʾtāmi/ in the nominative and /miʾtēmi/ in the genitive-accusative; cf. Arab. miʾatāni, H. mā(ʾ)táyim. The plural form written *mat* was probably pronounced /miʾāt-/; cf. Arab. miʾāt, H. mēʾōt < *miʾāt-.

The numeral "1,000," *alp*, is a noun of the qatl pattern (cf. Arab. ʾalf, Syr. ʾalpā, H. ʾǽlæp). It also occurs in the dual, *alpm* (cf. Hebr. ʾalpáyim), and in the plural, absolute *alpm* and construct *alp*, probably with a bisyllabic base, /ʾalap-/.

The numeral "10,000" is written *rbt*. The root is /r-b-b/ and second consonant of *rbt* is doubled (cf. H. and Aram. ribbō, H. rəbābā). This numeral occurs also in the dual: *rbtm* (cf. H. ribbōtáyim).

53.4. Ordinal numerals

Most of the numerals which function as ordinals are not distinct in written form from the corresponding cardinal.

53.5. Fractions

Fractions most often take the form of *m* prefix + numeral; this probably represents a passive participle of the factitive pattern of the verb derived from the numeral, cf. *mrbʿt* (pl.) 1.19:II:33–34 "quarters." Cf. also *mṯlṯt* . . . *mšbʿt* 1.14:I:16–20, "one third . . . one seventh." (For *mṯdṯt*, cf. the Eblaitic PN fem. mu-sa-ti-sa "she makes number 6".)

53.6. Multiplicative numerals

The multiplicatives are adverbs formed with the afformative *-id* /-ʾid-/ (or, with loss of /ʾ/, *-d* /-id-/): *ṯnid.šbʿd* 2.64:14 = **82.1** "twice seven times."

53.7. Quantitative expressions outside of the system of numerals

The notions "all" and "each" are expressed by the same term, *kl* /kull-/, e.g., *kl.dbrm* /kullu/ 2.32:7 "all things"(?); with suffixed pronoun *klhm* 1.43:26 "all of them" (cf. Arab. kull, H. kōl, kull-). A dualic expression has the root /k-l-ʾ/: *klat* 1.3:I:11 "both" (cf. H. kilʾayim "of two kinds"). Mention should also be made of *nṣp* 4.132:6 "half"(?) (cf. Arab. nuṣf?).

54. *Verbs*

54.1. Lexical and inflectional categories

The semantic characteristics of a verb are determined by the configuration of the root consonants and of some vowels between them. Even if not all of these occur in every form of the verb, they characterize it as a lexical unit and may therefore be called "lexical." These characteristics are in principle not affected by inflectional changes. Lexical categories include the system of characteristic vowels (for verbs of action, verbs of temporary state or quality, and verbs of permanent state or quality) and, with some qualification, that of verbal classes (strong verbs and various classes of weak verbs).

The verbal categories involved in the paradigm of a verb may be called inflectional. All the forms of one verbal root provided with markers of these categories constitute the paradigm of that verb. The paradigm contains both finite forms and non-finite forms. Those forms which exhibit markers of person are defined as finite; they are also marked for number and, in most second and third person forms, for gender. Verbal forms not marked for person are called non-finite. Substantive verbal nouns are infinitives, and adjective verbal nouns are participles. Other inflectional categories include aspect/tense (perfect, imperfect); mood (indicative; the volitive moods: jussive, subjunctive, energic, imperative); manner of action (simple, factitive, causative); and voice (active, reflexive, passive). The last two categories are combined in verbal patterns. (The term "verbal pattern"—corresponding to "nominal pattern"—is used here instead of less appropriate terms, such as "stem" (German "Stamm"), "conjugation," "form.")

Most verbal forms, finite and non-finite, can be provided with suffixed personal pronouns.

The forms quoted in the survey of the verbal system are generally those of strong (or regular) verbs in the simple pattern; forms of weak verbs and derived pattern forms are adduced as necessary.

54.11. System of characteristic vowels

The characteristic vowels, positioned between the second and third root consonants of the simple active pattern, serve to distinguish the following semantic types of verbs: verbs of action (perfect /a/–imperfect /u/; mostly transitive), verbs denoting a changeable state (/i/–/a/), and verbs denoting a permanent state (/u/–/a/).

54.12. System of verbal patterns

Every verbal form expresses a manner of action and at the same time a voice. Combinations of the various manners of action and voices produce different verbal patterns. A verbal pattern can be characterized as a morpheme which, together with the root and inflectional markers, forms the actual verbal forms. Like the root, the verbal pattern is a discontinuous morpheme.

The term "manner of action" (German "Aktionsart") refers to the different ways in which an action can be performed: (a) The simple manner of action carries no intrinsic notions. (b) The factitive manner indicates more action than does the basic form from which it is derived, be it verbal or nominal. Its marker is the doubling of the second root consonant (D-patterns) or, in some verbal classes, the lengthening of the vowel after the first root consonant (L-patterns) or repeating of some root consonants (R-patterns). (c) The causative manner of action indicates an action caused by another action. The regular marker is the prefix /š(a)-/. Forms of the internal causative—which are rare—are marked by vowels between root consonants.

The voices are marked by changes of vowels or by prefixes or infixes. (a) The active voice has a zero marker, i.e., it is unmarked. (b) The internal passive is marked with the vowel /-u/, either after or before the first root consonant. The evidence for these forms is limited. (c) The reflexive is marked with prefixed or infixed /t/. (d) The passive (originally reciprocal) is formed with the prefix /n-/. Reflexive and reciprocal were originally related to the category of the manner of action, but they shifted to the category of voice.

	voice	active	(internal) passive	reflexive	(reciprocal-) passive
manner of action	marker	Ø	/-u-/	/t-/ or /-t-/	/n-/
simple	Ø	G	Gp	Gt	N
factitive	$-C_2C_2-$	D	Dp	tD	
	$-C_1āC_2-$	(L)	(Lp)		
causative	/ša-/	Š	Šp	Št	
internal causative	imperf. $-C_2iC_3$	(C)			

54.13. Aspects/tenses: perfect and imperfect

The finite verbal forms are of two types, distinguished by the position and form of the person markers. Forms in which the personal marker appears only as an afformative belong to the perfect. Forms which express the person by both a prefix and an afformative belong to the imperfect and its moods. (The imperative has no prefix; its afformatives correspond to those of the jussive, one of the volitive moods.)

Personal afformatives of the first and second person perfect forms are related to those of the personal pronouns: /-tu/(?), /-ta/, /-ti/, /-na/(?), /-tum-/, /-tin(n)-/. Afformatives of certain third person perfect forms are similar to morphemes used in nominal inflection: /-a/, /-at/, /-ū/, /-ā/.

Personal prefixes of the imperfect and of the related moods consist of a consonant and a vowel; the vowel must be different from the characteristic vowel of the verb: /ᵓV-/, /tV-/, /nV-/, /yV-/. The prefixes are combined with personal and modal afformatives, /-u/ or /-a/(?) or /-Ø/, /-ī(na)/, /-ā(ni)/, /-ū(na)/.

The function of perfect and imperfect forms is at base aspectual, as can be observed in the older stages of the Ugaritic language reflected in the traditional poetry. In the later stage of the Ugaritic language, represented by the late prose texts, the function of these forms is temporal; perfect denotes the past, imperfect the non-past.

54.14. Moods: jussive and other volitive moods, imperative

The moods are related to the imperfect. The indicative imperfect has no special marker. The volitive moods are (a) the jussive, (b) the subjunctive (for which the evidence is equivocal), (c) the energic (possibly in two forms), and (d) the imperative. Modification of afformative vowels or omission of some components of the imperfect morphemes is used to form these four moods. The imperative is a special mood in that it has no prefixes; its afformatives correspond to those of the second person forms of the jussive (except in the plural feminine). The volitive moods are marked by these modifications of suffixes: instead of /-u/, jussive has /-Ø/, subjunctive /-a/(?), energic /-an(na)/(?); and instead of bisyllabic suffixes, shorter forms /-ī/, /-ā/, /-ū/ (except in the energic mood(s)).

54.15. Finite verbal forms: person, number, gender

The finite verbal forms may express the first person (the speaker[s]), or the second person (the one/those addressed by the speaker), or the third person. The expression of person is always combined with that of number. Gender is distinguished only in the forms of second and third persons, and perhaps not in all of them. The numbers are singular, plural and dual. The dual is consistently used in relation to dual subjects, even in the first person.

The markers of person, number, and gender are different for the forms of perfect, on the one hand, and for the forms of imperfect and related moods, including the imperative, on the other. The actual system of the markers is the result of a complicated process in which elements of quite different character and origin were put together. Different persons, numbers, and genders and their oppositions are indicated by various and often incongruous means.

54.16. Verbal nouns (infinitives and participles)

In addition to the finite verbal forms, there are two types of verbal nouns in the verbal paradigm. Verbal nouns of substantive character are of two types: the absolute infinitive and the construct infinitive; the latter can be connected with prepositions and with suffixed pronouns. Verbal nouns of adjective character are participles; these are inflected like other adjectives. Both infinitives and participles exhibit the markers of the verbal pattern to which they belong, i.e., markers of manner of action and of voice.

54.17. Verbal classes (strong and weak)

Nearly all verbs belong to the triconsonantal system: they either exhibit three root consonants or at least are adapted to the three-consonant verbal system. Verbs with three phonologically stable root consonants, i.e., three consonants which appear unchanged in all forms, are called "strong"; these are the most regular verbs. (This terminology differs from that of Indo-European linguistics: in Greek and the Germanic languages it is irregular verbs which are called "strong.") Those verbs which either have one or more root consonants susceptible to phonological changes (e.g., /n/, /w/, /y/), or exhibit traces of different formation in some patterns or forms, are called "weak" verbs.

The weak verbs with phonologically weak root consonants can be assigned to the following classes: I /n/, I /w/ or /y/, III /w/ or /y/. (I /n/ means the first root consonant is /n/, etc.)

Verbs with the second root consonant /w/ or /y/ are apparently derived from bases consisting of two consonants and one long vowel between them, $C_1\bar{V}C_3$. Similarly, verbs with identical second and third root consonants (II = III) developed from bases of the type $C_1VC_3C_3$. Both of these types have been adapted to the system of triconsonantal verbs, though some traces of original biconsonantal formations remain.

54.18. Verbal forms with suffixed personal pronouns

Both finite verbal forms and verbal nouns can be provided with suffixed personal pronouns. No changes in the basic form of the verb can be observed. The suffixed pronouns attached to finite verb forms correspond to those of the pronouns suffixed to nouns, except in the first person

Affixes of the perfect

			Ug.	(Arab.)	(Hebr.)	(Aram.)	(Akkad.) stative
sing.	1.	*-t*	/-tu/ (?)	-tu	-tī	-et	-(ā)ku
	2. m.	*-t*	/-ta/	-ta	-tā	-tā	-(ā)ta
	f.	*-t*	/-ti/	-ti	-tə < *-ti	-tī	-(ā)ti
	3. m.	-∅	/-a/	-a	-∅	-∅	-∅
	f.	*-t*	/-at/	-at	-ā	-at	-at
du.	1.	*-ny*	/-nayā/ (??)				
	2.	*-tm*	/-tumā/ (?)	-tumā			
	3. m.	-∅	/-ā/	-ā			} -ā
	f.	*-t*	/-tā/	-atā			
pl.	1.	not attested		-nā	-nū	-nā	-(ā)nu
	2. m.	*-tm*	/-tum(ū)/ (?)	-tum(ū)	-tæm	-tūn	-(ā)tunu
	f.	*-tm*	/-tin(na)/ (?)	-tunna	-tæn	-tēn	-(ā)tina
	3. m.	-∅	/-ū/	-ū	-ū	-ū	-ū
	f.	-∅	/-ā/	-na	{ -ū (-ā)	-ā	-ā

1. sing. cf. Old Can. nu-uḫ-ti EA 147:56; ša-par-ti EA 126:34; šap-ra-ti EA 96:30; 2. sing. m. cf. Old Can. na-ṣir-ta EA 112.9

singular, where the verb suffix is *-n* /-nī/ (against *-y* /-ya/ or -∅ /-ī/ with nouns). The suffixed pronouns indicate for the most part the direct (accusatival) object of the verb.

In some verbal forms with suffixed pronouns, *-n-* appears before the pronoun; the *-h-* of the pronoun can be then eliminated. Suffixes indicated by two letters are sometimes set off by a dividing wedge, e.g., *.nn.*

54.2. Simple active pattern (G)

The simple active pattern has no marker, in contrast to factitive and causative manners of action which are marked by prefixes and other markers.

54.21. Perfect

The base of perfect forms is apparently bisyllabic, and remains unaffected by the afformatives. The vowel of its first syllable is attested as /a/. The so-called characteristic vowel of the second syllable is in principle /a/ in verbs of action, /i/ in verbs denoting a changeable state or quality, and /u/ in verbs denoting a permanent quality.

This system is based on polarity in the characteristic vowels of the perfect and imperfect. A laryngeal consonant in the second or third position in the root requires that the imperfect vowel

Forms of the perfect

sing.	1.	*likt* /laʾiktu/ (?)
	2. m.	*likt* /laʾikta/
	2. f.	*ǵmit* /ǵamiʾti/
	3. m.	*yṣa* /yaṣaʾa/, *lik* /laʾika/
		na-qa-ma, ga-mi-ra
	3. f.	*yṣat* /yaṣaʾat/
		qpat, qa-pat /qapʾat/ (?)
du.	1.	▷ *qlny* /qilnayā/
	2.	D *mgntm* /maggantumā/ (?)
	3. m.	*mǵy* /maǵayā/
	3. f.	▷ *ylt* /yalattā/ < *-dt-
pl.	1.	—
	2. m.	▷ *ǵltm* /ǵalētum-/
	2. f.	*yritn* /yariʾtin(n)a/
	3. m.	*nšu* /našaʾū/
	3. f.	*tbʿ* /tabaʿā/

/g-m-r/ "to be complete"
/y-l-d/ "to bear (offspring)"
/y-ṣ-ʾ/ "to go out"
/y-r-ʾ/ "to fear"
/l-ʾ-k/ "to send"
/m-g-n/ D "to entreat"
/m-ǵ-y/ "to reach"
/n-q-m/ "to avenge"
/n-š-ʾ/ "to lift"
/ǵ-l-y/ "to lower"
/ǵ-m-ʾ/ "to be thirsty"
/q-w-l/ (?) "to fall down"
/q-p-ʾ/ meaning unknown
/t-b-ʿ/ "to go out/leave"
▷ weak and irregular forms

be /a/, regardless of the semantics. The /a/ imperfect vowel in turn requires an /i/ characteristic vowel in the perfect. Thus, because of the polarity, all the perfect forms of II /ʾ/ roots are attested as having /i/ as the characteristic vowel.

The consonants of the perfect afformatives can be determined from the alphabetic writing; the vowels can be determined in the alphabetic writing only if they are preceded by a glottal stop /ʾ/. Materials in syllabic writing are of limited assistance since only forms of the third person singular masculine and feminine are attested. Therefore the vowels after the consonants /t/ and /n/ can be reconstructed on the basis of analogies from other Semitic languages.

54.22. Imperfect

The base of the imperfect is monosyllabic; there is no vowel between the first and second root consonants. The vowel between the second and third root consonants depends on the character of the root; it is usually /u/ in verbs of action and /a/ in verbs denoting a state or a quality; it is /i/ in some weak verbs. A laryngeal in second or third position in the root requires that the characteristic vowel be /a/, regardless of the semantics of the root.

Prefixes and afformatives of the imperfect

		Ug.		(Arab.)		(Hebr.)		(Aram.)		(Akkad.)	
sing.	1.	*a-* /ʾa-/	-∅ /-u/	a-	-u	ʾæ-	-∅	ʾ-	-∅	a-	-∅
		i- /ʾi-/									
		u- /ʾu-/									
	2. m.	*t-*	-∅ /-u/	ta-	-u	ti-	-∅	t-	-∅	ta-	-∅
	2. f.	*t-*	*-n* /-īna/	ta-	-īna	ti-	-ī	t-	-īn	ta-	-ī
	3. m.	*y-*	-∅ /-u/	ya-	-u	yi-	-∅	y-	-∅	i-	-∅
	3. f.	*t-*	-∅ /-u/	ta-	-u	ti-	-∅	t-	-∅	ta-	-∅
du.	1.	*n-*	-∅? /-ā/ (??)								
	2.	*t-*	*-n* /-āni/	ta-	-āni						
	3. m.	*y-*	*-n* /-āni/	ya-	-āni					i-	-ā
		t-	-∅ /-ā/								
	3. f.	*t-*	*-n* /-āni/	ta-	-āni						
pl.	1.	*n.*	-∅ /-u/	na-	-u	ni-	-∅	n-	-∅	ni-	-∅
	2. m.	*t-*	-∅ /-ū/ (?)	ta-	-ūna	ti-	ū	t-	-ūn	ta-	-ā
	2. f.	*t-*	*-n* /-na/ (?)	ta-	-na	ti-	-nā	t-	-ān		
	3. m.	*t-*	*-n* /-ūna/	ya-	-ūna	y-	-ū	y-	-ūn	i-	-ū
			-∅ /-ū/								
	3. f.	*t-*	*-n* /-na/ (?)	ya-	-na	ti-	-nā	y-	-ān	i-	-ā
			-∅ /-ā/								

characteristic vowels	Arab.	Hebr.	Aram.	Akkad.
/-u-/ *amlk* /ʾamluka/	ʾaqtulu	ʾæmlōk < *ʾi-	niktub	aprus
/-a-/ *ilak* /ʾilʾaku/	ʾaslamu	ʾæšmāʿ(!) < *-a-	yilbaš	asbaṭ
/-i-/ *atn* /ʾatinu/	ʾaḥsimu	ʾættēn < *-i-	yintin-	apqid
/-ā-/ *uba* /ʾubāʾa/(?)		ʾābōʾ < *-āʾ		

The forms of the indicative imperfect are provided with both a prefix and an afformative.

The prefix consonants are /ʾ-/ in the first person singular, /n-/ in the first person dual and plural, /t-/ in all second-person forms (singular, dual, and plural, masculine and feminine) as well as in all third-person feminine forms (singular, dual, and plural). The same prefix consonant, /t-/, is also used in most forms of the third person masculine dual and plural. The prefix consonant /y-/ is used in the third person singular masculine regularly, and only rarely in the third person masculine in the dual and plural.

The prefix vowel is directly attested in the first person singular; in alphabetic writing the vowel is indicated by one of the three letters *a*, *i*, *u* expressing the vowel following a glottal stop. Some names in syllabic writing also indicate the quality of the prefix vowel. The prefix vowel /-a-/ occurs in imperfect forms which have the characteristic vowel /-u-/ or /-i-/. The prefix vowel /-i-/ occurs in forms which have the characteristic vowel /a/, whether on semantic grounds or because the second or third root consonant is a laryngeal. In the first singular forms it is indicated in alphabetic writing by the letter *i*. In syllabic writing the prefix of third singular

Forms of the imperfect

		/-u-/	/-a-/	/-i-/
sing.	1.	*amlk* /ʾamluku/	*ilak* /ʾilʾaku/	▷ *abky* /ʾabkiyu/
	2. m.	*ṯṯpṭ* /taṯpuṭu/		
	2. f.			D *taršn* /taʾarrišīna/
	3. m.	*yṯpṭ* /yaṯpuṭu/	*ylak* /yilʾaku/	
		ya-aš-p[u]*-ṭù*	*ig-ma-ra-*	
		yiḫd /yaʾḫudu/ (?)	▷ *yšu* /yiššaʾu/	
	3. f.	*tiḫd* /taʾḫudu/ (?)	▷ *tšu* /tiššaʾu/	
du.	1.			D *nmgn* /namagginā/ (??)
	2.			▷ *tǵẓyn* /taǵẓiyāni/ (?)
	3. m.		▷ *tša*(*n*) /tiššaʾā(ni)/	▷ *ytn* /yatinā/
	3. f.			▷ *tmǵyn* /tamǵiyāni/
pl.	1.			D *nmlu* /namalliʾu/
	2. m.		▷ *tšun* /tiššaʾūna/	
	2. f.		*tḫṭin* /tiḫṭaʾna/ (??)	
	3. m.	*tikl*(*n*) /taʾkulū(na)/	▷ *tšu* /tiššaʾū/	
	3. f.	*tǵṣ* /taǵǵuṣā/ (??)	N *tnǵṣn* /tinnaǵaṣna/ (??)	

/ʾ-ḫ-d/ "to seize"
/ʾ-k-l/ "to eat"
/ʾ-r-š/ D "to desire"
/b-k-y/ "to weep"
/g-m-r/ "to be complete"
/ḫ-ṭ-ʾ/ "to sin"(?)
/l-ʾ-k/ "to send"
/m-g-n/ D "to beseech"
/m-l-ʾ/ D "to (ful)fill"
/m-l-k/ "to reign"
/m-ǵ-y/ "to reach"
/n-ǵ-ṣ/ G "to quiver"(?) (or N?)
/n-š-ʾ/ "to lift"
/ǵ-ẓ-y/ "to entreat"
/ṯ-p-ṭ/ "to judge"
▷ weak and irregular forms

masculine /yi-/ is rendered by simple *i*-. (The prefix vowel /u/ is limited to verbs with a weak middle consonant, i.e., verbs of the type *CāC.)

The afformatives of the imperfect forms are these:

/-u/ in 1st sing. and pl., 2nd sing. masc., 3rd sing. masc. and fem.
/-īna/ in 2nd sing. fem.
/-āni/ in 2nd and 3rd du.
/-ūna/ in 2nd and 3rd pl. masc.

The form of the afformative of the second and third plural feminine, written with *-n*, may be reconstructed as /-na/(?) or as /-ān-/(??). Some short forms without /-ni/ or /-na/ with only the long vowel do occur: /-ā/, /-ū/. They can be observed directly in the verbs III /ʾ/: *tša* /tiššaʾā/ and *tšu* /tiššaʾū/ "they lift."

54.23. Volitive moods

The system of moods can be presented by examples of forms with short (or zero) afformatives: indicative imperfect yaqtulu, jussive yaqtul (zero afformative), perhaps a subjunctive yaqtula, and energic yaqtulan and/or yaqtulanna. The imperative also has a zero afformative.

Afformatives of volitive moods

short type: sing.: 1., 2. m., 3. m, 3. f.; pl.: 1.

			(Arab.)	(Old. Can.)	(Hebr.)
jussive		/-∅/	-∅	-∅	-∅
subjunctive (?)		/-a/	-a	-a	(-ā) coh.
energic	-*n*	/-an(na)/	-an(na)	-na	(-nnā) (?)

long type

	jussive & subjunctive	(Arab.)	energic	(Arab.)
sing. 2. f.	/-ī/	-ī		-inna
du. 2., 3.	/-ā/	-ā	-*n* /-ānni/ (?)	-ānni
pl. 2. m., 3. m.	/-ū/	-ū	-*n* /-ūnna/ (?).	-unna

The presumed subjunctive with *-a remains the most problematic mood. No instance of it appears in syllabic writing. The evidence from the rare forms in the alphabetic writing which may be relevant is equivocal: the forms could also be interpreted as jussives. Forms written with -*n* apparently belong to the energic mood (which may be compared to the two energic moods of Classical Arabic). The function of these forms is mostly volitive, but some probably do not differ in meaning from corresponding indicative forms.

The prefixes of the jussive, subjunctive and energic correspond to those of the indicative imperfect, while imperative forms have no prefix.

The afformatives of the jussive and of the subjunctive are mostly shorter than those of the indicative imperfect: zero and /-a/ against /-u/; /-ī/, /-ā/, /-ū/ against /-īna/, /-āni/, /-ūna/.

The afformatives of the energic mood contain /-n-/ or /-nn-/.

Forms of volitive moods

		jussive	subjunctive(?)	energic
sing.	1.	*ispi* /ˀispaˀ/ *ilak* /ˀilˀak/ ▷ *ašt* /ˀašīt/ (?)	*ispa* /ˀispaˀ(a)/ (?) *iqra* /ˀiqraˀ(a)/ (?)	*argmn* /ˀarguman(na)/ *iqran* /ˀiqraˀan(na)/
	2. m.	*tšmḫ* /tišmaḫ/ ▷ *tdu* /tadˀu/ (?)		
	2. f.	*tdḥl* /tidḥalī/		
	3. m.	*yspi* /yispaˀ/ *yṯbr* /yaṯbur/	*yqra* /yiqraˀ(a)/ (?)	▷ *ymǵyn* /yamǵiyan(na)/
	3. f.	▷ *tṣi* /taṣiˀ/ (?) ▷ *tšt* /tašīt/ (?)		▷ *tmǵyn* /tamǵiyan(na)/
du.	1.		*nlḥm* /nilḥamā/ (??)	
	2.	*tqrb* /taqribā/		
	3. f.			*tlsmn* /talsumānni/ (?)
pl.	1.	▷ *nšt* /ništē/ (?)		▷*ngln* /nagīlan(na)/
	3.	▷ *tǵr(k)* /taǵǵurū(-ki)/		▷ *tqln* /taqūlūnna/ (??)

/g-y-l/ "to jubilate"	/q-w-l/ (?) "to fall
/d-ˀ-y/ "to fly"	/q-r-ˀ/ "to call"
/d-ḥ-l/ "to fear"	/q-r-b/ "to approach"
/y-ṣ-ˀ/ "to go out"	/r-g-m/ "to say"
/l-ˀ-k/ "to send"	/š-y-t/ "to put"
/l-ḥ-m/ "to eat"	/š-m-ḫ/ "to rejoice"
/m-ǵ-y/ "to reach"	/š-t-y/ "to drink"
/n-ǵ-r/ "to guard"	/ṯ-b-r/ "to break"
/s-p-ˀ/ "to eat"	▷ weak forms

54.24. Imperative

The base of the imperative was probably identical to that of the imperfect, qtul, qtal, qtil, although it can be reconstructed as bisyllabic, i.e., qutul, etc. Possibly an anaptyctic vowel was pronounced before the first consonant: *lak* /ilˀak/(?) sing. m. "send!" (cf. Arab. ismaᶜ).

The imperative has no prefix, and the afformatives correspond to those of the second-person jussive forms for the most part. A possible exception: plural feminine probably ends in /-ā/ (?). (Cf. H. pəšṓṭā, rəgā́zā in Isa 32:11.) Singular masculine probably has two variant forms, /-∅/ and /-a/(?). See tables on p. 64.

The imperative expresses a command or appeal, addressed to second person(s). It is always positive; it cannot be negated.

Afformatives of the imperative

			(Arab.)		(Hebr.)		(Aram.)		(Akkad.)		
sing. m.	-∅	/-∅/	-∅	(u)qtul	-∅	qəṭōl	-∅		-∅	purus	limad
	-∅	/-a/ (??)									
f.	-∅	/-ī/	-ī	(u)qtulī	-ī	qiṭlī	-ī	ʾăkúlī	-i	pursī	limdī
du.	-∅	/-ā/	-ā	(u)qtulā							
pl. m.	-∅	/-ū/	-ū	(u)qtulū	-ū	qiṭlū	-ū		-ā	pursā	limdā
f.	-∅	/-ā/	-na	(u)qtulna	-nā	qəṭólnā	-ā				

Forms of the imperative

sing.	m.	*qra*	/qaraʾ(a)/ (?)	▷ *šu-ub-*	/ṯūb/	*sid*	siʾid/ (??)
		lak	/laʾak/ (?)				
		▷ *ša*	/šaʾ(a)/ (?)				
	f.	*sad*	/saʾadī/ (?)			▷ *ẓi*	/ẓiʾī/
du.		▷ *ša*	/šaʾā/	*rgm*	/rugumā/ (?)		
	m.	▷ *šu*	/šaʾū/			▷ *tn*	/tinū/
	f.	*šmᶜ*	/šamaᶜā/ (?)				

/y-ẓ-ʾ/ "to go out"
/y-t-n/ "to give"
/l-ʾ-k/ "to send"
/n-š-ʾ/ "to lift"
/s-ʾ-d/ "to serve"

/q-r-ʾ/ "to call"
/r-g-m/ "to say"
/š-m-ʾ/ "to hear"
/ṯ-w-b/ "to return"
▷ weak forms

54.25. Absolute infinitive

The vocalization of the absolute infinitive, qatālu, is attested directly in the quadrilingual vocabularies and indirectly in alphabetic texts. Generally an absolute infinitive can be recognized on the basis of its relationship with a finite form of the same verb or on other syntactic grounds.

ǵmu /ǵamāʾu/, *ba-ta-qú* /batāqu/, with *-m*: *lakm* /laʾākum-/
(cf. Akkad. parāsu(m), H. qāṭōl < qaṭāl-)

G /b-t-q/ "to cut off"(?); /l-ʾ-k/ "to send"; /ǵ-m-ʾ/ "to be thirsty"

54.26. Construct infinitive

The construct infinitive of the simple active pattern is attested only in alphabetic writings; the vocalization is not known. It is not impossible that several types of construct infinitive coexisted.

(b)nši /nušʾi/(?), *(b)šal* /šaʾ(a)li/(?) (cf. H. qəṭol, qåṭl-)

G /n-š-ʾ/ "to lift"; /š-ʾ-l/ "to ask"

54.27 Active participle

The structure of the simple active participle qātil- is reconstructed on the basis of forms in both alphabetic and syllabic writing; the quantity of the vowels is reconstructed on the basis of information from the other Semitic languages.

aḫd /ʾāḫidu/ "seizing, (one who is) seizing," etc.; *šiy* /šāʾiyu/; *la-i-ya*; *spu* /sāpiʾu/;
fem. *qrit* /qāriʾt-/;
pl. *a-ši-ru-ma* /ᶜāširūma/;
(cf. Akkad. pārisu(m), H. qōṭel < qāṭil, Aram. qāṭel, Arab. qātil-)

G /ʾ-ḫ-d/ "to seize"; /l-ʾ-y/ "to prevail"; /s-p-ʾ/ "to eat"; /ᶜ-š-r/ part. > "butler"; /q-r-ʾ/ "to call"; /š-ʾ-y/ "to shed"

54.28. Passive participle

In spite of its passive function, the passive participle is listed among the simple active forms for morphological reasons: its characteristic vowel is /-ī-/ (as opposed to the marker /-u-/ in the passive verbal patterns) and it has no prefix (against /mV-/ in the factitive and causative patterns and /na-/ in the reciprocal).

The structure of the simple passive participle qatīl is reconstructed from several forms in the syllabic writing. Two forms, both written *ḫa-ri-mu*, are explained in the quadrilingual vocabulary U:V:137 "split" (line II:40′), reflecting Ugaritic /ḫarīmu/ (with postvelar /ḫ/), and "separated" (line II:39′), reflecting /ḥarīmu/ (with pharyngeal /ḥ/).

ḫa-ri-mu /ḥarīmu/; *ḫa-ri-mu* /ḫarīmu/ (cf. Aram. qəṭīl < *qaṭīl-)

G /ḥ-r-m/ "to separate"; /ḫ-r-m/ "to split"

54.3. Simple patterns: passive, reflexive, and reciprocal/passive

54.31. Simple passive pattern (Gp)

Gp forms are marked by the vowel /-u-/ in the prefix, which is only rarely attested in alphabetic writing. The passive function of a verb form can often be determined from the context, but it is not always possible to specify whether the pattern is Gp, Dp, or N.

imperf.
sing. 3. m. *yrgm* /yurgamu/
3. f. *tuḫd* /tuʾḫadu/
du. 3. m. *tlakn* /tulʾakāni/

(cf. perf. Arab. qutila, H. quṭ(ṭ)al
imperf. Arab. yuqtalu, H. yåqṭal)

Gp /ʾ-ḫ-d/ "to be taken"; /l-ʾ-k/ "to be sent"; /r-g-m/ "to be said"

54.32. Simple reflexive pattern (Gt)

The Gt pattern is clearly distinguished by the infix /-t-/, which follows the first root consonant.

imperf.
  sing. 1. *iḥtrš* /ʾiḥtarašu/(?)
  3. m. *yitsp* /yiʾtasapu/(?), *yštal* /yištaʾalu/(?)
imper. sing. m. *ištm*ᶜ /ʾištamaᶜ/
inf. constr. (*il*)*štm*ᶜ, ilu-*iš-ta-mi* /ištamᶜi/

(cf. perf. Arab. iqtatala
imperf. Arab. yaqtatilu, Phoen. thtpk)

Gt /ʾ-s-p/ "to gather (for oneself)"; /ḥ-r-š/ "to perform magic"; /š-ʾ-l/ "to ask (for oneself)"; /š-m-ᶜ/ "to listen"

54.33. Reciprocal/passive pattern (N)

The N pattern is characterized by the prefix /n-/ at the beginning of the form in the perfect and the participle; in the imperfect the prefix is assimilated to the root consonant which immediately follows and is therefore not apparent in written forms. The original reciprocal function (manner of action) has changed to a passive one (voice).

perf.
  sing. 3. f. *nlqḥt* /nal(a)qaḥat/
imperf.
  sing. 3. m. *yadm* /yaʾʾadimu/
  du. 2. m. *tḫtan* /taḫḫatiʾāni/
  pl. 3. f. *tntkn* /tannatikna/(?)
part. sing. f. *nmrrt* /namrarat-/

(cf. perf. Arab. inqatala, H. niqṭal
imperf. Arab. yanqatilu, H. yiqqāṭel < *-nq-
part. H. niqṭāl)

N /ʾ-d-m/ "to rouge (oneself)"; /ḫ-t-ʾ/ "to be carried off"; /l-q-ḥ/ "to be taken"; /m-r-r/ "to be strengthened"; /n-t-k/ "to be shed"

54.4. Derived verbal patterns

The derived verbal patterns exhibit markers of both manner of action and voice. Some of these markers, such as doubled consonants and distinctive vowels, are scarcely recognizable in alphabetic writing.

The actual forms of derived patterns are generated by combining the markers with roots and with morphemes indicating the various finite and non-finite forms. The morphemes for the finite forms are similar to those used with the simple pattern. The polarity of characteristic vowels between perfect and imperfect may be supposed to exist in the derived patterns, as may the polarity in the imperfect between the characteristic vowel and the prefix vowel.

The participles of derived patterns are marked by the prefix /mV-/, while the base corresponds to that of the imperfect. The few attested infinitives seem to show a variety of forms.

The factitive manner of action is generally indicated by doubling the second root consonant. Causative forms with the prefix /ša-/ occur in both perfect and imperfect, while internal causatives, of the yaqtil- type, are limited to the imperfect.

54.41. Factitive active pattern (D)

Factitive forms are usually marked by the doubling of the middle root consonant. Since the doubling of consonants is not indicated in the alphabetic writing, this marker of the factitive is not directly attested. The forms in syllabic writing do not provide much help, since indications of doubling are far from consistent there.

The only factitive form which is clearly distinguished in alphabetic writing from forms of the simple pattern is the participle. It is provided with the prefix *m-* /mu-/.

perf.
 sing. 3. m. *mla* /mallaʾa/(?)
imperf.
 sing. 1. *arḫ̮p* /ʾaraḫḫipu/
 3. m. *yarš* /yaʾarrišu/, *ynšq* /yanaššiqu/
 pl. 1. *nmlu* /namalliʾu/
imper. sing. f. *kbd* /kabbidī/
part. act. *mnḥm*, *mu-na-ḫi-mu* /munaḥḥimu/

(cf. perf. Arab. qattala, Aram. qaṭṭil, H. qiṭṭel
imperf. Arab. yuqattilu, H. yəqaṭṭel)

D /ʾ-r-š/ "to desire"; /k-b-d/ "to honor"; /m-l-ʾ/ "to (ful)fill"; /n-ḥ-m/, "to comfort"; /n-š-q/ "to kiss"; /r-ḫ̮-p/ "to soar"

The factitive of several classes of weak verbs is formed, not by doubling the middle consonant, but by lengthening the vowel between the first and second root consonant (L factitive pattern) or by repeating the second and third root consonant (R factitive pattern).

54.42. Factitive reflexive pattern (tD)

In the tD pattern, the reflexive marker /t-/ appears before the first root consonant.

perf.
 sing. 3. m. *tkms* /takammasa/

(cf. perf. Arab. taqattala, H. (hi)tqaṭṭel
imperf. Arab. yataqattalu, H. yitqaṭṭel)

tD /k-m-s/ "to stretch (himself)"

54.43. Factitive passive pattern (Dp)

In Dp forms, the passive marker /-u-/ probably appears before or after the first root consonant.

jussive
 sing. 2. m. *tbšr* /tubaššar/(??)
part. sing. f. *mtrḫt* /mutarraḫat-/

(cf. perf. Arab. quttilla, H. quṭṭal
imperf. Arab. yuqattalu, H. yəquṭṭal)

Dp /b-š-r/ "to be provided with good tidings"; /t-r-ḫ/ "to be acquired (with a bride-price)"

54.44. Š-Causative active pattern (Š)

The prefix of the causative active pattern is clearly indicated by *š*: the prefix vowel, presumably /-a-/, is not directly attested. (Cf. Akkad. causative with š(a)- and some forms in Aram. and Syr.)

perf.
  sing. 3. m. *š^{c}ly* /ša^{c}laya/
  3. f. *š^{c}lyt* /ša^{c}layat/
imperf.
  sing. 1. *aš^{c}rb* /$^{\supset}$aša^{c}ribu/
  3. m. *yššil* /yašaš$^{\supset}$ilu/, *yš^{c}ly* /yaša^{c}liyu/
imper. sing. f. *šlḥm* /šalḥimī/
part. f. pl. *mšspdt* /mušaspidāt-/

(cf. Akkad. šaprus, Aram. hanpeq
Akkad. ušapris, Aram. yəhašpil)

Š /l-ḥ-m/ "to feed"; /s-p-d/ "to wail"; /^{c}-l-y/ "to lift/offer"; /^{c}-r-b/ "to make to enter, to introduce"; /š-$^{\supset}$-l/ "to let ask"

54.45. Š-Causative reflexive pattern (Št)

In Št forms, the marker of the reflexive voice /-t-/ follows the marker of the causative manner of action /š-/.

imperf.
  sing. 3. m. *yštḥwy* /yaštaḥwiyu/(?)
(cf. Akkad. šutaprus, Arab. istaqtala
Akkad. uštaprus, Aram. yištakləlūn, H. yištaḥăwǣ, Arab. yastaqtilu)

Št /ḥ-w-y/ "(to ask life for someone >(?)) to greet (by prostration)"

The form *yštḥwy* can also be explained as a reflexive from a root /š-ḥ-w/.

54.46. Š-Causative passive pattern (Šp)

The /-u-/ marker of the Šp probably precedes the first root consonant.

imperf.
  sing. 3. m. ▷ *yṯṯb* /yuṯaṯibu/ (?) < -*ša-

(cf. perf. Arab. uqtila, H. håqṭal
imperf. Arab. yuqtalu, yåqṭal
part. Aram. məhaḥsəpā)

Šp /ṯ-w-b/ "to be seated"

54.47. Causative internal pattern (C)

Forms of the internal causative, without any causative prefix, are directly and indirectly attested in the imperfect. The characteristic vowel of these forms is /-i-/, which is probably short in the forms of the strong verbs and long in the forms of the verbs with second root consonant /w/. (These forms correspond to the regular causative forms of the imperfect in Hebrew, e.g., yaqṭīl, yārīm, cf. Bibl.-Aram. yəqīm in addition to yəhāqēm; cf. also Arab. yuqtalu.)

imperf.

sing. 3. m. *yšlm*, *ya-aš-li-ma-* /yašlimu/, *ylḥm* /yalḥimu/

(cf. perf. Arab. ʾaqtala, H. hiqṭīl
imperf. Arab. yuqtalu, Aram. yəqīm, H. yaqṭīl
part. Aram. mašpil)

C /l-ḥ-m/ "to feed"; /š-l-m/ "to grant peace"

54.5. Verbal classes

The inflectional system of all Ugaritic verbs is uniform. The differences among the various verbal classes are due either to different qualities of root consonants or to different types of verbal bases. Strong verbs retain all the root consonants through the inflectional paradigm. There are a few minor exceptions involving roots which contain dental consonants: a dental other than /t/ may assimilate to an immediately following /-t-/ of a person marker. Verbs which do not show all three root consonants in all forms may be called "weak."

54.51. Identification of forms

There is no problem in determining the root of a verb form if in the written form all three root consonants are visible. However, there are many forms in which only two consonants and some in which only one consonant remains visible; these cannot always be assigned to a definite class.

If only two consonants are visible, there is a relatively high probability that the form belongs to the class II /w/ and /y/, since nearly all such forms are written with two letters only. In the other classes of weak verbs, forms with two letters are more frequent in the imperfect, imperative, and infinitive forms than in the perfect and participle forms.

54.52. Strong and weak verbs

The strong verbs are those in which all three root consonants remain unchanged through the inflectional paradigm. All consonants can serve as root consonants of the strong verbs, with the exception of /w/ and /y/ in all positions and of /n/ as the first root consonant; further, the second and third root consonant of a strong verb must not be identical.

The regular system of inflection applies to all strong verbs. There are a few exceptions, in which one of the root consonants is affected by an inflectional morpheme. A dental serving as a final root consonant may be assimilated to a following /-t-/. Thus, in /y-l-d/, *-dt > /-tt-/, yielding *ylt* /yalattā/ 1.23:53 "they (two) gave birth," and in /y-t-n/, *-nt- > /-tt-/, yielding *ytt* /yatattu/ 1.100:75 "I gave." The laryngeal root consonants are strong; the impact of these consonants on the adjacent vowels can often be observed indirectly.

The "weakness" of the weak verbs is caused by the changeability of one or more root consonants. Some of the changes are due to the sensitivity of the weak consonants to preceding or following phonemes in certain combinations. From a synchronic point of view, all verbal

Characteristic weak forms of verbs I /n/ and /l-q-ḥ/

		perfect	imperfect		other
G	sing. 1		*ask* /ʾassuku/	*iqḥ* /ʾiqqaḥu/	imper.
	3. m.		*yṣb* /yaṣṣubu/	*yšu* /yiššaʾu/	sing. m. *ša* /šaʾ(a)/
			ya-ṣu-ba	*yqḥ* /yiqqaḥu/	f. *sk* /sukī/
					pl. m. *šu* /šaʾū/
Gp	sing. 3. m.		*ysk* /yussaku/		
Gt	sing. 3. m.		*ytšu* /yittašaʾu/		
N	sing. 3. f.	*nlqḥt* /nal(a)qaḥat/(?)			
	du. 3. m.		*ynṯkn* /yannaṯikāni/(?)		

/l-q-ḥ/ "to take," N "to be taken"; /n-s-k/ "to pour," Gp "to be poured"; /n-ṣ-b/ "to set up"; /n-š-ʾ/ "to lift," Gt "to lift oneself"; /n-ṯ-k/ N "to bite one other"

forms deviating from the "strong" model can be explained this way. From the diachronic point of view, some classes of weak verbs developed from bases containing fewer than three root consonants. The consonants /n/ and /y/ in first root position can be considered secondary. The verbs now classified as II /w/ or /y/ probably developed from bases consisting of a long vowel between two consonants, $C_1\bar{V}C_3$. The verbs with repeated or doubled second root consonant ($C_1C_3C_3$) were probably derived from bases consisting of a consonant, a short vowel and a doubled consonant, $C_1VC_3C_3$. It is not clear whether the verbs III /w/ and /y/ developed from original bases of the type $C_1VC_2\bar{V}$, or whether the lack of the third root consonant in many forms is rather to be explained by its phonological "weakness."

54.53. Verbs I /n/ and /l-q-ḥ/

The class I /n/ contains verbs with initial /n-/ (except II /w/-/y/). The geminate verbs (those which have identical second and third root consonants) and verbs III /y/ share some characteristics of this class. The verb /l-q-ḥ/ is attached to this class because its first root consonant, /l/, is assimilated or eliminated in certain forms.

The "weakness" of verbs I /n/ is caused by two deviations from the regular model: the assimilation of /n/ to the immediately following consonant in many finite forms, and the omission (from a synchronic point of view) of the first root consonant in the imperative.

54.54. Verbs I /y/

The class I /y/ contains all verbs with first root consonant /y-/. The initial root consonant /y-/ is original only in some verbs of this class; in the majority of them /y-/ developed from original *w-. Some forms of the verbs /h-l-k/ "to go" (cf. H. h-l-k) and /h-l-m/ "to strike" are inflected as I /y/ forms.

The "weakness" of the I /y/ verbs is caused by two deviations from the regular model: the first results from the fact that /y/ (and /w/) formed with preceding vowels diphthongs which

Characteristic weak forms of verbs I /y/, /h-l-k/, /h-l-m/

		perfect	imperfect and jussive			other		
G	sing. 1.		*ard*	*idʿ*		imper.		
			/ʾaridu/	/ʾidaʿu/ (?)		sing. m.	*rd*	*lk*
			alk				/rid/	/lik/
			/ʾaliku/			f.	*ẓi*	
	3. m.		*yrd*	*yṣi*	*yru*		/ẓiʾī/	
			/yaridu/	/yiṣaʾ/(?)	/yīraʾu/	inf. constr.	*ṣat*	*lkt*
			ytn, ya-te-nu				/ṣiʾat-/	/lik(a)t/(?)
			/yatinu/					
			ylm					
			/yalimu/(?)					
Gt	sing. 1.		*itlk*					
			/ʾitalaku/					
Š	sing. 1.		*ašṣu*			inf. abs.	*šṣu*	
			/ʾašōṣiʾu/				/šōṣiʾu/(?)	
	sing. 3. m.	*šṣa*				partic.	*mšṣu*	
		/šōṣaʾa/					/mašōṣiʾu/	
C	sing. 3. m.		(juss.) *yṣi*					
			/yōṣiʾ/					

/h-l-k/ "to go," Gt "to walk"; /h-l-m/ "to strike"; /y-d-ʿ/ "to know"; /y-ṣ-ʾ/ and /y-ẓ-ʾ/ "to go out," Š and C "to cause to go out," "to provide"; /y-r-ʾ/ "to fear"; /y-r-d/ "to go down"; /y-t-n/ "to give"

were later monophthongized; the second is that the first root consonant does not appear in forms of the imperfect, the imperative, and the construct infinitive.

54.55. Verbs II /w/ and /y/

Verbs II /w/–/y/ have as their supposed second root consonant /w/ or /y/.

The "weakness" of verbs II /w/ and /y/ reflects the original base of these verbs, involving a long vowel between two consonants, $C_1\bar{V}C_3$. The verbs have been only partially adapted to the model of the strong verbs. Scarcely any of the forms attested in the Ugaritic texts show /w/ or /y/ as functional consonants; in nearly all forms, only the first and last root consonants are indicated in the alphabetic writing. Verbs II /w/ show medial /ū/ and verbs II /y/ show medial /ī/ in some forms, viz., in the imperfect and apparently also in the imperative and infinitive of the simple active pattern. In the imperfect some verbs have forms with medial /ā/. The factitive is formed according to the L-pattern; e.g. *trmm* /tarāmim(u)/ "you will/may erect" (cf. H. tərōmēm).

Characteristic forms of verbs II /w/ and /y/

		perfect	imperfect and jussive			other	
G	sing. 1.	*nḫt*	*amt*	*ašt*	*uba*	imper.	
		/nā́ḫtu/(?)	/ʾamūtu/	/ʾašītu/	/ʾubāʾa/	sing. m.	*ṯb, šu-ub-*
	3. m.	*qm*	*ykn, ya-ku-nu*	*ygl, ya-gi-li*			/ṯūb/
		/qāma/	/yakūnu/	/yagīlu/			*št*
		št					/šīt/
		/šāta/				inf.	*bu*
	3. f.	*bat*					/bāʾu/
		/bāʾat/					*ši-tu*
							/šītu/
						partic.	*qm*
							/qāmu/
							-da-nu
							/dānu/
Gp	pl. 3. m.	*šṯ*					
		/šītū/(?) < *šūtū(?)					
Gt	sing. 3. m.		*yṯtn*				
			/yaṯtīnu/				
	sing. 3. m.		*trmm*			imper.	
			/tarāmim(u)/			sing. m.	*rmm*
							/rāmim/
Š	sing. 1.		*aškn*			imper.	
			/ʾaškīnu/(?)			sing. m.	*ṯṯb*
	sing. 3. m.	*škn*	*yškn*			*ša- >	/taṯīb/
		/šakāna/(?)	/yaškīnu/(?)				
C			*ya-ri-mu, ya-ri-im-*				
			/yarīm-/				
			yṯb				
			/yaṯību/				

/b-w-ʾ/ "to come"; /g-y-l/ "to jubilate"; /d-y-n/ "to judge"; /k-w-n/ "to stand/be," Š(?) "to provide"; /m-w-t/ "to die"; /n-w-ḫ/ "to repose"; /q-w-m/ "to rise"; /r-w-m/ L "to make high," "to erect," C "to elevate"; /š-y-t/ "to put," Gp "to be put"; /ṯ-w-b/ "to (re)turn" intransitive, Š and C "to return, to send back"; /ṯ-y-n/ Gt "to urinate"

54.56. Verbs II = III ($C_1C_3C_3$)

This class, composed of verbs which have the same consonant in both second and third root position, is the least documented class of Ugaritic verbs; the lack of vocalized forms prohibits the recognition of different types.

Characteristic weak and strong forms of verbs II = III

		perfect	imperfect	other
G	sing. 2. m.	*rbt* /rabbāta/ (?)		partic. *mṣṣ* /māṣiṣu/
	3. m.	*ᶜz* /ᶜazza/ *ḥnn*, *ḫa-na-nu* /ḥanana/ (?)	*ysb* /yasubbu/ *yᶜzz* /yiᶜzazu/ (?)	inf. constr. *šrr* "to rule"
Gp				part. f. *mrrt* /marīrat-/
D/L(?)	sing. 1.		*arnn* /ᵓaranninu/ (?)	
	3. m.		*yšnn* /yašanninu/ (?), /yašāninu/ (?)	
Dp/Lp(?)	sing. 3. m.		*ymnn* /yumannanu/ (?), /yumānanu/ (?)	partic. + *-m* *mmnn*(*m*) /mumannanu(m)-/ (?), /mumānanu(m)-/ (?)

/ḥ-n-n/ "to favor"; /m-n-n/ Dp/Lp(?) "to be lowered"; /m-ṣ-ṣ/ "to suck"; /m-r-r/ Gp "to be strengthened"; /s-b-b/ "to turn"; /ᶜ-z-z/ "to be strong"; /r-b-b/ (?) "to be great"; /r-n-n/ D(?) "to shout with joy"; /š-n-n/ D/L(?) "to gnash one's teeth"; /š-r-r/ "to rule"(?)

The "weak" character of some forms of this class is not caused by phonetic weakness of the root consonants; rather it reflects the original base of the verbs, consisting of the first root consonant, a short vowel and a doubled consonant ($C_1VC_3C_3$). These "weak" forms (many of them motivated by the original characteristic vowel *u or *i) correspond to "strong" forms with /-a-/ between the second and third root consonants. The "weak" character of this class is also visible in the factitive patterns: L-pattern (lengthened vowel after the first consonant) and R-pattern (repetition of first and third root consonants).

D-pattern and L-pattern are not distinguished in the alphabetic writing: *arnn* /ᵓaranninu/ "I shall shout with joy" (cf. H. ᵓărannēn) and *tǵll* /taǵālilu/ "she sinks" (cf. H. ᶜōlaltī; cf. Arab. ǵ-l-l). The R-pattern is apparent: *ykrkr* /yakarkiru/ 1.4:IV:29 = **85.2** "he twiddles" (cf. H. məkarker).

Strong forms are those in which the second and third root consonants do not merge—each is indicated by one letter. "Weak" forms are those in which the second and third root consonant form a doubled consonant, which is indicated in alphabetic writing by only one letter.

54.57. Verbs III /y/ or /w/

All verbs with third root consonant /y/ as well as the few verbs with /w/ in third position belong to this class.

Forms of verbs III /y/ and /w/

		perfect		imperfect and jussive			other		
				/-i-/	/-a-/	/-u-/			
G	sing. 1.	*bnt*	*štt*	*abky*	*ištyn*	*ašlw*	imper.		
		/banētu/(?)	/šatītu/(?)	/ʾabkiyu/	/ʾištayan-/	/ʾašluwa/	sing. m.	*du*	*ṯny*
	3. m.	*ᶜly*	*ᶜl*	*ybky*	*yšt*			/duʾu/	/ṯan(a)ya/(?)
		/ᶜalaya/	/ᶜalā/	/yabkiyu/	/yištē/		f.	*di*	*ǵly*
		-mky	*-mk*	*ybk*				/duʾī/	/ǵal(a)yī/(?)
		-ma-ka-ya	*-ma-ka*	/yabkī/			pl. m.	*du*	*šty*
				yip				/duʾū/	/šit(a)yū/(?)
				/yaʾpī/			inf.		
				ybn, *ya-ab-ni*			abs.	*mǵy*	*bky*
				/yabni/				/maǵāyu/	/bakāyu/
	3. f.	*atwt*		*tdu*				*mǵ*	
		/ʾatawat/		/tadʾū/			constr.	(*l*)*šty*	(*b*)*bk*
	pl. 3. m.	*mǵy*	*šty*	*tbkn*	*tštn*			/šatyi/(?)	/bakī/(?)
		/maǵayū/	/šatiyū/	/tabkūna/	/tištūna/		partic.	*diy*	*la-i-ya*
				tity	*tšty*			/dāʾiy-/	
				/taʾtiyū/	/tištayū/				
Gp	sing. 3. m.			(juss.) *ybn*					
				/yubnā/(?)					
N	sing. 3. m.	*nkly*							
		/nak(a)laya/(?)							
D	sing. 1. m.	*klt*		*akly*	(juss.) *akl*		partic.	*mkly*	
		/kallētu/(?)		/ʾakalliyu/	/ʾakalli/			/mukalliyu/	
	3. m.			*ykly*	*yks*				
				/yakalliyu/	/yakassī/				
Š	sing. 2. m.			(juss.) *tšᶜl*			imper.		
				/tašaᶜli/			sing. f.	*ššqy*	
	3. m.	*šᶜly*		*yšᶜly*				/šašqiyī/	
		/šaᶜlaya/		/yašaᶜliyu/					
Št	sing. 3. m.			*yštḥwy*					
				/yaštaḥwiyu/					
C	sing. 3. m.			*yšqy*					
				/yašqiyu/					

/ʾ-p-y/ "to bake"; /ʾ-t-w/ "to come"; /b-k-y/ "to weep"; /b-n-y/ "to build," Gp "to be built"; /d-ʾ-y/ "to fly"; /ḥ-w-y/ Št "(to ask life for someone(?)), to greet (by prostration)"; /k-l-y/ N "to be spent," D "to destroy"; /k-s-y/ D "to cover"; /m-k-y/ meaning unknown; /m-ǵ-y/ "to reach"; /ᶜ-l-y/ "to go up," Š "to lift/offer"; /ǵ-l-y/ "to lower"; /š-l-w/ "to repose"; /š-q-y/ Š and C "to give drink"; /š-t-y/ "to drink"; /ṯ-n-y/ "to repeat"

The "weak" character of many forms of this class can be explained by the phonetic weakness of the semivowels /y/ and /w/. In some forms, they had formed diphthongs with preceding short vowels which were later monophthongized to long vowels. In other forms, the semivowels were elided between two vowels, which then contracted into a long vowel. In many instances comparable forms with and without /w/ or /y/ coexist.

"Strong" forms, those in which the consonant letter *y* or *w* is written, are distributed among different patterns and persons. The /y/ or /w/ is preceded by a short vowel and followed by another vowel, in most instances a long vowel and in some a short /a/.

54.58. Verbs with four root consonants

From triconsonantal roots bases of more than three consonants can be generated:

by dissimilation(?): *-ss- > /-rs-/: *yprsḥ* /yiparsaḥu/(?) 1.2:IV:22 = **88.51** "he collapses"
by repeating C_3: $C_1C_2C_3C_3$: *ṣḥrrt* /ṣaḥrarat/ 1.6:II:24 = **88.55** "she scorched"
by repeating C_1–C_3: $C_1C_3C_1C_3$: *k-r-r—*ykrkr* /yakarkiru/ 1.4:IV:29 = **85.2** "he twiddles"

54.6. Forms with suffixed pronouns

Suffixed pronouns attached to finite verb forms and to some infinitives and participles denote the object of the verbal action. Possessive suffixes can be attached only to some verbal nouns, viz., the construct infinitive and probably some participles.

The forms of the object suffixes correspond to those of the possessive suffixes attached to the nouns except in the first person sing., in which the object pronoun is /-nī/, indicated in the alphabetic writing by *-n*, while the possessive pronoun is /-ī/, not indicated in the consonantal writing, or /-ya/, written *-y*. In principle, a verb form is not affected by the addition of a suffixed pronoun; at least, the alphabetic writing does not show such change.

54.61. Finite forms

imḫṣh 1.19:I:14, 15 "I shall strike him"
atnk 1.17:VI:17 "I shall present you (with . . .)" (or "I shall give to you" ("datival"))
with /-n-/: *tšqynh* 1.19:IV:55 "she causes/gives him to drink"; *aqbrnh* 1.19:III:5 "I shall bury him"
with *.nn*: *yqbr.nn* 1.19:III:41 = **88.65** "he buries him"; *wgr.nn* 1.14:III:6 "and he attacked him"

54.62. Verbal nouns

infinitive: *bm.bkyh* 1.14:I:31 "in his weeping"
participle: *mᶜmsy* (with *-y*!) 1.17:II:20 "supporting me"; *mᶜmsk* 1.17:II:6 "supporting you"

55. *Adverbs*

55.1. Adverbs and other particles: forms and functions

In grammars of the Semitic languages, all those words which are neither nouns (in the broad sense, including pronouns and numerals) nor verbs are called particles. This large group is usually divided into adverbs, prepositions, conjunctions, and interjections, a division which reflects the function rather than the form of the words. The boundaries of these categories are not always clear, since one and the same word can be used as adverb, preposition or conjunction, e.g., *aḫr* "after."

The following distributional criteria can be applied:

Prepositions are always in the construct state, connected with a following noun in the genitive case.

Conjunctions (and related particles) either stand at the beginning of clauses or connect equivalent parts of clauses.

Adverbs are related to some other part of the clauses they are part of, usually the verbal predicate; adverbs can, however, occur in nominal clauses. The particles of negation and affirmation may be included among the adverbs; they are often connected with an immediately following verb. The expressions of existence and non-existence are traditionally classified as particles. Like some other adverbial expressions they can serve as nominal (non-verbal) predicates. In Ugaritic, no forms with suffixed pronouns are attested.

For the particles which remain outside the clause structure, the traditional term "interjections" may be used. Some of them serve to introduce a clause or a vocative noun which itself stands outside the sentence structure; others do not affect clause or sentence structure.

55.2. Nouns with adverbial markers

The accusative case ending /-a/ is not directly indicated in most written forms. Compare *mid* /maᵓda/(?), a noun in the accusative in 1.4:V:15 = **88.53**, "abundance, plenty" and the adverb *mid* /maᵓda/(?) in 2.16:10 = **84.1**, "very much."

The adverbial affix *-h* /-ah/(?) (cf. perhaps H. -ā(h), Akkad. -iš) indicates direction: *arṣh* /ᵓarṣah/(?) 1.14:I:29 "earthward"; *wᶜlmh* /wa-ᶜālamah/(?) 1.19:IV:6 = **87.4** "and to eternity."

The letter *-m* indicates several adverbial affixes, some of them related to the case system; two of these are accusatival /-am/(?) and locative /-um/(?). For *-m* /-am/, note *špšm* /šapšam/ 1.14:III:14 = **88.71** "at sun(set)" (cf. H. yōmām); *gm* /gam/(?) 1.6:III:22 "loudly" (from *g* "voice"). For *-m* /-um/, cf. the absolute infinitive *mtm* /mōtum/ 1.17:VI:38 = **88.63** "by dying."

55.3. Demonstrative adverbs

The majority of these are of local or modal character, e.g. *ṯm* /ṯam(ma)/ "there" (cf. H. šām); *kn* /kin-/ "so, thus" (cf. H. kēn).

55.4. Temporal adverbs

Some temporal adverbs are derived from the roots used also in the nouns for "time," e.g., *ᶜnt* and *ᶜtn* "now." (Cf. H. ᶜēt, root ᶜ-n-t.) Others contain deictic elements, e.g., *id*(*k*), *apnk*, *aphn*, all meaning "then" or "thereafter."

55.5. Interrogative adverbs

Most interrogative adverbs begin with /ᵓ-/, though some begin with the related /h-/. Some adverbial elements, e.g., /-k-/, and even the interrogative pronoun /mā/ are used to form interrogative adverbs.

The local interrogative adverbs begin with /ʾ-/. The element /y/ seems to be characteristic of adverbs related to staying in a place, while /n/ may indicate movement or direction. Compare *iy* /ʾiyy-/ < *ʾayy- 1.6:IV:16 "where?" and *an* /ʾan-/ 1.6:IV:22 "where (to)?"

The interrogative adverb of manner is *ik* "how?" or "why?", perhaps pronounced /ʾēka/.

The particle *hm* "whether, or" was perhaps originally an interjection. In interrogative function it is used in disjunctive and indirect questions.

55.6 Expressions of negation and affirmation

Identical or corresponding forms are used for both negation and affirmation. The opposite functions can be distinguished, though often not easily and clearly, from the context and situation.

The negative particle *l-* /lā/ "no(t)" and the affirmative particle *l-* /la/ "surely" are probably differentiated by the length of the vowel, /-ā/ for the negative, /-a/ for the affirmative particle. (Cf. Arab. and Aram. lā, H. lō(ʾ).)

The particle *bl* /bal/ (cf. H.) is used in negative and affirmative functions, "no(t)" or "surely," with no visible formal differentiation.

Negative and affirmative *al* /ʾal/, "no" (dynamic) or "surely," similarly exhibit no apparent formal differentiation. (For vocalization cf. H. ʾal.)

The affirmative particle *k-* "surely" is apparently related to the deictic element; the vocalization of it is not certain.

55.7. Expressions of existence and its modifications

The expression of existence *iṯ* /ʾīṯ-/ "there is" can be compared to H. yēš.

The expression of non-existence *in* /ʾēn-/ < *ʾayn "there is not" apparently originated from an interrogative adverb (cf. H. ʾáyin, Arab. ʾayna "where?").

56. *Prepositions*

56.1. General remarks

The prepositions are basically nouns used as adverbs. They are in the construct state, and nouns following them are in genitive (as in Arabic and Akkadian), e.g., *lksi* /lē kussiʾi/(?) 1.5:VI:12 = **87.3** "from the throne"; cf. *ki-a-bi* U:V:12:14 PN ("like the father").

In some prepositions, the nominal base is recognizable, while the short prepositions go back to basic elements. The prepositions can be divided according to the number of consonants in the base—one, two, three. Most prepositions can be provided with suffixed pronouns; the suffixes are attached to (quasi?)pluralic forms of some prepositions. Some prepositional expressions are compound, composed of a short preposition and a noun.

Prepositions can have many different meanings, depending on the governing verb or noun. This dependence helps to explain seemingly opposed meanings of the prepositions *b-*, *l-* and perhaps *ʿl*, on one hand "in," "to," "on," on the other hand "from." The forms are probably the same for both the seemingly opposite meanings.

56.2. One-consonant prepositions

The one-consonant prepositions *b-* "in," *l-* "to," and *k-* "as" are usually written together with the following noun. Variant forms with *-m* or *-n*, *bm*, *lm*, *ln*, *km*, appear usually as so-called B-words in the second colon of a verse.

56.21. Preposition *b-*

The usual form is *b-*, e.g., *bym ḥdṯ* 1.105:1 = **81.3** "on the day of the new moon"; *b.* also occurs: *b.rḥbn* 4.143:1 = **81.5** "in Raḥbān." The vocalization /bi-/ is indicated by the syllabic cuneiform *bi-i*[ ] U:V:130:III:6′, as well as by *by*, 2.38:13, 25 = **86.41.**

56.22. Preposition *l-*

The usual form is *l-*, e.g., *lpᶜn.bᶜly* 2.64:13 = **82.1** "to the feet of my lord"; *l.* also occurs: *ḫmšm.l.mitm* 4.143:2 = **81.5** "fifty (added) to two hundreds," i.e., "250"; cf. P:II:96. The vocalization is indicated by *le-e*[ ](?) U:V:130:III:5′.

56.23. Preposition *k-*

The usual form is *k-*, e.g., *klrmn* 1.23:50 = **88.2** "like a pomegranate"; *k.* also occurs: *k.sprt* 1.127:9 = **86.741** "according to the documents(?)." For the vocalization /ki/ cf. *ki-a-bi* U:V:12:14 PN ("like the father").

56.3. Biconsonantal prepositions

Prepositions with two simple consonants are *mn* "from," *yd* "with" (< "hand"), and apparently also *bl* "without."

The preposition *yd* /yada/(?) "with" developed from the word for "hand." (Cf. H. yad, Arab. yad, and possibly Phoen. dl "with.")

The preposition *bl* "without" may be related to the negation *bl* /bal/, but is probably not identical with it. The vocalization is not clear (cf. Akkad. balu(m), H. bəlī < *ba-).

56.4. Triconsonantal prepositions

The prepositions *ᶜm* /ᶜamm-/ "with, to" and *tk* /tōk-/ < *tawk "(in the) midst (of)" are derived from triconsonantal roots, as is *bn* /bēn-/ < *bayn. All three consonants are clearly indicated in the written forms of *aḫr*, *aṯr*, *bᶜd*, *qdm*, *qrb*. These prepositions appear with the word divider, e.g., *ᶜm* /ᶜamm-/ "with, to" in *ᶜm.bᶜl* 1.17:VI:28 "with Baal"; *ᶜm.il* 1.4:IV:21 = **85.2** "to Il"; *ᶜm.ᶜlm* 1.3:V:31 = **88.52** "with/to eternity."

56.5. Prepositions in *-ay/-ē/

The prepositions in /-ē/ have two—*ᶜd*, *ᶜl*—or three—*bn* (< *b-y-n), *tḥt*—root consonants. It may be supposed that they had an additional morpheme before the suffixed pronouns, though this morpheme is not indicated in the consonantal orthography. It may be reconstructed as *-ay- (cf. H. and Aram. *-ay-, Arab. ᶜalā(y), etc.) > /-ē/ (cf. Eblaitic a-dē).

The preposition *ᶜd* /ᶜad(ē)/(?) "until, to" (cf. Eblaitic a-dē) has the simple form *ᶜd*: *ᶜd.ᶜlm* 3.5:14 = **86.33** "until/to eternity, for ever"; *ᶜd.šbᶜ* . . . *ᶜd.škr* 1.114:3–4 = **88.3** "to satiety . . . to drunkenness."

The preposition *bn* /bēna/(?) "between" has the simple form *bn*: *bn.ᶜnm* 1.2:IV:22 = **88.51** "between the eyes"; *bn.nšrm* 1.18:IV:21 = **88.64** "between/among the eagles."

The preposition *tḥt* /taḥta/ "under, beneath" has the simple form *tḥt*: *tḥt.ṯlḥn* 1.114:6, 8 = **88.3** "under the table"; *ᶜbdil.tḥt ilmlk* 4.133:2 "ᶜAbdu-ᵓilu instead of Ilimilku."

56.6. Forms with suffixed pronouns

sing.	1.	*ly*	*ᶜmy*	*ᶜly*	du.	1.		*ᶜmny*	
	2.m.	*lk*	*ᶜmk*	*ᶜlk*		3.	*bhm*	*bᶜdhm*	
	2.f.	*lk*	*ᶜmk*	*ᶜlk*	pl.	1.	*ln*		*ᶜln*
	3.m.	*lh*	*bᶜdh*	*ᶜlh*		2.m.	*lkm*		
	3.f.	*bh*	*ᶜmh*	*ᶜlh*		3.m.	*lhm*		

l- "to"; *b-* "in"; *ᶜm* "with/toward"; *bᶜd* "behind"; *ᶜl* "upon"

Some forms have an additional *n* before the suffixed pronoun, e.g., *lnh* 1.100:5 = **86.73** "from him"; *ᶜmnk* 3.9:16 = **84.2** "with you"; *ᶜlnh* 1.4:IV:44 "upon him."

57. *Conjunctions*

57.1. Forms and functions

From a formal point of view, conjunctions can be divided into simple (e.g., *w*), extended (e.g., *wn*), and perhaps compound (cf. *k+d* 1.19:I:14). According to distribution and function, conjunctions can be divided into coordinating and subordinating. The coordinating conjunctions connect either elements within a clause or clauses; the subordinating conjunctions introduce subordinate clauses.

Some conjunctions are apparently primary, i.e., they occur only as conjunctions. Some prepositions, determinative pronouns/particles, and interjections are used as conjunctions.

57.2. Coordinating conjunctions

57.21. Conjunction *w-*

The usual form is *w-* /wa-/, usually written together with the following word: *wtn* 5.9:12 = **83.2** "and give!"; *w.b.spr* 4.338:3 = **82.4** "and in the list." There is an extended form, *wn*, e.g., *wn.in.bt* 1.4:IV:50 "and there is no house."

57.22. Other coordinating conjunctions

The coordinating conjunction *p-* /pa-/ "and" (cf. Arab. fa) is usually written together with the following word: *pdr.dr* 1.19:IV:6 = **87.4** "and (for) generation(s) of generation(s)."

Another coordinating conjunction is *ap* "also, but" (cf. H. ᵓap): *ap.krmm* | *ḫlq* 2.61:10–11=**86.44** "also the vineyards were destroyed"(?).

57.23. Disjunctive conjunctions

The conjunction *u* /ᵓō/ "or" (cf. H. ᵓō, Syr. and Arab. ᵓaw) is nearly always written together with the following word: *uilm.tmtn* 1.16:I:22=**88.73** "or do gods die?"

The disjunctive conjunction *hm* /him/(?) "or" occurs in disjunctive questions: *lḥm.hm.štym* 1.4:IV:35=**85.2** "eat or drink!"; *rǵbt. . .hm. . .ǵmit* 1.4:IV:33–34=**85.2** "are you hungry. . .or. . . are you thirsty?"

57.3. Subordinating conjunctions

Some subordinating conjunctions are particles of originally prepositional or interjectional character. The determinative/relative pronoun *ḏ*-, *d*- can also be used as a conjunction. The conditional conjunction *hm* is (at least in function) different from the disjunctive *hm*. The conjunction *k*- /kī/ is related to the deictic element *k*-.

The conjunction *k*- /kī/ "that, because, if," etc. (cf. H. kī) is usually written together with the following word: *ydᶜt.krḥmt* 1.16:I:33 "I know that you are compassionate"; *k.yiḫd* 1.72:16 "if he takes." There is a graphic variant *ky* /kī/: *ky.ᶜrbt* 2.16:7=**84.1** "that I entered."

The conjunction *hm* "if, whether" (cf. H. ᵓim, Arab. ᵓin, Aram. hēn < *hin) has the usual form *hm* /him/: *hm.yrgm.mlk* 2.33:30=**86.42** "if the king says." Variants include *im* and *-m*: *wm.ag*|*rškm* 3.9:6–7=**84.2** "and if I expell you."

The simple form of the conjunction *d* "since, because" is usually written with the following word (as is the determinative/relative pronoun, "that (of), who, which"): *din.bn.lh* 1.17:I:18 =**88.61** "since he has no son." There is an extended form, *dm*: *dm.rgm* | *iṯ.ly* 1.3:III:20–21 =**87.8** "because I have a word."

Some prepositions, instead of being connected with a noun, may be connected with a clause (which could be considered an attribute) and thus function as conjunctions: *k* (and *km*) "as (soon as)": *ktᶜrb* 1.148:18 "as soon as she enters"; *ᶜd* "until": *ᶜd.tšbᶜ.bk* 1.6:I:9 "until she is sated with weeping."

57.4. Particles introducing clauses

There are some particles which cannot properly be called conjunctions, but which have a similar function in that they determine the syntactic character of a following clause; they can be also classified as interjections.

The letter *l*- can indicate two different particles, a volitive /la-/ or /li-/ and a desiderative /lū/. (These particles cannot always be clearly distinguished from negative /lā/ and affirmative /la/). For desiderative *l*-, note *ltbrk* 1.15:II:14=**87.2** "may you bless."

58. *Interjections*

While most interjections are formed of primary deictic elements, a few may be related to a nominal or verbal base.

58.1. Interjections introducing a clause

The particles *hn* "behold, lo" and its derivatives *hnn*, *hnny*, and *hl* (and perhaps *hlm*) usually occur at the beginning of a clause.

The interjection introducing a vocative is *y-* /yā/ (cf. Arab.) "O!": *ybn* 1.16:VI:55 = **85.1** "O (my) son"; *ybtltm* 1.17:VI:34 = **88.63** "O young lady!" Note also the vocative use of a particle written *l*: *lkrt* 1.16:VI:41 = **85.1** "O Keret!"

58.2. Postpositive elements

The interjection *m*^{c} used for strengthening the imperative developed probably from *šm*^{c} "hear!"; *šm*^{c} *m*^{c} 1.16:VI:41 = **85.1** "hear, pray!"

Some short elements which appear at the ends of words may be interjections. (But some of the elements indicated in the consonantal writing by *-m* are of other than interjectional character, such as the generalizing /-mā/ [added, for example to the preposition /ki-/] or the /m/ of mimation after some case endings.) The so-called enclitic *m* attached to various words seems not, in many instances, to affect the meaning: *bqrbm.asm* 1.19:II:18 "in the midst of the granary"; *t*^{c}*rbm* 1.24:18 = **88.1** "may she enter." In some instances, its function may be euphonic: to separate vowels or identical consonants.

Postpositive elements indicated in writing include *-n*, *-h*, *-k*, *-y*, *-l*. These are added to various words and forms; their origin, form, and function is often unknown.

6. Function of Words in the Sentence

61. *Function of pronouns*

61.1. Independent personal pronouns

The character of the first- and second- person pronouns is more personal than that of the third-person pronouns, which are ultimately demonstrative in origin; these differences are reflected in the functions of the pronouns.

Personal pronouns of the first and second person often serve as subject, in nominal clauses by necessity, in verbal clauses often for emphasis.

at.aḫ 1.18:I:24 "you are my brother"
with inf. abs.: *ngš.ank.aliyn bᶜl* 1.6:II:21 = **88.55** "I crushed Victorious Baal"; *wan.mtm.amt* 1.17:VI:38 = **88.63** "and I, too, shall certainly die"
w.at | umy.al.tdḥl 2.30:20–21 = **83.4** "and you, my mother, do not be afraid!"

Personal pronouns of the third person in the genitive-accusative indicate either a direct object or an attribute.

kbd hyt 1.3:III:10 = **87.8** "honor her!"
tšqy.msk.hwt 1.19:IV:61 "she imbues/gives him (with) mixed wine (to drink)"
bᶜl.ṯbr.diy.hyt 1.19:III:37 = **88.65** "Baal broke her wings"

61.2. Suffixed personal pronouns

Personal pronouns suffixed to nouns—including numerals and prepositions—and to some verbal nouns are in the genitive case.

1. sing. with noun in gen.: *lksiy* 2.31:15 "to/from my throne"
acc.: *ṭḥ.ggy* 1.17:II:22 "plastering my roof"
nom.: *tnḫ. . . .npš* /napšī/ 1.17:II:13–14 "my soul will repose"; cf. *umy | tdᶜ* 2.16:6–7 = **84.1** "may my mother know"
3. sing. m.: *bm.bkyh* 1.14:I:31 "in his weeping"

Pronouns suffixed to finite verbal forms and to most verbal nouns indicate the accusative case. Only in the first person singular are the genitive and the accusative forms distinguished.

acc.: *al.tšrgn* 1.17:VI:34 = **88.63** "do not deceive me!"
gen.: *mᶜmsy* 1.17:II:20 "supporting me"/"supporter of mine"

61.3. Interrogative pronouns

The interrogative pronouns serve to introduce interrogative clauses. They can also be used in indirect questions and as the introductory pronouns of relative clauses.

interrogative function: *mh.ylt* 1.23:53 = **88.2** "what did they (du. fem.) bear?"; *mn.ib* 1.3:III:37 "what enemy?"
generalizing function: *mnm.irštk* 2.41:16 = **83.3** "whatever is your wish"

61.4. Determinative/relative pronouns

There are two forms, the basic form *d*, and *dt*. Their distribution and function are not clear, though it seems that *d* is used in relation to singular masculine antecedents, while *dt* is more frequent in relation to feminine forms, duals, and plurals. The two different functions of the pronoun are not formally distinguished.

determinative: *ᶜr.dqdm* 1.100:62 = **86.73** "city (that) of the East"
relative: *mrkbt.dt.* | *ᶜrb* 4.145:1–2 = **82.3** "chariots which entered"

61.5. Demonstrative pronouns

The basic form is *hnd* "this"; it serves as an adjectival attribute to governing nouns in the singular masculine and feminine, and in the plural.

l.ym hnd 3.4:1 = **86.32** "from this day on"
alpm.ššwm.hnd 2.33:32 = **86.42** "these two thousands horses"

The form with the feminine marker, *hndt*, refers to a noun: *hndt*. . .*mtt* 2.38:12–13 = **86.41** "this one (referring back to *anykn* "your vessel," line 10) died (became immobilized?)."

62. *Function of nouns*

The inflectional categories for substantive and adjective nouns are gender (masculine, feminine), number (singular—including collective nouns, dual, plural), case (nominative, accusative, genitive), and state (absolute, construct).

The category of indetermination is used occasionally: cf. **52.6** and **62.6**.

62.1. Substantive and adjective nouns

The differentiation of substantive and adjective nouns is not clearly indicated by formal means; they differ in function. Among the adjectives may be counted ordinal numerals, the cardinal numeral "1," participles, and the demonstrative pronoun *hnd*.

Substantive nouns occur in the following roles in the clause:

in the nominative—as subject, nominal predicate, complement to the subject; also as vocative
in the accusative—as object, complement to object, adverbial modifier
in the genitive—as nominal attribute, to nouns or to prepositions
in all cases—as nominal apposition.

Adjective nouns occur in these functions:

in all three cases—as adjectival attribute
in the nominative only—as nominal predicate, complement to subject.

Adjectival attributes usually follow the governing noun: *udm.rbt* (acc.) 1.14:III:30 = **88.71** "Great Udum" (object); *pǵt.aḥt* 4.349:3 = **81.4** "one girl." The nominal predicate occurs in nominal clauses: *špthm.mtqtm* 1.23:50 = **88.2** "their lips (are) sweet," while the complement to the subject occurs in verbal clauses: *alk.nmrrt* 1.19:IV:33 "I shall go strengthened."

The adjective noun can be provided with an adnominal adjunct.

ᶜz.mid 2.10:13 = **86.43** "very strong"
nᶜmt.bn.aḫt.bᶜl 1.10:II:16 = **88.56** "the (most) beautiful among Baal's sisters"

Some gradation is indicated by the prefix /ᵓa-/ in the adjectives: *agzr* 1.23:23 = **88.2** "voracious"; *aliy* 1.3:III:14 = **87.8** "(very) strong" (cf. H. ᵓakzāb "deceitful," ᵓakzār "cruel"; Arab. elative).

There are no special forms for the comparative or superlative; these relations are indicated by the context.

62.2. Gender

In principle masculine beings are represented by masculine nouns without a gender marker, while nouns for feminine beings are indicated as feminine by a marker containing /t/.

There are some feminine nouns without feminine marker:

females: *um* /ᵓumm-/ "mother" (note the plural form *umhthm* "their mothers"); *arḫ* "cow"
paired body parts: *yd* /yad-/ "hand"
natural entities: *arṣ* /ᵓarṣ/ "earth"; *špš* /šapš-/ "sun"
cities: *udm* /ᵓud(u)m-/: *udm.rbt* 1.14:III:30 = **88.71** "Great Udum"

62.3. Number

The Ugaritic language has, beside singular and plural, a dual.

The singular indicates individual animate beings or inanimate objects, as well as commodities, e.g., *yn* /yēn-/ "wine." A singular form can indicate more than one counted object: *ḫmšm.l.mitm.zt* 4.143:2 = **81.5** "250 olive (trees)." A noun in the singular can have collective meaning: *npš* 4.338:1 = **82.4** "persons."

The dual is widely used in Ugaritic, not only for natural pairs but also for other persons or objects occurring in number of two.

šptℎm.mtqtm 1.23:50 = **88.2** "their lips (are) sweet"
kdm.yn 4.279:4 = **86.24** "2 jars of wine"
iltm 1.102:13 "(two) goddesses"

62.4. Case

The case indicates the function of a noun in a clause; all nominal constituents and components have to be provided with the appropriate case marker. Since case markers are only rarely visible in the alphabetic writing, syntactic function is used along with form in determining the case of nouns.

The nominative is the case of the subject and of related constituents and components. Its marker, singular /-u/–plural /-ū/, as an expression of a statement may be related to the /-u/ marker of the indicative imperfect. The use of the nominative for the nominal predicate and for the complement to the subject points to the close relation to the subject of both components. The nominative is also used in the vocative function.

The accusative can be called an adverbial case. A noun in the accusative denotes the circumstances of an action or a state. Thus, the accusative is the case of a direct object depending on an active transitive verb. The circumstances related to actions expressed by other kinds of verbs can also be expressed by the accusative. The adverbial modifier as well as the adnominal adjunct consisting of a noun stand in the accusative.

The genitive is an adnominal case. It indicates that a noun is dependent on another noun and it is thus the case of the substantival attribute. A noun following a preposition is also in the genitive case: *lksi* 1.5:VI:12 = **87.3** "from the throne."

The case of nominal appositions and adjectival attributes is not fixed. It depends on the governing nominal constituent or component, since an apposition and an adjectival attribute have to agree with the governing noun in case as well as number and gender.

62.5. State

The form of the absolute is the same as that of the construct in the singulars of both masculine and feminine nouns and the plurals of feminine nouns. The construct state is formally differentiated from the absolute state by the lack of final morphemes, /-ma/ in the masculine plural, /-mi/ in both masculine and feminine duals. These morphemes are indicated by *-m* in the alphabetic writing.

The construct state is used for nouns followed by a genitival attribute consisting of a noun, and also for nouns provided with a suffixed possessive pronoun, which is virtually in the genitive. All prepositions and certain other particles provided with a genitival attribute, whether nominal or pronominal, are in the construct state.

62.6 Indetermination

For the occasional use of *-m* /-um/ in the nominal predicate cf. **52.6** and **73.21**.

63. *Function of numerals*

63.1. Cardinal numerals, simple and compound

The cardinal numerals, except for "1," are substantive nouns and are construed as such. They can appear in either the absolute or the construct state; forms with a suffixed possessive pronoun are related to those of the construct state. Cardinal numerals for "3"–"10" have two different forms, a form of masculine type (without a gender marker) and a form of feminine type (with a feminine marker).

In the compound numerals "11"–"19," the digit (with or without the feminine marker) is followed by one of the forms for "10," *ᶜšr*, *ᶜšrt*, *ᶜšrh* (cf. H ᶜæśrē).

arbᶜ.ᶜšr.ǵzrm 4.349:1 = **81.4** "14 young men"
barbᶜt.ᶜšrt 1.109:1 = **86.71**, cf. 1.46:10 "on the 14th (day of the month)"
ṯmn.ᶜšrh.mrynm 4.173:2 "18 warriors"

In the formation of larger numbers, the higher orders are usually followed by the lower ones, with or without the conjunction *w-* "and": *ḫmš.mat.arbᶜm* 4.338:10 = **86.26** "540" (= "500 (and) 40"). There is a variant, possessive construction, which adds tens to hundreds: *ḫmšm.l.mitm.zt* 4.143:2 = **81.5** "250 (50 to/belonging to 200) olive trees."

Cardinal numerals may be used in ordinal functions.

bšbᶜ.ymm 1.17:I:15 = **88.61** "on the seventh day"
barbᶜt.ᶜšrt 1.109:1 = **86.71** "on the fourteenth (day)"

63.2. Numerals and counted objects

The grammatical relation between substantive nouns and associated numerals is difficult to specify because the Ugaritic texts are not always clear about the case or number of the noun involved. There is a variety of expressions used for counted objects: they can be in the singular, dual, or plural. Further, they can be attached to cardinal numerals as appositions or as genitival attributes. Usage is free in the gender relationship between numerals and counted objects.

ṯṯ.ḥrṯm 4.630:6 = **82.2** "6 plowmen"
mitm.iqnu 4.247:28 "200 (pieces of) lapis lazuli"
mit.pḥm | *mit.iqni* 3.1:27–28 = **86.31** "100 gems, 100 (pieces of) lapis lazuli"
b.ᶜšrt 4.146:2 = **86.25** "for 10 (shekels)"

63.3. Other numerals

The ordinal numerals are adjectives and usually appear as adjectival attributes: *ṯdṯ.ym.* 1.14:III:3 "the sixth day." In some instances an ordinal numeral is used without a governing noun. This occurs often in date formulas: *brbᶜ* /bi-rābiᶜi/ 1.14:IV:46; 4.279:4 = **86.24** "on the fourth (day)."

Multiplicative numerals serve as adverbial modifiers.

63.4. The quantitive expression *kl* "all"

The expression *kl* /kull-/ is basically a noun meaning "wholeness." It is therefore construed as a substantive noun, and the counted objects are in genitive. It occurs before the singular (English "every"): *kl ǵr* 1.6:II:15–16 = **88.55** "every mountain"; perhaps 1.17:VI:38 = **88.63**.

It is used with suffixed pronouns, both singular: *il.klh* 1.17:V:31 = **88.62** "the god(s) of all of it (Egypt)"; and plural: *klhm* 1.14:II:42 "all of them."

64. *Function of verbal forms*

64.1. Finite verbal forms: person, number, gender

Verbal forms which indicate person and number are called finite. (All others are called verbal nouns.) The criterion for determining the syntactic function of finite verb forms is the expression of person and number. The only function of finite verb forms is to serve as verbal predicates in verbal clauses.

Every finite verbal form exhibits person (first, second or third) and number (singular, dual, or plural). In the second and third persons, there are separate masculine and feminine forms in most instances.

64.2. Finite forms: tenses

64.21. Perfect and imperfect

The two sets of verbal forms, the perfect, marked by afformatives, and the imperfect, marked by prefixes and afformatives, have different functions, aspectual in poetry and temporal in prose.

Ugaritic poetry was fixed in writing in the fourteenth century B.C., but preserves traditions going back several centuries. In poetry the function of the perfect and imperfect can be characterized by the notion of aspect. Aspect is by definition subjective, i.e., it expresses the subjective attitude of the speaker to an action or a state. The constative aspect is indicated by the perfect. The speaker is concentrating on noticing an action, without respect to its circumstances; usually actions which are independent of other actions or circumstances are expressed by the perfect. The cursive aspect is expressed by the imperfect. The speaker follows the action in its course, taking its circumstances into consideration. Actions dependent on other actions and those conditioned by circumstances may be indicated by the imperfect.

Most of the Ugaritic non-literary prose texts were written in the last stage of the city's existence, around 1200 B.C. In these texts the perfect and imperfect have temporal character. The tenses expressed by the perfect and imperfect indicate the relation of the action or state to the basic level of time, the present. The perfect of active verbs expresses actions which happened and were accomplished in the past or which were done in the past with consequences lasting into the present (like the Greek and English perfect tenses). The imperfect as a tense expresses the non-past, i.e., the present and the future. Actions or states expressed by the imperfect are considered unaccomplished or not yet accomplished.

The semantic character of the verb affects these functions, at least in the simple active pattern. Verbs of action may indicate aspects or temporal functions different from those of verbs of state or quality.

64.22. The perfect in poetry

Perfect forms of verbs of action in poetry indicate in principle the constative aspect: the speaker is calling attention to the independent and unconditional character of the action.

kn.npl.bᶜl 1.12:II:53 = **88.4** "thus Baal fell down"
bph.rgm.lyṣa 1.2:IV:6 = **88.51** "the word did not go out of her mouth"
dᶜlk.mḫṣ.aqht.ǵzr 1.19:IV:4 = **87.4** "because upon you(r territory) Aqhat, the young hero, was slain"
ik.atwt.qnyt.ilm 1.4:IV:32 = **85.2** "why did the creatrix of the gods come?"

A similar characteristic is true for the perfect forms of verbs of state or quality, but their temporal settings are more closely related to the present; the verbs tend to describe the results of past actions: *hm.ǵmu.ǵmit* 1.4:IV:34 = **85.2** "or have you been/are you very thirsty?"

There is, in addition to the aspectual usage, a performative usage of the perfect, an action is performed by saying the verb in the perfect (cf. H. Gen. 23:11, 13; 1:29): *ytt.nḥšm.mhrk* 1.100:75 = **86.73** "I (by saying this) gave snakes (as) your bride-price."

64.23. The imperfect in poetry

The aspectual character of the imperfect in poetry may be seen in its extension to all three temporal spheres: it can express an action expected or promised for the future; it can indicate a present action or state; and it is also used frequently in narrative for description of past actions.

future: *wykn.bnh.bbt* 1.17:I:25 = **87.1** "and his son will be in the house"; *wan.mtm.amt* 1.17:VI:38 = **88.63** "and I shall certainly die"
present: *ltdn* | *dn.almnt* 1.16:VI:45–46 = **85.1** "you do not judge the judgment of the widow"; *tlu.ḥ*(m)*t.km.nḫl* 1.100:68 = **86.73** "the venom(?) is as strong (flows out as strongly(?)) as a creek"
common narrative mode, action in the past: *ytbᶜ.yṣb* | *ǵlm* 1.16:VI:39 = **85.1** "Yaṣṣub the lad went out"; *yšu gh* | *wyṣḥ* 1.16:VI:40–41 = **85.1** "he raised his voice and shouted"
following a perfect: *mǵy.ḥrn.lbth* 1.100:67–68 = **86.73** "Ḥōrān reached his house
w | *yštql.lḥẓrh* and entered his court"

64.24. The perfect in prose

In the late non-literary texts, the perfect serves as a past tense for verbs of action.

iwrkl.pdy | *agdn* 3.4:2–3 = **86.32** "Iwrikalli redeemed Agdan"
anykn.dt | *likt.mṣrm* 2.38:10–11 = **86.41** "your ship, the one which you had sent/dispatched to Egypt"

In letters the perfect is used to describe an action from an addressee's point of view: *lpᶜn.bᶜly...qlt* 2.64:13 + 16 = **82.1** "down at the feet of my lord . . . I fell."

The perfect of verbs of state or quality seems to indicate the result of a past action lasting into the present.

mnm.irštk | *dḫṣrt* 2.41:16–17 = **83.3** "whatever (thing is) your desire, which you are lacking"

64.25. The imperfect in prose

The imperfect serves to express non-past actions and states in the prose texts; it generally indicates the future: *p.l.ašt.aṯty* 2.33:28 = **86.42** "and I shall not put my wife." It sometimes refers to the present. It also has a generic use, in regulations and ritual prescriptions: *id ydbḥ mlk* 1.115:1 = **82.5** "then the king (will/shall) sacrifice." (See also 1.109:1–2 = **86.71**; 3.5:15–18 = **86.33.**)

64.26. Some special functions of the aspects/tenses

The use of the perfect and imperfect in conditional sentences is determined by the relationship of the condition to the consequences rather than by the general functions of perfect and imperfect as aspects or tenses.

The perfect in the protasis of a conditional sentence indicates an unreal condition (cf. Greek and English): *w.hm.ḫt.* | *ᶜl.w.likt* | *ᶜmk* 2.30:16–18 = **83.4** "and if the Hittite were to come up, (then) I would send (a letter) to you." (See also 2.33:27 = **86.42.**)

The perfect may express a wish (cf. H. "precative perfect," e.g., nāpəlū in Ps 57:7):

lyrt 1.5:I:6 = **88.54** "may you descend"
ḥwt.aḫt 1.10:II:20 = **88.56** "may you live, my sister"

64.3. Moods

64.31. Indicative and volitive moods

The category of mood refers primarily to a set of finite verb forms related to the imperfect. (The category of mood may be relevant to the perfect in a few instances of forms modified after *w*-, as in H. consecutive perfect; cf., e.g., *wṯb.lunṯhm* 3.4:19 = **86.32** "and they will return to their labor duty"; perhaps also *wšmᶜ* 1.119:34 = **86.75** "and he will hear.")

The modal forms are derived from the same base as the imperfect. The volitive moods can be considered variants of the imperfect, differing from it in modal marker. The imperative also differs from the imperfect in lacking prefixes.

64.32. Jussive

The jussive, which is characterized by a zero suffix in many of its forms, expresses (a) a wish or desire aimed at changing reality, or (b) an indirect instruction, or (c) a prohibition aimed at keeping reality unchanged. It is probably used only in the second and third persons.

yṯbr.ḥrn | *rišk* 1.16:VI:55–56 = **85.1** "may Ḥōrān break your head"
yšlm.lk 2.16:4 = **84.1** "may peace be with you (sing. fem.)"

trtḥṣ.wtadm 1.14:II:9 "do wash yourself and be rouged/rouge yourself!"
ltbrk (with particle *l*-) 1.15:II:14=**87.2** "may you bless"

The jussive is negated with *al* /ʾal/.

al.yšt 2.38:27=**86.41** "may he not put"
al.tšrgn 1.17:VI:34=**88.63** "do not deceive me!"

64.33. Subjunctive

Forms of the subjunctive can be recognized, whether by the marker /-a/ or by other criteria, only in rare instances. In independent or main clauses, the subjunctive expresses a subjective wish. In dependent clauses it is probably used for volitive expressions for which the jussive or imperative would be used in independent clauses.

The main clause usage may be associated with the first person.

ašlw /ʾašluwa/ 1.14:III:45=**88.71** "I will repose"
iqra 1.23:1 "I will invoke"
bḥyk.abn.nšmḫ 1.16:I:14=**88.73** "let us rejoice in your life, O our father!"(?)

Dependent clause usage may extend to all persons.

ptḥ.bt.wuba 1.100:72=**86.73** "open the house, and/that I may enter"
tn nkl y|rḫ ytrḫ 1.24:17–18=**88.1** "give Nikkal (so that) Yarikh may marry (her)"

64.34. Energic

Even if there are two formally differentiated types of the energic mood in Ugaritic, they cannot be distinguished in the script, because the letter *-n* can indicate both /-an/ and /-anna/. The energic mood is apparently used in all three persons. In the second person it corresponds to the jussive, and in the first person to the subjunctive.

tqln 1.16:VI:57=**85.1** "may you fall down"
iqran 1.23:23=**88.2** (cf. *iqra* 1.23:1) "I will invoke"

In the third person the forms of the energic mood often do not differ in function from those of the indicative imperfect: *bkm.tmdln.ʿr* 1.19:II:8=**87.5** "weeping, she saddled the donkey." The energic can be used with suffixed pronouns:

aqbrnh 1.19:III:34=**88.65** "I shall bury him"; "let me bury him"
yqbr.nn 1.19:III:41=**88.65** "he buried him"

64.35. Imperative

The imperative is formally related to the jussive; the afformatives of both, those of the shortest type, are nearly identical. The imperative differs from all the other moods in that it lacks a prefix. The prefix is unnecessary, because all imperative forms indicate the second person. The imperative occurs in independent volitive clauses which express a command. It is often accompanied by a vocative. The imperative cannot be negated.

tn ks yn 5.9:15 = **83.2** "give a cup of wine!"
rgm 2.16:3 = **84.1** and often at the beginning of a letter "tell (the addressee)!"
špš.um.ql.bl 1.100:57 = **86.73** "Shapsh/Sun, my mother, bring the word (literally voice)!"

It can be strengthened by the particle *mᶜ*: *šmᶜ mᶜ.lkrt* | *ṯᶜ* 1.16:VI:41–42 = **85.1** "hear, pray/now, O Keret the Generous!" It is found in the main clause (apodosis) of conditional and related clauses.

ttn.wtn 5.9:12 = **83.2** "(if) you will give, (so) give!"
w.mnm | *rgm...w.št* | *b.spr.ᶜmy* 2.10:16–19 = **86.43** "and whatever is the word . . . put it in a letter to me!"

64.4. Verbal nouns

64.41. In general

The verbal nouns are the absolute infinitive, the construct infinitive, and the participles. Verbal nouns can express manner of action and voice in their patterns; their ability to express other categories is limited. Participles can indicate number (singular, dual or plural) and gender (masculine or feminine). The categories of person, number, and gender are not applicable for the infinitive, either absolute or construct.

The absolute infinitive is an adverb. In verbal clauses it usually serves as an adverbial modifier; it serves rarely as a nominal predicate, functionally corresponding to the imperative or to a finite form.

The construct infinitive is a noun which can be provided with an object. In a clause it can serve as an adverbial component, either as the object or, attached to and together with a preposition, as an adverbial modifier.

The participles are adjective nouns and therefore serve in the same functions as other adjective nouns, i.e., as predicates, complements to the subject, adjectival attributes, and, rarely, complements to the object.

Verbal nouns can be provided with adverbial components, objects and adverbial modifiers. All except the absolute infinitive can be provided with an adnominal component, i.e., a genitival attribute.

Construct infinitives and participles can function as substantive nouns in some positions in the clause.

The time referent is not formally expressed; it is indicated by context and situation.

64.42. The absolute infinitive

The absolute infinitive is used most frequently as an adverbial modifier. A particular form of this usage involves the absolute infinitive of the root from which the main verb of the clause is derived (cf. H. Num. 23:25).

bkm.tmdln.ʿr 1.19:II:8 = **87.5** "weeping, she saddles the donkey"
hm.ǵmu.ǵmit 1.4:IV:34 = **85.2** "or are you very thirsty?"; cf. also 1.17:VI:38 = **88.63**; 2.30:19–20 = **83.4**

The absolute infinitive is also used as a nominal predicate, frequently with a personal pronoun as subject (cf. also 2.38:23 = **86.41**; 2.61:5–7 = **86.44**. The pronoun is most often that of the first person singular.

ngš.ank.aliyn bʿl 1.6:II:21–22 = **88.55** "I attacked the Victorious Baal,
ʿdbnn.ank.imr.bpy I arranged him in my mouth (like/as) a lamb"
ḫtu hw 1.6:II:23 = **88.55** "he disappeared"

In a usage corresponding to the imperative, the absolute infinitive may express a command: *lḥm.hm.štym* 1.4:IV:35 = **85.2** "eat or drink!"

In principle the absolute infinitive should not be provided with suffixed pronouns; cf., however *ʿdbnn* 1.6:II:22 = **88.55**, cited above. (But this may be an imperfect 1. sing. ʿ- < *ʿaʾ-.)

64.43. The construct infinitive

The construct infinitive appears in both simple and derived verbal patterns.

The construct infinitive is a verbal noun which can be provided with an object or with a genitival attribute; either can be expressed by either a noun or a suffixed pronoun. The construct infinitive can appear in all three cases. In the genitive it can be attached to a governing noun or to a preposition (cf. also perhaps 1.80:4 = **86.51**).

mnt.nṯk.nḥš 1.100:4 = **86.73** "incantation against a snakebite (lit., incantation of the biting of a snake)"
tṣmt.adm.ṣat.špš 1.3:II:8 "she smites the men of sunrise (lit., of the going out of the sun)"
bm.bkyh 1.14:I:31 "in his weeping"
[km.yṯb] | *llḥm* 1.18:IV:18–19 = **88.64** "as soon as he sits down to eat" (cf. 1.18:IV:29)

In the accusative it can serve as an object.

hlk.kṯr. | *kyʿn* 1.17:V:10–11 "he really perceived the walking/arriving of Kothar"

64.5. Verbal nouns: Participles

64.51. Adjective verbal nouns

The participles are adjective nouns; they can express more categories than the other verbal nouns. Not only do the participles exhibit, through belonging to a certain verb pattern, manner of action and voice; they can also express number and gender, as other adjectives do.

As adjective nouns, the participles can serve in the clause as adnominal components, adjectival attributes, complements to the subject, or complements to the object. Active participles can also serve as substantive nouns, whether as objects or subjects.

ᶜrb.b|kyt.bhklh 1.19:IV:9–10 "wailing (women) entered his palace"
ṯġr | bt.il 1.114:11–12 = **88.3** "the janitor of Il's house" (cf. H. šōᶜēr)

64.52. Active participles

Active participles may govern a direct object, expressed by a noun or a suffixed pronoun.

aḫd.ydh 1.17:I:30 = **87.1** "holding his hand"
mᶜmsh 1.17:I:30 = **87.1** "supporting him"; *mᶜmsy* (with *-y*!) 1.17:II:20 "supporting me"

They may also govern adverbial modifiers.

Active participles may be used as

(a) subjects,

štk.šibt.ᶜn 1.12:II:59 = **88.4** "the (women) drawing (water of/from) the spring ceased"

(b) as nominal predicates,

pḥlt...qrit 1.100:1–2 = **86.73** "the young mare is calling"
nḥtm.ḫṭk 1.23:47 = **88.2** "your staff is going down"

(c) as complements to the subject,

wykn.bnh.bbt... 1.17:I:25–31 = **87.1** "and his son will be in the house,
mᶜmsh...spu supporting him ... eating"

(d) as objects,

imḫṣ.mḫṣ.aḫy 1.19:IV:34 "I shall smite the one who smote my brother"

(e) as complements to objects,

iqran.ilm...ynqm.bap... 1.23:23–24 = **88.2** "I will invoke ... gods ... suckling from the nipples..."

(f) as adjectival attributes:

pġt...ydᶜt.hlk.kbkbm 1.19:II:6–7 = **87.5** "Paghat ... knowing the paths (or knower of the paths) of the stars"

and (g) as genitival attributes (also after a preposition).

špk.km.šiy | dm 1.18:IV:23–24 = **88.64** "pour blood like a slaughterer(?)!
km.šḫṭ... ... like a butcher...!"
tspr.by|rdm.arṣ 1.4:VIII:8 "you will be counted among those who go down (in)to the earth"

64.53. Passive participles

Passive participles cannot govern an object; they can be provided with genitival attributes, expressed by a noun or a suffixed pronoun.

mtrḫt.yšrh 1.14:I:13 "(the espoused one of his legitimacy >) his rightful spouse"
ybʿr...lm.nkr | mddth 1.14:II:48–50 "he will entrust ... to a stranger his beloved one"

Passive participles may be used as (a) nominal predicates,

mmnnm.mṭ ydk 1.23:47 = **88.2** "weakened is the rod of your member (lit. hand)"

(b) complements to the subject,

alk.brktm(?)...*nmrrt* 1.19:IV:32–33 "I shall go blessed ... strengthened"

(c) adverbial attributes.

by | gšm.adr | nškḥ 2.38:13–15 = **86.41** "in/by the strong rainstorm which occurred"

64.6. Manners of action

64.61. Verbal patterns: manner of action and voice

Every verbal form, whether finite verb or verbal noun, belongs to one of the patterns. These indicate both manner of action (simple, factitive or causative) and voice (active, passive, or reflexive). The categories of both manner of action and voice determine the kind of the non-verbal components associated with a verbal form, such as objects and adverbial modifiers.

64.62. Kinds of manners of action

Manner of action is one of the two categories expressed by the verb pattern. The manners of action are (1) simple unmarked, (2) factitive, marked most often by doubling the second root consonant or rarely by lengthening or repeating some of the elements, and (3) causative, usually marked by a prefix or rarely by modification of the vowels between the root consonants.

64.63. Simple manner of action (G, Gp, Gt; N)

The simple manner of action is combined with the following voices in the verb patterns: active, internal passive, reflexive, and secondary passive (reciprocal/passive).

The simple active manner of action denotes an action emanating from the subject, or a state or quality associated with the subject.

64.64. The system of characteristic vowels

Only in the simple active pattern is there a system of characteristic vowels—those between the second and third root consonants of the perfect and imperfect—which indicate the character of the verb as (a) verb of action, (b) a verb denoting a changeable quality, or (c) a verb denoting a permanent quality. This feature is connected to the basic meaning of the root. Only some syntactic implications of this system are mentioned below.

The semantic characteristics of a verb, as indicated by the system of characteristic vowels, are reflected in the use and function of the perfect and imperfect in the simple manner of action. Verbs of action may be transitive, i.e., they may govern a direct object.

lqḥ šᶜrt 4.430:7 = **82.2** "they took wool(en blankets)"
yšu gh 1.16:VI:40 = **85.1** "he raised his voice"
lṯṯpṭ | ṯpṭ 1.16:VI:46–47 = **85.1** "you do not judge the judgment"
aštk 1.18:IV:17 = **88.64** "I shall put you"

Some verbs of action are intransitive, governing no object. Some of them can govern adverbial modifiers.

kn.npl.bᶜl 1.12:II:53 = **88.4** "thus fell Baal"
il.hlk.lbth 1.114:17 = **88.3** "Il went to his house"

Verbs of state/quality may govern adverbial modifiers.

bḥyk...nšmḫ 1.16:I:14 = **88.73** "in your life ... we shall/will rejoice"

64.65. Factitive manner of action (D, Dp, tD; L; R)

The factitive forms of strong verbs and some weak verbs are marked by doubling the middle root consonant; in some classes of weak verbs they are formed by lengthening the vowel after the first root consonant (the L forms), or by repeating the first and third root consonants (the R forms).

The term "factitive" seems to be more appropriate than the term "intensive," which is used in Hebrew grammars for Piᶜēl etc. As the term indicates, a factitive form involves more action than the simple pattern of the corresponding verb (or, since the factitive is the pattern of many denominative verbs, a factitive may indicate that action is involved).

wm.ag|rškm 3.9:6–7 = **84.2** "and if I expell you"
wykrkr | uṣbᶜth 1.4:IV:29–30 = **85.2** "and he twiddles his fingers"

The factitive manner of action of a verb of state or quality, like the factitive derived from a noun, indicates a action.

ykly.ṯpṭ.nhr 1.2:IV:27 = **88.51** "he finishes off Judge River"—from G /k-l-y/ "to be finished"
wyšnn 1.16:I:13 = **88.73** "and he gnashes his teeth"—from *šn* /šinn-/ "tooth"
yṯlṯ 1.5:VI:20 = **87.3** "he (divides in(to) three >) furrows"— from *ṯlṯ* "three"

64.66. Causative manner of action (Š, Šp, Št; C)

The causative manner of action is regularly indicated by the causative marker beginning with the consonant /š-/. There are some causative forms without this marker, formed by the characteristic vowel /-i-/ between the second and third root consonant; this internal causative is limited to the imperfect. There are no apparent differences in meaning between these two formal expressions of the causative manner of action.

The causative with /š-/ occurs in combination with the active, reflexive, and passive voices. The internal causative appears with the active voice and probably also with the passive voice.

The causative expresses an action which is caused by the subject of the verb. All causative forms are transitive; they are provided with direct accusatival objects.

skn.dšᶜlyt | ṯryl 6.13:1–2 = **86.72** "stele which Tharelli erected/offered"
rgm.ṯṯb 2.38:9 = **86.41** "return a word!, reply!"

Causatives may govern two objects, one of person, one of thing.

ašsprk.ᶜm.bᶜl | šnt 1.17:VI:28–29 = **86.63** "I shall make you count years with Baal"

There are some denominative causatives, i.e., verbs formed from nouns, substantive or adjective.

ibry | bᶜl.nšqdš 1.119:29–30 = **86.75** "we shall consecrate the buffaloes/bulls of Baal"

64.67. Reciprocal manner of action (N)

The original reciprocal function of the pattern with marker /n-/ is preserved in some poetic passages, e.g., *ynṯkn.kbṯnm* 1.6:VI:19 "they bite each other like snakes." However, in prose and generally in poetry the forms with /n-/ indicate the (secondary) passive voice.

64.7. Voice

64.71. Kinds of voice

Voice is indicated, along with manner of action, in verbal patterns: active, passive (primary, internal; secondary, with /n-/), and reflexive. Voice distinctions are important for syntax in many respects. Only active verbal forms can have an object. The real agent of a passive verb can be indicated only by an adverbial modifier.

64.72. Active voice

The active voice has no specific marker. It is attested for all manners of action, active, factitive and causative. The active voice indicates an action emanating from the subject, or a state or a quality ascribed to the subject. Only the active forms of a transitive verb can govern a direct object, e.g., *yᶜdb.ksa* 1.100:7 = **86.73** "he prepares the seat."

64.73. Passive voice (internal; with prefix /n-/)

The internal passive voice is formed by the modification of vowels, usually those between the root consonants. Such passive forms are plainly indicated in alphabetic writing only in rare instances, cf. *tuḫd* 1.127:29 = **86.741** "she/it will be taken." Otherwise the passive character of these forms has to be determined from the context. Though incontestable instances are rare, it seems that the internal passive is attested in both poetry and prose and that it is associated with all manners of action (simple, factitive, causative).

The secondary passive, with the marker /n-/, developed from the reciprocal manner of action: *yn...d.nkly.b.dbḥ* 4.213:24 = **86.23** "wine ... which was used up at the sacrifice."

Passive verbal forms express an action done on or to the subject. The subject is usually expressed or clear from the context (cf. also 1.23:47 = **88.2**; 1.4:VIII:8).

k.ibr.lbᶜl.yld 1.10:III:35 = **88.57** "that a buffalo was born to Baal"
tᶜbd.ksu | wyṯṯb 1.4:V:46–47 "a chair was prepared and he (Kothar-wa-Khasis, line 44) was seated"
w.b.spr.l.št 4.338:3 = **82.4** "and (persons, *npš*, line 1, who) were not put on the list"
hm qrt tuḫd 1.127:29 = **86.741** "if the city will be seized"
cf. also *wtadm* 1.14:II:9 "and be rouged/rouge yourself!"

The real agent of a passive verb can be expressed by an adverbial modifier.

ymlu | lbh.šmḫt 1.3:II:25–26 "her heart was filled with joy" (transformable into "joy filled her heart")

In some instances in which the identity of the real agent is not indicated, it is considered unknown and intentionally not indicated.

dᶜlk.mḫṣ.aqht.ǵzr 1.19:IV:4 = **87.4** "because upon you(r territory) Aqhat, the young hero, was slain (by an unknown murderer)"
ikm.yrgm.bn il | krt 1.16:I:20–21 = **88.73** "how can Keret be called son of Il?"

64.74. Reflexive voice

The reflexive voice, which is on the same level as the active and passive voice, was originally perhaps a reflexive manner of action, comparable to the reciprocal manner of action. The marker of the reflexive voice is /t/, infixed in the simple manner of action, prefixed in the factitive, and placed between the causative marker and the first root consonant in the causative.

The reflexive verbal form indicates that the action emanates from the subject and returns to the subject again. The reflexive subject may act in/on itself.

trtḥṣ 1.14:II:9 "do wash yourself!" (cf. also 1.109:2 = **86.71**)
wtkms.hd 1.12:II:54 = **88.4** "and Hadd stretched himself"

It may act for itself or to provide something for itself.

an.itlk 1.6:II:15 = **88.55** "I shall walk (for myself)"
tštḥwy 1.4:IV:26 = **85.2** "she asks life (for herself, by prostration)"(?) > "she prostrates herself"

It may separate itself from something.

wyrtqṣ.ṣmd.bd bˁl 1.2:IV:23 = **88.51** "and the club swirled from Baal's hand"

65. *Function of adverbs*

65.1. Kinds

Some adverbs developed from nouns in the accusative case; their adverbial character can be stressed by affixes such as *-m* and *-h*. Other adverbs are primary. Both primary and secondary adverbs can serve as adverbial modifiers, adnominal adjuncts, or nominal predicates. An adverb may be added to a preposition as a genitival attribute, and together they may function as an adverbial modifier.

65.11. In verbal clauses

ik.mǵyt 1.4:IV:31 = **85.2** "how/why did she arrive?"
ˁd lḥm.šty.ilm 1.4:VI:55 = **87.7** "the gods still ate and drank"
d.tšmˁ | ṯmt 2.10:17–18 = **86.43** "what you will hear there"

65.12 With prepositions

lht | wˁlmh 1.19:IV:5–6 = **87.4** "from now on and to eternity"

65.13. With nouns

ˁz.mid 2.10:13 = **86.43** "very strong"

65.2. Negative and affirmative particles

The negative and affirmative particles are so closely attached to the verb or noun that their function in the clause can be described as modification of the verb or noun; thus these particles have no special position in the structure of the clause. They may be classified as adverbial modifiers or adnominal adjuncts.

Some negative and affirmative particles are indicated by the same letters in alphabetic writing, e.g., *l-* for "not" and "certainly." This phenomenon makes the interpretation of certain passages difficult and uncertain. Consider *bl.nmlk* 1.6:I:48 (cf. also *blt.nmlk* 1.6:I:54): is the clause negative: "we shall/will not make king"; or interrogative: "shall we. . .?"; or affirmative: "yes, we shall make. . ."?

The most common negative particles are the static expression, *l-* /lā/, and the dynamic expression, *al* /ˀal/, both meaning "not." The negative particle *bl*, which occurs only in poetry, can be used in both static and dynamic functions.

65.21. Static negation *l-*

The static negative may stand before a verb.

bph.rgm.lyṣa 1.2:IV:6 = **88.51** "from her mouth the word did not go out"
bnš bnšm | *l.yqḥnn* 3.5:16–17 = **86.33** "absolutely no one will take it"

It is used in a question, expecting a positive answer.

lrgmt | *lk* 1.2:IV:7–8 = **88.51** "did I not tell you?"

It can also stand before an adjective noun.

yn.d.l.ṭb 4.213:2 = **86.23** "wine which is not good (i.e., spiced)"

65.22. Dynamic negation *al*

The dynamic negative is used only with the jussive and the subjunctive (not with the imperative).

al.tṣr 1.14:III:29 = **88.71** "do not besiege!"
w.uḫy.al.ybʿrn 2.41:22 = **83.3** "and may my brother not abandon me"

65.23. The negative particle *bl*

The particle *bl* is used to negate nominal clauses.

bl.iṯ.bn.lh 1.17:I:20 "he has no son"
bl.ṭl 1.19:I:44 "(there will be) no dew" (or "may there be no dew")

It is also used in negating a noun.

l.bl | *ḥrb* 1.96:4–5 = **82.6** "with no knife," "without a knife"
ḫpṯ.dbl.spr 1.14:II:37 "free men(?) without number"
umlk.ubl mlk 1.4:VII:43 "whether king or commoner (lit., a-not-king)"

65.24. Affirmative particles

The affirmative particles *l-* /la-/(?) and *bl* (perhaps a dynamic or volitive affirmative) are generally found before finite verb forms; affirmative *k-* is used before a verb which is not at the beginning of a clause.

idk.lttn.pnm 1.4:IV:20 = **85.2** "then she really directed (her) face"
bl.ašt 1.4:V:61 "I shall certainly put," "let me put"
hlm.il.kyphnh 1.4:IV:27 = **85.2** "as soon as Il really perceives her" (or "behold, Il, as he perceives her"(?))

Desiderative *l-* /lū-/(?) is similarly prefixed to verbs; it is difficult to distinguish the desiderative *l-* from the affirmative *l-*.

lyrt 1.5:I:6 = **88.54** "may you go down," "would that you would go down"
ltbrk 1.15:II:14 = **87.2** "may you bless," "would that you would bless" (or is this affirmative *l-* /la-/? or negative /lā/, introducing a question to which a positive answer is expected?)

65.3. Expressions of being and non-being

The particles of existence, *iṯ*, and non-existence, *in*, developed from nominal bases, and their nominal character is apparent in their syntactical use. They occur only as nominal predicates.

hm.iṯ.šmt 1.19:III:33 = **88.65** "whether there is fat"
rgm | *iṯ.ly* 1.3:III:20–21 = **87.8** "I have a word"
pd.in.bbty 1.14:III:38 = **88.71** "and/but that which is not in my house"

66. *Function of prepositions*

The prepositions are nominal elements to which nouns or pronouns in the genitive are attached.

66.1. Prepositional constructions

In syntactic terms, the preposition in a verbal clause appears as an adverbial modifier; the following noun or pronoun is its genitival attribute. Since a preposition can never stand alone, the preposition together with the following noun or pronoun may be considered a unit in syntactic analysis.

Prepositional constructions occur most frequently as adverbial modifiers; they occur quite rarely as nominal predicates or adnominal adjuncts. These three functions are similar; they are distinguished by the character of the clause.

nominal predicate: *bᶜdh.bhtm.mnt* 1.100:70 = **86.73** "behind him (are) the houses of incantation"; *ᶜšrm.ksp* | *ᶜl.šknt* 4.135:1–2 = **86.21** "20 shekels (are) (an obligation) on Sōkinat"
adnominal adjunct: *nᶜmt.bn.aḫt.bᶜl* 1.10:II:16 = **88.56** "the (most) beautiful among Baal's sisters"; *ḫmšm.l.mitm.zt* 4.143:2 = **81.5** "(50 to 200=) 250 olive trees"
adverbial modifier: *wyrgm.l* | *šmmn* 3.9.14–15 = **84.2** "and they will say to Shamuman"; *wykn.bnh.bbt* 1.17:I:25 = **87.1** "and his son will be in the house"

66.2. Function depending on the context

The function of prepositions depends on the other elements of the clause, especially the governing verb, and on the general situation. Some prepositions can indicate, on the one hand, being in a place or direction toward it, and on the other hand direction away from it; there can be similar variation with respect to time. (If there was any variation in the relevant vocalizations, the consonantal orthography does not reveal it.) Contrast these examples:

tbᶜ.bbth kṯrt 1.17:II:39–40 "the Kotharat(-deities) went away from his house"
ᶜrb.b|*kyt.bhklh* 1.19:IV:9–10 "wailing women entered his palace" (cf. 1.17:II:26)

The prepositions *b*- and *l*- can indicate direction toward a place, and *b* can also indicate being in a place.

wykn.bnh.bbt 1.17:I:25 = **87.1** "and his son will be in the house"
w.ap.mhkm | *b.lbk.al* | *tšt* 2.30:22–24 = **83.4** "and do not put anything/(worries?) into your heart"
lpʿn.il.thbr 1.4:IV:25 = **85.2** "she bows down to the feet of Il"

Both *b*- and *l*- can also indicate direction from, with respect to place and time.

wyqḥ.bhm | *aqht* 1.19:III:39–40 = **88.65** "and he took Aqhat out of them"
mr.ym | *lksih* 1.2:IV:19–20 = **88.51** "expel Yamm from his throne!"
lht | *wʿlmh* 1.19:IV:5–6 = **87.4** "from now and to eternity"
l.ym hnd 3.4:1 = **86.32** "from this day on"

66.3. Various functions of prepositions

local—being in a place: *b*- "in," "on"; *ʿl* "upon"; *bn* "between"; *bʿd* "behind"; *tḥt* "beneath"
local—direction "to": *b*- "in(to)"; *l*- "to"; *ʿm* "to(wards)"; *ʿd* "until," "to"; *bn* "between"; *aṯr* "behind"; *tḥt* "beneath"
local—direction "from": *b*-; *l*-; *min-, *m*- *mrḥqtm* 2.64:15 = **82.1** "from (two?) distance(s?)."
connection: *ʿm* "with"; *yd* "with"; cf. *bl* "without"
datival > possessive: *l*- "to" *bnšm.dt.iṯ.alpm.lhm* 4.422:1 = **83.1** "men to whom oxen belong," "men who have oxen"; *ʿl* "upon"
instrumental: *b*- "with" 1.6:II:31–32 = **88.55**; 1.5:VI:17–18 = **87.3**
time, being in/at: *b*-; also *k*- with an infinitive(?): 1.17:II:6, 20, cf. 1.17:I:30–31 = **87.1**
time, direction to: *ʿd* "until, to"
causal, "on account of": *b*- 2.38:13–14 = **86.41**; *ʿl* 1.19:I:14–15
comparison: *k*- "as, like"

66.4. Compound prepositions

bd (*b*- + *-d- "hand") and *byd* "in/from the hand(s)/power of"
b- + words for "midst": *bqrb*, *btk* "in the midst of"
lpn (*l*- + *pn* "face" pl. constr.) "before"

67. *Function of conjunctions*

67.1. Kinds

The conjunctions introduce clauses, coordinate and subordinate. Some coordinating conjunctions also connect equivalent constituents or components of a clause.

From a functional point of view, the conjunctions can be divided into coordinating and subordinating. The coordinating conjunctions introduce coordinate clauses and coordinate constituents or components of clauses. They also introduce the main clause if it follows a subordinate clause in a sentence. The subordinating conjunctions introduce subordinate clauses in subordinate sentences.

Conjunctions usually stand either at the beginning of a clause or before the second of the coordinate constituents or components.

67.2. Coordinating conjunctions

67.21. Conjunction *w-*

Most frequently the conjunction *w-* is used as a simple coordinating conjunction, i.e., it has no special connotation.

yšu gh | *wyṣḥ* 1.16:VI:40–41 = **85.1** "he raised his voice and he shouted"

It can also introduce elements or clauses which, though not exactly coordinate, continue preceding elements or clauses. These may be contrasting elements.

lht | *wᶜlmh* 1.19:IV:5–6 = **87.4** "from now on and to eternity"

Similarly, it is used to introduce concluding clauses which are coordinate from a formal point of view but are actually dependent on the main clause.

ptḥ.bt.wuba 1.100:72 = **86.73** "open the house and/that I may enter"

It can introduce a main verb following a subordinate clause or an infinitival construction.

ttn.wtn 5.19:12 = **83.2** "(if) you will give, (then) give!"
bnši.ᶜnh | *wyphn* 1.19:III:28–29 = **88.65** "and in lifting up his eyes (and) he perceives her"

In parallel cola, *w-* can connect parallel expressions; *aqht...wbn.dnil* 1.18:IV:18–19 = **88.64** "Aqhat . . . the son of Danel (= Aqhat)."

67.22. Other coordinating conjunctions

The conjunctions *p-* "and" and *ap* "also" also serve to coordinate clauses.

67.23. Disjunctive conjunctions

In principle, the disjunctive conjunctions belong among the coordinating conjunctions, since the conjoined elements can be considered independent.

u /ᶜo-/: "or" 1.16:I:22 = **88.73**
u- . . . *u-* "either . . . or" 1.4:VII:43
hm "whether?," "or?" 1.4:IV:34, 35 = **85.2**

67.3. Subordinating conjunctions

Subordinating conjunctions may be classified according to their function. An original adverbial character can be seen in some; the dividing line between the use as conjunctions and the use as adverbial modifiers is not always clear.

67.31. Conjunction *d*-

In addition to the basic subordinating conjunctions, the relative particle *d*—variant *dm*—and some secondary relative expressions (originally interrogative) are used to introduce subordinate causal clauses. For *d*- see 1.17:I:18 = **88.61**; 1.19:IV:4 = **87.4**; note also *k* + *d* > *kd* 1.19:I:14.

67.32. Conjunction *hm*

The conjunction *hm* is used in indirect questions.

> *waḥd.hm.iṯ.šmt* 1.19:III:33 = **88.65** "and I shall look (to see) whether there is fat"

It also occurs in conditional sentences.

> *hm.ḫry.bty* | *iqḥ* 1.14:IV:40–41 = **88.72** "if I take Hurray into my house"

67.33. Conjunction *k*-

The conjunction *k*- (variant *ky*, /kī/(?)) introduces clauses in content sentences (see also 1.6:III:8; 1.96:2–3 = **82.6**).

> *umy* | *tdᶜ.ky.ᶜrbt* 2.16:6–7 = **84.1** "and may my mother know that I entered..."

It also introduces conditional ("when/if": 1.71:23 = **86.62**; 1.119:20) and temporal ("as soon as": 1.148:18; 1.18:IV:18–19 = **88.64**) clauses.

67.34. Temporal conjunctions

Some temporal conjunctions are of deictic character. Their subordinating function is not always clear. They include *aḫr* "after" 1.4:III:23 and perhaps *hlm* "as soon as" (or "behold"(?)) 1.4:IV:27 = **85.2**.

68. *Function of interjections*

Interjections—like vocatives, to which they are frequently connected—are elements outside of, or on the periphery of clause and sentence structure. Some interjections, nonetheless, can be helpful in determining the character of a clause.

The interjections which introduce a vocative are *y*- /yā/ and *l*-.

> *ybn* 1.16:VI:55 = **85.1** "O (my) son!"
> *lkrt* 1.16:VI:41 = **85.1** "O Keret!"

The interjection following and strengthening an imperative is *m*ᶜ "pray."

> *šm*ᶜ *m*ᶜ 1.16:VI:41 = **85.1** "hear, pray!"

The deictic interjections, roughly "behold," are *hn* (2.33:27, 30 = **86.42**; 1.16:III:14–15); *mk* (1.15:III:22); and perhaps also *hlm* 1.4:IV:27 = **85.2**.

The desiderative interjections, roughly "O that!," are *aḫl* (1.19:II:15, 22); and *l*- /lū/ (1.17:I:23).

7. Sentence Structure

71. *Approaches*

71.1. Methods of syntactic analysis

The syntactic analysis of Ugaritic texts is based on the inflectional features of the Ugaritic language: the system of cases points to the syntactic functions of the nouns, the system of moods indicates syntactically relevant functions of verb forms, and so on. However, the alphabetic writing conceals many of these features, and therefore analogies with other Semitic languages must be relied on in considering certain syntactic phenomena. Arabic and Akkadian are especially helpful, because case and mood endings are clearly expressed in those languages; comparison with Hebrew also helps in studying some Ugaritic constructions.

Syntactic analysis is closely interconnected with the analysis of style, in the broad sense of that term. Different styles of non-literary and literary texts are reflected in considerable differences on the syntactic level. The spectrum goes from documents exhibiting virtually no syntactic features (e.g., name lists, labels) to highly structured poetic texts. The poetic texts are composed in a consistent parallelistic style; in general the verses coincide with sentences, and cola often with clauses. Syntactic and prosodic analyses have to be conducted simultaneously, and the results clearly show the interdependence of syntactic structure and verse structure. For texts in prose this relation between style and sentence structure is not so close, but the fixed formulas, especially in letters and legal texts, have to be taken into consideration in syntactic analysis.

71.2. Prose texts

Plain prose is represented by only a few samples; most of the texts in prose are highly formulaic. Many of the formulas are imitations or adaptations of the legal, epistolary, and other formulas of Akkadian documents.

71.21. Formulas in prose texts

Many formulas in letters and in legal, administrative, and economic documents are patterned after Akkadian models. Some formulas in the divinatory texts (e.g., 1.103=**86.744**; 1.127 =**86.741**; 1.142=**86.742**) are of Akkadian origin. The formulas in the ritual texts may be Canaanite since corresponding formulas can be found in Phoenician sacral inscriptions. For some formulas in letters, see 2.16:1–3, 4–6a, 14–20 = **84.1**; 2.38:1–9 = **86.41**; 2.10:1–4 = **86.43**. The formulas in legal texts include *l.ym hnd* 3.4:1 = **86.32** "from this day on" and *šḫr.ˁlmt* 3.5:15 = **86.33** "sometime in the future."

71.3. Poetry

There are long and short epic poems (1.1–22; 1.114 = **88.3**) as well as liturgical texts (1.23 = **88.2**; 1.24 = **88.1**; 1.100 = **86.73**; 1.119 = **86.75**; 1.96 = **82.6**) composed in their entirety or to a large extent in verse.

71.31. Principles

Since the verses (bicola or rarely tricola) in poetry coincide, with few exceptions, with sentences, they can be delimited by combined syntactic and prosodic analysis. Similarly, the cola of which the verses are composed frequently coincide with the clauses; this is especially true of the first colon in the verse. It is therefore possible to delimit the prosodic cola by applying both syntactic and prosodic criteria.

Ugaritic poetry is based on the principle of the parallelism of members (Latin "parallelismus membrorum"). A first colon is followed by a second colon exhibiting identical, similar or complementary syntactic structure but replacing some words by synonyms or complements.

A verse is a prosodic unit consisting of two or rarely three cola. Isolated cola (monocola) also occur.

The semantic relations between the full words serving as basic units of cola and verses can be characterized as identity or similarity. (The antithetic relationships represented in many biblical proverbs do not occur in Ugaritic poetry.) Frequently a word in the first colon, a so-called A-word, is paralleled in the second colon by a synonym, a so-called B-word. There are many fixed pairs of A and B words. In principle the A-word is a basic word, the B-word its synonym or variant. Examples of synonyms are *riš–qdqd* "head" 1.16:VI:56–57 = **85.1**; /d-y-n/–/ṯ-p-ṭ/ "to judge" 1.16:VI:45–46 = **85.1**. Complementary terms are also used: *ytm* "orphan"—*almnt* "widow" (persons requiring special legal protection) 1.16:VI:49–50 = **85.1**; /r-ǵ-b/ "to be hungry"–/ṣ-m-ˀ/ "to be thirsty" and /l-ḥ-m/ "to eat"–/š-t-y/ "to drink" (basic feelings of need and their satisfaction) 1.4:IV:33–35 = **85.2**. The expression in the B-colon may be extended with so-called "ballast-variants," e.g., *yn* "wine"–*dm.ˁṣm* "blood of trees/vines" 1.4:IV:37–38 = **85.2**; *bbt* "in the house"–*bqrb.hklh* "in the midst of his palace" 1.17:I:25–26 = **87.1**; *bˁl* "Baal"–*rkb.ˁrpt* "Rider on the cloud(s)" 1.10:III:34–37.

71.32. Colon and verse

The colon is a prosodic unit consisting, on the average, of three full words, i.e., nouns or verbs; short particles do not count. Cola consisting of two or four words are rare. Cola occur most frequently in combination of two, i.e., a bicolon. There are also combinations of three cola, i.e., a tricolon. Isolated cola and sequences of more than three related cola are rare.

The isolated colon (monocolon) is always a sentence. In combinations of two cola, the first colon is usually a self-contained clause, while the second colon either forms a parallel complete clause or gives some supplement to the clause expressed by the first colon. Two cola form a bicolon; from a syntactic point of view such a verse is a complete sentence in most instances. In a tricolon, a verse consisting of three cola, there is usually a basic structure consisting of two cola, supplemented by a third colon at the end or at the beginning. The tricolon, too, usually forms a complete sentence.

The isolated colon often consists of a formula introducing or initiating direct speech.

yšu gh | *wyṣh* 1.16:VI:40–41 = **85.1** "he raised his voice and shouted"
wyᶜny.krt ṯᶜ 1.16:VI:54 = **85.1** "and Keret the Generous answered"

Two short sentences within one colon are rare, e.g., 1.6:VI:17, 18–19. There are relatively few sentences extending beyond the limits of a tricolon; see 1.17:I:26–33 = **87.1**; 1.14:III:14–19 = **88.71**. Combinations of two bicola are found in 1.18:IV:18–21 = **88.64**; 1.14:IV:40–45 = **88.72**.

71.33. Bicolon

The bicolon, a verse consisting of two cola, is the most frequent unit in Ugaritic poetry. The first colon (A) is, with few exceptions, the basic colon, coinciding with a self-contained clause. The second colon (B) is either a parallel repetition of the first colon, or a repetition of some of its elements, frequently with the addition of further details.

A and B may be entirely parallel.

lḥm | *bṯlḥnt.lḥm* 1.4:IV:35–37 = **85.2** "eat from the tables bread,
št | *bkrpnm.yn* drink from the cups wine!"

The A-colon may be a complete clause while B contains only components depending on A-colon.

bph.rgm.lyṣa 1.2:IV:6 = **88.51** "from her mouth the word did not go out,"
bšpth.hwth from her lips her utterance"

A variant in B enriched by some additional elements is called a "ballast variant."

wykn.bnh.bbt 1.17:I:25–26 = **87.1** "his son will be in the house,
šrš.bqrb | *hklh* a root (descendant) in midst of his palace."

The second colon is not always parallel to the first, but it is always syntactically related to it. A clause may extend through two cola, e.g., 1.24:16–17 = **88.1**, and two clauses may form a sentence, e.g., 1.4:IV:27–28 = **85.2**; 1.17:VI:34–35 = **88.63**.

71.34. Tricolon

There are a few tricola in which all three cola (A, B, C) are parallel (A//B//C: 1.16:VI:45–48 = **85.1**); most tricola are essentially bicola expanded with one more colon (A + B//C: 1.4:IV:20–22 = **85.2**; 1.16:VI:54–57 = **85.1**). The additional colon is frequently a variant of the second colon (1.4:IV:35–38 = **85.2**). In some tricola the additional colon may be considered an introduction to the following bicolon (1.16:VI:54c–55a + 55b–56a//56b–57a = **85.1**).

72. *Sentences and their parts*

72.1. Definitions and terms

A sentence is a group of words forming an utterance which is complete in itself and independent. In traditional grammar, it is considered the maximum unit of syntactic analysis. Sentences may be simple or complex; complex sentences are either coordinate or subordinate. A simple sentence consists of one clause only, while complex sentences contain two, or, rarely, more than two clauses.

A clause is a string of words which contains a subject and a predicate. This traditional definition is suitable for the analysis of the rather simple syntactic structure of Ugaritic prose and poetry. A clause can be either a complete independent simple sentence or a part of a complex sentence. The clauses in complex sentences are either coordinate or subordinate. If the clauses are mutually independent, they are considered coordinate. The main clause in a complex sentence is the clause which can stand independently. Subordinate clauses depending on the main clause are usually marked by a subordinating conjunction or particle.

72.2. Parts of clause

Constituents of a clause are those parts which have to be represented in every clause, i.e., subject and predicate. All other parts of a clause are here called components.

72.21. Constituents

The subject is expressed by a noun, by a pronoun or by the personal marker of a verbal form. The predicate is expressed by a finite verb form in a verbal clause and by a noun in a nominal clause.

72.22. Components

Clause components may depend either on a verb (adverbial components) or a noun (adnominal components). Adverbial components include objects, adverbial modifiers, complements to the subject, and complements to the object. Adnominal components include appositions, adjectival attributes, nominal (genitival) attributes, and adnominal adjuncts.

72.3. Kinds of clauses and sentences

72.31. Kinds of clauses

The traditional (Greek and Latin) categories and terms can be used for Ugaritic clauses, with only a few modifications.

A statement or declarative clause is expressed by a nominal clause or by a verbal clause with the verb in the indicative mood. A question or interrogative clause is usually introduced by an interrogative pronoun, adverb, or particle. A volitive clause, i.e., a wish, command, or prohibition, usually contains a verb in one of the volitive moods (jussive, subjunctive, energic or imperative).

72.32. Kinds of sentences

In coordinate sentences the second clause is either introduced by a coordinating conjunction or attached asyndetically, i.e., without a conjunction.

In relative sentences, the relative clause is usually introduced by a relative pronoun, adverb or particle.

In content sentences (in which the main verb is one of knowing, perceiving, or saying), the content clause may be introduced by *k* /kī/ "that."

There are various types of modal sentences: comparative, temporal, causal, and final. In these the subordinate clause is usually introduced by a subordinating conjunction, though such sentences may involve clauses which are formally coordinated, beginning with a coordinating conjunction.

In conditional sentences, the subordinate clause (protasis) is introduced by a conditional conjunction or by a relative particle. The main clause (apodosis) may begin with *w*-.

73. *Clause constituents*

Subject and predicate are considered indispensable parts of a clause. If one of them is not expressed by a word, it is to be sought either in the context or in the reality outside the formal expression of words in the clause.

73.1. Subject

The subject is in principle expressed by a substantive noun. Other kinds of words, such as pronouns, numerals, and adjective nouns may be used. The subject can also be indicated by the personal morpheme of a finite verbal form. If the word for the subject is missing, the actual subject has to be supplied, either from the context or from the extralinguistic reality.

73.11. Subject expressed

The subject is mostly expressed by a noun: 1.16:VI:39=**85.1**; 3.9:11–12=**84.2**. A noun may be substituted for a pronoun of the second or first person in the polite style of letters: 2.16:6–7=**84.1**; 2.40:9–10. The subject can be expressed by a personal pronoun, often in nominal clauses, e.g., 1.18:I:24, especially those with the absolute infinitive, e.g., 1.6:II:21–22=**88.55**.

Personal pronouns are used in verbal clauses, even if the subject is indicated by the personal marker of a finite verbal form, because of some special construction (inserted vocative in 2.30:20–21=**83.4**) or for emphasis (2.41:17–18=**83.3**).

A subject alone can indicate existence or non-existence.

mṯb.il 1.4:I:12 "(there is) the residence of Il"
bl.ṭl 1.19:I:44 "(may there be) no dew"

A subject can be placed in the front of the relevant clause and referred to in that clause by a pronoun. Such a proleptic subject may be considered a clause in itself, a clause without a predicate. (In traditional Hebrew grammar, the pronoun is considered a connecting link or copula between the subject and predicate.) E.g., *anykn. . .hndt. . .mtt* 2.38:10–13 = **86.41** "(as for) your ship . . . it 'died' (has become immobile?). . . ."

73.12. Subject not expressed

The subject is not always represented by a particular word or personal morpheme. In such a case, the subject may have been mentioned before in the text (1.16:VI:39–41 = **85.1**; 2.30:16–19 = **83.4**) or may have to be supplied from the extralinguistic reality. The real subject may be the thing on which the text is inscribed: *skn.dšᶜlyt* | *ṯryl* 6.13:1–2 = **86.72** "(this stone is) the stela which Tharelli offered."

The construction may be impersonal, with no subject expressed.

> *yšlm.lk* 2.16:4 = **84.1** "(may) well-being/peace (be) to you (sing. fem.)"
> *lyrgm.laliyn.bᶜl* 1.4:V:12 = **88.53** "may it be said to Victorious Baal"

73.13. Vocative

The vocative may be considered a clause consisting of only a subject (in nominative). It can introduce or end another clause or be inserted into one. It can be provided with an apposition or attribute: 1.23:46 = **88.2**; 1.16:VI:41–42 = **85.1**; 1.16:IV:55; *laqht.ǵzr* 1.17:VI:26 = **88.63** "O Aqhat, young hero!"; cf. *umy* 2.30:21 = **83.4** "my mother!"

73.2. Predicate

The character of a predicate is determined by the ability of its basic part to express person. Finite verb forms, those indicating person (and number and often gender) serve as verbal predicates. All other words, even those belonging to a verb paradigm, such as participles and infinitives, are considered nominal predicates.

73.21. Nominal predicate

Every noun, in the broadest sense of the word, can serve as a nominal predicate. The predicate is represented frequently by a substantive noun, less frequently by an adjective noun, including verbal adjective nouns, i.e., the participles, a pronoun, a numeral. Particles of nominal character, i.e., adverbs, including the absolute infinitive and particles of existence and non-existence, can also serve as nominal predicates. Constructions consisting of a preposition and a noun or suffixed pronoun may be considered as one unit from syntactic viewpoint.

> *km.tsm.ᶜṯtrt.tsmh* 1.14:III:42 = **88.71** "her beauty (is) like the beauty of Ashtart"
> *dᶜmnk* 3.9:16 = **84.2** "which (is) with you"

Usually a nominal predicate follows the subject: 1.14:III:31 = **88.71**; 3.9:11–12 = **84.2**. The nominal predicate can be provided with the marker of indefiniteness *-m*: *nḥtm.ḫṭk* 1.23:47 = **88.2** "your staff (is) going down," especially if it precedes the subject.

73.22. Verbal predicate

A verbal predicate is expressed by a finite verb form. In forms of first and second persons the subject is specifically indicated by the personal morpheme. The imperative forms correspond to the second persons of jussive; cf. *wal ttn* | *tn* 5.9:14–15 = **83.2** ". . . so do not give; give (sing. m.). . . ."

73.23. Predicate not expressed

The subject alone can imply existence, cf. 1.4:I:12; 1.19:I:44. An ellipsis of the predicate may be supposed in such instances.

74. *Adverbial components*

By definition those components which depend on a verb should be considered adverbial. Such a definition is appropriate in languages with no nominal clauses, but in Ugaritic, which (like the other Semitic languages) has nominal clauses, so-called "adverbial" components may also be connected with some nominal elements of the clause as their modifiers or adjuncts.

Among adverbial components are reckoned the object, the complement to object (which depends on both the verb and the object), and the adverbial modifier. All of them can be expressed by a noun in the accusative.

74.1. Object

An object is here defined as an adverbial component depending on a transitive verb and expressed by a noun or noun-surrogate (pronoun or numeral) in the accusative case. Thus, the term is restricted to the direct or accusatival objects. (A so-called "indirect" or "datival object" may be counted with adverbial modifiers. As a criterion a simple transformation may be used: if a clause with a transitive verb governing a direct accusatival object is transformed into a passive construction, the direct object appears as the subject of the passive verb. An adverbial modifier remains unchanged.) The object can be attached to an active finite verb form, to an active participle, or to an active construct infinitive.

*y*ᶜ*db.ksa* 1.100:7 = **86.73** "he prepares the seat"
kbd hyt 1.3:III:10 "honor her!"
wm.agrškm 3.9:6–7 = **84.2** "and if I expell you"
*m*ᶜ*msy* 1.17:II:20 "supporting me"
*ṯnh.*k!*spm* | *atn* 1.14:IV:42–43 = **88.72** "I shall give double of her (weight) (object) in silver (complement to the object)
*ngš.ank.aliyn b*ᶜ*l* 1.6:II:21–22 = **88.55** "I attacked the Victorious Baal"

74.2. Complement to the object

Complement to the object basically depends on the verbal predicate and is attached to it through the object. Like the object, it is in the accusative case. E.g., *ytt.nḥšm.mhrk* 1.100:75 = **86.73** "I gave snakes (object) (as) your (bride-)price (complement to the object)."

74.3. Adverbial modifier

An adverbial modifier depends on the verb.

The adverbial modifier is in principle expressed by a noun or its surrogate in the adverbial case, i.e., accusative. The noun may be provided with an adverbial morpheme. Indeclinable adverbs may also serve as adverbial modifiers. A preposition with a following noun is in principle a nominal element in the adverbial case; preposition + noun can be considered one unit functioning as an adverbial modifier. The absolute infinitive used for strengthening a finite verb form is also an adverbial modifier.

d.tbᶜ.mṣrm 4.213:27 = **86.23** "who departed for Egypt"
hlmn.ṯnm.qdqd 1.18:IV:22 = **88.64** "strike him twice on the head!"
tlkn | ym.wṯn 1.14:IV:31–32 = **88.72** "they go a day and a second (day)"
aḫr | špšm.bṯlṯ | ymǵy.lqdš 1.14:IV:32–34 = **88.72** "afterwards, at sun(set), on the third (day), they arrive at the sanctuary"
ḥẓk.al.tšᶜl | qrth 1.14:III:12–13 = **88.71** "do not shoot your arrows (object) towards the city (adverbial modifier)!"

A "datival" adverbial modifier, indicating the recipient of giving, can be expressed by preposition *l-* "to" + noun or suffixed pronoun, or by suffixed pronoun only.

w.ytn.hm.lk 2.45:21 "and he gave them to you"
wrgm.laḫtk 1.16:I:38 "and say to your sister!"
lrgmt | lk 1.2:IV:7–8 = **88.51** "did I not tell you?"
tblk.ǵrm.mid.ksp 1.4:V:15 = **88.53** "the mountains will bring you plenty of silver"
dm.rgm | iṯ.ly.w.argmk 1.3:III:20–21 = **87.8** "because I have a word, and I shall tell (it) to you"

75. *Adnominal components*

Adnominal components are those parts of a clause which are dependent on a nominal constituent, be it a subject, a nominal predicate, or an adverbial component expressed by a noun, an object, or an adverbial modifier. Moreover, an adnominal component can be attached to another adnominal component which is expressed by a noun. Adnominal components can be divided into complements and attributes (in the broad sense of these terms).

Adnominal components dependent on a definite member of a clause are the complement to the subject (predicative), and the complement to the object, which, since it also depends on the governing verb, is also counted among adverbial components. Other adnominal components— appositions, adjectival attributes, genitival attributes, and adnominal adjuncts— can be attached to any constituent or component of a clause which is expressed by a noun.

The adnominal components differ in their congruence with the governing noun. Complements to the subject and to the object, apposition, and adjectival attribute agree with the governing noun in number, gender and case. Genitival attribute and adnominal adjunct need not agree with the governing noun. Their case is fixed as genitive for the genitival attribute and as accusative for the adnominal adjunct.

75.1. Complement to the subject

A noun, substantive or adjective, can serve as a complement to the subject (predicative) of either a nominal or verbal clause. It agrees with the subject in number, gender, and case which is always nominative.

dqt lṣpn.šrp wšlmm 1.109:10 = **86.71** "(one) head of small cattle (subject) for Ṣapān (as) burnt offering and peace offering(s) (complement to the subject)"
ikm.yrgm.bn il | *krt* 1.16:I:20–21 = **88.73** "how can Keret (subject) be called son of Il (complement to the subject)?"

75.2. Apposition

An apposition is a substantive noun, attached to a nominal constituent or component of a clause; a determinative pronoun followed by a genitival attribute can also serve as an apposition. An apposition agrees with the governing noun in number, gender and case, except if the governing noun is a cardinal numeral, in which case agreement in number and gender is not required. An apposition can be attached to a subject or vocative, to the predicate of a nominal clause or, to adverbial and adnominal components. Two or more appositions can be attached to a single governing noun, e.g., 1.100:1 = **86.73**; 3.5:2–4 = **86.33**. An apposition can be provided with an adjectival attribute, a genitival attribute or a determinative pronoun. The apposition usually follows the governing noun, but epithets, a major group of appositions, often precede the nouns that govern them.

rbt.aṯrt.ym 1.4:IV:31 = **85.2** "Lady (apposition) Athirat of the Sea (subject)"
bn.ilm.mt 1.6:II:13 = **88.55** "son of Il/god(s) (apposition) Mot (subject)"

75.3. Adjectival attribute

An adjectival attribute always follows the governing noun and agrees with it in number, gender, and case. In addition to adjective nouns, adjectival pronouns, the cardinal numeral "1," the ordinal numerals, and participles can be used as adjectival attributes.

An adjectival attribute can be attached to any constituent or component of a clause expressed by a noun, i.e., to a subject or vocative, to a nominal predicate, to an object, to the nominal element of a prepositional construction serving as an adverbial modifier, to an apposition, or to a genitival attribute. Two or more attributes can be attached to a single governing noun: *by* | *gšm.adr* | *nškḥ* 2.38:13–15 = **86.41** "in/by a strong rain(storm) (which) occurred." An adjectival attribute can be followed by another adnominal component, be it a genitival attribute or an adnominal adjunct. If the attribute is a participle, it may be followed by an object: *pǵt. . .ydᶜt.hlk.kbkbm* 1.19:II:6–7 = **87.5** "Paghat . . . knowing the course of the stars."

The superlative function can be expressed by an adjectival attribute followed by a genitival attribute: *ḥry* | *nᶜmt.špḥ.bkrk* 1.14:III:39–40 = **88.71** "Ḥurray, the most beautiful of the offspring of your first-born."

75.4. Genitival attribute

A genitival attribute is expressed by a noun, numeral, or pronoun and attached to a nominal constituent or component. A genitival attribute can be attached to a substantive or adjective noun, to a numeral, or to a determinative pronoun. If the genitival attribute indicates or points to a person, it is usually possessive. A personal pronoun serving as a genitival attribute usually appears in suffixed form, but cf. *diy* | *hyt* 1.19:III:31–32 = **88.65** "the wings of her(s)." If the genitival attribute is a thing, it frequently expresses a quality of the governing noun.

aṯt.ṣdqh 1.14:I:12 "his legitimate wife"
rᶜ ᶜlm 5.9:11 = **83.2** "the eternal friend"

The superlative function may be expressed by a genitival attribute.

bnš bnšm 3.5:16 = **86.33** "man of men"; negated: "absolutely nobody"
ᶜmq.nšm 1.17:VI:45 = **88.63** "the strong(est) of men"

All words governed by prepositions are in the genitive and are therefore genitival attributes. From a syntactic point of view, however, it is advisable to take preposition + following genitive as a unit.

A genitival attribute can be followed by another genitival attribute, usually a suffixed pronoun, rarely another noun. Cf. 1.14:III:39–40 = **88.71**; 1.14:III:16 = **88.71**; 6.24:1–2 = **81.2**.

75.5. Adnominal adjunct

An adnominal adjunct is expressed by an adverb or by a preposition followed by a noun in the genitive. Adjuncts attached to nominal components correspond to adverbial modifiers (for verbal clauses) and to predicates (for nominal clauses) expressed by a prepositional construction or by an adverb.

ᶜz.mid 2.10:13 = **86.43** "very strong"
ᶜnt | *nᶜmt.bn.aḫt.bᶜl* 1.10:II:15–16 = **88.56** "Anat, the most beautiful among Baal's sisters"
wdg bym 1.23:63 "and fish(es) from/of the sea" (parallel to *ᶜṣr.šmm* 1.23:62 "birds of the heavens")

76. *Clauses*

76.1. Kinds

A clause is either a complete independent sentence or a part of a sentence. It has as constituents a subject and a predicate. It may also have optional components. Clauses are differentiated according to the character of the predicate: a clause with a finite verb as predicate is called a verbal clause, and a clause with any other kind of predicate is called a nominal clause. According to their function and relation to reality clauses can be divided into declarative, interrogative, and volitive.

Exclamations can be considered either independent clauses or elements outside the sentence structure. Cf., e.g., *ylk* 1.19:IV:3 = **87.4** "woe to you!"

76.2. Declarative clauses

A declarative clause expresses a statement; it indicates the reality or possibility of an action or situation. Most declarative clauses exhibit a subject and nominal or verbal predicate; however, the titles of lists and introductions to letters can be considered subjects, while the predicate is the following text.

spr.npš. . . 4.338:1–3 = **82.4** "list of persons"
tḥm.mlk.ṣr.aḫk 2.38:3 = **86.41** "message of the king of Tyre, your brother"
cf. also 1.3:III:13–14 = **87.8**

76.3. Interrogative clauses

An interrogative clause expresses a question. A question may involve the reality of a clause (a "yes-no" question) or it may seek further information (an "item-specification" question) or instruction (an instruction-seeking question).

Yes-no questions usually have no introductory particle or other marking indicated in the text. (In the spoken language such a question could be indicated by intonation, etc.)

rǵb.rǵbt 1.4:IV:33 = **85.2** "are you very hungry?"
ik.mǵyt. . .aṯrt 1.4:IV:31 = **85.2** "why/how did Athirat arrive?"
mh.yqḥ.mt.aṯryt 1.17:VI:36 = **88.63** "what will (a) man get as (his) future?" (cf. line 35)

76.4. Volitive clauses

A volitive clause indicates an intention to change reality, usually by a wish or by a command. The forms of the volitive moods, jussive, subjunctive, energic, and imperative, are used to express various nuances.

A positive command or exhortation in the second person can be expressed by an imperative, a jussive, an energic form, and also by the appropriate perfect form used in a precative sense. The imperative cannot be negated; prohibitions are usually expressed by a negated jussive.

tn ks yn 5.9:15 = **83.2** "give a cup of wine"
tštḥwy.kbd hyt 1.3:III:10 = **87.8** "prostrate (yourself), honor her!"
al.tṣr | udm 1.14:III:29–30 = **88.71** "do not besiege Udum!"
lyrt (perfect) 1.5:I:6 = **88.54** "may you go down"

In the first person a wish or an intention may be expressed by a subjunctive or energic form.

ašr nkl wib 1.24:1 = **88.1** "I will sing (of) Nikkal-Ibb" (cf. H. cohortative, Isa 5:1)
iqran.ilm.nᶜmm 1.23:16 = **88.2** "I will invoke (energic) beautiful gods"

In the third person, a wish or an exhortation is expressed by a jussive or energic form; for a negative wish a negated jussive is used.

tṣi.km | rḥ.npšh 1.18:IV:24–25 = **88.64** "may his soul go out like wind"
w.aḫy. . .al.yšt 2.38:26–27 = **86.41** "may my brother not put. . ."

76.5. Some relations between parts of clauses

76.51. Coordinate constituents and components

Subjects are coordinated by the conjunction *w*-. Verbal predicates following each other are connected by *w*- or asyndetically, i.e., without conjunction; each of the predicates can be considered a kernel of a clause.

yšu gh | wyṣḥ 1.16:VI:40–41 = **85.1** "he raises his voice and he shouts"
ily | ugrt.tǵrk. | tšlmk 2.16:4–6 = **84.1** "may the gods of Ugarit protect you (and) give you peace."

76.52. Agreement

The structure of the Ugaritic language with its full system of markers of number and gender, exhibits agreement between those parts of the clause which belong together, especially between subject and predicate, and between governing noun and apposition or adjectival attribute; they agree in gender, number, and case.

77. *Sentences*

77.1. Kinds

A simple sentence is identical with an independent clause; a complex sentence is a combination of two or more clauses, either coordinate or subordinate. If every clause in a complex sentence can also appear independently, the sentence is coordinate. A subordinate complex sentence consists of one main clause and one or more subordinate clauses, the subordination usually indicated by a subordinating word. A subordinate clause may be related to its main clause as an object, an adverbial modifier, an adnominal attribute, or an adjunct.

77.2. Coordinate sentences

Coordinate sentences consist of clauses which can also appear independently. The clauses may be coordinated by the conjunction *w*- "and" or follow each other without a conjunction. A second clause can indicate action identical with, parallel to, or continuous with that of the first clause. Thus the clauses may be interchangeable as to position (identical or parallel action).

mǵy.ḥrn.lbth 1.100:67–68 = **86.73** "Ḥōrān reached his house
w|yštql.lḥẓrh (and) came to his court"

The clauses follow the order of actions.

irš.ḥym.watnk 1.17:VI:27 = **88.63** "ask for life, and (then) I shall give (it) to you"

In disjunctive sentences the clause introduced by the disjunctive marker follows the clause which is unmarked: *lḥm.hm.štym* 1.4:IV:35 = **85.2** "eat or drink!"

Some sentences which are formally coordinate can express subordination. Some subordinate sentences developed from and are related to coordinate sentences, e.g., the final sentence, which expresses a result or goal, e.g., *tn ks yn | wištn* 5.9:15–16 = **83.2** "give (me) a cup of wine, and I shall/that I may drink (it)."

77.3. Subordinate sentences with relative clauses

Relative clauses are usually marked by a relative pronoun or particle, but there are relative clauses with no marker: *rgm ltd^{c}.nšm* 1.3:III:27 = **87.8** "the word (which) men do not know" (cf. line 26).

The most frequent marker of relative clauses is the determinative/relative pronoun, "(that) which," written *d-* and *dt*. The relative marker always stands at the beginning of the clause, whether it serves as subject or object.

ṯmn.mrkbt.dt. | ^{c}rb 4.145:1–2 = **82.3** "8 chariots which (subject) entered"
mnm | ḫsrt 2.41:19–20 = **83.3** "whatever (object) I lack/need"

The original determinative character of the relative clause is indicated by its usual position at the end of the sentence; but cf. 1.14:III:38 = **88.71**; 2.16:16–20 = **84.1**; also 2.10:16–19 = **86.43**.

A relative clause can be attached as an apposition to various nominal constituents or components of the main clause, i.e., to subject, object, adverbial modifier, or genitival attribute. It can serve as a subject, or as an object; it may be referred to with a pronoun in the main clause: *wd lyd^{c}nn | y<.>lmn* 1.114:7–8 = **88.3** "and he whom he does not know, he strikes <him>."

77.4. Subordinate sentences with object clauses

Subordinate clauses which function as objects of the main clauses usually express the content of the main verb's action, e.g., knowing, perceiving, saying. The introductory marker may be interpreted as "that."

Object clauses are usually introduced by the conjunction *k-*, *ky* /kī/. There are also object clauses with no marker. Indirect questions may be counted among sentences with object clauses; the introductory conjunction is *hm* "whether."

umy | td^{c}.ky.^{c}rbt 2.16:6–7 = **84.1** "may my mother know that I entered"
wyḥd. | iṯ.šmt 1.19:III:38–39 = **88.65** "and he saw (that) there was fat"
waḥd.hm.iṯ.šmt 1.19:III:33 = **88.65** "and I shall see whether/if there is fat"

77.5. Subordinate sentences with clauses serving as adverbial modifiers

Subordinate clauses which can be considered adverbial modifiers of the main clause are usually introduced by a conjunction. Such sentences can be characterized as comparative, temporal, or causal.

77.51. Comparative sentences

Comparative subordinate clauses are introduced by the conjunction *k-* "as, like": *kb^{c}l.kyḥwy... ḥwy* 1.17:VI:30 = **88.63** "as Baal really grants life . . . you live(?)" (or imper.? or "if Baal, when he grants life. . ."(?)). Cf. also 1.6:II:28–30 = **88.55**.

77.52. Temporal sentences

A subordinate temporal clause usually precedes the main clause: cf. 1.4:IV:27–28 = **85.2**; 1.18:IV:18–19 = **88.64** (cf. 29–32); 1.4:V:44–45. Such a clause may be introduced by *hlm* "as soon as," *km* "as soon as," or *aḫr* "after that," among others. Temporal clauses with ^{c}*d* "until (to)" follow the main clause, e.g., 3.4:16–18 = **86.32**.

77.53. Causal sentences

Causal subordinate clauses are introduced by the conjunction *k-* "as, because" or by the relative particle *d-* (extended form *dm*) (cf. H. ʾăšær). Cf. 1.6:III:19–20; 1.19:IV:3–4 = **87.4**; 1.17:VI:34–35 = **88.63**.

77.6. Conditional sentences

In conditional sentences the subordinate clause (protasis) is usually marked by a conditional conjunction, *hm* "if" (variants *im* and *-m*) or rarely *k-*. There are also conditional clauses with no conjunction. The main clause (apodosis) is introduced, especially in prose, by the conjunction *w-* "and," which seems to indicate that the action in the main clause is considered a consequence of that expressed by the preceding subordinated clause.

The relationship of the condition to reality are indicated by the use of tense/aspect in the main and subordinate clauses. The use of the imperfect in the subordinate clause indicates a real condition; the action of the condition is set in the present or future.

> *hm.ḥry.bty* | *iqḥ...atn* 1.14:IV:40–43 = **88.72** "if I take Ḥurray into my house, . . . I shall give"
> *ttn.wtn* 5.9:12 = **83.2** "if you will give, (then) give!"

A nominal predicate in the subordinate clause also indicates the reality of the condition.

> *whm.ḥy...*[b^{c}l] | . . . *whm.iṯ...b^{c}l...šmm.šmn.tmṭrn* 1.6:III:2–6 "and if Baal . . . is alive, and if there is . . . . Baal . . . , heavens will rain oil"
> cf. also *win udn šma*<.>*l*.b[h] 1.103:37 = **86.744** "and (if) there is no left ear on him . . ."
> *hm.iṯ* [yn...w] *tn.wnšt* 1.23:72 "if there is [wine] . . . give, and/so that we may drink"

The use of the perfect in the subordinate clause may indicate an unreal condition.

w.hm.ḫt. | *ˁl.w.likt* | *ˁmk* 2.30:16–18 = **83.4** "and if the Hittite had come, I would have sent (a message) to you"

77.7. Some relations between clauses in the sentences

77.71. Clause order

In general the subordinate clause precedes the main clause. However, certain kinds of subordinate clauses follow the main clause: object clauses with *k* /kī/, indirect questions introduced by *hm*, causal clauses with *k* and *d(m)*, final clauses and some relative clauses.

77.72. Ellipses

The ellipsis of one constituent or component is quite frequent in poetry. In parallel cola one or two constituents or components from the first colon are not repeated or paralleled. They can be supplied from the first colon. E.g., in 1.17:VI:36–37 = **88.63** [l]*riš* "on (my) head" is parallel to *qdqdy* "my pate," and the -*y* is a "double-duty suffix." For ellipsis over a greater distance, see 1.14:III:33–34 = **88.71**, cf. *qḥ* "take!" in line 22.

78. *Some combinations of sentences*

78.1. Direct speech

Direct speech is characterized by prevalent use of the second person; first-person monologue is rather rare. In most instances direct speech is introduced by a stereotype formula. In both poetic and prose texts this usually involves a clause in the third person containing a verb of saying. The most frequent introductory formula in poetry is *yšu gh* | *wyṣḥ* 1.16:VI:40–41 = **85.1** "he raised his voice and shouted," with variations due to gender and number, e.g., 1.14:VI:38–39; note also the formula *wtˁn.btlt* | *ˁnt* 1.17:VI:25–26 = **88.63** "and Virgin ˁAnat answered." Messengers both in poetry and in letters are instructed to say the message to its recipient: *rgm* "say!" 1.3:III:11 = **87.8**; 2.16:2–3 = **84.1**. Direct speech without an introductory formula is rare, e.g., 1.19:II:15; 1.4:VI:36.

78.2. Parallel passages

Some sections of Ugaritic poems are worded in stereotype formulas which vary only the names of the actors and the consequent inflections. Also, a command and its fulfillment or a prediction and the description of the action are expressed as much as possible in identical words and constructions. Cf., e.g., the dream of Keret, 1.14:II:9–III:49 = **88.71**, and its fulfillment, 1.14:III:52–VI:35; and cf. also deliberations of Yaṣṣub, 1.16:VI:26–38, and the execution of his plans, 1.16:VI:39–54 = **85.1**.

Part 8

Selected Texts

The texts below are taken from KTU. Presentation differs in some minor points, cf. above, "How to Use This Book: Transliteration and transcription" (pp. xii–xiii). All words are listed in the glossary (**9**).

The autographs in section **84** and **85** give some idea of the appearance of Ugaritic texts. Other autographs and photographs are referred to in **81–83** and in the Bibliography, **B 41**. Texts in sections **81–85** are provided with commentary.

8. *List of Texts*

(Texts marked by ° are presented here completely, others in excerpts.)

81. *Texts containing only nominal forms* 129
81.1. Inscription on a bronze adze (°6.6) 129
81.2. Inscription on a cylinder (°6.24:1–2) 129
81.3. From a ritual: a sacrificial listing (1.105:1–2) 129
81.4. A list of persons (°4.349:1–4) 130
81.5. A record of olive trees and oil supplies (°4.143:1–5) 130
82. *Texts containing verbal forms* 131
82.1. From a letter: the obeisance formula (2.64:13–16) 131
82.2. From a ration roster (4.630:6–7) 131
82.3. From a chariot roster (4.145:1–2) 131
82.4. Heading for a list of persons (4.338:1–3) 132
82.5. From a ritual: two rubrics (1.115:1–2, 9–10) 132
82.6. From a ritual: ᶜAnat eats her brother (1.96:1–5a) 132
83. *Texts containing a variety of sentence types* 133
83.1. Heading of a list (4.422:1) 133
83.2. From a letter apparently written as a scribal exercise (5.9:7–16) 133
83.3. From a letter sent from one king to another (2.41:16–22) 134
83.4. From a letter to the Queen Mother from the King (2.30:16–24) 134
84. *Non-literary texts in autograph and transliteration* 135
84.1. A letter from Talmiyān to his mother Tharelli, Queen Mother of Ugarit (°2.16:1–20) 135
84.2. A document of a religious association (°3.9:1–21) 138
85. *Literary texts in autograph and transliteration* 141
85.1. From the Keret Epos (1.16:VI:39–59) 141
85.2. From the Baal Cycle (1.4:IV:20–39) 145
86. *Non-literary texts* 148
86.1. Lists and administrative texts 148
86.11. A list of soldiers (4.623:1–3, 8) 148
86.12 A list of persons (4.360:1–5) 148
86.13 Transfers of fields (4.356:1–2) 148
86.2. Economic texts 149
86.21. A record of a debt of silver (°4.135:1–2) 149
86.22. A receipt (°4.266:1–7) 149
86.23. Wine records (4.213:1–3, 24–30) 149

86.24. Wine rations (°4.279:1–5) 149
86.25. A list of clothes and their prices (°4.146:1–8) 149
86.26. A record of trade with the King of Byblos (bottomry loan?) (4.338:10–18) . 150
86.3. Contracts 150
86.31. Tribute for the Hittite king (°3.1:22–28) 150
86.32. Redemption of captives (°3.4:1–19) 150
86.33. Royal grant of real property (°3.5:1–21) 151
86.4. Letters 151
86.41. The King of Tyre to the King of Ugarit (°2.38:1–27) (Translated from Akkadian or transliterated from South Canaanite) 151
86.42. Commandant Irri-tharrūma to the Queen(?) (2.33:22–39) 152
86.43. Iwri-žarri to Pilsiya (2.10:1–19) 152
86.44. Report about looting to a superior (°2.61:1–13) 153
86.45. An informal letter (°2.15:1–10) 153
86.5. Records in substandard orthography 153
86.51. On the slaughter of small cattle (°1.80:1–5) 153
86.52. A list of persons (°4.277:1–5) 154
86.53. On oil; written right to left (4.31:1–2, 11) 154
86.6. Hippiatric texts 154
86.61. Heading of a hippiatric text (1.85:1) 154
86.62. A hippiatric remedy (1.71:23–26) 154
86.7. Ritual texts 154
86.71. A list of offerings to the gods (1.109:1–23) 154
86.72. A sacrificial stele (°6.13:1–3) 155
86.73. An incantation against snake bite (1.100:1–7, 57–76) 155
86.74. Divination texts 156
86.741. From an inscription on a clay lung model (1.127:1–9, 29–31) 156
86.742. Inscription on a clay liver model (°1.142:1–3) 156
86.743. A solar eclipse oracle (°1.78:1–6) 156
86.744. From an omen collection (1.103:1, 5, 16, 17, 37–42, 51, 54) 156
86.75. How to get Baal's protection against the attacker (1.119:26–36) 157
87. *Poetic texts: Recurrent passages* 157
87.1. The duties of a son (from Aqhat; 1.17:I:25–33) 157
87.2. A blessing (from Keret; 1.15:II:12–20) 157
87.3. Mourning (from the Baal Cycle; 1.5:VI:11–25b) 157
87.4. Cursing an unknown murderer (from Aqhat; 1.19:IV:1–7) 158
87.5. Saddling a donkey (from Aqhat; 1.19:II:5b–11) 158
87.6. Invitation (from the "Rephaim" Texts; 1.22:II:3–6a) 158
87.7. Entertaining guests (from the Baal Cycle; 1.4:VI:55–59) 158
87.8. A message for Anat (from the Baal Cycle; 1.3:III:8b–31) 159
88. *Poetic texts: Selected passages* 159
88.1. The Wedding of the Moon Deities (1.24:1, 16–23a, 30b–39) 159
88.2. The Birth of the Twin Gods (1.23:23–24, 46b–53) 160
88.3. The Feast of Il (1.114:1–23) 160
88.4. The Poem of Baal-Hadd (1.12:II:53b–61) 161
88.5. The Baal Cycle 161

88.51. Baal and Yamm fight (1.2:IV:6–10, 18b–27) 161
88.52. Anat intervenes on Baal's behalf (1.3:V:29b–34) 161
88.53. Il allows Baal to build a house (1.4:V:12–19) 162
88.54. Mot threatens Baal (1.5:I:1–8) 162
88.55. Anat's revenge on Mot (1.6:II:13–37a) 162
88.56. Anat visits Baal (1.10:II:10–25) 163
88.57. Baal's son-bull is born (1.10:III:32–37) 163
88.6. The Aqhat Legend 163
88.61. Il hears Daniel's requests (1.17:I:15b–19) 163
88.62. The artisan god brings the bow (1.17:V:21–33) 164
88.63. Anat asks for the bow (1.17:VI:25–45) 164
88.64. Anat plots Aqhat's death (1.18:IV:16–27a) 164
88.65. Daniel buries his son's remains (1.19:III:28b–45a) 165
88.7. The Keret Epos 165
88.71. From Keret's dream-vision (1.14:III:10b–49) 165
88.72. Keret's vow to Athirat (1.14:IV:31b–43) 166
88.73. Keret's illness (1.16:I:11b–30) 167
89. *Concordance of major texts* 168

81. *Texts containing only nominal forms*

81.1. Inscription on a bronze adze (°6.6)

rb khnm

/rabbu/ sing. nom. "great, leader" (or /rabbi/?, gen., depending on the unexpressed word for "adze")
/kāhinīma/ pl. gen.-acc. "priest"

81.2. Inscription on a cylinder (°6.24:1–2 = P:II:175)

(1) *spr.tbṣr* (2) *klt.bt.špš*

/sipru/ sing. nom. "written, text, document"
/tabṣiri/? PN f. gen.
/kallati/ fem. gen. "bride," apposition
/bēti/ gen. < *bayt- "house"
/šapši/ DN "Sun"; cf. *ša-ap-šu* U:V:138:3′

81.3. From a ritual: a sacrificial listing (1.105:1–2 = U:V:12)

(1) *yrḫ.ḫyr.bym ḥdṯ*
(2) *alp.wš.lbʿlt bhtm*

This text was perhaps a scribal exercise.

/yarḫu/ "month"
/ḫi(y)yāri/ gen. month name; cf. *ḫi-ya-ri* RS 25.455 (UT 19.959); attribute (cf. H. 1 Kgs 6:37, 38; 8:2)
/bi-/ prep. "in"; like all prepositions, with genitive; cf. *bi-i* U:V:130:III:6′
/yāmi/ "day"; cf. *ya-mu* U:V:138:2′
/ḥudṯi/ "new moon"; cf. *ḫu-dá-ši* (gen.) P:III:15.132:5 (p. 133); *ḫu-da-ši* U:V:95:4, PN; cf. *ḫu-ud*!-*ša-nu* P:III:16.257:I:17 (p. 199) PN; cf. Arab. ḥidṯān (ḥidaṯān)

/ˀalpu/ nom. "ox"
/wa-/ conj. "and"
/šū/(?) nom. "sheep"
/la-/(?) or /lē/(?) prep. "to"; datival; cf. *le-e*[?] U:V:130:III:5′
/baᶜlati/ gen. "lady, owner"
/bahatīma/(?) pl. gen.-acc. of *bt* "house, palace, temple"; cf. Akkad. bēlit ekallim "lady of the temple"

81.4. A list of persons (°4.349:1:4 = P:V:81)

(1) *arbᶜ.ᶜšr.ǵzrm*
(2) *arbᶜ.aṯt*
(3) *pǵt.aḥt*
(4) *w.pǵy.aḥ*(d)

/ˀarbaᶜu/ or /-a/(?) "4"
/ᶜaš(a)ri/(?) or /-a/? "10"; together "14"; cf. Arab. ˀarbaᶜata ᶜašara, H. ˀarbaᶜ ᶜæśrē(h)
/gazirūma/ (?) pl. nom. or /ǵazirīma/(?) pl. gen.-acc. "(young) warrior, hero"
/ˀaṯṯātu/(?) pl. nom. or /ˀaṯṯāti/(?) pl. gen. or acc. "woman"
/paǵītu/(?) < *paǵiyt-(?) "girl" (elsewhere PN fem.)
/ˀaḥattu/ f. "one"
/paǵiyu/(?) "boy"
/ˀaḥadu/ "one"

81.5. A record of olive trees and oil supplies (°4.143:1–5 = P:II:96)

(1) *b.gt.mlkt.b.rḥbn*
(2) *ḫmšm.l.mitm.zt*
(3) *w.bd.krd*
(4) *ḫmšm.l.mit*
(5) *arbᶜ.kbd*

For *l.* in line 2 cf. P:II:pl. XVII (to be corrected accordingly in KTU).

/gitti/ f. gen. < *gin-t- "press," also "land estate" (perhaps with a press)
/malkati/ gen. "queen"
/raḥbāna/ GN gen., diptote name; cf. *ra-aḫ-ba-na* (gen.) P:III:16.131:16, 21 (p. 139)
/ḫam(i)šūma/ "50"
/lē-/ cf. note to **81.3:2**
/miˀtēmi/ gen.-acc. "200"; *ḫmšm.l.mitm* "250"
/zēti/(?) sing. gen.(?) "olive (tree)"
/badi/(?) or /bīdi/(?) compound prep. < /b(i)-/ "in" + (*y*)*d* "hand"; "in the hand of"; cf. Old Can. ba-di-ú

/karrādi/ PN gen.; perhaps cf. GN *ḫlb krd* 4.48:2, *ḫal-bi kàr-ra-di* Syria 21:125:6
/mi$^{\supset}$ti/ gen. "100"; the number in lines 4–5 is "154"
/kabid-/(?) "heavy"; here probably "total" (cf. Mari Akkad. kabittum)

82. *Texts containing verbal forms*

82.1. From a letter: the obeisance formula (2.64:13–16 = P:V:115)

(13) *lp^{c}n.b^{c}ly* (14) *ṯnid.šb^{c}d* (15) *mrḥqtm* (16) *qlt*

/lē-pa^{c}nē/ prep. + noun, du. gen.-acc. constr. "feet"
/ba^{c}li-ya/ noun with suff. 1. sing. "lord"
/ṯ(i)nā$^{\supset}$id(a)/(?) multiplicative numeral "twice"
/šab^{c}id(a)/(?) "seven times"; together "fourteen times"; cf. Akkad. 2-šú 7-šú P:IV:17.391:5 (p. 226); Ug. *šb^{c}d* | *w.šb^{c}id* 2.12:8–9
/mir-raḥuq(a)ti-ma/(?) prep. /min-/ "from," /-rr-/ < *-nr- + noun f. gen. "distance" + particle *-ma* (or /-(a)tēmi/(??) du. gen.-acc.(?) "two distances"(??)); cf. H. mē-rāḥōq Exod 2:4; 20:18; Akkad. iš-tu ru-qiš P:IV:17.391:4 (p. 226)
/qultu/(?) or /qiltu/(?) or /qā́ltu/(?) perf. 1. sing. /q-w-l/(?) "I fall"; cf. Akkad. am-qut P:IV:17.391:5 (p. 226)

82.2. From a ration roster (4.630:6–7 = P:V:52)

(6) *ṯṯ.ḥrṯm* (7) *lqḥ š^{c}rt*

/ṯiṯṯu/ cardinal numeral, form without /-t/, with masc., "6"
/ḥāriṯūma/(?) pl. nom. or /ḥāriṯīma/(?) pl. gen.-acc. "plowman"
/laqaḥū/ perf. 3. pl. m. "to take, obtain"
/ši^{c}ar(a)ta/(?) (or /ša^{c}(a)rata/?) acc. "wool" (or /ši^{c}arāti/(?) pl. gen.-acc. "woolen blankets"(?))

82.3. From a chariot roster (4.145:1–2 = P:II:121)

(1) *ṯmn.mrkbt.dt.* (2) *^{c}rb.bt.mlk*

/ṯamānī/ cardinal numeral, form without /-t/ with fem. "8"
/markabātu/(?) fem. pl. nom. or /markabāti/(?) fem. pl. gen.-acc. "chariot"
/dātu/ relative pronoun f. pl. "which"
/^{c}arabā/ perf. 3. pl. f. "to enter"
/bēta/ "house"; acc. after a verb of movement
/malki/ "of the king"; genitival attribute

82.4. Heading for a list of persons (4.338:1–3 = P:V:106)

(1) *spr.npš.d.* (2) ᶜ*rb.bt.mlk.* (3) *w.b.spr.l.št*

/sipru/ "list, document" (see note to **81.2:1**)
/napši/ sing. gen. "breath" > "soul" > "(living) person"; here collective, "persons"
/dū/ relative pronoun
/ᶜarabū/ perf. 3. pl.
/bēta/ acc. "house"
/malki/ gen. "king"
/wa-/ conj. "and"
/bi-/ prep. "in(to)"
/sipri/ gen. after a prep.
/lā šītū/ or /šūtū/(?) negative particle "not" + perf. 3. pl. m., simple passive pattern, /š-y-t/ "to put"; thus, "were not put"

82.5. From a ritual: two rubrics (1.115:1–2, 9–10 = U:V:11)

(1) *id ydbḥ mlk* (2) *lušḫ*r ḫlmẓ. . .
(9) *š lilbt.šlmm* (10) *kll ylḥm bh*

/ᵓidā/ adv. "then" (or "when(ever)"?)
/yidbaḥu/ imperf. 3. sing. m. /d-b-ḥ/ "to sacrifice"
/malku/ "king"
/lē-ᵓušḫari/ DN f., cf. DN f. *iš-ḫa-ra* U:V:18:23
/ḫulmiẓẓi/ "lizard, dragon," apposition (cf. KTU; the autograph has a peculiar *ẓ*(?)/*ṭ*(?))
/šū/(?) see note to **81.3:2**
/lē-ᵓil(i) bēti/ prep. + DN "god of the house/family(?)/dynasty(?)"
/šal(a)mīma/ a kind of offering, adverbial acc. "as peace-offering"(?)
/kalīlu/ "whole" (cf. H. kālīl, esp. Jdg 20:40)
or *kl lylḥm* (?) /kullu lā yilḥamū/ (?) "all will/must not eat"; or cf. H. Lev 6:15–16 (?)
/yilḥamū/ jussive imperf.(?), probably 3. pl. masc.; predicate in pl. with a collective subject
/bihu/(?) prep. with suff. 3. sing. m. "in, from," instrumental or privative meaning

82.6. From a ritual: ᶜAnat eats her brother (1.96:1–5a = CRAIBL 1960, pp. 180–186)

(1) ᶜ*nt*!.*hlkt.wšnwt* (2) *tp.aḫh.wn*ᶜ*m.aḫh* (3) *kysmsm. tspi.širh* (4) *l.bl ḥrb.tšt.dmh* (5) *l bl.ks*

/ᶜanatu/ ᶜ*nt*! corrected for ᶜ*nn*, DN f.; cf. (d)*a-na-tum* U:V:18:20; cf. abdi-*a-na-ti* P:III:15.139:7 (p. 167), var. abdi-*an-ti* P:III:16.257:III:39 (p. 202) PN ("Servant of ᶜAnat")

/halakat/ perf. 3. sing. f. /h-l-k/ "to go"
/šanawat/(?) perf. 3. sing. f. G /š-n-w/ "to shine"(?) or Š /n-w-y/ (G "to be beautiful"(?)) Š "to consider beautiful, praise"
/t-p-/ imperf. 3. sing. f., short form, /p-h-y/ "to see" (or acc. of a noun *tp* "beauty," root /y-p-y/)
/ʾaḫa-ha/ acc. with suff. 3. sing. f. "brother"
/wa-/ conj. "and," introducing a circumstantial clause
/naʿīmu/(?) adj., "beautiful, pleasant" (cf. H. nāʿīm Song of Songs 1:16) (or /nuʿma/ acc. "loveliness," cf. 1.23:1–2)
/kī/(?) conj. "that" or affirmative particle "verily"; for *w-* + *k-* cf. *bnši.ʿnh.wtphn* | . . . | *ktʿn* 1.4:II:12–14 "in lifting her eyes, (and) she perceives him . . . verily/as she sees"
/yasamsamu/ adj. "(very) beautiful"; cf. H. f. yəpepīyā "very beautiful"
/tispaʾ/ imperf. 3. sing. f., short form, /s-p-ʾ/ "to devour"
/šiʾra-hu/ acc. "flesh" + suff. 3. sing. m.
/la/(?) affirmative particle "verily," or /lē/(?) prep. "to" (or /lā/ "not"?)
/balī/(?) prep. "without"
/ḥarbi/ gen. "knife, sword"
/tištē/ imperf. 3. sing. f. /š-t-y/ "to drink"
/dama-hu/ acc. + suff. 3. sing. m. "blood"
/kāsi/ gen. "cup"

83. *Texts containing a variety of sentence types*

83.1. Heading of a list (4.422:1 = P:V:23)

(1) *bnšm.dt.iṯ.alpm.lhm*

/bun(n)ōšūma/ pl. of *bnš* "(son of mankind >) man"; cf. *bu-nu-šu* U:V:131:7′
/dūtu/ relative pronoun, pl. m. "who, which"
/ʾīṯ(u/a)/ particle of existence, "there is/are"
/ʾalapūma/ m. pl. "oxen"; for ending cf. *ba-a-lu-ma* U:V:130:III:14′
/lē-hum(u)/ prep. with suff. 3. pl. m.

83.2. From a letter apparently written as a scribal exercise (5.9:7–16 = P:II:19)

(7) *iršt.aršt* (8) *laḫy.lrʿy*

---

(9) *wytnnn* (10) *laḫh.lrʿh* (11) *rʿ ʿlm.*
(12) *ttn.wtn* (13) *wlttn* (14) *wal ttn* (15) *tn ks yn* (16) *wištn*

/ʾirašta/ acc. "desire, wish"
/ʾarištu/(?) perf. 1. sing. "to desire"
/lē-ʾaḫi-ya/ gen. with suff. 1. sing. "brother" cf. *a-ḫu* U:V:135:rev.:19

/lē-ri^{c}i-ya/(?) "friend"; /ri^{c}u/(?) (or /ri^{c}ē/ < *ri^{c}ay(?)); apposition
/wa-yatinūna-n(ū/ā)/(?) imperf. 3. pl. m.(?) /y-t-n/ "to give" with suff. 3. sing. m./f.
/lē-$^{\supset}$aḫi-hu/ /lē-ri^{c}i-hu/ suff. 3. sing. m.; cf. notes to line 8
/ri^{c}i/(?) gen.; apposition
/^{c}ōlami/ "unlimited time, eternity"; cf. *ḫu-ul-ma-tum* U:V:137:III:15′ "future"; attribute
/tatinu/ imperf. 2. sing. m. /y-t-n/ "(if) you give"
/wa tin/ *w-* in a conditional sentence + imperative sing. m. "give!"
/wa lā tatinu/ "(if) you will not give"
/wa $^{\supset}$al tatin/ negative particle + jussive 2. sing. m., "do not give!"
/tin/ "give!"
/kāsa/ "cup," acc.; cf. Jer 25:15
/yēni/ < *yayni "wine"
/wa $^{\supset}$ištē-nū/ or /-nā/ subjunctive 1. sing. /š-t-y/ "to drink" with suff. 3. sing. m. or (f.(?)), or energic mood(?)

83.3. From a letter sent from one king to another (2.41:16–22 = P:V:65)

Cf. P:IV:17.116:25′–27′, 29′–30′ (pp. 133–134) and P:III:15.24:12–21 (p. 18); P:VI:16:rev.:1′–6′

(16) *mnm.irštk* (17) *dḫsrt.w.ank* (18) *aštn..l.iḫy*
(19) *w.ap.ank.mnm* (20) ḫ*srt.w.uḫy* (21) y*^{c}msn.ṯmn* (22) *w.*[u]*ḫy.al.yb^{c}rn*

/minūmē/(?) pronoun "whatever"
/$^{\supset}$iraštu-ka/ "wish, desire" with suff. 2. sing. m.
/dā(?) ḫasirta/ relative pronoun acc. + perf. 2. sing. m. /ḫ-s-r/ "to lack," a stative verb
/$^{\supset}$anāku/ personal pronoun 1. sing. "I"; here emphasizes the 1. person (cf. P:III:15.24:16 (p. 18))
/$^{\supset}$ašītan(na)/(?) or /$^{\supset}$ašītu-n(n)ū/ā/(?) energic mood 1. sing. or imperf. 1. sing. with suff. 3. sing. m.(?)/f.(?) in neuter function; /š-y-t/ "to put"
/lē-$^{\supset}$iḫi-ya/ "to my brother"; gen. case vowel motivates assimilation /a/ > /i/
/$^{\supset}$ap/ conj. "also"
/$^{\supset}$anāku/ pronoun 1. sing. "I"
/ḫasirtu/ perf. 1. sing.
/$^{\supset}$uḫu-ya/ "my brother"; nom. case vowel motivates assimilation /a/ > /u/, see note on /$^{\supset}$iḫi-ya/
/ya^{c}musu-n(n)ū/ā/(?) or /ya^{c}musan(na)/(?) imperf. 3. sing. m. with suffix 3. sing. m./f. or energic mood 3. sing. m. /^{c}-m-s/ "to carry," "he will carry"
/ṯamman/ adv. "there"; with /-n/
/$^{\supset}$al yib^{c}ar-nī/(?) dynamic negation + jussive /b-^{c}-r/ "to abandon"(?) with suff. 1. sing.: cf. U:V:38:13–14

83.4. From a letter to the Queen Mother from the King (2.30:16–24 = P:II:13)

(16) *w.hm.ḫt.* (17) *^{c}l.w.likt* (18) *^{c}mk.w.hm* (19) *l.^{c}l.w.lakm*
(20) *ilak.w.at* (21) u*my.al.tdḥ*l (22) *w.ap.mhkm* (23) *b.lbk.al* (24) *tšt*

/him-/(?) conditional conjunction "if"
/ḫattu/(?) or /ḫattī/(?) "Hittite"

/ᶜalā/ perf. 3. sing. m. /ᶜ-l-y/ "to come up"
/wa-/ "and" > "even then" in the apodosis of a conditional sentence
/laᵓiktu/(?) perf. 1. sing. "to send"; perhaps hypothetical, "I would send"
/ᶜamma-ki/ prep. "with, to" with suff. 2. sing. f.
/lā ᶜalā/ negative particle "not" + verb
/laᵓākum/ inf. absol. with /-m/; here strengthens the force of the following verb
/ᵓilᵓaku/ imperf. 1. sing. "I will send"
/ᵓatti/ personal pronoun 2. sing. f. "you"
/ᵓummī/ "mother" with suff. 1. sing. /-ī/ indicated by *-y*; nominative in vocative function
/ᵓal tidḫalī/ negative particle + jussive 2. sing. f., /d-ḫ-l/ "to be afraid"
/ᵓap/ conj. "also"
/mahakīma/(?) with *-m*(?) or (pseudo-)pl.(?) gen.-acc. *mhk* "whatever, anything"; cf. 2.38:26; cf. EA 170:78
/bi libbi-ki/ prep. "in" + gen. "in your heart"
/ᵓal tašītī/ negative particle + jussive 2. sing. f. /š-y-t/ "to put"

84. *Non-literary texts in autograph and transliteration*

84.1. A letter from Talmiyān to his mother Tharelli, Queen of Ugarit (°2.16:1–20 = P:II:15)

This tablet (p. 136), RS 15.08, was found in 1951 in the Eastern Archives of the Royal Palace. It was published by Ch. Virolleaud, in Palais Royal d'Ugarit II, nr. 15, pp. 30–31 and pl. IX, in autograph and transliteration, with French translation and notes; Cl. F.-A. Schaeffer discussed the correspondence of prince Talmiyān in the same volume, pp. XIX–XX. The style and formulas of the Ugaritic letters reflect the custom of the time: a letter was brought by the messenger to the addressee, and the messenger read it to the addressee.

(1) /taḫūmu/(?) "message"
/talmiyāna/ *tlmyn* 2.11:3; 2:12:4; 2.71:1; *tal-mi-ya-na* (gen.) P:III:16.145:5 (p. 169); PN in gen.-acc. /-a/; diptote name; cf. Hurrian talmu "great"
(2) /lē-ṯarelli/ prep. "to" (addressee of the letter) + PN f. (or title?), cf. (a-na) (f) *šar-el-li* (šarrati) (gen.) U:V:159:9–10, 12 "(to the queen) Š."; cf. Akkad. > Hurrian šarri "king" + Hurrian elli "sister"; cf. also 2.34, a letter addressed by a king (*mlk*) to his mother Tharelli, and also 2.30 = **83.4** and 2.13
/ᵓummi-ya/ gen. with suff. 1. sing. "my mother"; cf. **83.4:21**
(3) /rugum/ imperative active sing. m. "say!"
(4) /yišlam/ jussive 3. sing. m. (impersonal) /š-l-m/ "to be intact, healthy, at peace"; "may there be health/well-being!"; cf. Akkad. lu-ú šul-mu a-na muḫ-ḫi-ki P:III:12.33:4 (p. 14) "may there be health/well-being for you (lit., on your skull)!" and *l.umy | yšlm* 2.13:6–7; 2.30:5–6 "may there be health/well-being for my mother!"
/lē-ki/(?) prep. *l-* "to" with suff. 2. sing. f.
ily /ᵓilī/(??) pl. nom. constr. /ᵓil-/ "god"; cf. *il.mṣrm* 2.33:22 = **86.42** "the gods of Egypt" and the pl. absolute *ilm* 2.11:7; 2.21:5; 2.34:3. The expected form of the pl. nom. constr. is /ᵓilū/. The use of *-y*, apparently as a vowel letter, seems to indicate the pronunciation

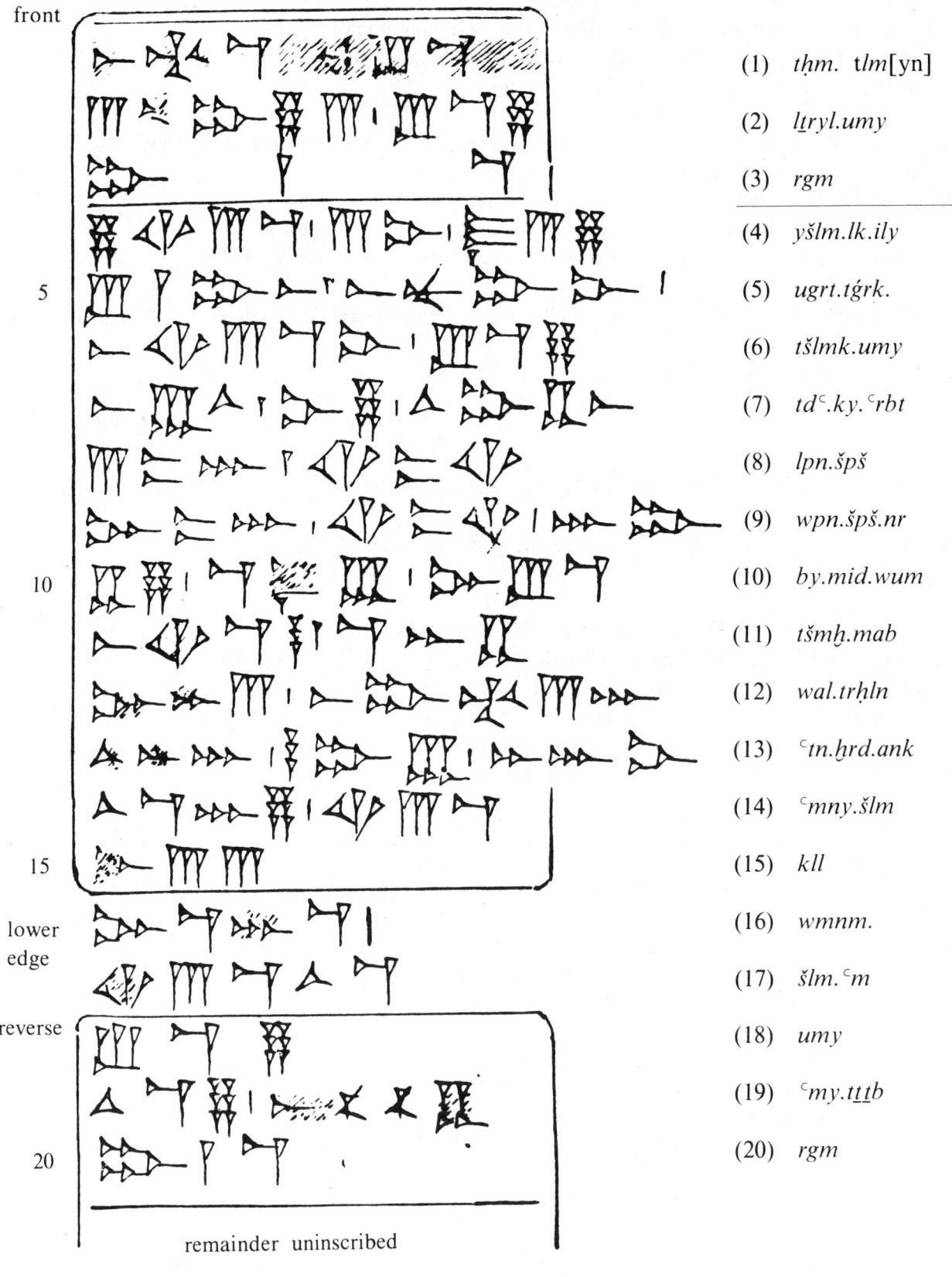

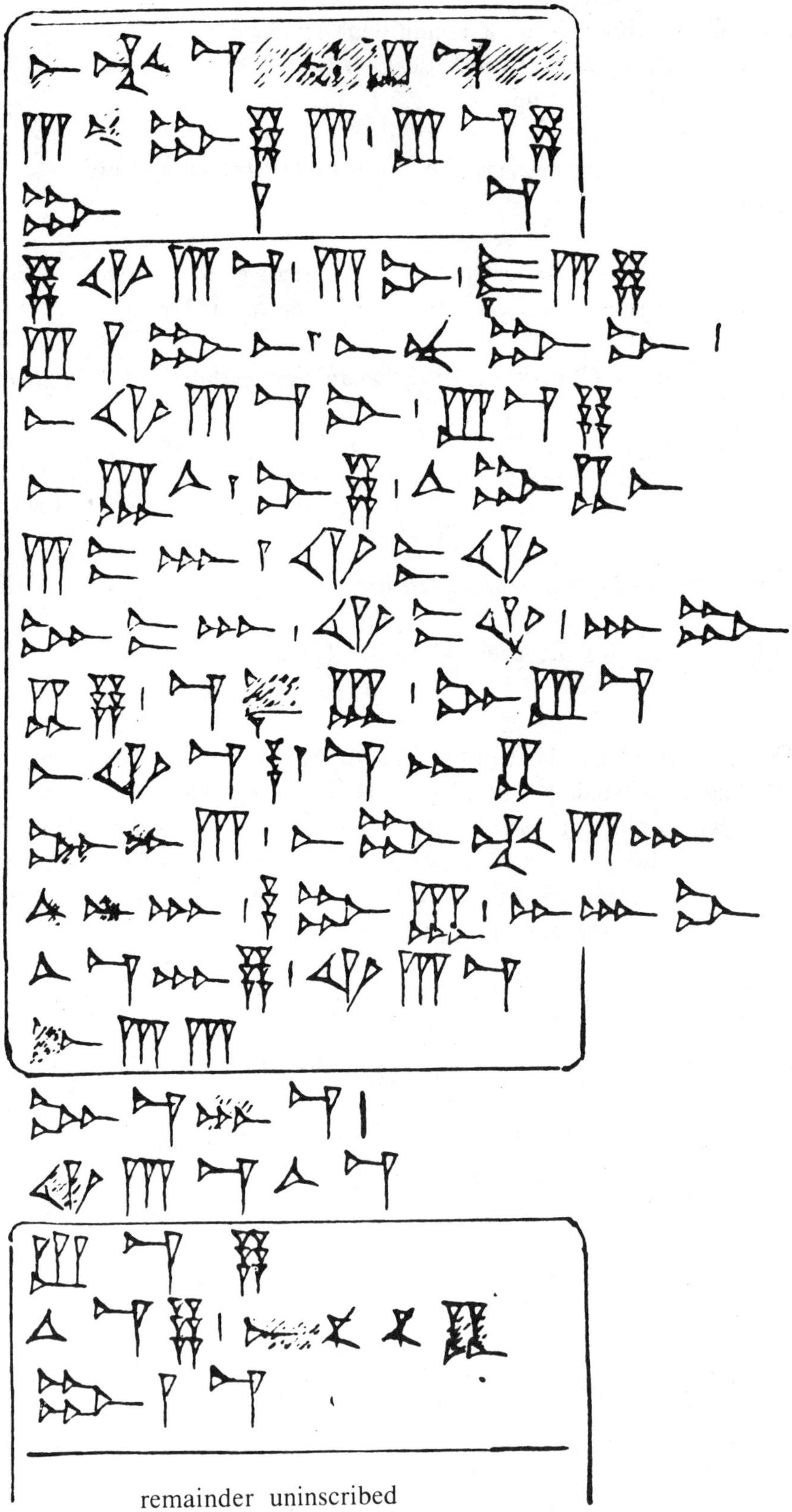

(1) *tḥm.* t*lm*[yn]

(2) *lṯryl.umy*

(3) *rgm*

(4) *yšlm.lk.ily*

(5) *ugrt.tǵrk.*

(6) *tšlmk.umy*

(7) *tdʿ.ky.ʿrbt*

(8) *lpn.špš*

(9) *wpn.špš.nr*

(10) *by.mid.wum*

(11) *tšmḫ.mab*

(12) *wal.trḥln*

(13) *ʿtn.ḫrd.ank*

(14) *ʿmny.šlm*

(15) *kll*

(16) *wmnm.*

(17) *šlm.ʿm*

(18) *umy*

(19) *ʿmy.ṯṯb*

(20) *rgm*

/ˀilī/; the use of this gen.-acc. form as subject would point to a weakening of the case system. The -*y* could also be a postpositive element or may reflect a scribal error.

(5) /ˀugarīta/(?) GN gen.; if a diptote name, cf. *u-ga-ri-ta* RS 6.198:5, Syria 16, 189; or if a triptote cf. (āl)*u-ga-ri-ti* P:III:15.122:14 (p. 131); cf. "the gods of Ugarit" in note to line 6

/taǵǵurū-ki/ jussive 3. pl. m. /n-ǵ-r/ "to guard, protect" with suff. 2. sing. f.

(6) /tašallimū-ki/ jussive 3. pl. m. D /š-l-m/ "to give/preserve in well-being/peace"; cf. H. Job 8:6; for the whole blessing in 4b–6a cf. ilānu (M) ša(māt)*u-ga-ri-it*...a-na šul-ma-ni liṣṣuru(ru)-ki P:III:16.111:4–6 (p. 13) "may the gods of Ugarit preserve you in well-being"

/ˀummī/ "my mother"; nom. with suff. 1. sing. shows -*y* for /-ī/, but cf. also *um*, line 10, perhaps also with suff. 1. sing.

(7) /tidaᶜ/ jussive 3. sing. f. /y-d-ᶜ/ "to know"; the third person was probably considered more polite than direct address in the second person, cf. line 6

/kī/ "that"; with the vowel letter -*y* for /-ī/

/ᶜarabtu/(?) perf. 1. sing. /ᶜ-r-b/ "to enter"

(8) /lē-panī/ prep. *l*- + pl. gen. constr. "face" (cf. H. pānīm); possibly a compound preposition "before" (cf. H. li-pnē), but cf. *pn* in line 9

/šapši/ gen. < *šamš cf. *ša-ap-šu* U:V:138:3′ "Sun," used as title of a Hittite (cf. 3.1:25 = **86.31**) or Egyptian (cf. 2.23:23) king

(9) /wa-panū/ conj. "and" + pl. nom. "face"; see note to line 8

/šapši/ see note to line 8

/nārū/(?) perf. 3. pl. m. /n-w-r/ "to shine"

(10) /bi-ya/ prep. *b*- "on" with suff. 1. sing.

mid /maˀda/(?) adv. "much"; < acc. of the noun *mid* "plenty"

/wa-ˀummu/ nom. without suff. (cf. (*m*)*ab*, line 11)(?) (or /ˀummī/(?) with suff. 1. sing. as in line 6)

(11) /tišmaḫ/ jussive 3. sing. f. /š-m-ḫ/ "to rejoice"

/miˀ-ˀ-/ prep. < *min-ˀ- "from"(?); "may (the/my) mother draw happiness from (the/my) father"; (cf. H. ū-śəmaḥ mē-ˀēšæt nəᶜūrǣkā Prov 5:18)

/ˀabī/(?) gen. *ab* "father" (cf. Arab. gen. ˀabī, H. constr. ˀăbī(?)); or read *mad*(?), cf. *mid*, line 10

(12) /wa-ˀal/ "and" + negative particle /ˀal/ "not" before jussive(?)

/t-r-ḥ-l(i)n(n)ū/(?) jussive 3. sing. f. apparently with suff. 3. sing. m. (or 1. sing. /-nī/?); /r-ḥ-l/ attested only here and its meaning is not clear; according to the context, the line may mean "do not make him (the father) uncomfortable" or vocalizing /taraḥḥil(i)-n(n)ū/(?), "do not frighten him/(me?)"; or perhaps read *td*!*ḥl*(?) (cf. 2.30:21 = **83.4**) "do not be afraid!"

(13) /ᶜattan/(?) adv. "now"(?), only here, < *ᶜanta + n; or an error for *ᶜnt* "now," cf. 1.19:IV:6 = **87.4**(?)

/ḫarādu/(?) absolute infinitive(?) /ḫ-r-d/ "to guard, be watchful"(?), cf. *ḫrd* "guard"(?) 4.179:15; 4.230:12; 4.683:1; *ḫrd* "(guarded) treasure"(?) 2.47:15, 17, 19, cf. Akkad. ḫarādu "to guard"; or /ḫaridu/ adj. "watchful"(?); or /ḫurādu/ < Hurrian "(a type/title of) soldier"(?); whatever the exact sense, cf. perhaps as a contrast *nḫt* 2.11:14 "I am quiet, relaxed"

/ˀanāku/ pronoun 1. sing. "I"

(14) *ᶜmny* /ᶜamma/ prep. "with, at" + -*ny* /-nayā/(?) suff. 1. du. "with both of us"(?); or an extended form -*n*- + -*y* of the suff. 1. sing.(?); or -*ny* adverbial affix, "here"(?)

/šalāmu/ "well-being, peace"

(15) /kalīlu/ subst. noun "whole," adj. "complete"; cf. also note to **82.5:10**
(16) /wa-minūmē/ "and" + pronoun "whatever"
(17) /šalāmu/ see note to line 14
/^{c}amma/ "with, at," see note to line 14
(18) /^{ɔ}ummi-ya/ gen. "my mother," see note to line 5
(19) /^{c}amma-ya/(?) or /^{c}ammī/(?) see note to line 14, with suff. 1. sing. "to(ward) me"
/tat̲at̲ib/ jussive 3. sing. f. Š-causative /t̲-w-b/ "to return"; instead of /š/ the causative prefix here is /t̲/, by assimilation to /t̲/, the first root consonant
(20) /rigma/ acc. "word"; "to return a/the word" > "to answer" (cf. H. hēšīb dābār).

84.2. A document of a religious association (°3.9:1–21=RS 1957.702)

This tablet, RS 1957.702, was not unearthed by a scientific excavation. It was taken illegally from the site, probably in 1957. Together with another alphabetic Ugaritic tablet (4.709) and four Akkadian tablets, this tablet was offered for sale in Paris and in 1970 was purchased for and given to the Institute for Antiquity and Christianity, in Claremont, California. The texts were edited by L. F. Fisher, in cooperation with M. C. Astour, M. Dahood, and P. D. Miller, The Claremont Ras Shamra Tablets (= Analecta Orientalia 48), Roma, 1971. Tablet 3.9 is presented in photographs (pl. IX–XI), with autograph copy, transliteration, translation and commentary by P. D. Miller; M. Dahood provides additional notes (pp. 51–54). The text is well preserved. Since it is the only text of its kind, interpretation depends more than usual on the individual approaches of interpreters. Recent discussion is surveyed by R. E. Friedman, Maarav 2 (1979–80):187–206; with photographs by K. A. Zuckerman, plates 1–12. The tablet is apparently a document establishing a religious association (club) which organized banquets for its members. (Cf. also an Aramaic ostracon from Elephantine, fifth cent. B.C., Répertoire d'épigraphie sémitique 1295).

Obverse

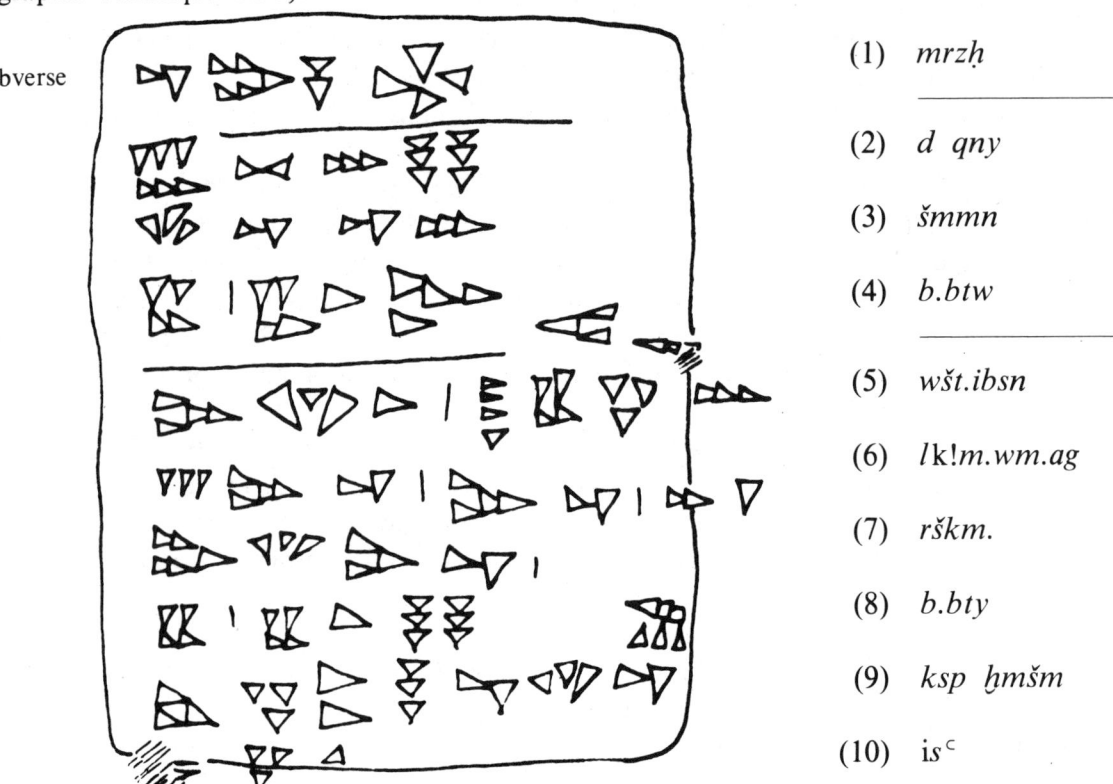

(1) *mrzḥ*

---

(2) *d qny*

(3) *šmmn*

(4) *b.btw*

---

(5) *wšt.ibsn*

(6) *l*k!*m.wm.ag*

(7) *rškm.*

(8) *b.bty*

(9) *ksp ḫmšm*

(10) is^{c}

Reverse

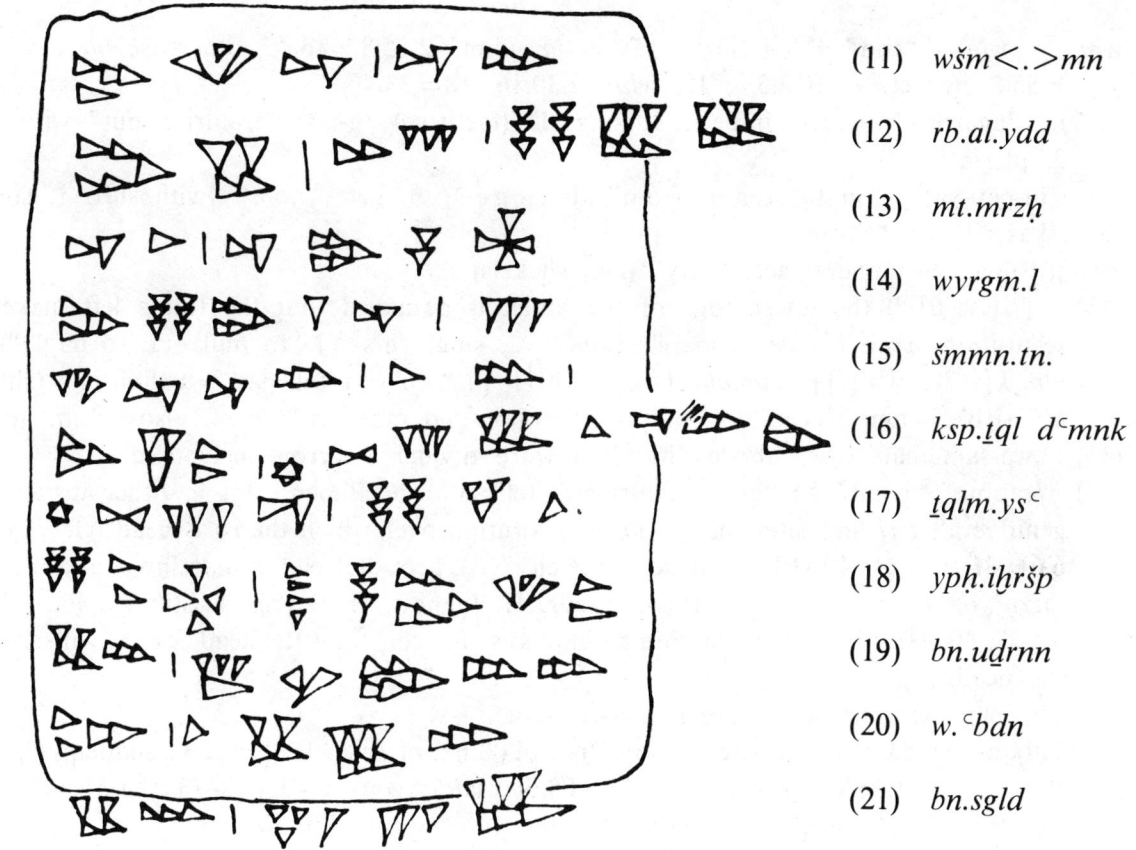

(11) *wšm<.>mn*

(12) *rb.al.ydd*

(13) *mt.mrzḥ*

(14) *wyrgm.l*

(15) *šmmn.tn.*

(16) *ksp.ṯql dᶜmnk*

(17) *ṯqlm.ysᶜ*

(18) *ypḥ.iḫršp*

(19) *bn.uḏrnn*

(20) *w.ᶜbdn*

(21) *bn.sgld*

(1) /marziḥu/ "(cultic) association, (religious) club"; cf. *ma-ar-zi-ḫi* (gen.) RS 14.16:3, Syria 28, 173; cf. also *mrzḥ.ᶜn*[t] 4.462:4–6 "marziḥu of ᶜAn[at(?)]"; *mrzḥh* 1.114:15 = **88.3** "his marziḥ" (of Il)

(2) /dā/(?) relative pronoun acc. "which"

/qanaya/ perf. 3. sing. m. /q-n-y/ "to create"; cf. *qnyt.ilm* 1.4:I:22 "creatrix of gods"; [b]*nm.aqny* 1.14:II:4 "I shall (pro)create sons"; here specifically "to establish"

(3) /šamūmānu/ cf. *ša-mu-ma-nu* (nom.) P:III:16.256:16 (p. 159); *ša-mu-ma-na* (gen.) P:III:16.256:8, 14 (p. 159); P:III:16.178:3 (p. 148); P:VI:38:7, 14, 16 (all referring to Š. son of *ta-la-a-bi*, who held estates given by the king); other persons of this name are: *šmmn.bn.ᶜdš* 4.261:12, a metal smith (cf. also *šmmn* 4.43:2); [š]*mmn. bn.gmz* 4.350:14

(4) /bi-bētiw(u)/(?) "in his house"; suff. 3. sing. m. after a genitive ending *-ihu > *-iu > /-iwu/(?) or /-iw/(?); or /bi-bēti/ + dittographic *w*(?)

(5) /wa-šâttu/ perf. 1. sing. /š-y-t/ "to put, set" (cf. wə-šattī Exod 23:31) conj. /wa-/ + perf. indicates a past tense or less probably a consecutive perfect, cf. *w.št* 2.10:18 = **86.43** "and you will put," or imperative(?); or 3. sing. m. /wa-šāta/(?), cf. line 6

/ʾib(ū)sāna/ acc. "storeroom(?), dining room"(?); feeding (place)"(?); cf. (amīl)bēl (bīt) a-bu-si P:III:11.732:A:8 (p. 181) "master of the horse stall"(?)); *ibsn* is a noun formed with the afformative /-ān/

(6) /lē-kum(u)/! the second letter looks much more like *w*, but the context requires k!; "to you"; if *w* is read: *lwm* /lē-wum(u)/ < *lē-um- < *lē-hum-(?) suff. 3. pl. m. "to them"; cf. *wšt*, line 5

wm /w(a)-/ "and" + /-(ʾ)im/ "if", cf. *im* /ʾim/ 2.15:8 = **86.45**, otherwise *hm* 1.4:IV:34 = **85.2** etc.; cf. *whm* 2.3:8, 18; *whm* 2.30:16, 18 = **83.4**

(6–7) /ʾagarrišu-kum(u)/, imperf. 1. sing. D (factitive) /g-r-š/ "to drive out" with suff. 2. pl. m.

(8) /bi-bēti-ya/ *b-* in the sense "from" after /g-r-š/ + gen. "house" with suff. 1. sing.

(9) /kaspa/ acc. "silver"

/ḫam(i)šīma/ numeral acc. "fifty" (i.e., shekels)

(10) /[ʾi]ssaʿu/(?) the lower edge of the tablet is damaged, but the traces left make the restitution of an i most probable; imperf. 1. sing. /n-s-ʿ/? "to pull out, to pay"(?); cf. *alp. k*[sp?] | *.tšʿn*[?] | *w.hm.alp* | *l.tšʿn* 3.8:11–14 "... you will pay(?) a thousand (shekels of) si[lver], and if you do not pay the thousand (shekels)"(?); cf. also *ysʿ* in line 18

(11) /wa-šamūmānu/ see above, line 3; a word divider is erroneously used

(12) /rabbu/ ("great" >) "head, chairman" (cf. H. rab, Phoen. rb); in other instances a genitive after *rb* indicates the group or institution over which the *rb* is head (cf. *rb khnm* 6.6 = **81.1**; *rb qrt* 4.141:III:3 "head of the city"(?)); here the head of marziḫu is meant (cf. rb mrzḥʾ on several Palmyrene tesserae, eds. H. Ingholt, H. Seyrig, J. Starcky, Paris 1955, nr. 27, 30–33). Lines 11–12 contain a nominal sentence, "Š., is the head" or "Š. will/shall be the head."

/ʾal/ negative particle, before a jussive "not"

/yiddad/ or /yiddadū/ jussive 3. sing.(?) or pl.(?) m., of /n-d-d/ "(to move suddenly(?) >) to flee, rise" (cf. *ydd.wyqm* 1.10:II:17 = **88.56**; *ydd...yqm* 1.4:III:12–13 "he rises ... he stands up"), cf. note to /yargum(ū)/, line 14

(13) /mutu/(?) or /mutū/(?) sing.(?) or pl.(?) constr. "man" or "men"

/marziḫi/ ("man/men, member(s) of") "the association"

(14) /wa-yargum(ū)/(?) "and" + jussive 3. sing.(?) or pl.(?) m. "to say" (cf. note to **84.1:3**). "he/they may not rise and say"; cf. Aram. mḥr ... tqm tmt wtʾmr Kraeling 2:9 "if tomorrow ... Tamut rises up (cf. note to *ydd*, line 12) and says"

(14–15) /lē-šamūmāna/ *l-* + PN gen., diptote; cf. *ša-mu-ma-na*, see note to line 3

(15) /tin(a)/ imperative sing. m. /y-t-n/ "to give"; cf. H. imperative tēn < *tin, from n-t-n!

(16) /kaspa/ see note to line 9

/ṯiqla/ acc. "weight (unit), shekel"; apposition

/dū/ relative pronoun nom. "which"; introducing a relative nominal clause

/ʿammanaka/(?) prep. "with" (see note to **84.1:14, 17**) with suff. 2. sing. m.

(17) /ṯiqlēmi/ acc. "two shekels"(?)

/yissaʿ(ū)/ jussive 3. sing.(?) or pl.(?) m. "he/they shall pay"; see note to line 10. The short clause on line 17 may be considered an apodosis; the protasis, "if he/they rise and say 'Give the silver ... deposited with you'" is to be understood.

(18) /yapiḫu/ "witness"

/ʾiḫī-rašapu/ PN ("my brother is (the god) Rašapu"); cf. *aḫršp* 4.370:7 and note the less correct variant *aḫrṯp* 4.277:5 = **86.52**; cf. aḫi-(il)rašap (written with logograms) P:VI:51:4 etc.; for the first part, cf. *iḫmn* 4.282:4; *i-ḫi-ma-nu* P:III:15.190:4 (p. 137); the spelling reveals the assimilation /ʾaḫ-/ > /ʾ-iḫ-/ before /-ī/; for the second part cf. *nu-ma-re-ša-ip* U:V:98:2 and Eblaitic ra-sa-ap

(19) /bunu/ constr., "son"; < *bin-; cf. *bu-nu-šu* ("son of man" >) "man" U:V:137:II:31′

udrnn PN gen.; cf. *bn.udrn* 4.428:8; cf. PN *idrn* 4.64:V:8

(20) /wa-ʿabdīnu/ "and" + PN; *ʿbdn* 4.313:4; 4.339:19; *ab-di-na* (gen.) P:III:11.839:7 (p. 194)

(21) /bunu/ "son (of)"

/sigilda/ PN gen., cf. *sgld* 4.309:3; 4.98:13; cf. *sí-gil-da* (gen.) P:III:16.201:4 (p. 151) and *sí-gil-da-na* (gen.) line 6; P:III:16.138:16 (p. 144); also P:VI:121:5

85. *Literary texts in autograph and transliteration*

85.1. From the Keret Epos (1.16:VI:39–59; cf. Gordon 127; II K, VI)

The last column of Keret (Kirta) epos (p. 142) was published by Ch. Virolleaud (Syria 23, 1942–3, pp. 1–20), and reedited by A. Herdner in CTA 16. The colophon (line 59) is written on the left edge of the tablet. Lines 39–54a tell how the prince Yaṣṣub carried out his intention, revealed in lines 27–38, of replacing his ailing father Keret on the throne.

(39a) imperf. 3. sing. m. /t-b-^{c}/ "to depart"

PN, /yaṣṣubu/(?) (cf. /n-ṣ-b/ "to erect"), cf. (bin-)*ya-ṣu-ba* P:III:16.386:2 (p. 165); cf. also *y*[a(?)]-*ṣa*-[bu](?) P:VI:138:15; cf. Amor. Ya-an-ṣí-bu-um

"boy, young man"

(39b–40a) prep. "upon; toward"

gen. /ʾabi-hu/ "father" + suff. 3. sing. m.

imperf. 3. sing. m. "to enter"

(40b–41a) imperf. 3. sing. m. /n-š-ʾ/ "to lift"

acc., *g* "voice," with suff. 3. sing. m.

"and" + imperf. 3. sing. m. /ṣ-w-ḥ/(?) "to shout, call"

This verse is a standard introduction of the direct speech, varied only in person and number.

(41b–42a) imperative sing. m., /š-m-^{c}/ "to hear"

m^{c} interjection, "please, pray"

/la-/(?) vocative particle "O!"

krt PN of a king; the usual vocalization, Keret, is not based on any textual or comparative evidence; cf. the name of the Mittanian king Ki-ir-ta, a name attested also in Alalaḫ; cf. perhaps also the PN *krty* 4.371:18 ("Cretan"(?))

ṯ^{c} an epithet of King *krt*, either "munificent" (or "offerer"?) (cf. ESA mṯ^{c}y "offering") or "of (the tribe) *ṯ*^{c}" (cf. also *ṯ*^{c}*y*, line 59; 1.90:22; and *bn.ṯ*^{c}*y* 4.76:7 PN)

(42b) imperative sing. m. Gt /š-m-^{c}/ "hearken!" (cf. H. GN ʾæštəmō(a)^{c})

/wa-tiqaǵ/ jussive 2. sing. m. /y-q-ǵ/ "to awake, be alert"

"ear" probably accusative of relation, "be alert (as concerns) the ear!"

(43) /ki-/ "as" or /kī/ "when, for, because"

ǵz and *ǵzm* meaning unclear, perhaps "raider"; parallel to *ǵrm* 44a; *ǵz.ǵzm*, perhaps "raider of raiders, the most ruthless raider"

imperf. 2. sing. m. /d-b-r/, perhaps D, "to administer"

(44a) *ǵrm* meaning unclear, perhaps "raiders," parallel to *ǵzm*, line 43 (but cf. note to 43–44a)

ṯṯwy imperf. 2. sing. m. /ṯ-w-y/, meaning unclear, perhaps "to govern" (cf. perhaps H. (^{c}ēmæq) šāwē Gen 14:17, GN, "Valley of the Ruler"(?), explained as (^{c}ēmæq) ham-mælæk "Valley of the king"; or "to dwell"(?); but cf. note to 43–44a)

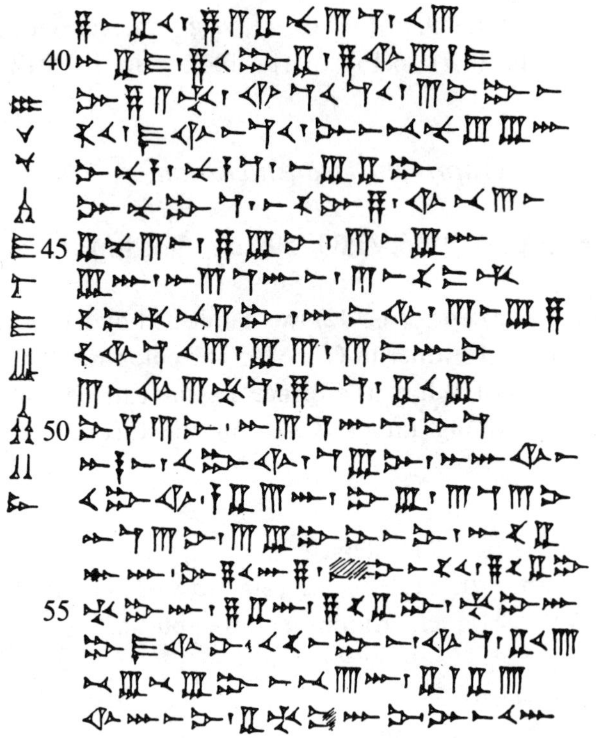

(39) *ytb^{c}.yṣb ǵlm.^{c}l*
(40) *abh.y^{c}rb.yšu gh*
(41) *wyṣḥ.šm^{c} m^{c}.lkrt*
(42) *ṯ^{c}.ištm^{c}.wtqǵ udn*
(43) *kǵz.ǵzm.tdbr*
(44) *wǵrm.tṯwy.šqlt*
(45) *bǵlt.ydk.ltdn*
(46) *dn.almnt.ltṯpṭ*
(47) *ṯpṭ qṣr.npš.ltdy*
(48) *ṯšm.^{c}l.dl.lpnk*
(49) *ltšlḥm.ytm.b^{c}d*
(50) *kslk.almnt.km*
(51) *aḫt.^{c}rš.mdw.anšt*
(52) *^{c}rš.zbln.rd.lmlk*
(53) *amlk.ldrktk.aṯb*
(54) *an.wy^{c}ny.*krt *ṯ^{c}.yṯbr*
(55) *ḫrn.ybn.yṯbr.ḫrn*
(56) *rišk.^{c}ṯtrt.šm.b^{c}l*
(57) *qdqd*k!.*tqln.bgbl*
(58) *šntk.bḥpnk.wt^{c}n*
(59) *spr.ilmlk.ṯ^{c}y*

(39a) /yitba^{c}u yaṣṣubu ǵalmu/
(39b–40a) /^{c}alē | $^{\supset}$abi-hu ya^{c}rubu/
(40b–41a) /yišša$^{\supset}$u ga-hu | wa-yaṣūḥu/
(41b–42a) /šama^{c} ma^{c} la k-r-tu | ṯ-^{c}u/
(42b) /ištama^{c} wa-tiqaǵ $^{\supset}$udna/
(43) /ki ǵ-z- ǵ-zīma tadabbiru/
(44a) /wa-ǵ-rīma taṯ-w-yu/
(44b–45a) /šaqilta | bi-ǵalīti yadaka/
(45b–46a) /lā tadīnu | dīna $^{\supset}$almanati/
(46b–47a) /lā taṯpuṭu | ṯapṭa qaṣiri napši/
(47b–48a) /lā taddiyu | ṯāšīma ^{c}alē dalli/
(48b–49a) /lē-panīka | lā tašalḥimu yatuma/
(49b–50a) /ba^{c}da | kaslika $^{\supset}$almanata/
(50b–51a) /kamā | $^{\supset}$aḫāti ^{c}aršu madwi/
(51b–52a) /$^{\supset}$anīšati | ^{c}aršu zabūlāni/
(52b–53a) /rid lē-mulki | $^{\supset}$amluka/
(53b–54a) /lē-darkatika $^{\supset}$aṯiba | $^{\supset}$anā/
(54b) /wa-ya^{c}niyu k-r-tu ṯ-^{c}u/
(54c–55a) /yaṯbur | ḥōrānu yā bun-ī/
(55b–56a) /yaṯbur ḥōrānu | ra$^{\supset}$ša-ka/
(56b–57a) /^{c}aṯtartu šumu ba^{c}li | qudqudaka/
(57b–58a) /taqīlan(na) bi-gabali | šan-ti-ka/
(58b) /bi-ḥ-p-nika wa ta^{c}nu/
(59a) /sāpiru $^{\supset}$ili-milku ṯ-^{c}-y-/

(43–44a) No interpretation offered for these lines is entirely satisfactory, including this one: "As/For you, you rule like the raider of raiders (the most ruthless raider), and you govern (like) attacker(s)"; this translation renders a parallelistic structure. The context, however, requires a meaning closer to that of the following line, 44b–45a, "You have let down in inactivity your hand." "In pits (*ǵrm*) you will dwell" could be proposed for 44a; for 43 a similar meaning could be postulated. But cf. also note to *ǵlt* 44b–45a.

(44b–45a) /šaqīltā/(?) perf. 2. sing. m., /q-y-l/(?) "to fall", Š "to let fall/sink"

ǵlt a noun derived from /ǵ-l-y/ "to lower, bow down" (1.2:I:23, 24), thus "lowering" > "inactivity"(?), or "baseness"(?)

ydk apparently acc., "hand," with suff. 2. sing. m.

(44b–45a) "You have sunk your hand into inactivity (or some impropriety)." Perhaps the use of so many /ǵ/ sounds in 43–45a has an expressive function, to induce a sombre mood.

(45b–46a) negative particle + imperf. 2. sing. m. /d-y-n/ "to judge," cf. 1.17:V:7–8; Jer 5:28; Ps 7:9

acc. /dīna/ "judgment, cause"

gen. "widow," cf. Isa 10:2

(46b–47a) negative particle + imperf. 2. sing. m. /ṯ-p-ṭ/ "to adjudicate," B-word to /d-y-n/, cf. 1.17:V:7–8; Jer 5:28; Ps 7:9

/ṯapṭ-/ "suit," "case"

gen. "short"

gen. "soul" (< "breath" < "throat"); adj. with a nominal attribute; ("short of/in spirit" >) "wretched"; cf. H. qəṣar rū(a)ḥ Prov 14:29 "impatient"; qoṣær rū(a)ḥ Exod 6:9 "crushed(ness of) spirit"; /q-ṣ-r/ + næpæš Judg 16:16 "to be miserable"

(47b–48a) negative particle + imperf. 2. sing. m. /n-d-y/ "to throw away, banish"

ṯšm pl. acc., probably "(de)spoilers"; cf. Egypt. š3š.w "(plundering) nomads"; H. šō(ʾ)sáyik Jer 30:16 Kt.; cf. Amos 5:11

ʿl most probably prep. "upon" or "from (upon)"; note that in H., š-s-y and š-s-s govern direct objects, e.g., Jdg 2:14; 1 Sam 23:1

gen. "poor"

(48b–49a) *l* + "face" with suff. 2. sing. m. "before you"; see note to **84.1:8**

negative particle + imperf. 2. sing. m. Š /l-ḥ-m/ "to eat," Š "to feed"

/yatum-/(?) "orphan"; cf. Ps 82:3

(49b–50a) /baʿdu/(?) or /baʿda/(?) "behind"

/kasl-/ "loin" (> "back")

/ʾalmanata/ "widow," acc. as object to "you do not feed" in line 49a and parallel to "orphan"; (cf. Isa 1:17; Deut 10:18)

(50b–51a) /ka-mā/ prep. "like"

/ʾaḫāti/ "sister," cf. *a-ḫa-tum*-milku PN fem. ("sister of M.") P:III:15.89:11 (cf. also 8) (p. 53); *km aḫt* serves as a nominal predicate

"bed" subject

/madwi/ or /-ī/ < *-iyi(?) gen. "sickness," noun with a prefix *m-* from the root *d-w-y "to be miserable"; attribute; cf. H. ʿæræś dəwāy Ps 41:4

(51b–52a) /ʾanīšat-/ "intimate friend (fem.)"; depends on *km*, line 50

zbln gen. "disease," meaning parallel to *mdw* "sickness"; etymology not clear (perhaps connected with *z-b-l "to carry," viz., a plague carrying off its victims(?) or *zbl* "prince, ruler," viz., a disease inflicted by some godly power)

(52b–53a) imperative sing. m. /y-r-d/ "to go down"

l- "from"; (cf. H. li-rkōb 2 Kgs 4:24)
/mulk/-(?) infinitive, "reigning" (cf. H. construct inf. məlōk)
/ˀamluka/ subjunctive 1. sing. /m-l-k/ "to reign"
(53b–54a) *l-* "from," as above in 52b–53a
drktk gen. with suff. 2. sing. m. "rule, government; authority"
/ˀaṯiba/ subjunctive 1. sing. /y-ṯ-b/ "to sit"
an(?) the photo indicates *an* (cf. line 38), the autograph *nn*; the pronoun /ˀanā/ "I" fits better in the context, reinforcing the 1. person of the verb
(54b) *w-yᶜny* conj. + imperf. 3. sing. m. /ᶜ-n-y/ "to answer"
see above to 41b–42a
(54c–55a) /yaṯbur/ jussive 3. sing. m. /ṯ-b-r/ "to break"
DN
/yā/ interjection, introducing vocative, "O!"
bn /bunī/ "my son," vocative (or /bunu/ "son"?)
(55b–56a) see above note to 54c–55a
/raˀša-ka/ acc., "head," with suff. 2. sing. m. (*i* here indicates the absence of a vowel after /ˀ/)
(56b–57a) DN fem.
/šumu/(?) "name" cf. PN *šu-um-a-na-ti* P:III:15.139:9 (p. 167); *šu-mu-a-bi* (gen.) P:III: 16.257:II:50 (p. 201); apposition
/baᶜli/ DN. gen., (< "lord," originally an epithet of Hadd)
"Astarte name of Baal" cf. Phoen. ᶜštrt šm bˀl KAI 14:18, Pun. tnt pn bᶜl "Tinit face of Baal"
*qdqd*k(!) instead of the *r* on the tablet, k /-ka/, suff. 2. sing. m., is to be read; acc. "pate"
(57b–58) /taqīlan(na)/(?) or /taqūlan(na)/(?) energic mood 2. sing. m. /q-y-l/(?) "to fall," see note to 44b–45a
b- "in" or "from"(?)
gbl gen.; /gabali/(?) "mountain, peak"(?) or /gubuli/(?) "boundary"?
šntk suff. 2. sing. m.; either f. pl. of *šnt* "year," /šanāt-/ or f. sing. *šnt* /šanīt-/ "loftiness" cf. perhaps H. Prov 5:9; Isa 11:11
(58b) *b-* "in"(?)
ḥpnk gen. with suff. 2. sing. m.; *ḥpn*, form and meaning unclear; cf. *yḥpn* 1.22:I:9, II:12(?); (cf. H. ḥåpnáyim "the hollow of both hands"; Akkad. upnu; Arab. ḥafnat); perhaps a word parallel to "loftiness," or a word meaning "nullity"(?) or "empty-handness"(??)
wtᶜn "and" + imperf. (jussive?) /ᶜ-n-w/(?) "to be downcast," or N in the same meaning (cf. H. Ps 119:107; Exod 10:3)
(59) Colophon on the left edge of the tablet
/sāpiru/ "scribe" cf. 3.8:23; 4.183:II:29
/ˀilumilku/(?) PN, cf. ilu-milku (written with logograms) U:V:9:252 etc.; cf. also ili-*mu-lik* P:VI:82:16
ṯᶜy probably the beginning of a clause which was not completed (cf. 1:4:VIII:49; [ṯᶜ]*y.nqmd.mlk.ugrt*), "he dedicated" perf. /ṯ-ᶜ-y/?); or "supervisor (of)"(?); or a tribal name(?), see note to 41b–42a (but cf. *ilmlk.šbny* 1.6:VI:54)

85.2. From the Baal Cycle (1.4:IV:20–39; cf. Gordon 51:IV; IIAB, IV)

This selection (p. 146) is taken from the most voluminous of the Ugaritic tablets. It was published by Ch. Virolleaud, Un nouveau chant de poème d'Aleïne-Baal, Syria 13, 1932, 113–163, with French translation and commentary, and reedited by Andrée Herdner in CTA 4. The passage depicts the trip to the residence of the supreme god Il undertaken by the goddess Athirat on donkeyback in the company of two divine servants and the welcome extended to her by Il. The purpose of the visit is to intervene for the young god Baal, who needs a palace. Lines 20–23, 25–29, 31–35 coincide with the cola of the verses.

(20) adverb "then"
l- affirmative particle "really"
imperf. 3. sing. f. /y-t-n/ "to give"
pl. acc. "face" (cf. **84.1.8**); with /y-t-n/ "to direct face, set out"
(21) *ᶜm* "with," here "to"
il DN (also used as a noun, "god," 1.17:V:31 = **88.62**, cf. *i-lu* U:V:133:I:14)
/mabbak-/ < *manbak- "source" (place from which the water flows out); cf. also *nbk* (GN? "source") 4.269:19 (cf. H. mibbəkē nəhārōt Job 28:11)
du. gen.-acc. "river"
(22) /qarba/ noun used as preposition; "(in) midst"
/ᵓapiqi/ gen., "headwater, channel"; cf. Arab. (< Aram.) GN ᵓAfqā, east of Byblos, supposed to be mythical abode of Il; cf. Ps 18:16
/tahām(a)t-/ du. gen. "(primeval) ocean"; cf. (DN f.) *ta-a-ma-tum* U:V:137:III:34″; cf. Job 38:16
(23a) imperf. 3. sing. f. /g-l-y/ "to go in/(out?)" cf. also 1.16:VI:4; parallel to /b-(w)-ᵓ/ "to come in"
d̲d /d̲ad-/ or /žad-/(?) "territory" (or "pavilion"(?), cf. 1.19:IV:51–52)
/ᵓili/ see note to 21
(23b–24a) /tubāᵓu/ imperf. 3. sing. f. /b-w-ᵓ/ "to come, enter"
qrš "precinct, domain" (or "pavilion"?)
/malki/ sing. gen. "king"; cf. *ma-al-ku* U:V:130:III:13′
/ᵓabī/ sing. gen. "father," apposition
šnm either pl. of *šnt* "year" (cf. H. šānīm), though Ug. pl. is otherwise *šnt*; or *ab.šnm* "exalted one"(?) or DN *šnm*, cf. *t̲knm wšnm* 1.123:8; 1.39:3, 6; 1.114:19 = **88.3**
(25) *pᶜn* du. gen.-acc. constr. "foot"
thbr imperf. 3. sing. f. /h-b-r/ "to bow down"
tql imperf. 3. sing. f. /q-w-l/(?) "to fall down"
(26) *tštḥwy* imperf. 3. sing. f. "she greets/prostrates herself"; the root is probably /ḥ-w-y/ "to live," Št "to ask life (for oneself)"
tkbdh imperf. 3. sing. f. with suff. 3. sing. m. /k-b-d/ "to be heavy, honored," D "to honor"
(27) *hlm* interjection "behold" or conjunction "as soon as"
k- /kī/(?) affirmative particle, "surely," before an imperfect which stands at the end of a clause; cf. H. kī Ps 49:16; 128:2

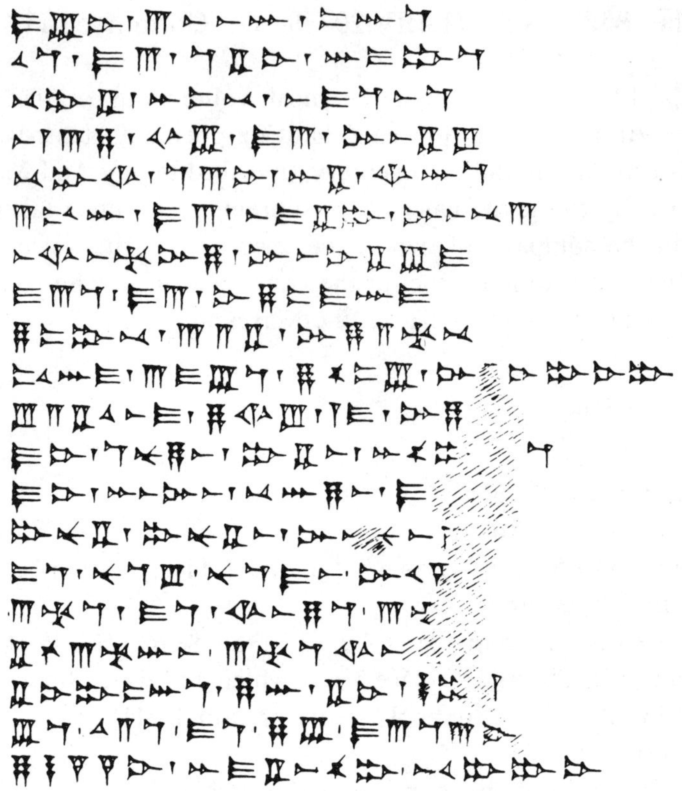

(20) *idk.lttn.pnm*
(21) *^{c}m.il.mbk.nhrm*
(22) *qrb.apq.thmtm*
(23) *tgly.ḏd.il.wtbu*
(24) *qrš.mlk.ab.šnm*
(25) *lp^{c}n.il.thbr.wtql*
(26) *tštḥwy.wtkbdh*
(27) *hlm.il.kyphnh*
(28) *yprq.lṣb.wyṣḥq*
(29) *p^{c}nh.lhdm.yṯpd.*wykrkr
(30) *uṣb^{c}th.yšu.gh.wyṣ*[ḥ]
(31) *ik.mǵyt.rbt.aṯ*r[t.y]m
(32) *ik.atwt.qnyt.i*[lm]
(33) *rǵb.rǵbt.*wtǵt[ ]
(34) *hm.ǵmu.ǵmit.w^{c}*s[ ]
(35) *lḥm.hm.štym.lḥ*[m]
(36) *bṯlḥnt.lḥm št*
(37) *bkrpnm.yn.bk*(s).*ẖ*rṣ
(38) *dm.^{c}ṣm.hm.yd.il m*lk
(39) *yẖssk.ahbt.ṯr.t^{c}*rrk

(20) /$^{\supset}$iddāka la-tatinu panīma/
(21) /^{c}amma $^{\supset}$ili mabbaka naharēmi/
(22) /qarba $^{\supset}$apiqi tahāmatēmi/
(23a) /tagliyu ḏada $^{\supset}$ili/
(23b–24a) /wa-tubā$^{\supset}$u | qarša malki $^{\supset}$abī š-n-m-/
(25) /lē-pa^{c}nē $^{\supset}$ili tahburu wa-taqūlu/
(26) /taštaḥwiyu wa-takabbidu-hu/
(27) /halum(ma) $^{\supset}$ilu kī-yiphēn-ha/
(28) /yaparriqu liṣba wa-yiṣḥaqu/
(29a) /pa^{c}nē-hū lē-hadāmi yaṯpudu/
(29b–30a) /wa-yakarkiru | $^{\supset}$uṣba^{c}āti-hu/
(30b) /yišša$^{\supset}$u ga-hu wa-yaṣūḥu/
(31) /$^{\supset}$ēka maǵayat rabbatu $^{\supset}$aṯiratu yammi/
(32) /$^{\supset}$ēka $^{\supset}$atawat qāniyatu $^{\supset}$ilīma/
(33) /raǵābu raǵibti wa t-ǵ-t-/
(34) /him ǵamā$^{\supset}$u ǵami$^{\supset}$ti wa ^{c}-s--/
(35a) /laḥāmu him šatāyuma/
(35b–36a) /laḥ(a)mī | bi-ṯulḥānāti laḥma/
(36b–37a) /šatī | bi-karpānīma yēna/
(37b–38a) /bi-kāsī ẖurāṣi | dama ^{c}iṣīma/
(38b–39a) him yaddu $^{\supset}$ili malki | yaẖassisu-ki/
(39b) /$^{\supset}$ahbatu ṯōri ta^{c}āriru-ki/

yphnh imperf. 3. sing. m. with suff. 3. sing. f. -(*n*)*h*, /p-h-y/ "to see, perceive"; cf. *phy* 3.1:15 "he saw"
(28) /yapruqu/ (or /yaparriqu/(?)) imperf. 3. sing. m. /p-r-q/ G (or D) "to sever, open wide"
lṣb "the narrowness"(?) (of mouth or throat); cf. *ᶜnh.blṣbh* 1.103:49 "his eyes (are) in his mouth(?)"
imperf. 3. sing. m. /ṣ-ḥ-q/ "to laugh"
(29a) du. gen.-acc. + suff. 3. sing. m. "his feet"
l- "to"
hdm gen. "footstool"
yṯpd imperf. 3. sing. m. /ṯ-p-d/ "to put, set"(?) or "to tap"(?); cf. *ṯn.mṯpdm* 1.1:III:20 "two jumps"(?)
(29a–30a) /yakarkiru/ imperf. 3. sing. m., D/R from the root /k-r-r/, or quadriliteral verb /k-r-k-r/ "to twiddle"
pl. /ᵓuṣbaᶜ-/ "finger"
(30b) cf. notes to **85.1**, 40b–41a
(31) /ᵓēka/ adv. "how, why"
perf. 3. sing. f. /m-ǵ-y/ "to reach, arrive"; cf. also /m-ṣ-ᵓ/ var. /m-ẓ-ᵓ/ "to reach"
/rabbatu/ "Lady"; cf. *rb* "great, head"
/ᵓaṯ(i)ratu/(?) DN f. constr.; cf. (d)*aš-ra-tum* U:V:18:19
/yammi/ gen. "sea"; "of the sea" (or "of the (god) Yamm/"Sea"?)
(32) 3. sing. f. /ᵓ-t-w/ "to come"
participle sing. f. constr. /q-n-y/ "to create" (cf. H. q-n-y Gen 14:19; Phoen. ᵓl qn ᵓrṣ)
/ᵓilīma/ pl. gen.-acc. "gods"; cf. 1.4:III:26
(33) /raǵābu/ absolute infinitive /r-ǵ-b/ "to be hungry"; the infinitive stresses the finite verb
/raǵibti/ perf. 2. sing. f.; apparently an interrogative clause, cf. *hm* "or," line 34
w- apparently a coordinating conjunction, meaning "and, while, since"
tǵt[--] traces of two vertical wedges indicated in the autograph may point to a *ṣ* or *l*. The context indicates forms of 2. person sing. f. here and in the line 35; *ᶜs*[ ] in line 35 may be restored as a perfect, *ᶜs*[t]. The interpretation of *tǵt* "you have journeyed afar," from /t-ǵ-y/ would provide a parallel to *ᶜs*[t] "you travelled (all the night)." (Perhaps the last word in line 33 is to be read m!*ǵt*, cf. *mǵyt* line 31.)
(34) /him/ "or" in a disjunction question
absolute infinitive and perf. 2. sing. f. /ǵ-m-ᵓ/ "to be thirsty"
ᶜs[t](?) perf. 2. sing. f.(?), see note to *tǵt*, line 33. Perhaps the word is to be read *ᶜr*[bt] "you entered," cf. *atwt* "she came," line 31 and m!*ǵt*(?), line 33.
(35a) /laḥāmu/ infinitive /l-ḥ-m/ "to eat," an expression of command
hm "or"
/šatāyum(a)/ infinitive absolute + *-m* /š-t-y/ "to drink"
(35b–36a) /laḥ(a)mī/ imperative sing. f. "eat!"
/bi-/ probably "from"
/ṯulḥānāti/ fem. pl. gen.-acc. /ṯulḥān-/ "table"
/laḥma/ acc. "food, bread"
(36b–37a) /šatī/ or, reading *št*[y], /šat(a)yī/ imperative sing. f. "drink!"
krpnm pl. (or sing. with *-m*?) gen.-acc. /karpān-/(?) "cup"

/yēna/ acc. *yn* "wine," see note to **83.2:15**

(37b–38a) *bk* is to be corrected to *bk*(s), cf. 1.5:IV:16 = **87.3** and 1.17:VI:5; pl. (or sing.?) gen.-acc. constr.; cf. **83.2:15**; /kās-/ "cup"

/ḫurāṣi/ gen. "gold" cf. U:V:137:II:4′ *ḫu-r*[a-ṣu]

/dama/ acc. "blood"

/ᶜiṣīma/ pl. gen.-acc. /ᶜiṣ-/ "tree, bush"

(38b–39a) *hm* conditional conjunction "if," for expressing a wish (cf. H. ᵓim tišmaᶜ Ps 81:9) (or introducing a question(?))

yd /yadd-/ "love, attention," parallel to *ahbt* "love," cf. 1.3:III:6–7 and H. Isa 51:8; the interpretation of /yad-/ as ("hand" >) "male organ," cf. 1.23:33–34, does not provide parallelism with *ahbt*

/ᵓili/ gen. DN

/malki/ gen. "king"; apposition

yḫssk imperf. 3. sing. m. with suff. 2. sing. f. /-ki/, /yaḫassisu/ D /ḫ-s-s/ (or /yaḫāsisu-/ L /ḫ-w-s/ or /ḫ-y-s/) "to excite, to stir"

(39b) /ᵓahbatu/ "loving, love"

gen. /ṯōr-/ "bull"; epithet of the god Il

tᶜrrk imperf. 3. sing. f. with suff. 2. sing. f. /-ki/ L /ᶜ-w-r/ "to arouse"; cf. Song of Songs 8:5

86. *Non-literary texts*

86.1. Lists and administrative texts

86.11. A list of soldiers (4.623:1–3, 8)

(1) m*ry*[n]m [ ]
(2) *bn rmyy* [ ]
(3) *yšril*[ ]

(8) *bn.išbᶜl*[ ]

86.12. A list of persons (4.360:1–5)

(1) *bn.bᶜln.biry*
(2) *ṯlṯ.bᶜlm*
(3) *w.adnhm.ṯr.w.arbᶜ.bnth*

---

(4) *yrḫm.yd.ṯn.bnh*
(5) *bᶜlm.w.ṯlṯ.nᶜrm.w.bṭ.aḥt*

86.13. Transfers of fields (4.356:1–2)

(1) *šd.bn.šty.l bn.ṭbrn*
(2) *šd.bn.ḫtb.lbn.yᶜḏrd*

86.2. Economic texts

86.21. A record of a debt (°4.135:1–2)

(1) *ᶜšrm.ksp*
(2) *ᶜl.s̀knt.syny*

86.22. A receipt (°4.266:1–7)

(1) *b.ym.ḥdṯ.*
(2) *b.yr*(ḫ)*.pgrm*
(3) *lqḥ.bᶜlmᶜḏr*
(4) *w.bn.ḫlp*
(5) *miḫd*
(6) *b.arbᶜ*
(7) *mat.ḫrṣ*

86.23. Wine records (4.213:1–3, 24–30)

(1) *ḫmš.ᶜšr.yn.ṭb*
(2) *w.tšᶜm.kdm.kbd.yn.d.l.ṭb*
(3) *w.arbᶜm.yn.ḫlq.b.gt.sknm*

---

(24) *mi*t*m.yn.ḥsp.d.nkly.b.db*ḥ[ ]
(25) *mit.arbᶜm.kbd.yn.ḥsp.l.m*[ṣb]
(26) *mit.ᶜšrm.*k*bd.yn.ḥsp.l.y*b?[ ]
(27) *ᶜšrm.yn.ḥsp.l.ql.d.tbᶜ.mṣ*r?*m*
(28) *mit.arbᶜm.kbd.yn.mṣb*
(29) *l.mḏrǵlm*
(30) *ᶜšrm.yn.mṣb*[––]*ḥ*[–––]*.l.gzzm*

86.24. Wine rations (°4.279:1–5)

(1) b*ym.prᶜ dnkly kd wk*d
(2) *wᶜl* y?m? *kdm*
(3) *wbṯlṯ.kd yn wkrsnm*
(4) *wbrbᶜ kdm yn*
(5) *wbḫmš kd yn*

86.25. A list of clothes and their prices (°4.146:1–8)

(1) *lbš.aḥd*
(2) *b.ᶜšrt*
(3) *w.ṯn.b.ḫmšt*
(4) *ṯprt.b.ṯlṯt*
(5) *mṯyn.b.ṯṯt*
(6) *ṯn.lbšm.b.ᶜšrt*
(7) *pld.b.arbᶜt*
(8) *lbš.ṯn.b.ṯnt.ᶜšrt*

86.26. A record of trade with the King of Byblos (bottomry loan?) (4.338:10–18)

(10) *ḫmš.mat.arbᶜm*
(11) *kbd.ksp.anyt*
(12) *d.ᶜrb.b.anyt*
(13) *l.mlk.gbl*
(14) *w.ḫmšm.ksp*
(15) *lqḥ.mlk.gbl*
(16) *lbš.anyth*
(17) *bᶜrm.ksp*
(18) *mḫrhn*

86.3. Contracts

86.31. Tribute for the Hittite king (3.1:22–28)

(22) [ḫ]mš.*mat pḥm*
(23) [ḫm]*š*[.m]*at.iqnu*
(24) *argmn.nqmd.mlk*
(25) *ugrt.dybl.lšpš*
(26) *mlk.rb.bᶜlh*
(27) *ks.ḫrṣ.ktn.mit.pḥm*
(28) *mit.iqni.lmlkt*

86.32. Redemption of captives (°3.4:1–19)

(1) *l.ym hnd*
(2) *iwr*kl*.pdy*
(3) *agdn.bn.n*wgn
(4) *wynḥm.aḫh*
(5) *w.bᶜln aḫh*
(6) *w.ḥṯṯn bnh*
(7) *w.btšy.bth*
(8) *w.ištrmy*
(9) *bt.ᶜbdmlk aṯ*t[h]
(10) *w.snt*
(11) *bt.ugrt*
(12) *w.pdy.h*[m]
(13) *iwrkl.*mit
(14) *ksp.b*yd
(15) *birtym*
(16) [wun]*ṯ inn*
(17) *l*hm *ᶜd tṯṯbn*
(18) *ksp.iwrkl*
(19) *wṯb.lunṯhm*

86.33. Royal grant of real property (°3.5:1–21)

(1) *lym.hnd*
(2) *ᶜmṯtmr.bn*
(3) *nqmpᶜ.ml*[k]
(4) *ugrt.ytn*
(5) *šd.kḏǵdl* [bn]
(6) uš–l? *d.bš*[ ]y
(7) *–m–*.[y]d *gth*
(8) yd gn*h* *yd*.[ ]
(9) [k]r*mh.yd*
(10) [k]*lklh*
(11) w*ytn.nn*
(12) *l.bᶜln.bn*
(13) *kltn.wl*
(14) *bnh.*ᶜd.*ᶜlm*
(15) *šḥr.ᶜlmt*
(16) *bnš bnšm*
(17) *l.yqḥnn.bd*
(18) *bᶜln.bn.kltn*
(19) *w.bd.bnh.ᶜd*
(20) *ᶜlm.wunṯ*
(21) *in.bn*

86.4. Letters

86.41. The King of Tyre to the King of Ugarit (°2.38:1–27)

Translated from Akkadian or transliterated from South Canaanite

(1) *l.mlk.ugrt*
(2) *aḫy.rgm*
(3) *tḥm.mlk.ṣr.aḫk*
(4) *yšlm.lk.ilm*
(5) *tǵrk.tšlmk.*
(6) *hnny.ᶜmn*
(7) *šlm.ṯmny*
(8) *ᶜmk.mnm.šlm*
(9) *rgm.ṯṯ*b
(10) *anykn.dt*
(11) *likt.mṣrm*
(12) *hndt.b.ṣr*
(13) *mtt.by*
(14) *gšm.adr*
(15) *nškḥ.w*
(16) *rb.tmtt*

(17) *lqḥ.kl.d̲rʿ*
(18) *bd*n*tm.w.ank*
(19) *kl*[.]*d̲rʿhm*
(20) k*l npš*
(21) k*lklhm.bd*
(22) *rb.tmtt.lqḥt*
(23) *w.ṯṯb.ank.lhm*
(24) *w.anyk.ṯt*
(25) *by.ʿky.ʿryt*
(26) *w.aḫy.mhk*
(27) *b.lbh.al.yšt*

86.42. Irri-tharruma to the Queen(?) (2.33:22–39)

(22) *w.mlk.bʿly*
(23) *lm.škn.hnk*
(24) *l.ʿbdh.alpm.*s̀s̀w*m*
(25) *rgmt.ʿly.ṯh.lm*
(26) *l.ytn.hm.mlk.*(b)*ʿly*
(27) *w.hn.ibm.šṣq.ly*
(28) *p.l.ašt.aṯty*
(29) *nʿry.ṯh.lpn.ib*
(30) *hn.hm.yrgm.mlk*
(31) *bʿly.tmǵyy.hn*
(32) *alpm.s̀s̀wm.hnd*
(33) *w.mlk.bʿly.bnš*
(34) *bnny.ʿmn.*
(35) *mlakty.hnd*
(36) *ylak.ʿmy*
(37) w.*tʿl.ṯh.hn*
(38) [a]l*pm*[.]*s̀s̀wm*
(39) [ ]*n.*[ ].*w.ṯb*

86.43. Iwri-žarri to Pilsiya (°2.10:1–19)

(1) *tḥm.i*wr*d̲r*
(2) l!.*plsy*
(3) *rgm*
(4) *yšlm.lk*
(5) *l.trǵds*
(6) *w.l.klby*
(7) *šmʿt.ḫti*
(8) *nḫtu.ht*
(9) *hm.in mm*
(10) *nḫtu.w.lak*
(11) *ʿmy.w.yd*

(12) *ilm.p.kmtm*
(13) *ᶜz.mid*
(14) *hm.nṯkp*
(15) *mᶜnk*
(16) *w.mnm*
(17) *rgm.d.tšmᶜ*
(18) *ṯmt.w.št*
(19) *b.spr.ᶜmy*

86.44. Report about looting to a superior (°2.61:1–13)

(1) *l.ḏrdn*
(2) *bᶜly.rgm*
(3) *bn.ḫrnk*
(4) *mǵy.*
(5) *hbṭ.hw*
(6) *ḫrd.w.šl hw*
(7) *qrt*
(8) *akln.b.grnt*
(9) *l.bᶜr*
(10) *ap.krmm*
(11) *ḫlq*
(12) *qrtn.ḫlqt*
(13) *w.dᶜ.dᶜ*

86.45. An informal letter (°2.15:1–10)

(1) *gnryn*
(2) *lmlkytn*
(3) *ḥnny lpn mlk*
(4) *šink itn*
(5) *rᶜy šṣa idn ly*
(6) *lšmn iṯr hw*
(7) *piḫdn gnryn*
(8) *im mlkytn yrgm*
(9) *aḫnnn*
(10) *wiḫd*

86.5. Records in substandard orthography

86.51. On the slaughter of small cattle (°1.80:1–5)

(1) *b gt ilštmᶜ*
(2) *bt ubnyn šh d.ytn.ṣtqn*
(3) *ṯut ṭbḫ ṣtq*n
(4) *b bz ᶜzm ḥbḫ š*
(5) *b kl ygz ḥḫ šh*

86.52. A list of persons (°4.277:1–5)

(1) *bnš.kld.*
(2) *kbln.ᶜbdyrǵ.ilgt*
(3) *ǵyrn.ybnn qrwn*
(4) *ypltn.ᶜbdnt*
(5) *klby.aḥrṯp*

86.53. On oil; written right to left (4.31:1–2, 11)

(1) *ᶜbdrŠ.bt*[bq]
(2) *bŠŠ ᶜŠr Šmn.*r[qḪ]
(11) *bḪmŠ ᶜŠr Šmn*[ ]

86.6. Hippiatric texts

86.61. Heading of a hippiatric text (1.85:1)

(1) *spr.nᶜm. śśwm*

86.62. A hippiatric instruction (1.71:23–26)

(23) *kyraš wykhp mid*
(24) *dblt yṯnt wṣmqm yṯn*[m]
(25) *wqmḥ bql yṣq aḥdh*
(26) *bap*h

86.7. Ritual texts

86.71. A list of offerings to the gods (1.109:1–23)

(1) *barbᶜt.ᶜš*r[t]
(2) *yrtḥṣ.mlk.*b[rr]
(3) *bym.mlat*
(4) *tqln.alpm.*
(5) *yrḫ.ᶜšrt.lbᶜ*[l ṣpn]
(6) *dqtm.wynt.qr*[t]
(7) *wmtntm.š lrmš*
(8) *wkbd.wš.lšlm* kbd
(9) *alp.wš.lbᶜl ṣpn*
(10) *dqt lṣpn.šrp.wšlmm*
(11) *kmm.wbbt.bᶜl.ugrt*
(12) *k*b!*dm.wnpš.ilib*
(13) *gdlt.il š.bᶜl š.ᶜnt*
(14) *ṣpn.alp.wš.pdry.š*

(15) *šrp.wšlmm ilib š*

(16) *bʿl ugrt š.bʿl ḫlb š*

(17) *yrḫ š.ʿnt ṣpn.alp*

(18) *wš.pdry š.ddmš.š*

(19) *wburbt.ilib.š*

(20) *bʿl.alp wš*

(21) *dgn.š.il tʿḏr.š*

(22) *bʿl š.ʿnt š.ršp š*

(23) *šlmm.*

86.72. A sacrificial stele (°6.13:1–3)

(1) *skn.dšʿlyt*

(2) *ṯryl.ldgn.pgr*

(3) [š] *walp lakl*

86.73. An incantation against snake bite (1.100:1–7, 57–76)

(1) *um.pḥl.pḥlt.bt.ʿn.bt.abn.bt.šmm wthm*

(2) *qrit.lšpš.umh.špš.um.ql.bl.ʿm*

(3) *il.mbk nhrm.bʿdt.thmtm*

(4) *mnt.nṯk.nḥš.šmrr.nḥš*

(5) *ʿqšr.lnh.mlḫš abd.lnh.ydy*

(6) *ḥmt.hlm.yṯq.nḥš.yšlḥm.ʿqšr*

(7) *yʿdb.ksa.wyṯb*

(57) *tqru lšpš.umh.špš.um.ql.bl*

(58) *ʿm.ḥrn.mṣdh.mnt.nṯk nḥš*

(59) *šmrr.nḥš.ʿqšr.lnh.mlḫš*

(60) *abd.lnh.ydy.ḥmt.*

(61) *bḥrn.pnm.trǵnw.wtṯkl*

(62) *bnwth.ykr.ʿr.dqdm*

(63) *idk.pnm.lytn.tk aršḫ.rbt*

(64) *waršḫ.ṯrrt.ydy.bʿṣm.ʿrʿr*

(65) *wbšḥt.ʿṣ.mt.ʿrʿrm.ynʿrnh*

(66) *ssnm.ysynh.ʿdtm.yʿdynh.yb*

(67) *ltm.yblnh.mǵy.ḥrn.lbth.w*

(68) *yštql.lḥẓrh.tlu.ḥ*(m)*t.km.nḫl*

(69) *tplg.km.plg*

(70) *bʿdh.bhtm.mnt.bʿdh.bhtm.sgrt*

(71) *bʿdh.ʿdbt.ṯlṯ.ptḥ.bt.mnt*

(72) *ptḥ.bt.wuba.hkl.wištql*

(73) *tn.km.*(mhry.)*nḥšm.yḥr.tn.km*

(74) *mhry.wbn.bṯn.itnny*

(75) *ytt.nḥšm.mhrk.bn bṯn*

(76) *itnnk*

86.74. Divination texts

86.741. From an inscription on a clay lung model (1.127:1–9, 29–31)

(1) *dbḥ kl yrḫ*

(2) *ndr*

(3) *dbḥ*

(4) *dt nat*

(5) *wytnt*

(6) *ṯrmn w*

(7) *dbḥ kl*

(8) *kl ykly*

(9) *dbḥ k.sprt*

(29) *hm qrt tuḫd.hm mt yʿl bnš*

(30) *bt bn bnš yqḥ ʿz*

(31) *wyḥdy mrḥqm*

86.742. An inscription on a clay liver model (°1.142:1–3)

(1) d*bḥt.byy b*n

(2) š*ry l*ʿ*ṯt*r?[ ]

(3) *d.bqbr*

86.743. A solar eclipse oracle (°1.78:1–6)

(1) *bṯṯ.ym.ḥdṯ*

(2) *ḫyr.ʿrbt*

(3) *špš ṯǵrh*

(4) *ršp*

(5) *kbdm tbqrn*

(6) *skn*

86.744. From an omen collection (1.103:1, 5, 16, 17, 37–42, 51, 54)

(1) [kt]*l*d a(ṯ)*t.abn.mad tntqln bḥwt*

(5) [ ]r*ǵbn ykn bḥwt*

(16) [w]i[n].i*bn.yḫlq bhmt* ḥw*t*

(17) [ ]*.ṯnn ʿz yuḫd ib mlk*

(37) *win udn šma*<.>*l.*b[h.]mlkn[.y]*šdd ḥwt i*b

(38) *wyḥslnn*

(39) *wqṣrt.pʿnh.bʿln yǵt*r[.ḫ]r*d wuḫr*

(40) *y.ykly* rš*p*

(41) waph.kap.ʿṣr.*ilm.tb*ʿrn.*ḥwt*

(42) [ ]*št.wydu*

(51) [ ]*bh.bph.yṣu.ibn.yspu.ḥwt*

(54) [ ]–*ḥrh.bpith.mlkn.yšlm libh*

86.75. How to get Baal's protection against the attacker (1.119:26–36)

(26) kgr ^{c}z. ṯǵrkm[.]qrd
(27) ḥmytkm.^{c}nkm.l[.]b^{c}l tšun
(28) yb^{c}lm.[a]l[.]tdy ^{c}z.ṯǵrn
(29) y.qrd [l]ḥmytny.ibr y
(30) b^{c}l.nšqdš.mḏr b^{c}l
(31) nmlu.[d?]kr b^{c}l.nš[q]dš
(32) ḥtp b^{c}l[.]nmlu.^{c}šrt.b^{c}l[.n^{c}]
(33) šr.qdš b^{c}[l.]n^{c}l.ntbt bt[.b^{c}l]
(34) ntlk.wšm[^{c}.b]^{c}[l.]l.ṣlt[km]
(35) ydy.^{c}z.lṯǵrkm[.qrd]
(36) lḥmytkm[ ]

87. *Poetic texts: Recurrent passages*

87.1. The duties of a son (from Aqhat; 1.17:I:25–33)

(25) wykn.bnh.bbt.šrš.bqrb
(26) hklh.nṣb.skn.ilibh.bqdš
(27) ztr.^{c}mh.larṣ.mšṣu.qṭrh
(28) l^{c}pr.ḏmr.aṯrh.ṭbq.lḥt
(29) niṣh.grš.d.^{c}šy.lnh
(30) aḫd.ydh.bškrn.m^{c}msh
(31) [k]šb^{c} yn.spu.ksmh.bt.b^{c}l
(32) [w]mnth bt.il.ṭḥ.ggh.bym
(33) [ṯi]ṭ.rḥṣ.npṣh.bym.rṯ

87.2. A blessing (from Keret; 1.15:II:12–20)

(12) [w]y^{c}n.aliy[n.]b^{c}l
(13) [ ]tb^{c}.llṭpn
(14) [il.]dpid.ltbrk
(15) [krt.]ṯ^{c}.ltmr.n^{c}mn
(16) [ǵlm.]il.ks.yiḫd
(17) [il.b]yd.krpn.bm
(18) [ym]n.brkm.ybrk
(19) [^{c}bdh].ybrk.il.krt
(20) [ṯ^{c}.ym]rm.n^{c}m[n.]ǵlm.il

87.3. Mourning (from the Baal Cycle; 1.5:VI:11–25b)

(11) apnk.lṭpn.il
(12) dpid.yrd.lksi.yṯb
(13) lhdm.wl.hdm.yṯb

(14) *larṣ*.y*ṣq*.^{c}*mr*
(15) *un*.*l*rišh.^{c}*pr*.*plṯt*
(16) *l*.*qdq*dh.*lpš*.*yks*
(17) *mizrtm*.*ǵr*.*babn*
(18) *ydy*.*psltm*.*by*^{c}r
(19) *yhdy*.*lḥm*.*w*dq*n*
(20) *yṯlṯ*.*qn*.*ḏr*^{c}h[.]*yḥrṯ*
(21) *kgn*.*ap lb*.*k*^{c}*m*q.*yṯlṯ*
(22) *bmt*.*yšu*.*gh*[.]*wyṣḥ*
(23) *b*^{c}*l*.*mt*.*my*.*lim*.*bn*
(24) *dgn*.*my*.*hmlt*.*aṯr*
(25) *b*^{c}*l*.*ard*.*barṣ*

87.4. Cursing an unknown murderer (from Aqhat; 1.19:IV:1–7)

(1) *ymǵ*.*lqrt*.*ablm*.*ab*lm
(2) *qrt*.*zbl*.*yrḫ*.*yšu* *g*h
(3) *wyṣḥ*.*ylk*.*qrt*.*ablm*
(4) *d*^{c}*lk*.*mḫṣ*.*aqht*.*ǵzr*
(5) ^{c}*wrt*.*yštk*.*b*^{c}*l*.*lht*
(6) *w*^{c}*lmh*.l^{c}*nt*.*pdr*.*dr*
(7) ^{c}*db*.*uḫry*.*mṭ*.*ydh*

87.5. Saddling a donkey (from Aqhat; 1.19:II:5b–11)

(5) *tš*[m^{c}]
(6) *pǵt*.*ṯkmt*.*my*.*ḥspt*.l[š^{c}]r.*ṭ*l
(7) *y*d^{c}*t*.*hlk*.*kbkbm*
(8) bk*m*.*tmdln*.^{c}*r*
(9) *bkm*.*tṣmd*.*pḥl*.*b*km
(10) *tšu*.*abh*.*tštnn*.*l*[b]*mt* ^{c}*r*
(11) *lysmsm*.*bmt*.*pḥl*

87.6 Invitation (from the Rephaim Texts; 1.22:II:3–6a)

Cf. 1.21:II:1–4, 9–12, 1.22:II:8–11

(3) *lk bty*.r[pim(rpim.bty.)aṣḥ]
(4) *km*.*iq*r[akm.ilnym.bhkly].
(5) *aṯrh*.r[pum.ltdd.aṯrh]
(6) *ltdd*.*il*[nym]

87.7. Entertaining guests (from the Baal Cycle; 1.4:VI:55–59)

Cf. 1.4:III:40–44, 1.5:IV:12–16

(55) ^{c}*d*.*lḥm*.*šty*.*il*m
(56) *wpq*.*mrǵṯm*.ṯd

(57) *bḫrb.mlḥt.qṣ*[.m]r
(58) *i.tšty.kr*p[nm.y]n
(59) [bk]s.ḫrṣ.d[m.^{c}ṣm]

87.8. A message for Anat (from the Baal Cycle; 1.3:III:8b–31)

(8) *km ǵlmm*
(9) *w.^{c}rbn.lp^{c}n.^{c}nt*.h*br*
(10) *wql.tštḥwy.kbd hyt*
(11) *w.rgm.lbtlt.^{c}nt*
(12) *ṯny.lymmt.limm*
(13) *tḥm.aliyn.b^{c}l.hwt*
(14) *aliy.qrdm.qryy.barṣ*
(15) ml*ḥmt št.b^{c}pr*m*.ddym*
(16) *sk.šlm.lkbd.arṣ*
(17) *arbdd.lkbd.šdm*
(18) *ḥšk.^{c}ṣk.^{c}bṣk*
(19) *^{c}my.p^{c}nk.tlsmn.^{c}my*
(20) *twtḥ.išdk.dm.rgm*
(21) *iṯ.ly.wargmk*
(22) *hwt.w.aṯnyk.rgm*
(23) *^{c}ṣ.w.lḫšt.abn*
(24) *tant.šmm.^{c}m.arṣ*
(25) *thmt.^{c}mn.kbkbm*
(26) *abn.brq.dl.td^{c}.šmm*
(27) *rgm ltd^{c}.nšm.wltbn*
(28) *hmlt.arṣ.atm.wank*
(29) *ibǵyh.btk.ǵry.il.ṣpn*
(30) *bqdš.bǵr.nḥlty*
(31) *bn^{c}m.bgb^{c}.tliyt*

88. *Poetic texts: Selected passages*

88.1. The Wedding of the Moon Deities (1.24:1, 16–23a, 30b–39)

(1) ašr *nkl wib*
(16) *ylak yrḫ* nyr *šmm.^{c}m*
(17) ḫr[ḫ]*b mlk qẓ.tn nkl y*
(18) *rḫ ytrḫ.ib t^{c}rbm bbh*
(19) *th.*watn *mhrh la*
(20) *bh.*alp *ksp wrbt ḫ*
(21) *rṣ.*išl*ḥ ẓhrm* iq
(22) *nim.*atn *šdh k*rm[m]
(23) *šd dd*h *ḥrnq*[m.]
(30) *wy^{c}*n
(31) *yrḫ nyr šmm.wn^{c}*n

(32) ʿmn nkl ḫtny.a[ḫ]r
(33) nkl yrḫ ytrḫ.adnh
(34) yšt mṣb.mznm.umh
(35) kp mznm.iḫh yṯʿr
(36) mšrrm.aḫtth la
(37) bn mznm.nkl wib
(38) dašr.ar yrḫ.wy
(39) rḫ yark

88.2. The Birth of the Twin Gods (1.23:23–24, 46b–53)

(23) iqran.ilm.nʿmm[.agzrym.bn]ym
(24) ynqm.bap zd.aṯrt.[ ]

(46) whn.aṯtm.tṣḥn.y.mt.mt
(47) nḥtm.ḫṭk.mmnnm.mṭ ydk.hl.ʿṣr
(48) tḥrr.lišt.wṣḥr(r)t.lpḥmm.aṯtm.aṯ[t.il]
(49) aṯt.il.wʿlmh.yhbr.špthm.yšq
(50) hn.špthm.mtqtm.mtqtm.klrmn[m]
(51) bm.nšq.whr.bḥbq.ḥmḥmt.tqt[nṣn w]
(52) tldn.šḥr.wšlm.rgm.lil.ybl.aṯ[ty]
(53) il.ylt.mh.ylt.yldy.šḥr.wšl[m]

88.3. The feast of Il (1.114:1–23)

(1) il dbḥ.bbth.mṣd.ṣd.bqrb
(2) hklh.ṣḥ.lqṣ.ilm.tlḥmn
(3) ilm.wtštn.tštn.y(n) ʿd šbʿ
(4) trṯ.ʿd.škr.yʿdb.yrḫ
(5) gbh.km.klb.yqṯqṭ.tḥt
(6) ṯlḥnt il.dydʿnn
(7) yʿdb.lḥm + d mṣd + lh.w d l ydʿnn
(8) + bqr(ʿ?) + y<.>lmn.ḫṭm.tḥt.ṯlḥn
(9) ʿṯtrt.wʿnt.ymǵy
(10) ʿṯtrt.tʿdb.nšb lh
(11) wʿnt.ktp.[-]bhm.ygʿr.ṯǵr
(12) bt.il.pn.lm.k!lb.tʿdbn
(13) nšb.linr.tʿdbn.ktp
(14) bil.abh.gʿr.yṯb.il.wl
(15) aṯr[t.]il.yṯb.bmrzḥh
(16) yšt.[y]n.ʿd šbʿ.trṯ. ʿd škr
(17) il.hlk.lbth.yštql.
(18) lḥẓrh.yʿmsn.nn.ṯkmn
(19) wšnm.wngšnn.ḥby.
(20) bʿl.qrnm wḏnb.ylšn
(21) bḫrih.wṯnth.ql.il.km mt
(22) il.kyrdm.arṣ.ʿnt
(23) wʿṯtrt.tṣdn.[ ]

88.4. The Poem of Baal-Hadd (1.12:II:53b–61)

(53) *kn.npl.b^{c}l*
(54) *km ṯr wtkms.hd.*
(55) *km.ibr.bt*k.*mšmš* b^{c}l
(56) *i*(š)*tt*k.*lawl*
(57) *išttk.lm.ttkn*
(58) *štk.mlk.dn*
(59) *štk.šibt.^{c}n*
(60) *štk.qr.b*t.*il*
(61) *wmṣlt.bt.ḥ*rš

88.5. The Baal Cycle

88.51. Baal and Yamm fight (1.2:IV:6–10, 18b–27)

(6) [b]*ph.rgm.lyṣa.bšpth.hwth.wttn.gh.yǵr*
(7) *tḥt.ksi.zbl.ym.w^{c}n.kṯr.wḫss.lrgmt*
(8) *lk.lzbl.b^{c}l.ṯnt.lrkb.^{c}rpt.ht. ibk*
(9) *b^{c}lm.ht.ibk.tmḫṣ.ht.tṣmt ṣrtk*
(10) *tqḥ.mlk.^{c}lmk.drkt.dt.drdrk.*

---

(18) *kṯr.ṣmdm.ynḥt.wyp^{c}r.šmthm*
(19) *šmk.at.aymr.aymr.mr.ym.mr.y*m
(20) *lksih.nhr.lkḥṯ.drkth.trtqṣ*
(21) *bd b^{c}l.km.nšr buṣb^{c}th.hlm.qdq*
(22) *d.zbl ym.bn.^{c}nm.ṯpṭ.nhr.yprsḥ ym*
(23) wy*ql.larṣ.wyrtqṣ.ṣmd.bd b^{c}l*
(24) km[.]*nšr.buṣb^{c}th.ylm.qdqd.zbl*
(25) ym.*bn ^{c}nm.ṯpṭ.nhr.yprsḥ.ym.yql*
(26) *larṣ.tnǵṣn.pnth.wydlp.tm*nh
(27) *yqṯ b^{c}l.wyšt.ym.ykly.ṯpṭ.nhr*

88.52. Anat intervenes on Baal's behalf (1.3:V:29b–34)

(29) *wt*[^{c}]n.*btlt.^{c}n*t
(30) *tḥmk.il.ḥkm*[.]*ḥkmk*
(31) *^{c}m.^{c}lm.ḥyt.ḥẓt.tḥmk*
(32) *mlkn.aliyn.b^{c}l.ṯpṭn*
(33) *in.d^{c}lnh.klnyy.qšh*
(34) *nbln.klnyy.nbl.ksh*

88.53. Il allows Baal to build a house (1.4:V:12–19)

(12) *lyrgm.lali*yn *b*^{c}*l*
(13) *ṣḥ.ḫrn.bbh*t!*k*
(14) ^{c}*ḏbt.bqrb.hklk*
(15) *tblk.ǵrm.mid.ksp.*
(16) *gb*^{c}*m.mḥmd.ḫrṣ*
(17) *yblk.udr.ilqṣm*
(18) *wbn.bht.ksp.wḫrṣ*
(19) *bht.ṭhrm.iqnim*

88.54. Mot threatens Baal (1.5:I:1–8)

(1) *ktmḫṣ.ltn.bṯn.brḥ*
(2) *tkly.bṯn.*^{c}*qltn.*
(3) *šlyṭ.d.šb*^{c}*t.rašm*
(4) *tṯkḥ.ttrp.š*mm*.krs*
(5) *ipdk.ank.ispi.uṭm*
(6) *ḏrqm.amtm.lyrt*
(7) *bnpš.bn ilm.mt.bmh*
(8) *mrt.ydd.il.ǵzr*

88.55. Anat's revenge on Mot (1.6:II:13–37a)

(13) *w*^{c}*n.*bn*.ilm.mt.mh*
(14) *taršn.lbtlt.*^{c}*nt*
(15) *an.itlk.waṣd.kl*
(16) *ǵr.lkbd.arṣ.kl.gb*^{c}
(17) *lkbd.šdm.npš.ḫ*srt
(18) *bn.nšm.npš.hmlt.*
(19) *arṣ.mǵt.ln*^{c}*my.arṣ*
(20) *dbr.ysmt.šd.šḥlmmt*
(21) *ngš.ank.aliyn b*^{c}*l*
(22) ^{c}*dbnn ank.imr .bpy*
(23) *klli.bṯbrn q*(n)*y.ḫtu hw*
(24) *nrt.il*m*.špš.ṣḥrrt*
(25) *la.šmm.byd.bn ilm.mt*
(26) *ym.ymm.y*^{c}*tqn.lymm*
(27) *lyrḫm.rḥm.*^{c}*nt.tngṯh*
(28) *klb.arḫ.l*^{c}*glh.klb*
(29) *ṯat.limrh.km.lb*
(30) ^{c}*nt.aṯr.b*^{c}*l.tiḫd*
(31) *bn.ilm.mt.bḥrb*

(32) *tbq^{c}nn.bḫṯr.tdry*
(33) *nn.bišt.tšrpnn*
(34) *brḥm.tṭḥnn.bšd*
(35) *tdr^{c}nn.širh.ltikl*
(36) ^{c}ṣrm.*mnth.ltkly*
(37) *npr*[m].š*ir.lšir.yṣḥ*

88.56. Anat visits Baal (1.10:II:10–25)

(10) *tšu knp.btlt.*^{c}n[t]
(11) *tšu.knp.wtr.b^{c}p*
(12) *tk.a*ḫ *šmk.mlat* rumm
(13) *wyšu.^{c}nh.aliyn.b^{c}l*
(14) *wyšu.^{c}nh.wy^{c}n*
(15) *wy^{c}n.btlt.^{c}nt*
(16) *n^{c}mt.b*n.*aḫt.b^{c}l*
(17) *lpnnh.ydd.wyqm*
(18) *lp^{c}nh.ykr^{c}.wyql*
(19) *wyšu.gh.wyṣḥ*
(20) *ḥwt.aḫt.wnar*k
(21) *qrn.dbatk.bt*lt.^{c}nt
(22) *qrn.dbatk.b^{c}l.ymšḥ*
(23) *b^{c}l.ymšḥ.hm.b^{c}p*
(24) *nṭ^{c}n.barṣ.iby*
(25) *wb^{c}pr.qm.aḫk*

88.57. Baal's son-bull is born (1.10:III:32–37)

(32) *ql.lb^{c}l.ttn*n
(33) *bšrt.il.*bš[r.b]^{c}*l*
(34) w*bšr.*ḥ*tk.*dgn
(35) k.*ibr.lb^{c}l*[.]yld
(36) wr*um.lr*kb[.]^{c}rpt
(37) *yš*m*ḫ.a*l*iyn.*b^{c}*l*

88.6. The Aqhat Legend

88.61. Il hears Daniel's requests (1.17:I:15b–19)

(15) *mk.bšb^{c}.ymm*
(16) [w]*yqrb.b^{c}l.bḥnth.abyn*at
(17) [d]n*il.mt.rpi anḫ.ġzr*
(18) mt.*hrnmy.din.bn.lh*
(19) *km.aḫh.w.šrš.km.aryh*

88.62. The artisan god brings the bow (1.17:V:21b–33)

(21) *tšmʿ*
(22) *mṯt.dnty.tʿdb.imr*
(23) *bpḫd.lnpš.kṯr.wḫss*
(24) *lbrlt.hyn.dḥrš*
(25) *ydm.aḫr.ymǵy.kṯr*
(26) *wḫss.bd.dnil.ytnn*
(27) *qšt.lbrkh.yʿdb*
(28) q*ṣʿt.apnk.mṯt.dnty*
(29) *tšlḥm.tššqy ilm*
(30) *tsad.tkbd.hmt.bʿl*
(31) *ḥkpt il.klh.tbʿ.kṯ*r
(32) *lahlh.hyn.tbʿ.lmš*
(33) *knth*

88.63. Anat asks for the bow (1.17:VI:25b–45)

(25) *wtʿn.bt*lt
(26) *ʿnt.irš.ḥym.laqht.ǵzr*
(27) i*rš.ḥym.watnk.blmt*
(28) w*ašlḥk.ašsprk.ʿm.bʿl*
(29) *šnt.ʿm.bn il.tspr.yrḫm*
(30) *kbʿl.kyḥwy.yʿšr.ḥwy.yʿš*
(31) *r.wyšqynh.ybd.wyšr.ʿlh*
(32) *n*ʿmn[.wt]*ʿnynn.ap ank.aḥwy*
(33) *aq*ht[.ǵz]r.*wyʿn.aqht.ǵzr*
(34) *al.t*šr*gn.ybtltm.dm.lǵzr*
(35) *šrgk.ḫḫm.m*t!.*uḫryt.mh.yqḥ*
(36) *mh.yqḥ.mt.aṯryt.spsg.ysk*
(37) [l]r*iš.ḥrṣ.lẓr.qdqdy*
(38) [ky?]m*t.kl.amt.wan.mtm.amt*
(39) [ap.m]*ṯn.rgmm.argm.qštm*
(40) [ ]m*hrm.ht.tṣdn.tinṯt*
(41) [ ]m.*tṣḥq.ʿnt.wblb.tqny*
(42) [ ]*ṯb.ly.laqht.ǵzr.ṯb ly wlk*
(43) [ ]h?*m.laqryk.bntb.pšʿ*
(44) [ ].*bntb.gan.aš*q*lk.tḥt*
(45) [pʿny.a]n!*k.nʿmn.ʿmq.nšm*

88.64. Anat plots Aqhat's death (1.18:IV:16–27a)

(16) w*tʿn.btlt.ʿnt.ṯb.yṭp.w*[ ]
(17) *lk.aštk.km.nšr.bḥ*b[šy]
(18) *km.diy.btʿrty.aqht.*[km.yṯb]

(19) *lḥm.wbn.dnil.lṯ*rm.[^{c}lh]
(20) *nšrm.trḫpn.ybṣr.*[ḥbl.d]
(21) *iym.bn.nšrm.arḫp.a*n[k.^{c}]l
(22) *aqht.*^{c}*dbk.hlmn.ṯnm.q*dq*d*
(23) *ṯlṯid.*^{c}*l.udn.špk.km.šiy*
(24) *dm.km.šḫṭ.lbrkh.tṣi.km*
(25) *rḥ.npšh.km.iṯl.brlth.km*
(26) *qṭr.baph.u*/b!*ap.mp*/h!*rh.ank*
(27) *laḥwy*

88.65. Daniel buries his son's remains (1.19:III:28b–45a)

(28) bn*ši.*^{c}*nh.*
(29) w*yphn.yḥd.ṣml.*um*.nšr*m
(30) y*š*u*.gh.*w*yṣḥ.kn*p*.ṣm*l.
(31) *b*^{c}*l.yṯbr.b*^{c}*l.yṯ*br.di*y*
(32) *hyt.tql.tḥt.p*^{c}*ny.i*bq^{c}
(33) kb*d*h.*waḥd.hm.iṯ*.š*m*t*.iṯ*
(34) ^{c}*ẓm.abky.waqbrnh.aštn*
(35) b*ḫrt.ilm.arṣ.bph.rgm.l*y[ṣ]*a*
(36) b*špth.hwth.knp.ṣm*l.*b*^{c}[l]
(37) b^{c}*l.ṯbr.diy.hyt.tq*l.tḥt
(38) *p*^{c}*nh.ybq*^{c}*.kbdh.w*y*ḥd*
(39) *iṯ.šmt.iṯ.*^{c}*ẓm.w*yqḥ.b*hm*
(40) a*qht.yb.l*lq*ẓ.ybky.*wyqbr
(41) *yqbr.nn.b*mdg*t.b*knr?*t*
(42) *wyšu.gh.wyṣḥ.knp.nšrm*
(43) *b*^{c}*l.yṯbr.b*^{c}*l.yṯbr.diy*
(44) *hmt.hm.t*^{c}*pn.*^{c}*l.qbr.b*ny
(45) *tšḫṭa.nn.bšnth*

88.7. The Keret Epos

88.71. From Keret's dream-vision (1.14:III:10b–49)

(10) *dm.ym.wṯn*
(11) *ṯlṯ.rb*^{c}*.ym.*ḫ!*mš*
(12) *ṯdṯ.ym.ḥẓk.al.tš*^{c}*l*
(13) *qrth.abn.ydk*
(14) *mšdpt.whn.špšm*
(15) *bšb*^{c}*.wl.yšn.pbl*
(16) *mlk.lqr.ṯigt.ibrh*
(17) *lql.nhqt.ḥmrh*
(18) *lg*^{c}*t.alp.ḫrṯ.zġt*
(19) *klb.ṣpr.wylak*
(20) *mlakm.lk.*^{c}*m.krt*

(21) *mswnh.tḥm.pbl.mlk*
(22) *qḥ.ksp.wyrq.ḫrṣ*
(23) *yd.mqmh.wʿbd.ʿlm*
(24) *ṯlṯ.sswm.mrkbt*
(25) *btrbṣ.bn.amt*
(26) *qḥ.krt.šlmm*
(27) *šlmm.wng.mlk*
(28) *lbty.rḥq.krt*
(29) *lḥẓry.al.tṣr*
(30) *udm.rbt.wudm ṯrrt*
(31) *udm.ytn*t!*.il.wušn*
(32) *ab.adm.wṯṯb*
(33) *mlakm.lh.lm.ank*
(34) *ksp.wyrq.ḫrṣ*
(35) *yd.mqmh.wʿbd*
(36) *ʿlm.ṯlṯ.sswm.mrkbt*
(37) *btrbṣt.bn.amt*
(38) *pd.in.bbty.ttn*
(39) *tn.ly.mṯt.ḥry*
(40) *nʿmt.špḥ.bkrk*
(41) d*k.nʿm.ʿnt.nʿmh*
(42) *km.tsm.ʿṯtrt.ts*mh
(43) *dʿqh.ib.iqni.ʿp*[ʿp]h
(44) *sp.ṯrml.tḥgrn.*[ ]d*m*
(45) *ašlw.bṣp.ʿnh*
(46) *dbḥlmy.il.yt*n
(47) *bḏrty.ab.adm*
(48) *wld.špḥ.lkrt*
(49) *wǵlm.lʿbd.il*

88.72. Keret's vow to Athirat (1.14:IV:31b–43)

(31) *tlkn*
(32) *ym.wṯn.a*ḫ*r*
(33) *špšm.bṯlṯ*
(34) *y*m[ǵy.]*lqdš*
(35) *aṯ*[r]t[.]*ṣrm.wlilt*
(36) *ṣd*[y]n*m.ṯm*
(37) *yd*r[.]k*rt.ṯʿ*
(38) *iiṯt.aṯrt.ṣrm*
(39) *wilt.ṣdynm*
(40) *hm.ḥ*r*y.bty*
(41) *iqḥ.ašʿrb.ǵlmt*
(42) *ḥẓry.ṯnh.*k!*spm*
(43) *atn.w.ṯlṯh.ḫrṣm*

88.73. Keret's illness (1.16:I:11b–30)

(11) ^{c}*l*
(12) *abh.y*^{c}rb!.*ybky*
(13) *wyšnn.ytn.gh*
(14) *bky.bḥyk.abn.*nšm*ḫ*
(15) *blmtk.ngln.kklb*
(16) *b*bt*k.n*^{c}*tq.kinr*
(17) *a*p! *ḫštk.ap.ab.kmtm*
(18) *tmtn.uḫštk.lntn*
(19) ^{c}*tq.bd.a*t̲*tab.ṣrry*
(20) i*km.yrgm.bn il*
(21) kr*t.špḥ.lṭpn*
(22) *wqdš.uilm tmtn*
(23) *špḥ.lṭpn.lyḥ*
(24) wy^{c}*ny.krt.*t̲^{c}
(25) *b*n*.al.tbkn.al*
(26) *t*d*m.ly.al tkl.bn*
(27) qr.^{c}*nk.mḫ.rišk*
(28) *udm*^{c}*t.ṣḥ.aḫtk*
(29) *t̲tmnt.bt..ḥmḥh*
(30) *da?n.tbkn.wtdm.ly* tt̲(?)b

89. *Concordance of major texts*

In addition to the major texts in the Ugaritic language, all texts presented in this book are included (BGUL) following the order of KTU. The items in the first column are incomplete unless marked °; the listings in the other columns refer to complete texts. The sigla used in Virolleaud's publications of the great literary texts are given here because they are used in a variety of old but still valuable treatments. Some texts have several UT numbers: only the actual text number is given here.

The following numbering conventions should be noted:

KTU 1.1–25 = CTA 1–25
UT 601–614 = U:V:1–14
UT 1001–1189 = P(RU):II:1–189
UT 2001–2172 = P(RU):V:1–172

Differences in the numbering of individual lines, most of them minor, are not noted here. Roman numerals indicate columns of the original tablets; Arabic numerals after the colon refer to the lines.

1. Literary and religious texts

BGUL	KTU	UT	Virolleaud	Content
				1.1–6 Baal Cycle
	1.1	^{c}nt *in part*	VI AB	Baal and Yamm
	II:1–III:30	pl. ix	pl. ix	
	IV:1–V:28	pl. x	pl. x	
	1.2			Baal and Yamm
	I:1–17	137	III AB,B	
	II:1–15			
	III:1–24	129	III AB,C	
88.51 = IV:6–10, 18–27	IV:1–40	68	III AB,A	
	1.3	^{c}nt *in part*	V AB	Baal and Anat
	I:1–II:41	I.1–II.41		
	III:1–3	II:42–44		
87.8 = III:8–31	III:4–47	III:1–44		
	IV:1–46	IV:45–90		
	IV:48–55	pl. vi:IV:1–8		
88.52 = V:29–34	V:1–43	V:9–51		
	VI:1–25	VI:1–25		

BGUL	KTU	UT	Virolleaud	Content
	1.4	51	II AB	Baal's Palace
85.2 = IV:20–39	I:1–IV:62	I:1–IV:62		
88.53 = V:12–19	V:1–65	V:63–127		
87.7 = VI:55–59	VI:1–VIII:49	VI:1–VIII:49		
	1.5	67	I* AB	Baal and Mot
88.54 = I:1–8	I:1–III:30	I:1–III:29		
87.3 = VI:11–25	IV:1–VI:31	IV:1–VI:31		
	1.6		I AB	Baal and Mot
	I:1–28	62:1–28		
	I:29–67	49:I:1–39		
88.55 = II:13–37	II:1–III:24	49:II:1–III:24		
	IV:1–27	49:IV:25–51		
	V:1–VI:38	49:V:1–VI:38		
	VI:39–58	62:38–57		
	1.10	76	IV AB	Baal and the Cow
	I:1–18	I:1–18		
	I:20–24	I:19–23		
88.56 = II:10–25	II:1–38	II:1–38		
88.57 = III:32–37	III:1–37	III:2–38		
	1.12	75	BH	The Poem of Baal-Hadd
	I:1–II:6	I:1–II:6		
88.4 = II:53–61	II:7–61	II:8–62		
	1.13	6		Hymn to Anat
	1–36	1–36		
				1.14–16 Keret Epos
	1.14	Krt	I K	
	I:1–43	1–43		
	II:1–51	54–104		
88.71 = III:10–49	III:1–59	105–163		
88.72 = IV:31–43	IV:1–52	164–215		
	V:1–28	216–243		
	V:30–45	246–261		
	VI:1–41	266–306		

BGUL	KTU	UT	Virolleaud	Content
87.2 = II:12–20	1.15 I:1–VI:9	128 I:1-VI:9	III K	
88.73 = I:11–30 85.1 = VI:39–59	1.16 I:1–62 II:1–58 III:1–17 IV:1–17 V:1–36 V:37–52 VI:1-59	 125:1–62 125:63–120 126:III:1–17 126:IV:2–18 126:V:1–36 126:V:38–53 127:1–59	 II K, I–II II K, III–V II K, VI	
				1.17–19 Aqhat Legend
 88.61 = I:15–19 87.1 = I:25–33 88.62 = V:21–33 88.63 = VI:25–45	1.17 I:1–47 II:1–47 V:1–VI:55	2 Aqht I:2–48 II:1–47 V:1–VI:55	II D	
88.64 = IV:16–27	1.18 I:1–34 IV:1–42	3 Aqht "rev.": 1–34 "obv.":1–42	III D	
  87.5 = II:5–11 88.65 = III:28–45 87.4 = IV:1–7	1.19 I:1–49 II:1–57 III:1–56 IV:1–61	1 Aqht 1–49 50–106 107–162 163–223	I D	
				1.20–22 "Rephaim" Texts
	1.20 I:1–II:12	121 I:1–II:12	I Rp.	
	1.21 II:1–13	122 1–13	II Rp	
  87.6 = II:3–6	1.22 I:1–28 II:1–26	 124:1–28 123:1–26	 III Rp. B III Rp. A	

BGUL	KTU	UT	Virolleaud	Content
88.2 = 23–24, 46–53	1.23 1–76	52 1–76	SS	The Birth of the Twin Gods
88.1 = 1, 16–23, 30–39	1.24 1–50	77 1–50	NK	The Wedding of the Moon Deities
			CTA	
	1.39	1	34	sacrifices
	1.40	2	32	protective ritual
	1.41	3	35	sacrifices
	1.47	17	29	god list
86.62 = 23–26	1.71	55	160	hippiatric text
°86.743 = 1–6	1.78	143		solar eclipse oracle
°86.51 = 1–5	1.80	1153		slaughter of small cattle
	1.82	1001		poetry
86.61 = 1	1.85			hippiatric text
	1.86	2158		dream oracle
	1.87	173	App. II	sacrifices (cf. 1.41)
	1.92	2001		poetry
82.6 = 1–5	1.96			poetry/ritual
86.73 = 1–7, 57–76	1.100	607		poetry/snake-bite incantation
	1.101	603		poetry
86.744 = 1, 5, 16, 17, 37–42, 51–54	1.103			omen collection
81.3 = 1–2	1.105	612		ritual
	1.107	608		poetry/incantation (cf. 1.100)
	1.108	602		poetry
86.71 = 1–23	1.109	613		ritual
88.3 = 1–23	1.114	601		poetry/feast of Il
82.5 = 1–2, 9–10	1.115	611		offerings
	1.118			god list
86.75 = 26–36	1.119			ritual seeking Baal's protection
	1.124	606		poetry
86.741 = 1–9, 29–31	1.127	801		oracle/lung model

BGUL	KTU	UT	CTA	Content
°86.742=1–3	1.142	802		oracle/liver model
	1.148	609		offerings
	1.161			evocation of the dead

2. Letters

BGUL	KTU	UT	CTA	Content
	2.4	18	55	to the high priest
°86.43=1–19	2.10	54	53	Iwri-žarri to Pilsiya
	2.11	95	51	Talmiyan to the Queen Mother
	2.12	89	52	Talmiyan to the Queen
	2.13	117	50	the King to the Queen Mother
	2.14	138		from Iwri-žarri
°86.45=1–10	2.15	1020		*gnryn* to *mlkytn*, an informal letter
°84.1=1–20	2.16	1015		Talmiyan to the Queen Mother
	2.19	1005		contract(!)
	2.26	1010		the King's order
83.4=16–24	2.30	1013		the King to the Queen Mother
86.42=22–39	2.33	1012		Commandant Irri-tharruma to the Queen
	2.34	2009		the King to the Queen Mother
°86.41=1–27	2.38	2059		the King of Tyre to the King of Ugarit
	2.39	2060		the Hittite king to the King of Ugarit
	2.40	2063		to the King of Ugarit
83.3=16–22	2.41	2065		one king to another
	2.42	2008		a commandant to the king

BGUL	KTU	UT	CTA	Content
	2.47	2062		to the King of Ugarit
°86.44=1–13	2.61	2114		report about looting to a superior
82.1=13–16	2.64	2115		a double letter
	2.70			to *yrdm*
	2.71			Talmiyan to *pzr*
	2.72			to the Queen Mother

3. Contracts

BGUL	KTU	UT	CTA	Content
86.31=22–28	3.1	118	64	tribute for the Hittite king
	3.2	1009		royal grant of a house
	3.3	1161		a list of pledges
°86.32=1–19	3.4	1006		redemption of captives
°86.33=1–21	3.5	1008		royal grant of real property
	3.8	2116		on payment
°86.53=1–21	3.9	702		a document of a /marziḥu/ association

4. Lists and administrative documents

BGUL	KTU	UT	CTA	Content
86.53=1–2, 11	4.31	57	207	on oil; written from right to left
	4.63	321	119	a list of soldiers
	4.68	113	71	a list of villages
	4.69	400	113	a list of soldiers
	4.103	300	82	a list of fields
	4.126	169		a list of guilds/professions
°86.21=1–2	4.135	1132		a record of a debt of silver
81.5=1–5	4.143	1096		a record of olive trees and oil supplies

BGUL	KTU	UT	CTA	Content
82.3=1–2	4.145	1121		a chariot roster
°86.25=1–8	4.146	1108		a list of clothes and their prices
86.23=1–3, 24–30	4.123	1084		wine records
°86.22=1–7	4.266	1156		a receipt
86.52=1–5	4.277	1045		a list of persons; in substandard orthography
°86.24=1–5	4.279	1086		wine rations
82.4=1–3 86.26=10–18	4.338	2106		a list of persons a record of trade with the king of Byblos bottomry loan(?)
81.4=1–4	4.349	2081		a list of persons
86.13=1–2	4.356	2089		transfers of fields
86.12=1–5	4.360	2080		a list of persons
	4.369	2107		a list of tribute
83.1=1	4.422	2023		a list of persons
82.2=6–7	4.630	2052		a rations roster involving wool

5. *Alphabets and scribal exercises*

cf. **21.5**	5.6	401		an alphabet tablet
83.2=7–16	5.9	1019		a letter/exercise
	5.10			cf. 5.9, letter/exercise
	5.11			cf. 5.9, letter/exercise
cf. p. 21	5.14	1189		an alphabet with syllabic equivalents

6. *Short inscriptions*

°81.1=1	6.6	b		bronze adze
86.72=1–3	6.13	69		offering stele
	6.14	70		offering stele
	6.23			royal seal (U:III, p. 81)
°81.2=1–2	6.24	1175		dossier label

Part 9

Glossary

Glossary

91. *Arrangement*

The lexical items are arranged according to the sequence of the Hebrew alphabet with the distinctive Ugaritic letters inserted (between dashes): /ᵓ/: *-a, i, u-*; *b*; *g*; *d*; *-ḏ-*; *h*; *w*; *z*; *ḥ*; *-ḫ-*; *ṭ*; *-ẓ-*; *y*; *k*; *l*; *m*; *n*; *s* and *-ś-;* ᶜ; *-ǵ-*; *p*; *ṣ*; *q*; *r*; *š* and *-Š-*; *t*; *-ṯ-*.

Nouns and particles are given in their basic form, while verbs are represented by roots, cited between slashes. For nouns not attested in singular, non-suffixed form, the actually attested forms are given. If a verbal root cannot be determined with sufficient certainty, only two root consonants are given, e.g., /-b-d-/. The actual verb forms are quoted after a colon.

Cognate words from other Semitic languages are quoted only when they help in determining the form and meaning of the Ugaritic lexical items: Canaanite languages: Hebrew (abbreviated H.); Phoenician (Phoen.); occasionally Old Canaanite (the language reflected in the El-Amarna letters; forms from the texts are cited with the siglum EA); Aramaic languages: Aram. (if no other characteristic is added, this means Biblical Aramaic), Syriac (Syr.); Arabic: Classical (Arab.), and dialects; Epigraphic (or Ancient) South Arabian (ESA); Ethiopic (Ethiop.); Akkadian (Akkad.). Akkadian forms are those of the dictionaries and grammars, unless a citation follows—this indicates forms attested at Ugarit—or the term Mari precedes—this indicates forms from the Mari texts.

92. *Words and meanings*

The meanings of Ugaritic words have been determined to some extent by trial and error. There are still many uncertainties, especially concerning words which do not appear frequently in the texts. The number of simple and double question-marks in the glossary should perhaps be even larger than it is.

Especially early in Ugaritic studies, the formal similarity between Hebrew words known from the biblical tradition and Ugaritic words was used for determining the values. Other Semitic languages were also found helpful, notably Arabic, because of the richness of both its phoneme inventory and its lexical resources, and Akkadian, because of its antiquity and its role as cultural and commercial language. Aramaic and Ethiopic also provided meaningful equivalents. The results reached by this comparative method have to be carefully tested against the Ugaritic texts. Combinatory methods have been used alongside comparative study and have led to viable determinations of meaning.

In some instances relations between words attested in the Ugaritic texts and archeological finds at Ras Shamra or other sites can be referred to. The syllabic cuneiform vocabularies give words in four languages (Sumerian, Akkadian, Hurrian and Ugaritic) (cf. U:V:130–137). These became available after many meanings and forms had already been determined by other methods.

93. *Glossary to selected texts in part* 8

/ʾ/: ***a, i, u***

i particle 1.14:IV:38 = **88.72**, perhaps /ʾē/ "where?" or "o!" (Arab. ʾay) or /ʾī/ introducing an oath (Arab. ʾī)

u /ʾō/ "or" (H. ʾō, Arab., Syr. ʾaw, Akkad. ū)

ab /ʾab-/ "father" (H. ʾāb)

ib: ***iby, ibk, ibm*** /ʾēb-/ "enemy" (H. ʾōyēb, Akkad. ayyābu)

ib /ʾibb-/(?) 1.14:III:43 = **88.71** "splendor" > "gem" (Akkad. ebbu "bright, pure")

ib /ʾibb-/ DN f. *nkl.wib*

uba 1.100:72 = **86.73** see /b-w-ʾ/

abd 1.100:5 = **86.73** "destruction"(?) or verb /ʾ-b-d/ "to destroy"(?) (cf. H. ʾ-b-d)

abyn 1.17:I:16 = **88.61** "wretched, poor" (H. ʾæbyōn "poor") or *abyn*<a>t "misery" (cf. Postbibl. H. ʾæbyōnūt "distress")

ablm see *qrt. ablm*

abn /ʾabn-/ 1.103:1 = **86.744** "stone," 1.24:36–37 = **88.1** "(stone) weight," 1.14:III:13 = **88.71** "(stone) projectile" (thrown by a sling) (H. ʾǽbæn, Syr. ʾabnā, Akkad. abnu)

ubnyn PN

ibsn /ʾib(ū)sān-/ 3.9:5 = **84.2** "dining room"(?), "store room"(?) (cf. H. ʾēbūs "manger," maʾăbūs "granary," ʾ-b-s "to feed, fatten"; Akkad. abūsu "store room, manger") (or *ibs* + *-n* suff. 1. pl.(?))

ibr "(humped) buffalo" (cf. H. ʾabbīr "strong"; ʾăbīr Gen 49:24; Isa 1:24)

agdn PN (Hurrian)

agzr 1.23:23 = **88.2** "voracious" (cf. H. g-z-r as in Isa 9:19)

ugrt GN, gen.-acc. *u-ga-ri-ta* RS 6.198:5, Syria 16, 189; *ú-ga-ri-it* P:III:15.33:5 (p. 15)

id "then" (Arab. ʾiḏā)

idk "then"

adm "man(kind)" (H. ʾādām)

udm GN fem. (cf. H. ʾædōm, Akkad. udumu)

udmʿt /(ʾ)udmaʿāt-/ or /-muʿ-/(?) pl. "tears" (cf. H. dimʿā sing. coll., dəmāʿōt pl.)

adn /ʾadān-/ cf. *a-da-nu* U:V:130:II:9′, 1.24:33 = **88.1** "father (head of household)"; "lord" (cf. H. ʾādōn; Ug. PN *a-du-nu* /ʾadōnu/ P:VI:139:2)

idn 2.15:5 = **86.45** "hearing, audience"(?) (cf. *udn* "ear," H. ʾ-z-n Hi. "to hear"); "permission"(?) (cf. Arab. ʾiḏn)

udn /ʾudn-/ "ear" (Jew.-Aram. ʾudnā, H. ʾózæn, Arab. ʾuḏn, Akkad. uznu)

adr /ʾad(d)ūr-/ cf. *a-du-rum* U:V:137:II:34′ "mighty"

udr "camel caravan"(?) (cf. Akkad. udru); "precious stone(s)"(?)

udrnn PN

ahbt /ʾahbat-/ "loving, love" (H. ʾahăbā)

ahl /ʾahl-/ "tent" (cf. H. ʾóhæl; Arab. ʾahl "tent" > "family, people")

awl 1.12:II:56 = **88.4** "help"(?)

iwrḏr /(ʾ)iwrižarru/ PN (Hurrian, cf. ibri-šarru P:VI:86:I:13)

iwrkl /(ʾ)iwri-kalli/ PN (Hurrian)

aḥd /ʾaḥad-/, fem. *aḥt* /ʾaḥatt-/ "one" (H. ʾæḥād < *ʾaḥ(ḥ)ad, f. ʾaḥat < *-dt; Arab. ʾaḥad)

aḥdh with adverbial *-h* "at once, together" (cf. H. yaḥdāw)

aḫrṯp (sic) 4.277:5 = **86.52** (cf. the correct form *aḫršp* 4.370:7) PN /ʾaḫu-rašap(i)/ ("Brother of the (god) Rašap"): cf. *iḫršp* 3.9:18 = **84.2**

aḥt see *aḥd*

aḫ /ʾaḫ-/: *iḫh, iḫy, uḫy* cf. *a-ḫu* U:V:135:rev.:19 "brother" (H. ʾāḥ, Aram. ʾaḥ-, Yaʾudi-Aram. ʾyḥy, ʾyḥ(y)h, Arab. ʾaḫ(ū), Akkad. aḫu)

aḫ 1.10:II:12 = **88.56** ("reeds"(?) >) "swamp" (cf. H. ʾāḥū; cf. Early Aram. ʾḥw(h))

/ʾ-ḫ-d/: imperf. *iḫd, yiḫd, yuḫd* 1.103:17 = **86.744**, *tiḫd*, part. *aḫd* "to seize, take hold"; Gp imperf.(?) *tuḫd* 1.127:29 = **86.741** "to be seized" (H. ʾāḥaz, yæʾĕḥōz and yō(ʾ)ḥēz, Anc.-Aram. ʾ-ḥ-z and ʾ-ḥ-d, Arab. ʾaḫaḏa, yaʾḫuḏu, Akkad. aḫāzu)

iḫh and ***iḫy*** see *aḫ*

uḫy see *aḫ*

aḫr adv. "afterwards" 1.24:32 = **88.1** (or "with"?); 1.17:V:25 = **88.62** (or conj. "after"?); 1.14:IV:32 = **88.72** (or prep. "after the sun(set)"?) (cf. H. ʾaḥar, ʾaḥărē)

uḫry 1.19:IV:7 = **87.4** "the other/next world" (cf. Arab. al-ʾuḫrā(y)); 1.103:39 = **86.744**

"posterity" (cf. H. ᵓaḥărīt; Anc.-Aram. ᵓḥrt; Akkad. aḫrūtu)

uḫryt 1.17:VI:35 = **88.63** "latter end, future" (cf. H. ᵓaḥărīt)

iḫršp PN, see *aḥrṯp*

aḫt: pl. *aḫt*, *aḫtth* "sister" (H. ᵓāḥōt, Phoen. A-ḫu-ut (in PN), Jew.-Aram. ᵓāḥātā, Akkad. ᵓaḫātu)

uṭm 1.5:I:5 = **88.54** sing.(?) or pl. (i.e., of *uṭ*)(?) "morsel, bite"(?), "funeral meal"(?) (cf. Arab. waṭm) (or cf. H. ᵓiṭṭīm pl.(?) "ghosts"(?), Akkad. eṭemmu "ghost")

aymr 1.2:IV:19 = **88.51** name of an ax/club, "(O-what-a-) Driver," "Ho, expel!" cf. /-m-r-/

ik, *ikm* "how?, why?" (cf. H. ᵓēk(ā))

/ᵓ-k-l/: *tikl* "to eat" (H. ᵓākal, yō(ᵓ)kel, Aram. ᵓăkálū, yō(ᵓ)kul, Arab. ᵓakala, yaᵓkulu)

akl /ᵓakl-/ "food" (cf. Arab. akl)

ikm see *ik*

al /ᵓal/ "not" with jussive (H. ᵓal, Phoen. ᵓl)

al /ᵓal/ "verily" 1.119:28 = **86.75**

il /ᵓil-/: *ilm* sing. with *-m* 1.5:I:7 = **88.54**; *ilm* du. and pl. abs.; *il* du. constr. 1.17:V:31 = **88.62**; *il* pl. constr. 2.23:22 (cf. 1.148:9 and U:V:18:25); *ily* pl. constr. 2.16:4 = **84.1** "god, deity" (H. ᵓēl, Phoen., Aram. ᵓl, Arab. ᵓil, Akkad. ilu)

il /ᵓil-/ cf. ilum(*lum*) U:V:18:2, DN (cf. H. ᵓēl, Phoen. ᵓl, ēlos, ilos); for *il.ṣpn* see *ṣpn*; see also *ilbt*

ilib DN (/ᵓil-/ + /ᵓib-/ < *ᵓab-, "god of the father"?)

aliy "(very) strong, strongest," root /l-ᵓ-y/ (cf. Akkad. leᵓū "to prevail," lēᵓū "able"; Phoen. (ᶜbd)lᵓt PN); *aliy.qrdm* "strongest among the heroes"

aliyn /ᵓalᵓiyān-/(?) "victorious," an epithet of Baal

ilbt DN ("god of the house/dynasty"?)

ilgt PN 4.277:2 = **86.52** (in substandard orthography; perhaps -d at the end would be correct, cf. *ilgdn* 4.277:13?)

ilmlk PN, cf. ilu-milku (written in logograms) U:V:9:22, etc.; cf. ili-*mu-lik* P:VI:82:16

almnt /ᵓalmanat-/ "widow" (H. ᵓalmānā vs. Phoen. ᵓlmt, Akkad. almattu)

ilnym pl. 1.22:II:(4), 6 = **87.6** (cf. 1.21:II:4) "(netherworld) gods" (cf. Phoen. pl. ᵓlnm, alonim)

alp /ᵓalp-/ "ox" (H. ᵓǽlæp, Akkad. alpu; cf. the name of the first letter, H. ᵓā́læp, Gr. alpha)

alp: du. *alpm* "1000" (cf. H., Aram. ᵓǽlæp, ᵓalp-, Arab. ᵓalf)

ilqṣm pl. "precious stones"

*ilštm*ᶜ GN, cf. (al) ili-*iš-tam-i* P:III:10.044:8′ (p. 189) (cf. H. ᵓæštəmō(a)ᶜ)

ilt 1.14:IV:35, 39 = **88.72** "goddess" (Phoen. ᵓlt, cf. Akkad. iltu)

im /ᵓim/ "if" 2.15:8 = **86.45** variant of standard *hm*; cf. *wm* 3.9:6 = **84.2** /w-(ᵓ)im/ "and if" (cf. H. ᵓim, Phoen. ᵓim, Arab. ᵓin)

um /ᵓumm-/ "mother" (H. ᵓem < ᵓimm-, Arab. ᵓumm, Akkad. ummu)

imr /ᵓimmar-/(?) "lamb" (Aram. pl. ᵓimmərīn, Akkad. emmeru)

amt /ᵓam(a)t-/ "handmaid" (H. ᵓāmā, Syr. ᵓamtā, Akkad. amtu)

an /ᵓanā/(?) "I" (H. ᵓănī, Aram. ᵓănā, Arab. ᵓanā)

in /ᵓēn-/: *inn* 3.4:16 = **86.32**, cf. *inmm* 2.10:9 = **86.43** "there is not" (H. ᵓáyin, ᵓēn-, Phoen. ynny, Akkad. yānu)

un /ᵓōn-/ "mourning" (cf. H. ᵓōnī(m), root ᵓ-n-y?; Old Canaan. a-un-nu? EA 116:11)

anḫ "sighing" (< part. or inf.?) (cf. Heb. ᵓ-n-ḥ Ni., Syr. ᵓenaḥ, Akkad. anāḫu II)

any sing. and pl., *anyt* f. sing. 4.338:11,17; pl. 4.125.1(?) "ship" (cf. Old Canaan. a-na-ya EA 245:28, -yi line 8; H. coll. ᵓŏnī, ᵓŏnīyā); with suff. 2. sing. m. *anyk* 2.38:24 = **86.41** and *anykn* 2.38:10 = **86.41**, with additional *-n*

ank /ᵓanāku/, cf. *a-na-ku* U:V:130:III:12′, "I" (cf. H. ᵓānōkī, Old-Canaan. anuki EA 287:66,69, Phoen. ᵓnk(y), anec(h), Yaᵓudi-Aram. ᵓnk(y), Akkad. anāku); *lm.ank.ksp* 1.14:III:33 = **88.71**; *ngš.ank* 1.6:II:21 = **88.55**

inmm 2.10:9 = **86.43** see *in* and *mm*

inn see *in*

inr 1.114:13 = **88.3**; 1.16:I:16 = **88.73** "cur"(?)

ansṫ /ᵓanīšat-/(?) fem. "intimate friend" (cf. Arab. ᵓanīs)

unṯ "duty (of forced labor)" (cf. Akkad. unuššū)

ap /ᵓap/ "also, but" (H., Aram. ᵓap)

ap /ᵓapp-/ "nose" 1.18:IV:26 = **88.64**; "beak" 1.103:41 = **86.744**; *ap.zd* 1.23:24 = **88.2** "nipple"; *u/b!ap* 1.18:IV:26 = **88.64** is perhaps a dittography to *baph* (or "anger"?) (H. ᵓap(p-),

Akkad. appu, Aram. ʾanp-, Arab. ʾanf)

aplb "(front part of the heart >) breast"

ipd "robe" (cf. H. ʾēpōd, Syr. ʾapūdā, Akkad. epattu (epādu?))

apnk "afterward, thereupon"

apq /ʾapīq-/ "headwater, stream" (cf. H. GN ʾăpeq < ʾapiq, constr. ʾăpīq "streambed," Arab. (< Aram.) GN ʾAfqā)

uṣbʿt /ʾuṣbaʿāt-/ or /-buʿ-/ (?) pl. "fingers" (H. ʾæṣbaʿ, pl. ʾæṣbāʿōt, Syr. ṣebʿā, Arab. iṣbaʿ, uṣbaʿ)

aqht /ʾaqhatu/ (?) PN (cf. H. qəhāt PN)

iqnu /ʾiqnaʾ-/ pl. *iqnim* "lapis-lazuli" (Akkad. uknu/uqnu; cf. Syr. qūnāyā "(sky)blue"?)

/-ʾ-r-/ ?: *yark* 1.24:39 = **88.1** imperf. 3. sing. m. /ʾ-w-r/ "to shine" with suff. 2. sing. (m. or f.) (or /ʾ-r-k/ (?)); for *nar*k 1.10:II:20 = **88.56** see /ʾ-r-k/

ar /ʾār-/ "light, shine" 1.24:38 = **88.1** (cf. H. ʾōr)

arbdd 1.3:III:17 = **87.8** "a kind of offering(?), love offering" (< Hurrian), parallel to *šlm* "peace-offering"

arbʿ /ʾarbaʿ-/, *arbʿt* /ʾarbaʿat-/ "4"; *arbʿ(t)*. *ʿšr(t)* "14" (H., Arab. ʾarbaʿ)

arbʿm /ʾarbaʿūma/, /-īma/ "40" (H. ʾarbāʿīm, Arab. ʾarbaʿūna, -īna)

urbt /ʾurubbat-/ (?) "opening, hatch" (in a horizontal surface, not a window in a vertical wall) (H. ʾărubbā)

argmn /ʾargaman(n)-/ "tribute" (< Hittite argaman, cf. H. ʾargāmān "purple," Akkad. argamannu "tribute, purple")

arḫ /ʾarḫ-/ "cow" (Akkad. arḫu)

ary "kinsman"

/ʾ-r-k/: *yark* 1.24:39 = **88.1** (or /-ʾ-r-/ ?); *nar*k 1.10:II:20 = **88.56** "to be long"

arṣ /ʾarṣ-/, cf. *ar-ṣum* U:V:137:III:14′, "earth" (H. ʾæræṣ, Aram. ʾarqā, ʾarʿāʾ, Arab. ʾarḍ)

/ʾ-r-š/: D? *taršn* (2. sing. f.), *irš* "to request" (see *iršt*)

aršḫ /ʾaraššiḫ-/ (?) GN (cf. Hurrian Aransiḫ etc., river Tigris)

iršt /ʾirašt-/ (?) "request," cf. /ʾ-r-š/ (H. ʾărǽšæt, Akkad. erištu)

išbʿl cf. gen. *i-ši-*(il)baʿal P:III:12.34:25 (p. 193), PN (H. ʾæšbáʿal)

išd /ʾišd-/ "leg" (cf. Akkad. išdu "foundation, base")

ušḫr DN, cf. *ušḫry*; *iš-ḫa-ra* U:V:18:23

ušn "gift" (cf. Arab. ʾaws; cf. PN ESA ʾwśn, H. Y(əh)ōʾāš)

išt "fire" (H. ʾēš, Jew.-Aram. ʾiššātā, Akkad. išātu)

ištrmy PN fem.

at /ʾatta/, cf. *at-ta* U:V:130:II:4′ "you (sing. m.)" (H. ʾattā, Aram. ʾnth); for 1.17:I:16 = **88.61**, cf. also *abyn*<a>t, but cf. 3. person *-h* in lines 18 and 19

at /ʾatti/ "you (sing. f.)" (H. ʾattə, Imper.-Aram. ʾt(y), Akkad. atti)

/ʾ-t-w/: *atwt*, *atm* 1.3:III:28 = **87.8** imper. sing. fem. + *-m* "to come" (H. ʾātā, Aram. ʾătā, Arab. ʾatā(y) and ʾatā(w), ESA ʾtw, Eth. ʾatawa)

itn 2.15:4 = **86.45** probably a substandard form of imperf. 1. sing. /y-t-n/ "to give" (cf. correct *atn* 1.24:19 = **88.1**); cf. also PN *itn* 4.616:9 (cf. Akkad. itinnu "builder"; cf. U:V:99:2, 12)

itnn "gift" (H. ʾætnan)

iṯ /ʾiṯ-/ "there is" (Aram. ʾītay, H. yēš)

iṯl "breath"

aṯr /ʾaṯr-/ "place" 1.22:II:5 = **87.6**; 1.17:I:28 = **87.1**; for 1.5:VI:24(?) = **87.3** see below (Aram. ʾătar, ʾatr-, Akkad. ašru; cf. Phoen. ʾšr "(holy) place")

aṯr /ʾaṯr-/ prep. "after" 1.6:II:30 = **88.55**; perhaps 1.5:VI:24 = **87.3**, see above (cf. Aram. ʾătar, bā(ʾ)tar; Arab. ʾiṯra)

aṯr 2.15:6 = **86.45** "pure butter"(?) (cf. Arab. ʾiṯr); or imperf. 1. sing. /ʾ-ṯ-r/ "to trace"(?)

aṯryt "future, destiny" (cf. Arab. ʾaṯar "destiny," ʾaṯrīyat "inheritance")

aṯrt /ʾaṯir(a)t-/ (?) DN f., cf. (d) *aš-ra-tum* U:V:18:19 (cf. Old Canaan. Aširat, PN Abdi-Aširta, H. ʾăšērā)

aṯt /ʾaṯṯat-/ (< *-nṯ-) "woman" (Akkad. aššatu, H. ʾiššā, Aram. ʾnth, Syr. ʾa(n)ttā, Arab. ʾunṯā(y))

iṯt "vow"(?) 1.14:IV:38 = **88.72** (cf. 2.13:15; 2.30:14)

b

b-, *b.* /bi/, cf. *bi-i* U:V:130:III:6; variants: *by* 2.38:13, 25 = **86.41**; *bm* 1.23:51 = **88.2**;

1.15:II:17 = **87.2**; with suff. *bh*, *bhm*, *by* prep. "in" (place and direction, time), "with," "for" (price) 4.146:2 = **86.25**; 4:266:6 = **86.22**; "from" 1.115:10 = **82.5**; 3.9:8 = **84.2**; 1.2:IV:6 = **88.51**; 1.18:IV:26 = **88.64**; 3.4:14 = **86.32**; the preposition can coalesce with an initial *b*- of the following word: *bty* < *bi-bētiya 1.22:II:3 = **87.6**, cf. *bhkly* 1.22:II:4 = **87.6** (H., Aram. b-, Arab. bi-)

biry adj. from a GN "from *bir*" (cf. (al)*bi-i-ri* (gen.) GN, P:III:16.244:7 (p. 93); cf. H. bəᵓērī, from bəᵓēr (also GN), Arab. biᵓr "well")

birty adj. from GN "from *birt*- (Beirut)" (cf. (kur)*bi-ru-ú*/*ut-ti* GN P:IV:17.341:14′, 17′ (p. 162)); /biᵓirōt-/ (cf. H. bəᵓērōtī from GN bəᵓērōt)

bbt 1.109:11 = **86.71**; *bbtk* 1.16:I:16 = **88.73**, see *b*-, *bt* "house"

bd 1.2:IV:21 = **88.51**; 3.5:17, 19 = **86.33** *b* + *d* "from the hand" (cf. Akkad. iš-tu qāti P:III:16.353: 11, 12 (p. 113)); 4.143:3 = **81.5**; 1.17:V:26 = **88.62** "in the hand(s) of" (cf. Old Canaan. ba-di-ú EA); 1.16:I:19(?) = **88.73** "through"

/-b-d-/: *ybd* 1.17:VI:31 = **88.63**; perhaps *bd* 1.16:I:19 = **88.73** "to sing, recite"(?) (cf. H. badd- "idle talk," Postbibl. H. badda(ᵓ)y "fiction")

bht see *bt* "house"

/b-w-ᵓ/: *tbu*, *uba* imperf. 1. sing. 1.100:72 = **86.73**, "to come, enter" (H. b-w-ᵓ: bā(ᵓ), yābō(ᵓ); cf. Akkad. bāᵓu, Arab. bāᵓa, yabūᵓu)

bz 1.80:4 = **86.51** "plunder"(?) (cf. H. baz?)

by 2.38:13, 25 = **86.41**, see *b*- "in"

byy 1.142:1 = **86.742** PN (also 4.170:25; 4.334:2)

/b-y-n/: *abn*, *tbn* 1.3:III:26, 27 = **87.8** "to understand" (H. bīn, yābīn)

/b-k-y/: *abky*, *tbkn*, *ybky* "to weep"; inf. abs. *bky* 1.16:I:14 = **88.73**, with *-m*: *bkm* 1.19:II:8,9 = **87.5** "weeping, in tears" (H. bākā, tibkǣ, inf. abs. bākō, noun bəkī "weeping," Akkad. bakū, Eth. bakaya)

bkr /bukr-/ (?) "first-born" (H. bəkōr, Akkad. bukru)

bl "no," "without" (H. bĕlī), see also *blmt*

/-b-l-/, see /y-b-l/

blmt "immortality" < *bl*- "no" or *bl* "without" + *mt* "death"

bm see *b*- "in"

bmt /bamat-/ (?), /bāmt-/ (?) "back" (H. bāmā, bwmt, Akkad. bāmtu)

/-b-n-/, see b-y-n

bn /bēn-/ 1.2:IV:22 = **88.51**; 1.10:II:16 = **88.56**; 1.18:IV:21 = **88.64** "between, among" (H., Aram. bēn, Arab. bayna)

bn /bun-/ "son" (Phoen. BYN < *bun-; against H. bēn < *bin, Arab. ibn), see also *bnš*

bnwt 1.100:62 = **86.73** "engendering power, virility" (cf. Arab. banā, yabnī, Akkad. banū "to build"; Akkad. banū 'to cohabit")

/b-n-y/: *bn* 1.4:V:18 = **88.53** imper. sing. m.(?) "to build" (H., Aram. b-n-y; for Arab., Akkad. cf. *bnwt*)

bnny 2.33:34 = **86.42** *bnš.bnny* "intermediary, middleman" (cf. Postbibl. H. bē(y)nōnī "central; middle; average")

bnš /bun(n)ōš-/ (?) (or /bunuš-/ (?), pl. *bnšm*; *bu-nu-šu* U:V:131:7′ "man" (< /bun-/ "son" + /nōš-/ < *nāš "mankind") (cf. bæn-ᵓænōš Ps 144:3; Aram. bar ᵓænāš); *bnš bnšm* 3.5:16 = **86.33** "every man"

bnt 4.360:3 = **86.12**, see *bt* "daughter"

bᶜd /baᶜd-/ "behind" (H. báᶜad, Arab. baᶜdu)

bᶜl /baᶜl-/ (cf. *ba-a-lu* DN U:V:137:IVb:17) "owner, lord," pl. *bᶜlm*, /baᶜalūma/, cf. *ba-a-lu-ma* U:V:130:III:14′ "lord(ship)" (H. báᶜal, Phoen. bᶜl, bal, Arab. baᶜl); word of relation *bᶜl.qrnm* 1.114:20 = **88.3** "(owner >) that of/with (two) horns"

bᶜl: with *-m* *bᶜlm* 1.2:IV:9 = **88.51**; 1.119:28 = **86.75** DN (< epithet of god Hadd, cf. 1.12:II:53 and 54 = **88.4**); *bᶜl.ugrt* 1.109:11 = **86.71**; *bᶜl.ṣpn* 1.109:9 = **86.71**

bᶜlmᶜḏr PN ("Baal + *ᶜḏr* "(to) help"; *-m* is an asseverative particle

bᶜln /baᶜlān-/ PN, cf. *ba-a-la-nu* U:V:86:18; (il)baᶜala(*la*)-*na* P:IV:17.393:23 (p. 227) gen.-acc.

bᶜlt /baᶜlat-/ "owner, lady" (H. baᶜălā, constr. baᶜălat, Phoen. bᶜlt, Arab. baᶜlat)

/b-ᶜ-r/: *l-bᶜr* D? 2.61:9 = **86.44** inf.? "to burn"(?), "to plunder(?)" (cf. H. b-ᶜ-r I and lə-bāᶜēr Num 24:22; Isa 5:5 "to be plundered(?)")

/b-ᶜ-r/: *ybᶜrn* D? 2.41:22 = **83.3** "to abandon"(?)

bᶜrm D? 4.338:17 = **86.26** inf. + *-m*? "to remove"(?) (cf. H. b-ᶜ-r II "to remove," "to graze") (or read *arb^{c}m*(?) "40"; or *b* + *^{c}rm* GN(?))

/b-ǵ-y/: *ibǵyh* "to seek out" (Arab. baǵā(y), yabǵī "to seek," Aram. bə^{c}ā, yib^{c}ē "to seek, inquire," H. b-^{c}-y I "to inquire") or "to reveal" (cf. Arab. faǵā "to be divulgated")

/b-ṣ-r/: *ybṣr* 1.18:IV:20 = **88.64** "to soar" (cf. PN *tbṣr* 6.24:1 = **81.2**)

bql: *qmḫ.bql* 1.71:25 = **86.62** "grouts"(?) (cf. Syr. bu(q)qālā "sprout," Arab. baql "vegetables, leguminous plants, pulse," also ESA bql, Akkad. buqlu "malt")

/b-q-^{c}/: *ibq^{c}*, *tbq^{c}nn* "to split" (H. bāqa^{c}, yibqa^{c})

bqr D/Dp(?) 1.78:5 = **86.743** "to examine (entrails for divination)"

brḥ 1.5:I:1 = **88.54** "writhing" (parallel to *^{c}qltn*) (cf. H. bārī(a)ḥ Isa 27:1; Job 26:13); or "(fleeing >) swift"(?) (cf. H. b-r-ḥ)

/b-r-k/: D *tbrk*, *brkm* inf. + *-m* "to bless" (H., Phoen. b-r-k Pi., Arab. b-r-k)

brk "knee" (H. bǽræk, bwrk, Syr. burkā, Jew.-Aram. birkā, Akkad. birku, burku)

brlt 1.17:V:24 = **88.62** "throat" > "appetite"; 1.18:IV:25 = **88.64** "breath, soul"

brq "lightning" (cf. H. bārāq, Syr. barqā, Arab. barq)

brr "pure" (H. bārūr, Akkad. barru); for 1.109:2 = **86.71** see 1.46:10

/b-š-r/: *bšr* "to get news" (most frequently good news) (cf. H. b-ś-r Pi., Arab. baššara, Akkad. bussuru "to bring news")

bšrt 1.10:III:33 = **88.57** "(good) news" (H. bəśōrā, Akkad. bussurtu)

bt /bēt-/ "house," pl. *bhtm*, *bht!k* (the tablet has *bhmk*) 1.4:V:13 = **88.53**, cf. lines 18, 19; with prep. *b-*: *bbt* 1.109:11 = **86.71**; *b.btw* 3.9:4 = **84.2**; or /bb/ > *b*: *bt.b^{c}l* 1.17:I:31 = **87.1** (cf. also 32); (cf. H., Aram. báyit, bēt; H. pl. bātīm; Aram. pl. bāt-; Arab. bayt; Akkad. bītu)

bt /bitt-/ (?) "daughter"; pl. *bnt* 4.360:3 = **86.12** (H. bat, pl. bānōt; Arab. bint; pl. banāt; Akkad. bintu, bun(a)tu(m))

btlt /batūlat-/, with vocative *y* and *-m* *ybtltm* 1.17:VI:34 = **88.63** "girl" (H. bətūlā, Jew.-Aram. bətūltā, Akkad. batultu; Arab. batūl)

btšy PN fem. (/bitt-/ "daughter" + *šy*; cf. perhaps *šu-ya* PN fem. P:III:16.135:4 (p. 89))

bṯn /baṯn-/ (?) "snake"(cf. Akkad. bašmu, "(mythical) snake"; Syr. patnā and H. pǽtæn (< Aram.) "viper")

bṯṯ 1.78:1 = **86.743** "to be ominous, sorrowful" (cf. Arab. baṯṯ "grief, sorrow")

g

g /gū, gī, gā/ (?) "voice"; with suff. *gh* (cf. H. gam Ps 137:1?)

gan /ga$^{\supset}$ān-/ "pride" (H. gā$^{\supset}$ōn)

gb 1.114:5 = **88.3** "back (animal, human)"(?) (cf. H. gab, Jew.-Aram. gabbā; cf. also Akkad. gabbu)

gbl 1.16:VI:57 = **85.1** "peak, mountain" (Arab. ǧabal; H. gəbūl Ps 78:54); or "boundary" (Phoen. pl. gubulim "boundaries")

gbl /gubl-/ (?) GN, "Byblos," Arab. Ǧubail 4.338:13, 15 = **86.26** (Old-Canaan. Gubla, Phoen. gbl, H. gəbāl)

gb^{c} /gab^{c}-/ "hill" (H. gǽba^{c})

gg /gag-/ "roof" (H. gāg)

gdl "big"; f. *gdlt* 1.109:13 = **86.71** "(a female head of) large (cattle), cow" (H. gādōl)

/g-w-r/: *gr* 1.119:26 = **86.75** "to attack" (H. g-w-r, yāgūr)

/g-z-z/: *ygz* part. pl. n. *gzzm* "to shear" (H. g-z-z, tāgōz, Syr. gaz, Arab. ǧazza, Akkad. gazāzu)

/-g-l-/: /g-y-l/: *ngln* 1.16:I:15 = **88.73** "to rejoice, jubilate" (H. g-y-l)

/g-l-y/: *tgly* 1.4:IV:23 = **85.2** "to go in (and also out?)" (cf. H. g-l-y "to go away/in exile," cf. also Aram. g-l-y)

gn /gann-/ "garden" (H. gan(n-))

gnryn PN (probably Hurrian)

/g-^{c}-r/: *yg^{c}r*, *g^{c}r* 1.114:14 = **88.3** inf. abs. (or a noun?) "to rebuke" (H. gā^{c}ar, yig^{c}ar, Syr. g^{c}ar)

g^{c}t "lowing" (cf. H. g-^{c}-y, Jew.-Aram. and Syr. g^{c}ā)

grn /gurn-/, pl. *grnt* "threshing floor" (H. góræn, pl. gərānōt)

/g-r-š/: *grš* part.; D *agrškm* "to drive out" (H. g-r-š Qal part. and Pi.)

gšm /gašm-/ (?) "(torrent of) rain" (H. gǽšæm)

gt /gitt-/ (?) "(wine)press," "estate (with press)"(?) (cf. Old-Canaan. GN Gimtu, Ginti-, Gitt-EA; H. gat, also GN)

d

d-, *d.* 4.213:2 = **86.23**; 1.5:I:3 = **88.54** /dū, dī, dā/, cf. *du-ú* U:V:137:II:29′ (cf. *ḏ* 1.24:45), determinative-relative pronoun "that of," "which"; with *-m*: *dm* 1.3:III:20 = **87.8**; 1:17:VI:34 = **88.63**; fem. *dt* 1.2:IV:10 = **88.51**; 2.38:10 = **86.41**; pl. m. *dt* 4.422:1 = **83.1**; pl. fem. *dt* 4.145:1 = **82.3**; in combination with other particles: *dk* 1.14:III:41 = **88.71**; *pd* 1.14:III:38 = **88.71**; function: determinative "that of" 1.5:I:3 = **88.54**; 1.2:IV:10 = **88.51**; 1.100:62 = **86.73**; relative "which," e.g., 4.338:1 = **82.4**; 1.114:7, 8 = **88.3**; 1.14:III:38 = **88.71**; 2.38:10 = **86.41**; 4.422:1 = **83.1**; conjunction "for": *dm* 1.17:VI:34 = **88.63** (cf. Arab. ḏā)

d see *bd*, *yd* "hand"

/d-ᵓ-y/: *ydu* "to fly"

diy /dāᵓiy-/ "(the flying one >) bird" 1.18:IV:18 = **88.64** (cf. H. dāᵓā(h) "(fork-tailed) kite"; d-ᵓ-y "to fly")

diy "wing, pinion" 1.19:III:31, 37 = **88.65** (cf. H. d-ᵓ-y "to fly")

da?n 1.16:I:30 = **88.73**, see *dnn*

dbat: dbatk 1.10:II:21,22 = **88.56** "strength" (cf. H. dåbᵓ- Deut 33:25)

/d-b-ḥ/: *ydbḥ*, *dbḥ* 1.114:1(?) = **88.3** "to sacrifice" (H. zābaḥ, yizbaḥ; Aram. d-b-ḥ; Arab. ḏabaḥa, yiḏbaḥu "to slaughter"); cf. perhaps *dbḥ* 1.127:3 = **86.741** part. > "sacrificer"(?)

dbḥ /dabḥ-/, cf. *da-ab-ḫu* U:V:137:III:6 "festival"; pl. *dbḥt*; "sacrifice" 1.127:9 = **86.741**; 1.142:1 = **86.742**; 4.213:24(?) = **86.23**; "slaughter, banquet" 1.114:1 = **88.3**; *dbḥ* 1.127:3 = **86.741** "sacrifice"(?) or "sacrificer," see above (cf. Syr. dabḥā, Arab. ḏibḥ "victim," ḏabḥ "slaughter")

dblt sing. (?)/pl.(?) 1.71:24 = **86.62** "cake of (pressed) figs" (H. dəbēlā, pl. dəbēlīm)

/d-b-r/: *tdbr* D? 1.16:VI:43 = **85.1** "to administer"(?) (cf. Syr. d-b-r Pa., Arab. d-b-r II) or "to flee"(?) (cf. Arab. d-b-r I)

dbr 1.6:II:20 = **88.55** "pasture" (cf. 1.5:V:18) (H. dåbr-)

dgn /dagān-/ cf. *da-gan* U:V:18:3 DN (H. Dāgōn, Phoen. dgn)

dgt(?) see *mdgt*

dd 1.24:23 = **88.1** "love" (cf. 1.3:III:7); (cf. 1.101:17; 1.3:III:5 "breast"(?); cf. H. dadd- "breast") (cf. *yd* 1.4:IV:38 = **85.2** "love"; cf. H. dōd "(be)love(d)," Qumran-Aram. dd, Akkad. dādu)

ddym pl. 1.3:III:15 = **87.8** "mandrake" (H. dūdāᵓīm)

ddmš cf. *dá-ad-mi-iš* U:V:18:27, DN

/d-ḥ-l/: *tdḥl* 2.30:21 = **83.4** "to be afraid" (Aram. d-ḥ-l, Early Aram. z-ḥ-l, H. zāḥal- Job 32:6)

/d-y-n/: *tdn*, *dn* 1.12:II:58 = **88.4** part.? "to judge" (H., Aram., Arab. d-y-n, Akkad. d(iᵓ)ānu)

dk 1.14:III:41 = **88.71** see *d-* and *k*

dkr cf. [d]*kr* 1.119:31 = **86.75** "ram"

dl /dall-/ "poor" (H. dal, Akkad. dallu)

/d-l-p/: *ydlp* 1:2:IV:26 = **88.51** "to be shaky, crumbled"(?) (cf. Akkad. dalāpu "to disturb"; perhaps H. yidlōp Ecclesiastes 10:18 "becomes shaky" or "sags")

dm 1.3:III:20 = **87.8** see *d-*

dm /dam-/ 1.4:IV:38 = **85.2**; 1.4:VI:59 = **87.7**; 1.18:IV:24 = **88.64** "blood" (H. dām, dam, pl. constr. dĕmē; Syr. dĕmā; Arab. dam; Akkad. damu)

[-]*dm* 1.14:III:44 = **88.71**, perhaps [u]*dm* GN(?) or "rubies"(?) or a verb(?)

/d-m-m/ (or /d-w-m/?): *dm* imper. sing. m. 1.14:III:10 = **88.71** "to stand still" (H. d-m-m I: dōm; cf. H. d-w-m I and II, Arab. dāma, yadūmu "to last")

/d-m-m/: *tdm* 1.16:I:26 = **88.73**; *tdm* 1.16:I:30 = **88.73** "to wail, grieve" (H. d-m-m II, Akkad. damāmu)

dn /dīn-/ "judgment, cause" (H., Aram., Arab., Akkad. dīn)

dnil /dānī-ᵓil-/(?) PN (cf. Dānīy(ᵓ)ēl Ezek 14:14, 20; 28:3; Amorite Da-ni-AN)

dnn(?) KTU *da*(?)*n* 1.16:I:30 = **88.73**, probably perf. 3. sing. m. /d-n-n/ "to be strong" (cf. Akkad. danānu) (or adj. "strong"(?), cf. Akkad. dannu)

dnt du.(?) 2.38:18 = **86.41** "store"(??), cf. *nt*

dnty PN fem. (wife of *dnil*)

dq /daqq-/ "small" (cf. H. daq(q-), Akkad. daqqu): fem. *dqt*, du. *dqtm* 1.109:6 = **86.71** "(a female head of) small (cattle), ewe"

dqn "beard" (H. zāqān, Syr. daqnā, Arab. ḏaqan, ḏiqan, ḏaqn, Akkad. ziqnu)

drdr 1.2:IV:10 = **88.51**; *dr.dr* 1.19:IV:6 = **87.4**

"long time, eternity" (cf. Akkad. dāru, dūru "duration, eternity," a-na da-ri du-ri P:III:16.282:13 (p. 161), dūr dāri "forever"; cf. also H. dōr (wā-)dōr; for H. dōr, Aram. dār "generation," cf. also Ug. *dr* 1.39:7; 1.40:33; 4.357:24 "assembly")

/d-r-y/: ***tdrynn*** with suff. 3. sing. m. "to winnow, scatter" (H. z-r-y, Syr. drā, Arab. ḏarā(y) and ḏarā(w), Akkad. zarū)

drkt "rule, authority" (cf. H. d-r-k Hos 10:13, parallel to rob gibbōrǣkā "multitude of your warriors"; Septuagint reads for drkk harmasi(n) sou = ? rkbk; Prov 31:3, parallel to ḥēlǣkā; Ps 138:5; Jer 3:13; cf. also Arab. dark "overtaking")

/d-r-ᶜ/: ***tdrᶜnn*** with suff. 3. sing. m. "to sow; scatter?" (cf. H., Anc.-Aram. z-r-ᶜ, Arab. zaraᶜa, yizraᶜu and ḏaraᶜa, Akkad. zarū; cf. also H. Hos 2:25; Lev 25:3)

dt see *d-*

ḏ

ḏd /žad-/ (?) "territory"(?) (cf. *šd* "field"?); "pavillion"(?)

/ḏ-m-r/: ***ḏmr*** part. "to guard, protect"(?), "to strengthen"(?) (cf. *ḏmr* 1.3:II:34 "soldier, guardian"; cf. Arab. ḏamīr "brave," H. zimrā Exod 15:2 "strength/protection"?)

ḏnb "tail" (H. zānāb, Jew.-Aram. danbā, dunbā, Arab. ḏanab)

ḏrᶜ /ḏirāᶜ-/ (?) "arm" (H. zərō(a)ᶜ, Aram. ᵓædrāᶜ, Syr. drāᶜā, Arab. ḏirāᶜ)

ḏrq: ***uṭm.ḏrqm*** 1.5:I:6 = **88.54** "crude, bloody (meat)"(?) (cf. H. z-r-q "to sprinkle (blood)"?) or "filthy"(?) (cf. Arab. ḏarq "excrement (of birds)"?)

ḏrt "vision"

h

/h-b-ṭ/: ***hbṭ.hw*** inf. abs.(?) 2.61:5 = **86.44** "to be low(?)/poor(?)" (cf. Arab. habaṭa, yahbuṭu, yahbiṭu "to go down, to sink") or D "to deprive"(?)

/h-b-r/: ***thbr, yhbr, hbr*** imper. du. m. "to bow down" (cf. Arab. hab(ī)r "depressed ground")

hd /hadd-/ 1.12:II:54 = **88.4** DN, original name of Baal, see *bᶜl*

/h-d-y/: ***yhdy*** "to cut, gush" (cf. Arab. hadā(y) "to cut"?)

hdm "footstool" (H. hădōm constr.)

hw /huwa/ "he" (Arab. huwa, H. hūᵓ)

hwt "word" (Akkad. awātum)

hyn 1.17:V:24 = **88.62** DN or epithet (cf. Syr. hawwīnā "skilled")

hyt /hiyati/ gen.-acc. "her" (cf. Arab. hiya, Spanish Arab. hiet, Eth. yeᵓetī, Akkad. šiᵓāti)

hkl /hēkal-/ "palace" (cf. Akkad. ekallu < Sumer. e-gal; cf. H. hēkāl, Aram. hēkal)

hl "behold"

/h-l-k/: G ***hlk, tlkn, lk*** "to go" (cf. H. h-l-k, lēk, Phoen. lech, Akkad. alāku; cf. Arab. halaka, yahliku "to perish"); Gt *itlk, ntlk* "to walk, stroll" (cf. H. Hitpa., Akkad. Gtn)

hlk /hilk-/ (?) "course" (cf. H. hēlæk)

hlm /halum(ma)/ (?) 1.4:IV:27 = **85.2** "behold" or "as soon as"; 1.100:6 = **86.73** "there" (cf. H. hălōm, Arab. halumma)

/h-l-m/: imper. ***hlm, hlmn***; imperf. ***ylm, ylmn*** "to strike" (cf. H. hāləmā, yahălōmūn!)

hm /humā/ (?) 1.10:II:23 = **88.56** "them (du.)" suffixed pronoun (Arab. -humā)

hm /hum(u)/ (?): *ytn.hm* 2.33:26 = **86.42** "them (pl. m.)," (suffixed?) pronoun, (Arab. -hum(u), H. -hæm)

hm /him/ "if; or; whether"; see also *im*; in disjunctive questions "or" 1.4:IV:35 = **85.2**; in indirect questions "whether" 1.19:III:33 = **88.65**; in conditional clauses "if" 2.33:30 = **86.42**; 2.30:16 = **83.4**; 1.19:III:44 = **88.65**; 1.17:VI:43 = **88.63**; 1.14:IV:40 = **88.72**; perhaps also 1.4:IV:38 = **85.2** or perhaps introducing a wish (cf. H. Ps 81:9) (cf. ESA hm, Aram. hēn < *hin; H. ᵓim)

hmlt "multitude, folk" (H. hămullā)

hmt "army"(?) 1.103:16 = **86.744** (cf. H. hāmōn)

hmt 1.17:V:30 = **88.62** "them (du.)"(?)

hmt /humat-/ (?) 1.19:III:44 = **88.65** "them (pl.)" (cf. Phoen. hmt, Spanish Arab. humat)

hn /hina/ (?) 2.33:31 = **86.42** "hither"(?) (cf. H. hḗnnā, Arab. hunā)

hn /hin/ (?) 1.23:46 = **88.2**; 2.33:27, 30(?) = **86.42**; 1.14:III:14 = **88.71** interjection "behold"; > "this"(?) (cf. H. hēn, Arab. ᵓinna(?), Akkad. annū(?))

hnd: after a m. noun *ym.hnd* 3.4:1 = **86.32**; 3.5:1 = **86.33**; after a f. noun *mlakty.hnd* 2.33:35 = **86.42**; after a pl. noun 2.33:32 = **86.42** "this" (*hn* + *d*); fem. *hndt* 2.38:12 = **86.41** "this (ship)" (cf. perhaps H. haz-zǣ, haz-zōt)

hnk 2.33:23 = **86.42** "that"(?) (*hn* + *k*?)

hnny 2.38:6 = **86.41** "here"

hr "conception" (cf. *hry* 1.11:5) (cf. H. h-r-y "to conceive")

hrnmy derived adj. (from a GN?)

ht "now"

w

w-, *w.* "and" (H., Aram. wə-, Arab. wa; Akkad. ū); coordinating conjunction

/w-ḥ-y/ (?) see /w-t-ḥ/

/w-l-d/: *wld* 1.14:III:48 = **88.71** Gp perf.(?) "is born" or inf. abs./noun(?) "bearing, birth"; cf. /y-l-d/ (cf. Arab. walada, yalidu; Akkad. (w)alādu; for H., Aram. see /y-l-d/)

wm 3.9:6 = **84.2** see *im*

wn 1.24:31 (?) = **88.1**, cf. 1.4:IV:50 "and," *w-* + *-n*

/w-t-ḥ/ (?): D *twtḥ* 1.3:III:20 = **87.8** "to hurry" (cf. Arab. w-t-ḥ IV "to push"?) or Gt /w-ḥ-y/ (?) (cf. Arab. waḥā(y), yaḥī "to despatch"?)

z

zbl "prince(ship)" (cf. H. PN zəbūl, zəbūlūn)

zbln 1.16:VI:52 = **85.1** "disease"; etymology not clear (connected with *z-b-l "to carry," cf. Akkad. zabālu, so, a plague carrying off its victims; or with *zbl* "prince," used as an epithet of gods, e.g., *zbl.bᶜl.arṣ* 1.5:VI:10, so, a disease inflicted by a godly power)

zd 1.23:24 = **88.2** "breast"; cf. *ḏd* 1.23:61 and *ṯd* 1.4:VI:56 = **87.7** (cf. H. zīz, Akkad. zīzu "teat")

zǵt 1.14:III:18 = **88.71** "barking" (cf. Arab. zaǵā(w) "to cry")

zt /zēt-/ "olive (tree)" (H. záyit, Syr. zaytā, Arab. zayt)

ztr 1.17:I:27 = **87.1** "monument"(?), parallel to *skn* "stele"; or part. /z-t-r/ "to protect"(?), "to let go out"

ḥ

ḥbḫ 1.80:4 = **86.51** error for *ṭbḫ*

ḥby 1.114:19 = **88.3** "steward"(?) (cf. Eth. ḥabī); or DN or epithet of a deity?

ḥbl "flock (of birds)" (H. ḥ-b-l 1 Sam 10:5, 10)

/ḥ-b-q/: *(b)ḥbq* 1.23:51 = **88.2** inf. constr. D(?) "to embrace" (cf. H. ḥ-b-q Pi; Syr. ḥbaq)

ḥbš "belt, sash"(?) (cf. Akkad. abšu?; cf. H. ḥ-b-š "to bind up"?)

/ḥ-g-r/: *tḥgrn* "to gird" (H. ḥāgar-, yaḥgōr)

/ḥ-d-y/: *aḥd*, *yḥd*, *(w)yḥdy* "to look, regard, scrutinize, examine" (cf. H. ḥ-d-y?: yaḥad Ps 33:15; 49:11; Job 34:29?; cf. H. ḥōzǣ "seer," Arab. ḥāzin "augur"; cf. H., Aram. ḥ-z-y, Arab. ḥazā(y))

ḥdṯ /ḥudṯ-/ "new moon" (H. ḥódæš < *ḥudṯ-)

/ḥ-w-y/: G (or D?) *yḥwy* 1.17:VI:30 = **88.63**; *ḥwy* 1.17:VI:30 = **88.63** imper.? (or erroneously repeated part of a preceding word?); G *ḥwt* 1.10:II:20 = **88.56** precative perfect 2. sing. f.; *yḥ* 1.16:I:23 = **88.73** jussive? "to live"; D: *aḥwy* 1.17:VI:32 = **88.63**; 1.18:IV:27 = **88.64** "to keep alive"; "to grant life"; "to revive"(?); Št: *tšthwy* ("to ask life for oneself" >) "to greet/prostrate oneself"; cf. *ú-wu* U:V:137:II:28′ "to be alive" (Phoen. ḥwʾ, avo; cf. H., Aram. ḥ-y-y, Arab. ḥay(i)ya; D: cf. H. ḥ-y-y Pi.; Št: cf. H. hištaḥăwā, yištaḥăwǣ (or derived from š-ḥ-y(?), cf. H. š-ḥ-y, š-ḥ-ḥ "to bow down," š-w-ḥ "to sink," Old-Canaan. ištaḫaḫin)

ḥḫ 1.80:5 = **86.51** apparently an error, cf. *ḥbḫ* 1.80:4 = **86.51**; read ṭb*ḫ* "to slaughter"

ḥwt 1.103:1 = **86.744** "land" (H. ḥawwā, cf. ḥawwōt, Num 32:41)

ḥẓ /ḥiẓẓ-/ "arrow" (cf. H. ḥēṣ, ḥiṣṣ-, Imper. Aram. ḥṭ-)

ḥẓ: fem. *ḥẓt* 1.3:V:31 = **88.52** "lucky"(?) or "good fortune"(?) (cf. Arab. ḥaẓẓ)

ḥẓr "court" (H. ḥāṣēr, Phoen. ḥṣr)

ḥym plural only 1.17:VI:27 = **88.63**; *ḥyk* 1.16:I:14 = **88.73** "life," cf. *ḫé-ya-ma* U:V:131:6′ (H. ḥayyīm, Aram. ḥayyīn)

ḥyt 1.3:V:31 = **88.52** "life"(?) (cf. *ḥym*)

ḥkm 1.3:V:30 = **88.52** "wise" (H. ḥākām, Aram. ḥakkīm, Arab. ḥakīm)

ḥkm: ḥkmk 1.3:V:30 = **88.52** "wisdom" (cf. *ḥkmt* 1.4:IV:41 (cf. Arab. ḥukm "decision, wisdom"; cf. H., Aram. ḥåkmā)

ḥkpt GN "Egypt"(?) (cf. ḫi-ku-up-ta-aḫ EA "Memphis")

ḥlm "dream" (H. ḥălōm, Aram. ḥḗlæm, Arab. ḥulm)

ḥmḥ: *ḥmḥh* 1.16:I:29 = **88.73** (< *ḥmḥm?) "affection"(?); "compassion"(?)

ḥmḥmt 1.23:51 = **88.2** "ardor; orgasm(?); impregnation"(?) (cf. H. ḥ-m-m Ni. Isa 57:5; Syr. ḥ-m-m Gen 30:39; cf. H. y-ḥ-m, Arab. waḥam "sexual desire")

ḥmyt see *ḥmt* "wall"

ḥmr "ass" (H. ḥămōr, Syr. ḥmārā, Arab. ḥimār)

ḥmt "venom" 1.100:6 = **86.73** (H. ḥēmā, Syr. ḥemtā, Akkad. imtu)

ḥmt /ḥāmīt-/, pl. *ḥmyt* /ḥāmiyāt-/ "wall" 1.119:27 = **86.75** (cf. H. ḥōmā, Phoen. pl. ḥmyt)

/ḥ-n-n/: *ḥnny* G(?) or D(?) imper. 2.153 = **86.45** "to make agreeable" (cf. H. ḥ-n-n Pi., Arab. ḥ-n-n II; cf. Akkad. enēnu "to bestow favor")

ḥnt "compassion" (Arab. ḥannat, cf. PN fem. H. Ḥannā, Phoen. Anna)

/ḥ-s-l/ "to plunder" (H. ḥ-s-l)

/ḥ-s-p/: *ḥspt* "to pour (water)" (Arab. ḥasufa, yaḥsafu)

ḥsp 4.213:25 = **86.23** adj., a kind of wine, cf. /ḥ-s-p/?

ḥpn 1.16:VI:58 = **85.1** "loftiness"(?); "nullity"(?)

ḥrb /ḥarb-/ "sword, knife" (H. ḥǽræb, ḥarb-, Syr. ḥarbā)

ḥry PN fem.

ḥrn /ḥōrān-/ DN (cf. Aurōnas; cf. GN H. Byt Ḥ(w)r(w)n—Bēt Ḥōrōn; Ḥwrnym—Ḥōrōnáyim; cf. the mountain Ḥawrān Ezek 46:16; Akkad. Ḫaurānu, Arab. Ḥawrān)

ḥrnq "orchard"(?) (cf. Akkad. urnuqqu, a plant)

ḥrṣ 1.17:VI:37 = **88.63** "quicklime"(?), "potash"(?) (cf. Arab. ḥurūḍ "potash")

/ḥ-r-r/: *tḥrr* 1.23:48 = **88.2** "to roast" (cf. H. ḥ-r-r "to glow")

ḥrš /ḥarrāš-/ (?) 1.17:V:24 = **88.62** "craftsman" (cf. H. ḥārāš)

ḥrš 1.12:II:61 = **88.4** "magic, divination"(?) (cf. *ḥršm* 1.19:IV:60; cf. Syr. pl. ḥeršē and ḥaršē "magic," "enchantments")

/ḥ-r-ṯ/: *yḥrṯ* "to plow," cf. [ḫ]*a-ra-š*[u] U:V:137:III:18′ "to plow"; *alp.ḥrṯ* gen.-acc. pl. 1.14:III:18 = **88.71** "plow oxen" (cf. *alpm. ḥrṯm* 2.45:22) (cf. H. ḥ-r-š: ḥăraš-, yaḥrōš, Arab. ḥaraṯa, yaḥriṯu and yaḥruṯu)

ḥrṯ: *ḥrṯm* 4.630:6 = **82.2** "plowman" (cf. Arab. ḥarrāṯ, H. ḥōrēš)

ḥš: *ḥšk* 1.3:III:18 = **87.8** inf. /ḥ-w-š/ "to hurry"(?) (cf. H. ḥ-w-š, Akkad. ḫ(i)āšu(m)) (or an object?, cf. *ᶜbṣ*, *ᶜṣ*)

ḥtk /ḥatūk-/ (?), /ḥatīk-/ (?) 1.10:III:34 = **88.57** "descendant"

ḥtp 1.119:32 = **86.75** a kind of offering (Akkad. ḫitpu, cf. ḫatāpu "to slaughter"; Aram. ḥtpy)

ḥtṯn /ḥat(t)uṯān-/ (?) PN (cf. *ḥtṯ* 1.14:II:18 "silver," Hittite ḫattuš)

ḫ

ḫḫ: *ḫḫm* 1.17:VI:35 = **88.63** "refuse"(?) (cf. Akkad. ḫaḫḫu I?)

ḫṭ /ḫaṭṭ-/ "staff, scepter" (Akkad. ḫaṭṭu)

/ḫ-ṭ-ᵓ/: *tšḫṭann* Š "to disturb (from sleep)"(?) (cf. H. ḥ-ṭ-ᵓ "to lead astray"?, cf. Arab. ḫ-ṭ-ᵓ IV, Akkad. ḫaṭū) or /ḫ-ṭ-/ "to awake"(?), cf. *yḫṭ* 1.14:III.50

ḫyr /ḫiyār-/ cf. *ḫi-ya-ri* RS 25.455, name of a month (Phoen. ḥyr, cf. Akkad. ayyāru > Postbibl. H. ᵓiyyār)

ḫlb /ḫalb-/ GN *bᶜl.ḫlb* 1.109:16 = **86.71**, cf. (il)adad *ḫal-pí* U:V:170:18

ḫlmẓ 1.115:2 = **82.5** "lizard, dragon"(?) (cf. Akkad. ḫulmiṭṭu "dragon"; Syr. ḥulmāṭā, H. ḥómæṭ(?) "lizard")

ḫlp PN (cf. Akkad. ḫalpu "substitute"?)

/ḫ-l-q/: *ḫlq* 2.61:11, 12 = **86.44** G "to perish"(?) or D "to destroy"(?); D 1.103:16 = **86.744** (cf. Akkad. ḫalāqu G and D)

ḫlq 4.213:3 = **86.23** "bad"(?) (cf. Akkad. ḫulqu "lost property"?)

ḫmš /ḫam(i)š-/: *ḫmšt* "5" (H. ḥāmēš, Arab. ḫams, Akkad. ḫamšu, ḫamištu)

ḫms /ḫāmiš-/ (?) 4.279:5 = **86.24** "fifth"

ḫmšm /ḫam(i)šūma/, /-īma/ "50" (H. ḥămiššīm, Arab. ḫamsūna)

/ḫ-n-n/: *aḫnnn* 2.15:9 = **86.45** D "to let spoil"(?) (cf. Syr. ḥa(n)nīnā "rancid")

/ḫ-s-s/: *yḫssk* D "to excite, stir" (cf. Akkad. ḫasāsu "to think," D "to remind") (or L /ḫ-w-s/, /ḫ-y-s/?)

ḫss /ḫasīs-/ (?) in *kṯr.wḫss* (cf. Akkad. (d) Ḫa-si-su DN, ḫasīsu "wisdom")

/ḫ-s-r/: *ḫsrt* "to lack, want" (H. ḥāsēr, yiḥsar)

ḫru: ḫrih gen. + suff. *-h* 1.114:21 = **88.3** "excrement" (cf. Syr. ḥeryā, Arab. ḫurᵓ and ḫarāᵓ)

/ḫ-r-d/: *ḫrd* inf. abs. 2.16:13 = **84.1** "to guard, be watchful"(?) (cf. Akkad. ḫarādu "to guard")

ḫrd 2.61:6 = **86.44** "watchful"(?); 1.103:39 = **86.744** "guard, body-guard, soldier" (cf. Akkad. ḫardu)

ḫrḫb 1.24:17 = **88.1** DN (Hurrian?)

ḫrn 1.4:V:13 = **88.53** "caravan"(?) (cf. Akkad. ḫarrānu); perhaps also with suff. 2. sing. m. *bn.ḫrnk* 2.61:3 = **86.44** "member(s) of your caravan"(?)

ḫrnk 2.61:3 = **86.44** see *ḫrn*(?) or PN?

ḫrṣ /ḫurāṣu/, cf. *ḫu-r*[a-ṣu] U:V:137:II:4 "gold" (cf. H. ḥārūṣ, Phoen. ḥrṣ, Akkad. ḫurāṣu; cf. Greek chrysos)

ḫrt "hole" (cf. Akkad. ḫurratu, ḫurru; H. ḥōr, Arab. ḫurr)

ḫšt: ḫštk 1.16:I:17, 18 = **88.73** "vault"(?) (cf. Akkad. ḫaštu "pit, grave"; Palestinian-Arab. ḫušše "family vault")

ḫt "(land of) Hittites" (cf. (māt) ḫa(t)-ti P:VI: 14:15, 17); 2.30:16 = **83.4** "the Hittite(s)"

/ḫ-t-ᵓ/: *ḫtu* 1.6:II:23 = **88.55** inf. abs.(?), *ḫti* 2.10:7 = **86.43** inf. const. "to disappear"(?); G or N: *nḫtu* 2.10:8, 10 = **86.43** imperf. 1. pl. "to disappear"(?) or "to be vanquished" (cf. Akkad. ḫatū "to vanquish"(?); cf. Arab. ḫ-t-ᵓ: iḫtataᵓa "to be carried away"(?)

ḫtb PN

/ḫ-t-n/: *ḫtny* 1.24:32 = **88.1** inf. + suff., "to become related by marriage, marry" (cf. H., Syr. ḥ-t-n Hitpa./Etpa., cf. H. ḥātān, Akkad. ḫat(a)nu "son-in-law")

ḫṯr "sieve" (cf. Postbibl. H. and Jew.-Aram.(!) ḥ-š-r "to sift")

ṭ

ṭb /ṭāb-/ "good" (Aram. ṭāb, Akkad. ṭābu; cf. H. ṭōb); 4.213:2 = **86.23** "spiced (wine)" (cf. H. Song of Songs 7:10 and 8:2)

/ṭ-b-ḫ/: *ṭbḫ* 1.80:3 = **86.51**; to be read also in 1.80:4,5 = **86.51** (instead of the erroneous *ḥbḫ*) "to slaughter" (H. ṭābaḥ-, Syr. ṭ-b-ḥ Pa., Akkad. ṭabāḫu)

/ṭ-b-q/: *ṭbq* part. "to drive away"(?), "to smother, extinguish"(?), "to scorch"(?) (cf. Arab. ṭabaqa "to cover"?; cf. Syr. ṭabqā "frying pan"?)

ṭbrn PN

ṭhrm pl. 1.4:V:19 = **88.53** /ṭuhr-/ ("purity, brightness" >) "gem," cf. *ṭu-ú-ru* U:V:137:II:1 "pure" (cf. H. ṭóhar); cf. var. *ẓhrm*

/ṭ-w-ḫ/ see /-ṭ-ḫ-/

/ṭ-ḥ-n/: *tṭḥnn* "to grind" (H. ṭ-ḥ-n, yiṭḥan, Arab. ṭaḥana, yaṭḥanu)

/-ṭ-ḫ-/, /ṭ-w-ḫ/ (?): *ṭḫ* part. "to plaster" (H. ṭāḥ, ṭū(a)ḥ, cf. Arab. ṭāḫa, yaṭīḫu "to smear")

ṭl /ṭall-/ "dew" (H. ṭal(l-), Syr. ṭallā, Arab. ṭall)

/ṭ-ᶜ-n/: *nṭᶜn* 1.10:II:24 = **88.56** "to pierce" (H. ṭ-ᶜ-n, Arab. ṭaᶜana, yaṭᶜunu, yaṭᶜanu) or /n-ṭ-ᶜ/ "to plant"(?) (cf. H. n-ṭ-ᶜ)

ẓ

ẓhrm pl. 1.24:21 = **88.1** "gem"; var. of *ṭhrm*

ẓr 1.17:VI:37 = **88.63** "top, back" (cf. Arab. ẓahr)

y

y-, *y.* /yā-/ 1.16:VI:55 = **85.1**; 1.23:46 = **88.2** "O!" (cf. Arab. yā)

y-: ylk 1.19:IV:3 = **87.4** "woe (to you)!" (cf. Arab. way) (or cf. *yl*)

yb 1.19:III:40 = **88.65**, perhaps read *yb*(ky); cf. /n-b-y/ (?)

/y-b-l/: G *ybl* 3.1:25 = **86.31**, *yblnh* 1.100:67 = **86.73**, *nbl*(*n*), *bl* imper. 1.100:2 = **86.73**, *ybl* 1.23:52 = **88.2** G or Gp? "to bring"; 1.100:67 = **86.73** "to carry (away)" (cf. Akkad. (w)abālu; cf. H. y-b-l Hi.)

ybltm du. 1.100:66–67 = **86.73** a (soap?) plant (equivalent to Akkad. maštakal)

ybmt 1.3:II:33, variant (or error) *ymmt* 1.3:III:12 = **87.8**; usually in *ybmt.limm* "progenitress of nations"(?) (cf. H. y-b-m Pi. "to procreate (from a levirate marriage)"; cf. Arab. wabama "to procreate"; cf. H. yəbimt- "(widowed) sister-in-law")

ybnn PN, cf. *ya-ab-na-na* (gen.) U:V:12:9; *ya-ab-ni-in* RS 19.102

yd /yad-/ "hand" (cf. *d* in *bd*) (cf. H. yād, constr. yad, Aram., Arab. yad); 1.14:III:13 = **88.71** "portion" (cf. Akkad. qātu); *ydk* 1.23:47 = **88.2** "(member >) penis"; in the prepositional expression *byd* 3.4:14 = **86.32** "from (the hand of)"; 1.6:II:25 = **88.55** "because of"

yd /yad-/ preposition "(together) with" 3.5:8, 9 = **86.33**; 4.360:4 = **86.12** (cf. Akkad. qa-du P:III:16.353:7–8 (p. 113))

yd /yadd-/ "love, affection" 1.4:IV:38 = **85.2**, probably also 2.10:11 = **86.43** (cf. H. yədīdūt; cf. Arab. wadda "to love")

ydd 1.5:I:8 = **88.54** "beloved" (H. yādīd)

/y-d-y/: *ydy* 1.5:VI:18 = **87.3** "to scratch" (cf. Arab. waḏā(y))

/y-d-ᶜ/: *ydᶜnn*, *tdᶜ*, *dᶜ* imper., "to know" (H. yādaᶜ, yēdaᶜ, Aram. yədaᶜ, Akkad. edū, idū)

yḥr 1.100:73 = **86.73** "snake" or an epithet for snake (nominal prefix *y*-, cf. /ḥ-r-r/)

yṭp 1.18:IV:16 = **88.64** shortened form of PN *yṭpn* 1.18:IV:27

yl: *ylk* 1.19:IV:3 = **87.4**, cf. *y*- "woe!" (or cf. Arab. wayl, with suff. waylaka "woe to you!")

/y-l-d/: *ylt* 1.23:53 = **88.2** perf. du. 3.f., *tldn* "to bear" (H. yālad, tēlēd, Arab. walada, yalidu, Akkad. (w)alādu); Gp *yld* /yulida/ 1.10:III:35 = **88.57** "to be born" (cf. H. yullad, ywld Isa 9:5)

yld "child, boy" (H. yǽlæd; cf. Arab. walad)

ylt 1.23:53 = **88.2** see /y-l-d/

ym /yām-/ (?), cf. *ya-mu* U:V:138:2, pl. *ymm* "day" (cf. H. yōm, pl. yāmīm; cf. Aram. yōm, pl. yōmīn, Arab. yaum, Akkad. ūmu)

ym /yamm-/ "sea"; 1.2:IV:7 = **88.51** DN (perhaps also 1.4:IV:31 = **85.2**) (H. yam, yamm-, Aram. yammā, Arab. yamm)

ymmt 1.3:III:12 = **87.8** see *ybmt*

ymn /yamīn-/ "right (hand)" (H. yāmīn, Arab. yamīn)

yn /yēn-/ "wine," *y*(n) 1.114:3 = **88.3** (H. yáyin, constr. yēn, Arab. wayn, cf. Greek (w)oinos)

ynḥm /yanḥamu/ PN, cf. *ya-an-ḫa-am-mu* P:VI:49:18′; *ya-an-ḫa-mu* U:V:81:42

/y-n-q/: *ynqm* part. du. m. "to suck" (H. yānaq-, yīnaq, Syr. īneq, Akkad. enēqu)

ynt "dove" (H. yōnā)

ysmsm "pleasant, beautiful" (cf. Arab. wasīm "pretty")

ysmt "beauty" (cf. Arab. wasāmat)

yᶜḏrd /yaᶜḏur-addu/ (?) PN ("may (H)addu help!") (cf. Phoen. PN mlkyᶜzr)

yᶜr 1.5:VI:18 = **87.3** "razor" (cf. H. táᶜar)

ypḥ 3.9:18 = **84.2** "witness" (cf. H. (w-)īpē(a)ḥ Ps 27:12)

/y-p-y/ see *tp*

ypltn 4.277:4 = **86.52**, cf. correct *ypltn* 4.215:5; cf. *ya-ap-lu-ṭá-nu* P:III:16.257:III:57 (p. 202), PN (cf. *pu-la-ṭu* U:V:137:II:20′ "to rescue")

/y-ṣ-ᵓ/: *yṣa*, *yṣu*, *tṣi* "to go out"; Š: *šṣa*, part. *mšṣu* part. "to bring out" (H. yāṣāᵓ, yēṣēᵓ, Akkad. (w)aṣū; cf. (Akkad. >) Aram. šēṣī "to bring to end")

yṣb /yaṣṣub-/ (?) 1.16:VI:39 = **85.1** PN, cf. *ya-ṣu-bu* P:III:16.386:2 (p. 165) (cf. Amorite PN Ya-an-ṣi-bu-um)

/y-ṣ-q/: *yṣq* 1.71:25 = **86.62** inf. abs. (?), imper. (?); *yṣq* 1.5:VI:14 = **87.3** imperf.; "to pour" (H. yāṣaq, yiṣṣōq)

/y-r-d/: *yrt* 1.5:I:6 = **88.54** perf. 2. sing. m., *yrd*, *ard*, *rd* imper., *yrdm* part. pl. "to go down" (H. yārad, yērēd, rēd; cf. Arab. warada, yaridu "to come"; cf. Akkad. (w)arādu)

/y-r-w/ (?): *tr* 1.10:II:11 = **88.56** imperf. 3. sing. f. "to shoot"(?), "to take off"(?) (cf. H. y-r-y "to shoot"; ESA wrw, Eth. warawa "to throw")

yrḫ /yarḫ-/ "month" 1.105:1 = **81.3**; 1.109:5 = **86.71**; 4.266:2 = **86.22** (H. yǽraḥ < yarḥ-, Akkad. (w)arḫu)

yrḫ /yariḫ-/ (?) DN ("Moon") 1.24:16, 17, 33 = **88.1**; 1.114:4 = **88.3**; 1.109:17 = **86.71**; 1.19:IV:2 = **87.4** (cf. H. yārē(a)ḥ, Akkad. (w)arḫu)

yrḫm PN, cf. *ya-ri-ḫi-ma-nu* U:V:86:24

yrq 1.14:III:22 = **88.71** "yellow (color), yellow/pale (gold)" (cf. H. yǽræq "yellow/green thing"; cf. Eth. warq "gold")

/y-š-n/: *yšn* "(to go) to sleep" (H. y-š-n: yī(y)šan, yāšēn, cf. Arab. wasina, yawsanu)

yšril 4.623:3 = **86.11** PN (cf. H. Yiśrāᵓēl?)

ytm /yatum-/ (?) "orphan" (H. yātōm, Syr. yatmā, Arab. yatīm)

/y-t-n/: *ytt* 1.100:75 = **86.73** perf. 1. sing. *ytn*, *ttn*, imperf. 1. sing. *atn* 1.24:19 = **88.1**;

1.17:VI:27 = **88.63** (also *itn*?, 2.15:4 = **86.45**), imper. *tn*, "to give" (Phoen. y-t-n: yaton (perf.), cf. H. nātan, yittēn, tēn)

ytnt 1.14:III:31 = **88.71** "gift"; 1.127:5 = **86.741** "gift"(?) or PN(?) (cf. PN *ytn* 6.17:2, 4.609:35; [y]*a-ta-nu* P:III:16.245:4 (p. 94))

/y-ṯ-b/: *yṯb*, *aṯb*, *ṯb* "to sit" (H. yāšab, yēšēb, šēb; Aram. yĕtib; cf. Akkad. (w)ašābu; cf. Arab. waṯaba, yaṯibu "to jump" (all with crossed legs?))

yṯn /yaṯan-/ (?) 1.71:24 = **86.62** "old" (H. yāšān)

/y-ṯ-q/: *yṯq* 1.100:6 = **86.73** imperf. "to bind" (cf. Arab. w-ṯ-q IV "to bind") or "to overfeed"(?) (cf. Arab. waṯaqa (?))

k

k-, *k*. /ki-/ "as, like" 1.23:50 = **88.2**; 1.16:VI:43 = **85.1**, etc.; "according to" 1.127:9 = **86.741** (H. kə-, kā-, Arab. ka); with *-m*: *km* /kimā/ (H. kəmō, Arab. kamā, cf. Akkad. kīma); conj. "as" 1.18:IV:(18), 29 = **88.64**

k- /ki/ (?) affirmative particle "surely, verily," before imperfect 1.4:IV:27 = **85.2**, 1.17:VI:30 = **88.63**, cf. also 1.5:I:1 = **88.54**, 2.15:4 = **86.45**(?) (cf. H. kī Ps 49:16; 128:2; cf. H. ᵓak)

k- /kī/ "when, if" 1.71:23 = **86.62**; *ky* 2.16:7 = **84.1** (H. kī, Phoen. chy, Anc. Aram. ky, Akkad. kī)

/k-b-d/: D *tkbd* "(to consider heavy >) to honor" (cf. H. k-b-d Pi; cf. Akkad. kabātu D)

kbd 4.143:5 = **81.5**, 4.338:11 = **86.26** "total"(?) (cf. Mari Akkad. kabittum "main part"(?), "total"(?) and below)

kbd /kabid-/ du. *kbdm*, pl. *kbdt* 1.6:II:16, 17 = **88.55**; 1.109:8, 12 = **86.71**; 1.19:III:33, 38 = **88.65** "liver" (H. kābēd, Arab. kabid, cf. Akkad. kabattu, kabittu)

kbkb /kabkab-/ "star" (cf. Akkad. kakkabu < *kabkab-; cf. H. kōkāb < *kawkab- < *kab-, Arab. kawkab)

kbln PN (Hurrian?)

kd /kadd-/ "jar" (H. kad(d-), Greek kados)

kd̠ǵdl PN (Hurrian; DN Kušuḫ + adal)

khn /kāhin-/ "priest" (Arab. kāhin, H. kōhēn)

/k-h-p/: *ykhp* 1.71:23 = **86.62** "to snort" (of a horse)(?)

/k-w-n/: *ykn* "to be" (Phoen. kn, chon, ykn; Old-Canaan. ku-na imper. EA 147:36; Arab. kāna, yakūnu; cf. H. k-w-n Ni. "to be firm," cf. Akkad. kānu "to stay")

kḫṯ "chair" (cf. Old-Canaan. ka-aḫ-šu, Hurrian kešḫi)

ky 2.16:7 = **84.1** see *k-* /kī/

kl /kull-/ "every, all"; *klh*, *klhm*; *kl yrḫ* 1.127:1 = **86.741** "every month"(?) (cf. also *klyrḫ* PN); *kl* | *kl* 1.127.7–8 = **88.741** "sacrifice of all, all will be consumed" (or *klkl*?) (cf. H. kōl, kål-, kull-, Aram. kål-, kǒllā, Arab. kull-)

klb 1.16:I:15 = **88.73** (cf. 1.114:12 = **88.3**!?) "dog"(?) /kalb-/ (cf. H. kǽlæb, Arab. kalb, Akkad. kalbu)

klby PN, cf. *kal-bi-ya* P:III:15.136:4 (p. 121)

kld PN(?) or title of official(?)

/k-l-y/: N *nkly* "to be spent"; D *ykly*, *tkly*, *tkl* "to finish with, annihilate" (cf. H. k-l-y)

klkl 3.5:10 = **86.33**, 2.38:21 = **86.41** "everything" (cf. Akkad. (qa-du) gab-bi mim-mu-šu P:III:16.353:8 (p. 113)); for 1.127:7–8 = **86.741**(?) see *kl*

kll /kalīl-/ (?) "whole" 1.115:10 = **82.5** (cf. H. kəlīl constr. Judg 20:40)

klt /kallat-/ "bride" (H. kallā, Syr. kallṯā, Akkad. kallātu)

kltn PN (Hurrian)

km "as, like" see *k-*

kmm 1.109:11 = **86.71**, adv. "likewise"(?)

/k-m-s/: tD *tkms* 1.12:II:54 = **88.4** "to be prostrate" (cf. Akkad. kamāsu)

kn /kin-/ (?) 1.12:II:53 = **88.4** "so" (H. kēn)

kn 2.38:10 = **86.41** in *anykn*, suff. 2. sing. m. *-k* + *-n* "your"(?)

knp /kunap-/ (?) "wing" (H. kānāp, Arab. kanaf)

knrt(?) 1.19:III:41 = **88.65** pl. of *knr* (cf. 1.108:4) "lyre" (cf. H. kinnōr, pl. kinnōrōt) or GN? (cf. H. kinnæræt) or read *knkt*(?) "jar/urn"(?) (cf. *kknt* 1.6:I:67) (cf. Arab. kankan "barrel")

ks /kās-/ "cup" (H. kōs, f. cf. Ps 23:5, Syr. kāsā, Akkad. kāsu, Arab. kaᵓsu)

ksu (nom. cf. 1.4:VIII:12), *ksi* gen., *ksa* acc. /kussiᵓ-/ (?) "throne, seat" (cf. Old Akkad. kussīum, Akkad. kussūm < Sumer. gu-za, H. kissēᵓ, Aram. kårsēᵓ)

/k-s-y/: *yks* D? 1.5:VI:16 = **87.3** "to cover, put on," cf. [ku-u]*s*(?)-*sú* U:V:137:I:21′ "to cover"

(cf. H. k-s-y Pi.)

ksl /kasl-/ "(loins >) back" (H. kǽsæl)

ksm 1.17:I:31 = **87.1** "portion"(?) (cf. Akkad. kasāmu "to cut to pieces")

ksp /kasp-/, cf. *kàs-pu*, *ka-as-pu* U:V:137:II:2′, 3′, "silver"; with *-m* 1.14:IV:42 = **88.72** (cf. H. kǽsæp, Aram. kaspā, Akkad. kaspu)

kp /kapp-/ "palm (of hand)"; 1.24:35 = **88.1** "tray/pan (of scales)" (H. kap(p-), and Akkad. kappu "palm"; cf. Arab. kaff "palm; tray/pan (of scales)")

krd PN

/k-r-k-r/: *ykrkr* "to twiddle" (cf. Arab. karkara "to turn" > "to repeat"; cf. H. k-r-r "to dance": məkarker)

krm /karm-/ "vineyard" (H. kǽræm, Syr. karmā, Arab. karm)

krs 1.5:I:4 = **88.54** "belly"(?) (cf. H. kərēś-?, Syr. karsā, Arab. kariš?) or *k-* + *rs*, perhaps to be corrected to *r*(k)*s*(?) "belt," cf. /r-k-s/ "to bind" 1.1:V:10, 23 (cf. H. r-k-s, Akkad. rakāsu)

krsn: du. *krsnm* 4.279:3 = **86.24** a kind of jar(?) or a liquid measure(?)

/k-r-ʿ/: *ykrʿ* "to kneel down" (H. kāraʿ, yikraʿ)

/k-r-r/(?) see /k-r-k-r/

krpn /karpān-/(?) "goblet" (cf. Akkad. karpāniš "like an earthen vessel," karpatu "(earthen) vessel")

krt PN (the form "Keret" is not based on ancient tradition; cf. Ki-ir-ta, the name of a Mitannian king, attested also at Alalaḫ; cf. perhaps *krty* 4.371:18 "Cretan"(?), and H. k-r-(w)-t Zeph 2:6(?))

ktn pl. *ktnt* 3.1:21, a kind of robe (cf. Syr. kuttīnā, H. kuttónæt, Akkad. kititu, kitintu, cf. Greek khitōn)

ktp /katip-/ "shoulder" (H. kātēp, Arab. katif)

kṯr /kōṯar-/ DN ("skillful"), *kṯr.wḫss* 1.2:IV:7 = **88.51**, cf. *ku-šar-ru* U:V:137:IVa:19 (cf. PN *ku-šar-a-bu* U:V:96:27) (cf. Phoen. Chousōr; cf. Arab. kawṯar, a fountain in Paradise)

l

l-, *l.* /lē-/(?), cf. *le-e*[?] U:V:130:III:5′, with suff. *ly*, *lk*, *lnh* "to, at, from"; local 2.10:5, 6 = **86.43**, 1.5:VI:12, 13 = **87.3**, 1.14:III:28, 29 = **88.71**; temporal: 3.4:1 = **86.32**, 3.5:1 = **86.33**, 1.19:IV:5, 6 = **87.4** (H., Aram. lə-, Arab. li, Amorite la, Akkad. < Aram. la); with *-m*: *lm* (cf. 1.14:II:49) probably 1.12:II:57 = **88.4** (cf. PN Ləmō-ʾel Prov 31:4?)

l- /la-/(?) affirmative "yea" 1.4:IV:20, V:12; 1.2:IV:6, 7 = **88.51**; 1.100:63 = **86.73**; perhaps 1.17:VI:43 = **88.63** (cf. Arab. la)

l- /lā/ negative "not" 1.2:IV:6 = **88.51** ("not (yet)"); 1.16:I:23 = **88.73**, 1.114:7 = **88.3**, 3.5:17 = **86.33**, 4.338:3 = **82.4**, 1.14:III:15 = **88.71**, *la-a* U:V:130:II:7′, 12′ (Aram., Arab., Akkad. lā, H. lō)

l- /la/(?) interjection "O!" 1.2:IV:8 = **88.51**, 1.16:VI:41 = **85.1**, 1.15:II:13 = **87.2**, 1.17:VI:42 = **88.63** (cf. Arab. la-)

l- /lū/ "if only," "O that" 1.5:I:6 = **88.54**, 1.22:II:5, 6 = **87.6**, 1.15:II:14, 15 = **87.2** (H. lū, cf. Akkad. lū, Arab. law, Syr. lway)

la: la.šmm 1.6:II:25 = **88.55**, probably perf. 3. du. (but. cf. *šmm: ša-mu-ma*!) "to shine"(?) (cf. Arab. laʾlaʾa) or "to be tired"(?) (cf. H. l-ʾ-y, Arab. laʾā(y), Akkad. laʾū) or "to be soiled"(?) (cf. Akkad. luʾʾū D "to soil" and luʾʾū "soiled"; cf. also *ṣḥrr*)

/l-ʾ-w/ (or /l-ʾ-y/): *tlu* imperf. 3. sing. f. 1.100:68 = **86.73** "to be strong, victorious"; cf. *aliy*(*n*) (cf. Akkad. leʾāʾum, leʾū)

/l-ʾ-k/: *likt*, *ilak*, *ylak*, *lak* 2.10:10 = **86.43** imper.(?), inf.(?); *lakm* 2.30:19 = **83.4** inf. abs., "to send" (see also *mlak* and *mlakt*)

lim: pl. *limm* "people, nation" (cf. H. ləʾōm, ləʾumm-; cf. Akkad. līmu, liʾmu "thousand")

lb /libb-/ "heart, mind" (cf. H. lēb < libb-, Aram. libb-, Arab. libb, Akkad. libbu), see also *aplb*

/l-b-š/: *lbš* 4.338:16 = **86.26** "to dress" (H. lābēš, yilbaš, Arab. labisa, yilbasu, Akkad. labāšu) or *l* + *b*(n)*š*(?)

lbš 4.146:1 = **86.25** "garment," cf. *lpš* 1.5:VI:16 = **87.3** (cf. H. ləbūš, Akkad. lubūšu)

lḥ(y): *lḥm* du. 1.5:VI:19 = **87.3** "jaw, cheek" (cf. H. ləḥī, du. ləḥāyáyim, Akkad. laḫū, Arab. laḥy) or "whisker(s)"(?) (cf. Arab. liḥyat)

/l-ḥ-m/: G *ylḥm*, *tlḥmn*, *lḥm* 1.4:IV:35 = **88.2** inf. abs. "to eat"; Š *tšlḥm*, *yšlḥm* "to feed" (cf. H. l-ḥ-m "to feed": tilḥam, Akkad. laʾāmum, lēmu); cf. *lḥm*

lḥm /laḥm-/ "food, bread" (H. lǽḥæm, Phoen.

lḥm, Aram. ləḥem, Syr. laḥmā, "bread," but cf. Arab. laḥm "meat"); 1.114:7 = **88.3** probably "meat"

lḥt 1.17:I:28 = **87.1** "insult"(?) (cf. Arab. laḥw and laḥy) or "freshness, vigor" (cf. H. lēḥ- "sap"; Postbibl. H. lēḥā "moisture")

/l-ḫ-š/: "to whisper" D part. *mlḫš* "conjurer" (cf. H. l-ḥ-š, məlaḥăšīm Ps 58:6; Akkad. laḫāšu G and D, mulaḫḫišu)

lḫšt "whisper" (cf. H. láḥaš)

lṭpn "kind, kindly one" 1.15:II:13 = **87.2**, 1.16:I:21, 23 = **88.73**, epithet of the god Il (cf. Arab. laṭīf)

llu (nom. 1.86:15), *lli* gen. "kid" (Akkad. laliu, lalū)

lm 1.12:II:57 = **88.4** see *l*- prep.

lm /lē-mā/ (?) 2.33:23 = **86.42**, 1.14:III:33 = **88.71** "why?"

ln 1.17:I:29 = **87.1** (?) "look, appearance"(?) (cf. Akkad. lānu; cf. Arab. lawn "color")

lnh 1.17:I:29 = **87.1** (?) "from" + suff., see *l*- prep.

/l-s-m/: *tlsmn* "to run" (Akkad. lasāmu)

lpš "garment" see *lbš*

lṣb 1.4:IV:28 = **85.2**, 1.103:49 "mouth"(?) (cf. Arab. liṣb "narrow passage, strait")

/l-q-ḥ/: *lqḥ*, *lqḥt*, *iqḥ*, *tqḥ*, *yqḥnn*, *qḥ* "to take" (H. lāqaḥ, yiqqaḥ, qaḥ, Anc. Aram. lqḥ, yqḥ, Akkad. leqū, laqū)

/l-q-ẓ/ 1.19:III:40 = **88.65** "to gather" (cf. H. and Arab. l-q-ṭ?)

lrmn- 1.23:50 = **88.2** "pomegranate" (cf. Akkad. lurmū, lurimtu; cf. H. rimmōn, Arab. rummān)

/-l-š-/: *ylšn* 1.114:20 = **88.3** imperf. 3. sing. m. + suff. m.(?) "to knead"(?), or "to wallow" or "to soil"(?) (cf. H. l-w-š and Akkad. lāšu "to knead"(?); cf. Jew.-Aram. lišluštā "foam (of nostrils)" and Postbibl. H. lišlǽšæt "chicken's dirt," "spittle"(?))

ltn 1.5:I:1 = **88.54** "sea dragon" (H. liwyātān)

m

m- /mi(n)-/: *mab* "from" 2.16:11 = **84.1**; *mrḥqtm* 2.64:15 = **82.1** (cf. H., Aram. min, mēʾ-)

-*m*: *wm* 3.9:6 = **84.2** see *im*

mid /maʾd-/ (?) 1.4:V:15 = **88.53** "plenty"; adv. "much" 2.10:13 = **86.43**, 2.16:10 = **84.1**

mad /maʾād-/ 1.103:1 = **86.744** "plenty," cf. *ma-a-duma* U:V:137:II:36′ (cf. H. məʾōd; Akkad. mādu adj.)

mizrt: *mizrtm* du. 1.5:VI:17 = **87.3** a garment, probably loin-cloth, consisting of two pieces (cf. Arab. miʾzar and H. ʾēzōr "loin-cloth")

miḫd 4.266:5 = **86.22** a precious object

mat 4.266:7 = **86.22** see *mit*

mit /miʾt-/ "100"; du. gen.-acc. *mitm* /miʾtēmi/ 4.213:28 = **86.23**; pl. *mat* /miʾāt-/ 4.266:7 = **86.22** (cf. H. mēʾā, Phoen. mʾt, Aram. məʾā, Arab. miʾat)

mbk /mabbak-/ (< -*nb-) "source" (cf. H. mibbəkī Job 28:11, nibkē Job 38:16)

mdgt: *b mdgt* (or *bm dgt*?) 1.19:III:41 = **88.65** "darkness"(?) or "grave"(?) (cf. Arab. duǧǧat "darkness")

mdw /madw(ī)-/ "sickness" (H. constr. madwē; cf. dəwāy Ps 41:4)

/m-d-l/: *tmdln* "to saddle"

mḏr 1.119:30 = **86.75** a kind of vow/offering

mḏrǵl "soldier armed with *mḏrn* (cf. 4.167:11)" (-*ǵl*/-*uḫ-lu* is a Hurrian affix)

mh /mah/ "what?" (H., Aram., Arab. mā)

mhk 2.38:26 = **86.41**, (pseudo-)pl.(??) or + -*m* *mhkm* 2.30:22 = **83.4** interrog. gener. pron. "whatever"(?)

mhmrt 1.5:I:7–8 = **88.54** "gullet" (< "pit filled with rain-water"(?), cf. H. pl. mahămōrōt; Arab. hamara "to pour," hamrat "rain")

mhr 1.100:73, 74 = **86.73** "bride-price" (H. móhar, Arab. mahr)

mhr: pl. *mhrm* 1.17:VI:40 = **88.63** "soldier"; cf. *m*[a]-*aḫ-ḫu-ram* U:V:137:II:24′ "young hero"(?) (cf. Phoen. PN mhrbʿl, Maharbal); cf. also *mh!rh* 1.18:IV:26 = **88.64** (the tablet has *mprh*) or "for his insolence"(?) < "haste" (cf. H. məhērā)

/m-w-t/: *mt*, *mtt*, *amtm*, *tmtn*, inf. abs. *mtm* "to die" (H. mōt, yāmūt, Arab. māta, yamūtu)

mznm du. only "scales" (H. mō(ʾ)znáyim, Aram. mō(ʾ)zanyā, Arab. mīzān, pl. mawāzin, cf. wazana "to weigh")

mḥmd 1.4:V:16 = **88.53** "desirable, precious (thing)" (cf. H. maḥmad, maḥmūd-)

mḫ 1.16:I:27 = **88.73** "marrow, brain" (H. mō(a)ḥ, Arab. muḫḫ; cf. Akkad. muḫḫu "skull")

/m-ḫ-ṣ/: *mḫṣ*, *tmḫṣ* "to smite, slay" (H. māḥaṣ, yimḥaṣ, Akkad. maḫāṣu; cf. Arab. maḫaḍa); Gp(?) 1.19:IV:4 = **87.4**

mḫṣ 1.19:IV:4(?) = **87.4** "murder"(?)

mḫr /maḫīr-/ "price" (H. məḥīr, Akkad. maḫīru)

mṭ "staff" (H. maṭṭǣ)

my /miya/ 1.5:VI:23 = **87.3** "who?" (H. mī, Old Canaan. miya)

my 1.19:II:6 = **87.5** "water" (cf. H. pl. máyim, Syr. mayyā)

mk 1.17:I:15 = **88.61** "lo!" (cf. Akkad. muk(u)?)

/m-l-ʾ/ D "to (ful)fill" (H. m-l-ʾ Pi.)

mlu(?): f. *mlat* 1.10:II:12 = **88.56** "full" (H. mālēʾ, Syr. mlē(ʾ), Arab. maliʾ)

mlak /malʾak-/ "messenger" (H. malʾāk, Arab. malʾak, cf. l-ʾ-k IV)

mlakt /malʾakat-/ "mission" (cf. H. məlā(ʾ)kā "mission, business, work")

mlat 1.109:3 = **86.71** "fullness, full moon"; see also *mlu*

mlḥ f. *mlḥt* 1.4:VI:57 = **87.7** "good"(?), "pleasant"(?), cf. *uz.mrat.mlḥt* 4.247:20 "a good fat goose" (cf. Arab. malīḥ)

mlḥmt "fight, war" (H. milḥāmā, Arab. malḥamat)

/m-l-k/: *amlk* "to reign, rule" (H. mālak, yimlōk, cf. Arab. malaka, yamliku)

mlk /milk-/ (?), /mulk-/ (?) 1.2:IV:10 = **88.51**; 1.16:VI:52 = **85.1** "ruling, kingship" (cf. Arab. mulk?)

mlk /malk-/, cf. *ma-al-ku* U:V:130:III:13′; 137:II:32′ "king" (H., Aram. mǽlæk, malk-; cf. Akkad. mal(i)ku, Arab. malik)

mlkytn PN (cf. Phoen. PN mlkytn, in Cypriote syllabary mi-li-ki-ya–to-no-(se))

mlkt /malkat-/ "queen" (H. malkā, Phoen. mlkt, Aram. malkətā)

mm 2.10:9 = **86.43** "water"(?), cf. *my*(?); or is *inmm* an extended form of *in* "there is not"?; or to be read *m*(n)*m*(?)

mn prep. "from," see *m-*

mnm "whatever" 2.10:16 = **86.43**, 2.16:16 = **84.1**, 2.38:8 = **86.41**, 2.41:16 = **83.3** (cf. Akkad. mīnummē)

/m-n-n/: D passive, *mmnnm* part. + *-m* 1.23:47 = **88.2** "to be weakened/lowered"(?) (cf. Arab. m-n-n IV "to weaken"; cf. Eth. mannana "rejected")

mnt 1.17:I:32 = **87.1** "portion" (H. mānā and mənāt); perhaps also 1.6:II:36 = **88.55**; or "limb(s)"? (cf. Akkad. pl. of minītu)

mnt 1.100:4, 70 = **86.73** "incantation" (cf. Akkad. minūtu "recitation (of an incantation)")

mswn 1.14:III:21 = **88.71** "camp"(?)

mʿ interj. "pray"

mʿn 2.10:15 = **86.43** "answer, reply" (H. maʿănǣ)

/m-ǵ-y/: *mǵy*, *mǵyt*, *mǵt*, *ymǵ*, *ymǵy*, *tmǵyy* 2.33:31 = **86.42** "to reach, arrive" (cf. Arab. maḍā(y), yamḍī "to go out/further," Aram. mĕṭā (mṭy Kt.), Syr. mṭā, mṭī "he reached"; also H. māṣāʾ "he found")

mpr: *mprh* 1.18:IV:26 = **88.64** "destruction" (??); cf. *apr* 1.15:III:30 (cf. H. p-w-r and p-r-r "to break"); or read *mh*!*rh*(?)

mṣb 1.24:34 = **88.1** "stand (for scales)," cf. /n-ṣ-b/ (cf. H. maṣṣāb)

mṣb 4.213:28 = **86.23** a quality of wine (< C passive part. /n-ṣ-b/?, "settled down"(?) or a place for storing wine?

mṣd 1.100:58 = **86.73** "fortress, inaccessible place"(?) (cf. H. məṣād, məṣūdā?) or "hunting place"?, cf. /ṣ-w-d/ (?)

mṣd 1.114:1, 7 = **88.3** "banquet, food" (cf. H. ṣáyid II) or "(sacrifice of) prey, game" (cf. H. məṣūdā Ezek 13:21; ṣáyid I)

mṣlt 1.12:II:61 = **88.4** "bell"(?) (cf. H. pl. constr. məṣillōt) or part. pl. f. constr. of /ṣ-l-l/ (?) "ringing bells" (cf. H. ṣ-l-l)

mṣrm GN "Egypt" (H. miṣráyim)

mqm 1.14:III:23 = **88.71** "place; estate"(?) (H. māqōm, Arab. maqām)

/-m-r-/: *mr* 1.2:IV:19 = **88.51** imper. "to expel"; /y-m-r/ (?) cf. *aymr* 1.2:IV:19 = **88.51**; or /m-r-y/ (?) (cf. Arab. marā(y) "to drag forth")

/-m-r-/: *tmr* 1.15:II:15 = **87.2** see /m-r-r/

mri gen. /marīʾ-/ (?) "fatted, fatling" (H. mərīʾ; cf. Akkad. marū)

mrzḥ /marziḥ-/, cf. *ma-ar-zi-ḫi* RS 14.16:3, Syria 28, 173; 3.9:1 = **84.2** "(religious) association"; 1.114:15 = **88.3** "banquet" (cf. Phoen. mrzḥ "festival," Punic, Aram. mrzḥ(ʾ) "(cultic) association," H. marzē(a)ḥ, mirzaḥ Amos 6:7; Jer 16:5 "banquet, cult festival"; cf. Greek thiasos)

mrḥq pl. 1.127:31 = **86.741** "distance; future"(?) (cf. H. mærḥaq), cf. *rḥq*

mryn cf. *mar-ya-nu* P:III:16.239:17 (p. 80), pl. *mar-ya-nu-ma* P:VI:93:1 "warrior" (< Sanskrit marya- "young man")

mrkbt /markabt-/, cf. *mar-kab-te* gen. P:III: 16.249:28 (p. 98) "chariot" (cf. H. mærkābā, constr. mirkæbæt, cf. Akkad. narkabtu < *ma-)

/m-r-r/: ***tmr*** 1.15:II:15 = **87.2** "to strengthen, bless" (cf. Arab. marīr "strong")

/m-r-r/ Š: ***šmrr*** inf. 1.100:4 = **86.73** "to poison" (cf. H. mərōr "bitter," mərōrat pətānīm Job 20:14 "poison of vipers"; Anc. Aram. mryr and Syr. mrīr "bitter," Syr. martā "bile, poison")

mšdpt 1.14:III:14 = **88.71** part. Dp /š-d-p/ "to be thrown on high"(?) (cf. Arab. š-d-p "to be tall"?) or "citadel"

/m-š-ḥ/: ***ymšḥ*** "to anoint" (H. māšaḥ, yimšaḥ; cf. Aram. məšaḥ "oil")

mškn pl. *mšknth* 1.17:V:32–33 = **88.62** "dwelling" (H. miškān, pl. miškānōt)

mšmš 1.12:II:55 = **88.4** "swamp"(?)

mšṣu 1.17:I:27 = **87.1** see /y-ṣ-ʾ/: Š

mšrrm pl. 1.24:36 = **88.1** a part of a scale, "beam"(?) or "ingot"? (cf. Syr. š-r-r Pa. "to stabilize")

mt /mut-/ 1.23:46 = **88.2**, 3.9:13 = **84.2**, 1.17:I:17 = **88.61**, 1.17:VI:35 = **88.63** (written erroneously *mm*), 36; pl. *mtm* 1.16:I:7 "man" (cf. PN *mu-ut-*(il)baᶜal(*al*) P:III:16.155:6 (p. 209)) (cf. H. pl. mətē, mĕtū- in PN, Amor. mu-tu-in PN, Akkad. mutu)

mt /mōt-/ 1.100:65 = **86.73**; *mtm* 2.10:12 = **86.43** "death" (H. mā́wæt, constr. mōt, Aram. mōt, Arab. mawt); DN 1.100:65 = **86.73**(?); 1.6:II:13 = **88.55**

mtntm du. 1.109:7 = **86.71** "loins" (cf. Syr. matnātā, H. måtnayim)

mtq /matuq-/: *mtqtm* du. f. 1.23:50 = **88.2** "sweet" (H. mātōq, Akkad. matqu, f. matuqtu)

mṯyn 4.146:5 = **86.25** a kind of garment

mṯn "repetition," cf. *ma-aš-nu-ú* U:V:137:II:41′; "replica"(?), cf. /ṯ-n-y/ (cf. H. mišnǣ); *mṯn.rgmm* 1.17:VI:39 = **88.63** "repetition of words"(?) or "another word"(?)

mṯt "lass, lady" (cf. *mṯ* "lad")

n

/n-ʾ-ṣ/: ***niṣ*** part. "to revile" (H. nāʾaṣ, yinʾaṣ, Akkad. nāṣu)

nat 1.127:4 = **86.741** PN f.(?); a kind of offering(?) (cf. H. naʾăwā "the seemly, proper")

/n-b-y/: ***yb*** 1.19:III:40 = **88.65** "to take out"(?) or is *yb* from /n-b-b/ "to hollow"? (cf. H. nābūb "hollowed") or read *yb*(ky)(?)

/n-g-y/: ***ng*** imper. 1.14:III:27 = **88.71** "to depart" (cf. Arab. naǧā(w), yanǧū)

/n-g-š/: ***ngš*** inf. abs. 1.6:II:21 = **88.55** "to press"; D(?) *ngšnn* 1.114:19 = **88.3** "to press/drive"(?) (cf. H. nāgaś, yiggōś; cf. Arab. naǧaša "to rouse/drive (game)")

/n-g-ṯ/: N ***tngṯh*** 1.6:II:27 = **88.55** "to approach" (cf. H. n-g-š Q. and Ni., Akkad. nagāšu; cf. Arab. naǧaṯa "to seek out"?)

/n-d-d/: ***ydd***, ***tdd*** "to move suddenly/fast"; 3.9:12 = **84.2** "to rise (suddenly?)"; 1.10:II:17 = **88.56**, 1.22:II:5, 6 = **87.6** "to hurry" (cf. H. n-d-d: nādā́dū, yiddōd, Aram. nadd-, Arab. nadda "to flee"; cf. Akkad. nadādu?)

/n-d-y/: ***ydy*** 1.119:35 = **86.75**, *tdy* 1.119:28 = **86.75** "to throw/drive away, to remove" (cf. Postbibl. H. n-d-y Pi. "to banish," Akkad. nadū "to throw (away)")

/n-d-r/: ***ydr*** 1.14:IV:37 = **88.72** "to vow" (H. nādar, yiddōr, cf. Arab. naḏara, yanḏuru)

ndr 1.127:2 = **86.741** "vow" (H. nǽdær, nédær; cf. Arab. naḏr)

nhqt "braying" (cf. H. n-h-q, Arab. nahaqa)

nhr /nah(a)r-/ "river" 1.4:IV:21 = **85.2**; 1.100:3 = **86.73** (H. nāhār, Aram. nəhar, Arab. nahr, Akkad. nāru); DN 1.2:IV:20 = **88.51**

nwgn 3.4:3 = **86.32** PN or read *nrgn*?

/n-w-y/: Š ***šnwt*** 1.96:1 = **82.6** "to consider beautiful," "to praise" (cf. H. n-w-y, Exod. 15:2)

/n-w-r/: ***nr*** 2.16:9 = **84.1** "to shine" (cf. Akkad. nawāru "to be light, to shine"; cf. Arab. n-w-r "to light (up)," cf. H. mənōrā "lampstand")

nḥlt /naḥlat-/(?) "inheritance" (H. naḥălā; cf. Arab. niḥlat "gift")

nḥš "snake" (H. nāḥāš)

/n-ḥ-t/: ***nḥtm*** part. + *-m* 1.23:47 = **88.2** "to go down"; D *ynḥt* 1.2:IV:18 = **88.51** "to bring down" (cf. H. n-ḥ-t: yēḥat, Aram. n-ḥ-t, Syr. nḥēt, neḥōt)

nḫl /naḫl-/ "torrent, wady" (H. náḥal, Akkad.

naḫ(al)lu)

nyr 1.24:16 = **88.1** "illuminator," cf. /n-w-r/ (cf. Syr. nayyar Pi. "to illuminate"; cf. Arab. nayyir "shining")

nkl /nik(k)al-/ DN f. 1.24:1, 17, 33 = **88.1** (cf. PN *ᶜbdnkl* 4.63:II:43; abdi-*ni-kál* U:V:6:31, cf. Sumer. NIN-GAL); double name *nkl.wib* 1.24:1 = **88.1**

/n-k-r/: N(?) ***ykr*** 1.100:62 = **86.73** "to estrange oneself" (cf. H. n-k-r Ni. and Hitpa., Akkad. nakāru)

nn: yᶜmsn.nn 3.5:11 = **86.33**, *ytn.nn* 1.114:18 = **88.3** suffixed pronoun 3. sing. m./f. "him"/"her"

/n-s-y/ (?): ***ysynh*** 1.100:66 = **86.73** "to remove" (cf. Akkad. nesū "to be distant," D nussū "to remove"; cf. Arab. nassa "to drive away")

/n-s-k/: ***sk*** imper. 1.3:III:16 = **87.8**; *ysk* Gp/N 1.17:VI:36 = **88.63** "to pour" (H. nāsak, yissəkū, cf. Arab. nasaka, yansuku, cf. Akkad. nasāku)

/n-s-ᶜ/: ***ysᶜ, isᶜ*** "to pull out" > "to pay"(?) 3.9:10, 17 = **84.2** (cf. perhaps *tšᶜn* 3.8:12, 14) (cf. H. nāsaᶜ, yissaᶜ "to pull out, depart")

/n-ᶜ-/ (?): ***(w)nᶜ*** 1.24:31 = **88.1** (?) "to require, ask" (cf. Arab. nāᶜa) (?)

nᶜm: f. *nᶜmt* 1.10:II:16 = **88.56**; du. m. *nᶜmm* 1.23:23 = **88.2** "pleasant" (H. nāᶜīm, Arab. naᶜīm)

nᶜm 1.3:III:31 = **87.8** "loveliness"; 1.85.1 = **86.61** "health"(?) (cf. H. nóᶜam)

nᶜmy /-ay/ 1.6:II:19 = **88.55** "loveliness, lovely place" (cf. Arab. nuᶜmā(y))

nᶜmn /naᶜmān-/ 1.15:II:15 = **87.2**, 1.17:VI:45 = **88.63** "(a) gracious (person)" (also PN, cf. H. PN Naᶜămān); epithet of heroes (cf. H. niṭᶜē naᶜămāmīm "gardens of Adonis")

/n-ᶜ-r/: D ***ynᶜrnh*** 1.100:65 = **86.73** "to shake off" (H. n-ᶜ-r Pi.)

nᶜr /naᶜr-/ 2.33:29 = **86.42**; 4.360:5 = **86.12** "boy, servant" (H. náᶜar, Phoen. nᶜr)

/n-ǵ-ṣ/: N ***tnǵṣn*** 1.2:IV:26 = **88.51** "to shake" (cf. Arab. naǵaḍa; cf. Arab. tanaǵǵaṣa "to be disquieted")

/n-ǵ-r/: ***tǵrk*** 2.16:5 = **84.1**, cf. *ni-iḫ-rum* U:V:137:I:11′, "to preserve, protect" (cf. H. nāṣār-, tiṣṣōr; Aram. n-ṭ-r; Arab. naẓara, yanẓuru)

/n-p-l/: ***npl*** "to fall" (H. nāpal, yippōl, Aram. nəpal, yippel)

npṣ 1.17:I:33 = **87.1** "garment" (cf. Arab. nifāḍ "smock")

npr 1.6:II:37 = **88.55** "sparrow" (cf. Arab. naffār)

npš /napš-/ 1.109:12 = **86.71** "lung"; 1.18:IV:25 = **88.64** "(throat >) breath"; 4.338:1 = **82.4** "soul; person" (H. nǽpæš, Arab. nafs)

/n-ṣ-b/: ***nṣb*** part. "to set up" (cf. H. n-ṣ-b Hi., Arab. naṣaba, yanṣubu)

nqmd /niqmaddu/, cf. *níq-ma*-(il)adu P:VI:45:2, cf. *ni-iq-ma*(!)-*du* on the seal of the dynasty (RS 17.378B), U:III,70, PN, name of several kings of Ugarit

nqmpᶜ /niqmēpaᶜ/, cf. *níq-me-pa* P:III:15.126:2 (p. 112), PN, name of a king of Ugarit

nr 2.16:9 = **84.1** see /n-w-r/

nrt 1.6:II:24 = **88.55** "luminary" (cf. H. nēr, pl. nērōt "lamp")

nš- pl. *nšm* 1.6:II:18 = **88.55**; 1.3:III:27 = **87.8** "men" (cf. H. pl. ᵓănāšīm, cf. Aram. coll. nāšā, Arab. coll. nās; cf. Akkad. pl. nišū)

/n-š-ᵓ/: ***nša, yšu, tšu, nši*** inf. constr. "to lift" (H. nāśāᵓ, yiśśāᵓ, Aram. nəśāᵓ, śēᵓ, Akkad. našū)

nšb 1.114:10, 13 = **88.3**, a kind of meat, "haunch"(?)

nšm see *nš-*

/n-š-q/: ***yšq, nšq*** inf. "to kiss" (H. nāšaq, yiššāq, Akkad. našāqu)

nšr "eagle, vulture" (H. nǽšær, Aram. nəšar, Arab. nasr)

nt(?): pl. *ntm*(?) 2.38:18 = **86.41** "seaman"(??); cf. *dnt*

ntb: pl. *ntbt* 1.119:33 = **86.75** "path" (cf. H. nātīb)

ntn 1.16:I:18 = **88.73** "mourning" (cf. *bky* 1.16:II:41 "weeping")

/n-ṯ-k/: ***nṯk*** inf. 1.100:4 = **86.73** "to bite"; "biting" (cf. H. nāšak, yiššōk, Akkad. našāku)

s and *ś*

/s-ᵓ-d/: ***tsad*** 1.17:V:30 = **88.62** "to serve, honor"

sgld 3.9:21 = **84.2** PN, cf. *si-gil-da* P:III:16.201:4 (p. 151)

sgrt "(closed) room" (cf. H. s-g-r "to close," səgōr "enclosure"; cf. Akkad. sekēru "to close") *syny* 4.135:2 = **86.21** derived adj.(?), cf. GN *syn* 4.382:34, *si-ya-na* U:V:44:14(?); cf. PN *sí-ni-ya* gen. U:V:159:3(?)

skn 6.13:1 = **86.72**, 1.17:I:26 = **87.1** "stele, monument" (cf. Akkad. šiknu)

skn 1.78:6 = **86.743** "concern, jeopardy"(?) (cf. H. s-k-n Ni.)

skn /sākin-/: pl. *sknm* 4.213:3 = **86.23**; cf. *sà-ak-ki-ni* gen. P:III:15.33:2 (p. 15), "steward; governor" (cf. H. sōkēn, Phoen. skn, Old-Canaan. zu-ki-ni)

śknt /sōkinat-/ 4.135:2 = **86.21** PN fem. (cf. PN m. *sà-ki-ni* gen. P:III:15.41:4 (p. 38)?) (cf. *skn*?)

snt 3.4:10 = **86.32** PN fem. (cf. PN m. *sny* 4.412:I:29?)

ssw: pl. *sswm* 1.14:III:24 = **88.71**; and *śśw:* pl. *śśwm* 2.33:24 = **86.42**, 1.85:1 = **86.61** "horse" (cf. H. sūs, Syr. sūsyā, Old Canaan. zū[zi] EA 263:25, Akkad. sīsu)

ssnm pl. 1.100:66 = **86.73** "fruit stalks (of a date palm)" (cf. H. sansinn-, Akkad. sissinnu)

sp /sapp-/ "bowl" (H. sap, sipp-, Akkad. sappu "a metal vessel")

/s-p-ʾ/: *ispi*, *yspu*, *spu* part. "to eat" (cf. H. mispōʾ "fodder"; cf. Postbibl. H., Jew.-Aram. s-p-ʾ and s-p-y "to give a portion to eat")

spsg 1.17:VI:36 = **88.63** cf. [ś]*pśg* 4.182:8 "glaze" (cf. H. Prov 26:23 (k)sp-s(y)gym; < Hittite zapzaga(y)a?)

/s-p-r/: *tspr* 1.17:VI:29 = **86.63** "to count"; Š: *ašsprk* 1.17:VI:28 = **86.63** "to make to count" (H. sāpar, yispōr)

spr /sāpir-/ 1.16:VI:59 = **85.1** "scribe" (H. sōpēr, Aram. sāpar, Akkad. šāpiru)

spr /sipr-/ "written text, document" 6.24:1 = **81.2**; "list" 4.338:1 = **82.4**; "treatise" 1.85:1 = **86.61** (H. sḗpær, Aram. səpar, siprīn, Akkad. (< Aram.) sipru)

sprt 1.127:9 "recitation"(?) (cf. /s-p-r/ 1.23:57; *mspr* 1.4:V:42)

ᶜ

ᶜbd /ᶜabd-/, cf. *ab-du* U:V:137:III:4, "servant, slave" (H. ᶜǽbæd, Aram. ᶜabd-, Arab. ᶜabd)

ᶜbdyrǵ 4.277:2 = **86.52** (cf. correct *ᶜbdyrḫ* 4.98:12) PN ("Servant of (god) Yrḫ")

ᶜbdmlk 3.4:9 = **86.32** PN (cf. H. PN ᶜæbæd-mælæk)

ᶜbdn 3.9:20 = **84.2**, cf. *ab-di-na* gen. P:III: 11.839:7 (p. 194), PN

ᶜbdnt 4.277:4 = **86.52** (cf. correct *ᶜbdᶜnt* 4.151:I:6), cf. abdi-*a-na-ti* P:III:16.129:19 (p. 33), PN

ᶜbdrš 4.31:1 = **86.53**; cf. abdi(*dì*)-*ir-ši* gen. P:III:16.257:IV:8 (p. 203), PN (cf. Phoen. ᶜbdʾrš)

/ᶜb-ṣ/: *ᶜbṣk* inf. 1.3:III:18 = **87.8** "to make haste" (< Proto-Semitic ᶜ-b-ḍ(?), cf. Imper.-Aram. ᶜ-b-q "to make haste")

ᶜgl /ᶜigl-/ "calf" (H. ᶜḗgæl, Syr. ᶜeglā, Arab. ᶜiǧl)

ᶜd /ᶜad(ē)/(?) 1.114.3, 4 = **88.3**, 3.4:17 = **86.32**, 3.5:14 = **86.33** "until" (H., Aram. ᶜad, Eblaitic a-dè, Akkad. adi)

ᶜd 1.4:VI:55 = **87.7** adv. "still, yet" (cf. H., Aram. ᶜōd)

/ᶜ-d-b/: *ᶜbd*, *yᶜdb*, *tᶜdbn*, imperf. 1. sing. *ᶜdbnn* 1.6:II:22 = **88.55**, *ᶜdbk* 1.18:IV:22 = **88.64**: (*ʾaᶜd- > ᶜad-) "to prepare, set" (*ᶜ-ḏ-b?, cf. H. ᶜ-z-b Exod 23:5?)

ᶜdbt 1.100:71 = **86.73** "installation, building"

/ᶜ-d-y/: *yᶜdynh* 1.100:66 = **86.73** "to remove" (cf. H., Aram. ᶜ-d-y Hi./Ha.)

ᶜdt 1.100:3 = **86.73** "assembly" (H. ᶜēdā, Syr. ᶜidtā)

ᶜdtm du. 1.100:66 = **86.73** "reed bulbs"(?) (cf. Akkad. adattu "succulent part of reed"?)

ᶜḏbt 1.4:V:14 = **88.53** "caravan"(?) (cf. Imper.-Aram. ᶜdb "group"(?))

/ᶜ-w-p/: *tᶜpn*, inf. constr. *ᶜp* "to fly" (H. ᶜ-w-p)

/ᶜ-w-r/: L *tᶜrrk* 1.4:IV:39 = **85.2** "to arouse" (cf. H. ᶜ-w-r "to be aroused," Polel ᶜōrēr "to arouse, stir" Song of Songs 8:5)

ᶜwrt "blindness" (H. ᶜawwǽræt)

ᶜz /ᶜazz-/ 2.10:13 = **86.43** "strong" (H. ᶜaz(z-))

ᶜz /ᶜuzz-/ "strength," "army"(?) 1.103:17 = **86.744**, 1.119:26 = **86.75** (H. ᶜōz)

ᶜz /ᶜizz-/ 1.127:30 = **86.741**, 1.80:4 = **86.51** "goat" (H. ᶜēz, ᶜizzīm, Aram. pl. ᶜizzīn, cf. Arab. ᶜanz, Akkad. enzu, ezzu, izzum)

ᶜẓm /ᶜaẓm-/ "bone" (H. ᶜǽṣæm, Syr. ᶜaṭmā, Arab. ᶜaẓm)

/ᶜ-y-n/: *yᶜn* 1.10:II:14, 15 = **88.56** "to behold"; cf. *ᶜn* "eye" (cf. H. ᶜ-y-n)

ʿky gen. 2.38:25 = **86.41** GN, cf. (al)*a-ki-ya* P:VI:79:16 (H. ʿakkō)

ʿl /ʿal(ē)/, with suffixes: *ʿly*, *ʿlk*, *ʿlh*, *ʿlnh* "upon" 1.16:I:1, "toward"; 1.16:VI:39 = **85.1** "from (upon)"(?); expression of duty or indebtedness 4.135:2 = **86.21**; 2.33:25 = **86.42**(?) (cf. H., Aram. ʿal, Arab. ʿalā(y), Akkad. eli)

ʿl 4.279:2 = **86.24** "second"(?) or *ʿl* /ʿal(ē)/ "over"(?) or "upon"(?)

/ʿ-l-y/: *ʿl* 2.30:17 = **83.4**, *ʿly* 2.33:25 = **86.42**(?), *tʿl*, *yʿl* "to go up"; Š: *šʿlyt* 6.13:1 = **86.72** "to offer" (or "to erect"?), *tšʿl* 1.14:III:12 = **88.71** "to bring up; shoot" (cf. H. ʿ-l-y Q., Hi.)

ʿlm "unlimited time, eternity"; *ʿlmh* 1.23:49 = **88.2**, 1.19:IV:6 = **87.4** "to eternity"; *ʿd.ʿlm* 3.5:14 = **86.33** (cf. Akkad. a-di da-ri-ti P:III:16.353:10 (p. 113)); cf. *ʿlmt* (cf. H. ʿōlām, Aram., Arab. ʿālam)

ʿlmt /ʿulmat-/, cf. *ḫu-ul-ma-tum* U:V:137:III:15′ "future"; *šḥr.ʿlmt* 3.5:15 = **86.33** "tomorrow (and) in the future" (cf. Akkad. ur-ra-am še-ra-am P:III:15.155:19 (p. 118), cf. Imper.-Aram. (l)mḥr (ʾw) ywm ʾḥrn)

ʿm /ʿamma/(?) "with, to"; + *-n*: *ʿmn* 1.24:32 = **88.1**, 1.3:III:25 = **87.8**; with suffixes *ʿmy*, *ʿmk*, *ʿmnk* 3.9:16 = **84.2**, *ʿmny* 1. sing.(?) 2.16:14 = **84.1**, *ʿmn* 1. pl.(?) 2.38:6 = **86.41**; *ʿm.ʿlm* 1.3:V:31 = **88.52** "to eternity" (cf. H. ʿim(m-), Syr. ʿam "with," Aram. ʿim(m-) Dan 3:33 "to")

ʿm /ʿamm-/ 1.17:I:27 = **87.1** "closest male paternal relative" (cf. Arab. ʿamm, ESA ʿm "paternal uncle"); cf. PN *ʿmrpi* gen. 2.39:2; *am-mu-ra-pí* gen. U:V:23:2; PN *ʿmṯtmr* 3.5:2 = **86.33** (cf. H. PN ʿammī-nādāb)

ʿmn 1.24:32 = **88.1**; 2.33:34 = **86.42**; 1.3:III:25 = **87.8** see *ʿm* "with"

ʿmny 2.16:14 = **84.1** see *ʿm* "with"

ʿmnk 3.9:16 = **84.2** see *ʿm* "with"

/ʿ-m-s/: *yʿmsn* "to carry"; D part. *mʿmsh* 1.17:I:30 = **87.1** "to carry" (H. ʿ-m-s, yaʿămōs; Phoen. ʿ-m-s)

ʿmq 1.5:VI:21 = **87.3** "valley; plain (between mountains)" (cf. H. ʿḗmæq, Amorite ḫamqum, Arab. ʿamq)

ʿmq 1.17:VI:45 = **88.63** "strong, wise"(?) (cf. H. ḗmæq Job 39:21 "strength"(?); cf. Akkad. emqu "wise, skilled"; cf. H. ʿāmōq, Arab. ʿamīq "deep")

ʿmr 1.5:VI:14 = **87.3** "earth"(?) (cf. Arab. ʿāmir "cultivated (land)"(?); or "hay, sheaves (of mown grain)"(?) (cf. H. ʿāmīr; cf. Syr. ʿmīrā "grass, hay")

ʿmṯtmr 3.5:2 = **86.33**; cf. *a-mis-tam-ru* P:III:15.126:2 (p. 112) PN, name of several kings of Ugarit

ʿn /ʿēn-/: du. *ʿnm* 1.2:IV:22 = **88.51**, *ʿnk* 1.16:I:27 = **88.73** "eye" (H. ʿáyin, ʿēn, Aram. constr. ʿēn, Arab. ʿayn, Akkad. īnu); *ʿn* 1.12:II:59 = **88.4**, 1.100:1 = **86.73** "spring, well" (cf. H., Syr., Akkad.)

/ʿ-n-w/(?): *tʿn* 1.16:VI:58 = **85.1** "to be downcast" (cf. H. ʿ-n-y and ʿānāw "humble"; cf. ESA ʿnw, Arab. ʿanā(w), yaʿnū, ʿunuw "to be humble(d)")

/ʿ-n-y/: *yʿn*, **(*wn*)***ʿn*(?) 1.24:31 = **88.1** "to answer" (cf. H. ʿ-n-y)

ʿnt 1.19:IV:6 = **87.4** "now" (cf. Aram. ʿǽnæt; cf. H. ʿáttā)

ʿnt 1.109:13 = **86.71**, 1.3:III:9 = **87.8**, 1.96:1 = **82.6**; cf. *a-na-tum* U:V:18:20, DN fem. (cf. H. (bæn-)ʿănāt)

/-ʿ-s-/(?): **ʿs[?]** 1.4:IV:34 = **85.2** "to travel by night"(?) (cf. Arab. ʿašā(w)) or "to explore"(?) (cf. Syr. ʿas) or read ʿr[bt](?)

ʿp see /ʿ-w-p/

ʿpʿp du. 1.14:III:43 = **88.71** "eyes"(?); "eyelids"(?) (cf. H. ʿapʿappē du. constr. "eyelids")

ʿpr /ʿapar-/(?) "dust, earth" (H. ʿāpar, Syr. ʿaprā, Arab. ʿafar)

ʿṣ /ʿiṣ-/, cf. *iṣ-ṣú* U:V:130:III:8′, "tree, bush, wood" (H. ʿēṣ, Akkad. iṣ(ṣ)u; cf. ESA ʿḍ, Imper. Aram. ʿq, Bibl. Aram. ʾāʿ)

/ʿ-ṣ-ṣ/(?): *ʿṣk* 1.3:III:18 = **87.8** inf. with suff. "to hurry(?); to press"(?) (cf. Syr. ʿ-ṣ-ṣ "to press, compel," cf. also ʿṣā "to compel"; Jew.-Aram. ʿ-ṣ-y "to press"; cf. Arab. ʿassa "to be hard; press") or *iṣ* + *-k* "wood"(?)

ʿṣr "bird" (Akkad. iṣṣūru)

ʿq: *ʿqh* 1.14:III:43 = **88.71** du. + suff. "eyebrow" cf. Arab. ʿaqīqat "hair of new-born child"?)

ʿqltn 1.5:I:2 = **88.54** "crooked" (H. ʿăqallātōn)

ʿqšr 1.100:5 = **86.73** "scaly"(?) (cf. H. ʿaqrāb "scorpion"; cf. Arab. qišr(at) "scale") or "tortuous"(?)

ʿr /ʿīr-/ 1.100:62 = **86.73** "city" (H. ʿīr)

ʿr /ʿēr-/ 1.19:II:8 = **87.5** "(he-)ass" (cf. H. ʿáyir

"(he-)ass," Arab. ᶜayr "(wild) ass"; cf. ḫārum, ayarum in Mari Akkad. text "he-ass")

/ᶜ-r-b/: *ᶜrb*, *ᶜrbn*, *tᶜrbm* 1.24:18 = **88.1** "to enter"; 1.78:2 = **86.743** "to set (of sun)" (cf. Arab. ǵaraba "to enter," H. maᶜărāb "entering (of sun), (sun)set, west"); "to enter (as a pledge)," cf. 4.338:12 = **86.26**(?); Š: *ašᶜrb* 1.14:IV:41 = **88.72** "to bring (in)" (H. ᶜārab, Akkad. erēbu)

ᶜryt fem. 2.38:25 = **86.41** "naked, laid bare" (cf. H. ᶜæryā "nakedness")

ᶜrᶜr "tamarisk" (H. ᶜărᶜār "wild tamarisk(?)"; Arab. ᶜarᶜar "juniper")

ᶜrpt "cloud(s)" (Akkad. urpu, pl. urpāti "cloud(s)"; cf. H. ᶜărāpæl "darkness," Syr. ᶜarpelā "dark cloud"; cf. H. rōkēb bā-ᶜărābōt Ps 68:5)

/ᶜ-r-r/ (?) see /ᶜ-w-r/

ᶜrš /ᶜarš-/ "bed" (H. ᵓæræś, Akkad. eršu)

/ᶜ-š-y/: *ᶜšy* 1.17:I:29 = **87.1** "to do something bad (to a person)"(?) (cf. H. ᶜ-ś-y "to do, make"; cf. H. Pi. ᶜiśśū "to press" Ezek 23:3, 8(?)) or "to disturb"(?) (cf. Akkad. ešū, ašū?)

/ᶜ-š-r/: *yᶜšr* 1.17:VI:30, 30–31 = **88.63** (the second occurrence may be the result of dittography) "to feast"(?) (cf. Eth. ᶜaššara "to invite (to a party)," ᶜašūr "banquet")

/ᶜ-š-r/ D?/C? 1.119:32–33 = **86.75** "to give the tithe" (H. ᶜ-ś-r Hi.)

ᶜšr /ᶜaš(a)r-/ 4.213:1 = **86.23**, 4.349:1 = **81.4**, *ᶜšrt* 4.146:2, 6 = **86.25** "10" (H. ᶜāśār, ᶜæśrē, Aram. ᶜăśar, Arab. ᶜašr, ᶜašarat)

ᶜšrm /ᶜišrūma/, /-īma/ 4.135:1 = **86.21** "20" (H. ᶜæśrīm, Arab. ᶜišrūna)

ᶜšrt 1.109:5 = **86.71** "tenth (part)," 1.119:32 = **86.75** "tithe" (or "meal," cf. /ᶜ-š-r/) (cf. Akkad. ešrētum; cf. H. ᶜiśśārōn)

ᶜtn /ᶜattan/(?) "now" (cf. H. ᶜáttā, Aram. (kĕ)ᶜæt, (kĕ)ᶜænæt)

/ᶜ-t-q/: *ᶜtq*, *nᶜtq*, *yᶜtq* "to pass" (H. ᶜ-t-q, yæᶜtaq; cf. H., Aram. ᶜattīq "old")

ᶜṯtr(?) 1.142:2 = **86.742** DN(?)/PN(?)

ᶜṯtrt /ᶜaṯtart-/ DN fem. (cf. GN Aš-tar-tu EA 197:10, H. ᶜaštārōt, cf. LXX Gr. Astartē; Latin Astarthe; traditional H. vocalization ᶜAštṓræt is patterned after bṓšæt "shame")

ǵ

ǵz: (*k*)*ǵz.ǵzm* 1.16:VI:43 = **85.1** "raider"(?) (cf. Arab. ǵāzi(n) "raider," ǵazw "raid, razzia")

ǵzr "young man; hero, warrior" (cf. H. ᶜ-z-r 1 Chr 12:1, 22(?); cf. Arab. ǵazīr "rich"(?))

ǵryn 4.277:3 = **86.52** (cf. correct *ḫyrn* 4.307:5) PN (cf. *ḫyr*)

ǵlm "boy" (H. ᶜǽlæm; cf. Syr. ᶜlaymā, Arab. ǵulām)

ǵlmt "girl" 1.14:IV:41 = **88.72** (H. ᶜalmā)

ǵlt 1.16:VI:45 = **85.1** "lowering, inactivity" (cf. /ǵ-l-y/ "to lower" 1.19:III:54 etc.) or "hatred"(?) (cf. Arab. ǵill) or "transgression"(?) (cf. Arab. ǵalā(w)?) or "assassination"(?) (cf. Arab. ǵīlat?))

/ǵ-m-ᵓ/: *ǵmit*, *ǵmu* inf. abs. "to be thirsty" (cf. H. ṣāmēᵓ, yiṣmāᶜ, Arab. ẓamiᵓa, yaẓmaᵓu, Akkad. ṣamū)

/-ǵ-r-/: *yǵr* 1.2:IV:6 = **88.51** "to sink"(?) (cf. Arab. ǵāra, yaǵūru) or "to groan"(?)

ǵr 1.5:VI:17 = **87.3** , cf. [ú(?)]-*ru* U:V:130:II:6′, "skin" (H. ᶜōr)

ǵr 1.6:II:16 = **88.55**, 1.3:III:29 = **87.8** "mountain" (cf. Aram. ṭūr; cf. H. ṣūr "rock")

ǵr(?): *ǵrm* pl. 1.16:VI:44 = **85.1** "raider"(?) (cf. Arab. ǵ-w-r IV "to raid"; ǵārat "raid") or "pit"(?) (cf. Arab. ǵār "cave") or *ǵr* "mountain"(?), see above.

/ǵ-t-r/ 1.103:39 = **86.744** "to slaughter"(?) (cf. Arab. ᶜatara(?) "to slaughter for sacrifice")

p

p /pa-/ "and" 2.33:28 = **86.42**, 2.15:7 = **86.45**, 1.19:IV:6 = **87.4**; *pd* /pa-/ + *d*- (Anc.-Aram. p-, Arab. fa)

p 2.10:12 = **86.43** adv. "here" (H. pō, Phoen. pho)

p (cf. 1.107:34): *py* 1.6:II:22 = **88.55**; *ph* 1.2:IV:6 = **88.51** "mouth" (H. pǽ, Akkad. pū, Arab. fū, fī, fā; cf. Aram. pum)

/-p-/: *tp* 1.96:2 = **82.6**, see /-p-h-/ "to see"

pid /piᵓd-/ 1.15:II:14 = **87.2** "heart, compassion" (Arab. fiᵓd, fuᵓād "heart")

pit 1.103:54 = **86.744** "temple(s), border(s) of the head" (cf. H. pēᵓā)

pbl PN (Hurrian)

pgr 6.13:2 = **86.72** "offering (for the dead?)" (cf. H. pǽgær, Akkad. pagr "corpse"?)

pgrm 4.266:2 = **86.22** a month name

pd 1.14:III:38 = **88.71** see *p* /pa-/ and *d-*

/p-d-y/: *pdy*, *pdyh*[m] "to ransom" (H. p-d-y, Arab. fadā(y), Akkad. padū)

pdry 1.109:19 = **86.71** DN fem., cf. [pa-ad(?)-r]*i-ya-m*[a(?)] U:V:137:IVb:5 (cf. Akkad. pi-id-di-r[i-ya])

/-p-h-/: *yphn(h)*, *tp* 1.96:2 = **82.6** 3. sing. f., *iph* 2.25:4, *phy* 3.1:15 "to perceive, see" (cf. Arab. bāha "to observe"(?))

pḥl 1.100:1 = **86.73**, 1.19:II:9 = **87.5** "stallion" (Arab. faḥl, Akkad. puḫālu) or "jack-ass"(?)

pḥlt 1.100:1 = **86.73** "mare" (cf. *pḥl*) or "she-ass"(?)

pḥm pl. *pḥmm* "live coal(s);" 3.1:22 = **86.31** "carbuncle" (H. pæḥām, Arab. faḥm)

pḫd "flock" (cf. Arab. faḫid, Palmyr.-Aram. pḥd, pḥz "clan"; cf. Akkad. puḫādu "lamb")

/p-l-g/: *tplg* 1.100:69 = **86.73** "to stream," cf. *plg* (cf. H., Aram. p-l-g "to divide")

plg 1.100:69 = **86.73** "canal, stream" (H. pǽlæg, Akkad. palgu)

pld 4.146:7 = **86.25** a kind of garment

plsy 2.10:2 = **86.43**, cf. *píl-sí-ya* gen. P:III: 11.839:2 (p. 194), *píl-sú-ya* gen. U:V:12:11, PN

plṯt 1.5:VI:15 = **87.3** "wallowing" (cf. H. p-l-š Hitpa.)

pn 1.114:12 = **88.3**(?) expression of preventing, "lest; you may not!" (cf. H. pæn- Isa 36:18, Job 32:13) or read h!*n*(?) "behold!"(?)

pn pl. constr., *pnm* pl. abs., with suffix *pnnh* 1.10:II:17 = **88.56** "face"; *lpn* "before" (H. pl. pānīm, li-pnē, Phoen. lpn, Akkad. panū pl.)

pnt pl.(?) 1.2:IV:26 = **88.51** "vertebrae" (cf. H. pinnā "corner"?)

psltm du. 1.5:VI:18 = **87.3** "sideburns"(?) (cf. Arab. fasl "low")

*p*ᶜ*n* "foot" (cf. H. páᶜam, Phoen. pᶜm)

/p-ᶜ-r/: *yp*ᶜ*r* "to proclaim (a name)" (cf. H. pāᶜar-, Syr. pᶜar, nepᶜor, Arab. faᶜara "to open wide (the mouth)")

pǵy "boy" 4.349:4 = **81.4**

pǵt "girl" 4.349:3 = **81.4** (cf. *pǵy*); PN fem. 1.19:II:6 = **87.5**

/-p-q-/: *pq* 1.4:VI:56 = **87.7** "to swallow"(?) (cf. Arab. fāqa, yafūqu; cf. Syr. pāq "to gasp")

/p-r-s-ḫ/: *yprsḥ* "to collapse" (cf. Akkad. N napalsuḫu; cf. Arab. faršaḥa "to straddle, have one's legs spread apart"?)

*pr*ᶜ 4.279:1 = **86.24** "first"(?)

/p-r-q/: *yprq* G(?)/D(?) 1.4:IV:28 = **85.2** "to open" (< "to sever"(?)) (cf. H. pāraq "to tear away," Pi. "to pull off"; Aram. pəruq imper. "to remove"; Arab. faraqa, yafruqu, Akkad. parāqu "to sever")

*pš*ᶜ "rebellion" (H. pǽšaᶜ)

/p-t-ḥ/: *ptḥ* imper. "to open" (H. pātaḥ, yiptaḥ, Arab. fataḥa, yaftaḥu)

ṣ

ṣd 1.114:1 = **88.3** "game"(?) or "food"(?) (cf. H. ṣáyid I "food," II "game") or "banquet"(?) (from /ṣ-w-d/)

ṣdynm pl. 1.14:IV:36, 39 = **88.72** "Sidonians" (cf. GN *ṣi-du*-[na] P:III:11.723:2 (p. 9); Phoen. ṣdn, Sidōn, H. ṣīdōn, Old-Canaan. ṣidun(n)u)

/ṣ-w-d/: *tṣdn* 1.114:23 = **88.3**, 1.17:VI:40 = **88.63** "to hunt" (H. ṣād, yāṣūd, Akkad. ṣādu, cf. Arab. ṣāda, yaṣīdu); *ṣd* 1.114:1 = **88.3**(?) "to give a banquet"(?)

/ṣ-w-ḥ/ (or /ṣ-y-ḥ/): *ṣḥ*, *aṣḥkm*, *ṣḥn*, *yṣḥ* "to shout, call" (cf. H. ṣ-w-ḥ, yiṣwāḥū, ṣəwāḥā, Syr. ṣwaḥ, Arab. ṣāḥa, yaṣīḥu; Akkad. ṣīḫtu "lamentation")

/ṣ-ḥ-q/: *tṣḥq*, *yṣḥq* "to laugh" (H. ṣāḥāq-, yiṣḥaq; cf. Arab. ḍahiqa)

/ṣ-ḥ-r-r/: *ṣḥrrt* 1.23:48 (41, 45) = **88.2** "to roast" (cf. Arab. ṣ-ḥ-r XI iṣḥarra "to be yellow/red (in color)"; cf. ṣaḥrāᵓ "yellow/red; desert"; cf. Sahara)

/ṣ-y-ḥ/ (?), see /ṣ-w-ḥ/

ṣlt 1.119:34 = **86.75** "prayer" (cf. /ṣ-l-y/: *yṣly* 1.19:I:39 "he prays"; Jew.-Aram., Syr. ṣ(ə)lōtā "prayer")

/ṣ-m-d/: *tṣmd*(?) "to harness" (cf. H. ṣ-m-d Ni., Pu., Hi., ṣǽmæd "span," Akkad. ṣamādu)

ṣmd: du. *ṣmdm* "club, mace" (cf. Syr. ṣemdā "band"(?))

ṣml 1.19:III:29 = **88.65** name of the mother-eagle in Aqhat (cf. Arab. ṣumullu "hard, tough")

ṣmqm pl. 1.71:24 = **86.62** "(cakes of) dried grapes" (H. ṣimmūqīm)

/ṣ-m-t/: *tṣmt* (D?) "to silence; to kill" (cf. H. ṣ-m-t "to exterminate," Arab. ṣ-m-t II "to silence")

ṣp 1.14:III:45 = **88.71** "glamor"(?) or "glance"(?) (cf. Arab. ṣafw and ṣafāʾ "purity, brightness"(?); cf. H. ṣ-p-y "to look out")

ṣpn /ṣapān-/(?) GN, holy mountain, *bˁl.ṣpn* 1.109:9 = **86.71** "Baal of Ṣapān" (cf. (d)adad be-el ḫuršān ḫa-zi U:V:18:4); also DN, *ṣpn* 1.109:10 = **86.71**; 1.118:14; *il.ṣpn* 1.3:III:29 = **87.8** "the god Ṣapān" (cf. (d)ḫuršān ḫa-zi U:V:18:14) (cf. H. ṣāpōn, Phoen. ṣpn)

ṣpr 1.14:III:19 = **88.71** "hunger"(?) (cf. Arab. ṣafar "hunger," ṣafira "to be empty") or "watch(dog)"(?)

/-ṣ-q-/: Š *šṣq* "to oppress" (cf. H. ṣ-w-q Hi., Arab. ḍ-y-q II)

/-ṣ-r-/: *tṣr* 1.14:III:29 = **88.71** "to besiege; to press hard"(?) (cf. H. ṣ-w-r I: ṣar-, tāṣūr "to surround, besiege"; cf. H. ṣ-w-r II: ṣar-, tāṣar(!) "to press hard," cf. Arab. ḍāra, yaḍūru "to damage")

ṣr 2.38:3 = **86.41** GN, Tyre (Phoen. ṣr, Ṣur-ri, Tyros), see also *ṣrm*

ṣrm pl. 1.14:IV:35, 38 = **88.72** "Tyrians"; cf. (al)*ṣu-ri-ya* P:VI:79:6 (cf. H. ṣōrī, Phoen. ṣry)

ṣrry /-ay/ 1.16:I:19 = **88.73** "height" (cf. Akkad. ṣerrēti) or "radiance"(?) (cf. Akkad. ṣerru "clear light") or "lamentation"(?) (cf. Akkad. ṣāriru "singer of lamentation," Arab. ṣarra "to cry"?)

ṣrt 1.2:IV:9 = **88.51** ("enmity" >) "enemy" (cf. H. ṣar, Aram. ˁār, Arab. ḍarr, Akkad. ṣēru)

ṣtqn 1.80:2, 3 = **86.51** PN (cf. the correct form, *ṣdqn* 4.286:2)

q

/q-b-r/: *aqbrnh*, *yqbrnh* "to bury" (H. qābar, imper. qəbōr, Arab. qabara, yaqburu, Akkad. qebēru)

qbr /qabr-/ "grave" (H. qǽbær, Arab. qabr, Akkad. qabru)

qdm 1.100:62 = **86.73** "east" (H. qǽdæm)

qdqd "pate" (H. qådqōd < *qudqud, Akkad. qaqqad < *qadq-)

/q-d-š/ Š "to consecrate, offer" (H. q-d-š Hi.)

qdš 1.17:I:26 = **87.1**, 1.14:IV:34 = **88.72**, 1.3:III:30 = **87.8**, 1.119:33 = **86.75** "sanctuary," cf. *qi*-[i]*d*(?)-[š]*u*(?) U:V:137:III:29′ (H. qṓdæš, Syr. qudšā, Arab. quds)

qdš "holy" 1.16:I:22 = **88.73**, epithet of the god Il (cf. H. qādōš, Aram. qaddīš, Arab. qiddīs, qaddūs, Akkad. qaššu < *-dš-)

/q-w-l/(?), /q-y-l/(?), /q-l-l/(?): *ql*, *qlt*, *yql*, *tqln* "to fall"; Š: *šqlt* 1.16:VI:44 = **85.1**; *ašqlk* 1.17:VI:44 = **88.63** "to let fall down"; Št: *ištql* 1.114:17 = **88.3**; *yštql* 1.100:68 = **86.73** "to enter" (cf. Arab. qāla, yaqīlu "to rest (at noon)"; cf. Arab. maqīl and ESA mqwl "resting place"; cf. Eth. qalqal "falling down (of a mountain)," qwalā "low land"; cf. Akkad. qiālu "to fall"?)

/q-w-m/: *yqm* 1.10:II:17 = **88.56** "to rise" (H. qām, yāqūm, Aram. qām, yəqūm, Arab. qāma, yaqūmu); part. *qm* 1.10:II:25 = **88.56** ("one who is rising against" >) "adversary" (H. qām)

/-q-ḥ-/ see /l-q-ḥ/

qṭr "smoke, incense" (H. qīṭōr, qəṭóræt, Akkad. quṭru)

qẓ 1.24:17 = **88.1** "(late) summer" (H. qáyiṣ, Aram. qáyiṭ, Arab. qayẓ)

qy 1.6:II:23 = **88.55** see *qn*

/q-y-l/ see /q-w-l/

/-q-l-/ see /q-w-l/

ql /qōl-/ 1.10:III:32 = **88.57**, 1.100:2 = **86.73** (for *bl* see /y-b-l/); 1.14:III:17 = **88.71** "voice" (H. qōl, Aram. qāl, Arab. qawl)

ql 4.213:27 = **86.23** PN (cf. PN *qln* 4.609:34)

/q-l-l/ see /q-w-l/

/-q-m-/ *qm* 1.10:II:25 = **88.56** see /q-w-m/

qmḥ /qamḥ-/ "flour" (H. qǽmaḥ; cf. Arab. qamḥ "wheat")

qn "reed; shaft"; *qn.ḏrˁh* 1.5:VI:20 = **87.3** "the (humeral) bone of the arm" (cf. ʾæzrōˁī miq-qānā(h) Job 31:22); *ṯbrn q*(n)*y* 1.6:II:23 = **88.55** (cf. *ṯbrn qnh* 1.4:VIII:19–20) "breach/opening of my/his throat" (cf. H. qānǽ, Syr. qanyā, Akkad. qanū)

/q-n-y/: *qny*, *tqny*, "to establish, create"; 3.9:2 = **84.2** "to establish"; 1.4:IV:32 = **85.2** part. fem. *qnyt* "creatrix" (cf. Phoen. ʾl qn ʾrṣ, H. qōnǽ Gen 14:19)

/q-n-ṣ/: Gt *tqt*[nṣn] 1.23:51 = **88.2** (cf. 1.23:58) "to travail(?), conceive"(?) (cf. Arab. qaniṣat "the lower part of a bird's belly")

/-q-ǵ-/: *tqǵ* 1.16:VI:42 = **85.1** "to awake, be alert" (cf. H. /y-q-ṣ/: yīqāṣ, cf. q-y-ṣ Hi.; cf. Arab. yaqiẓa and yaquẓa, yayqaẓu)

qṣ 1.4:VI:57 = **87.7**; 1.114:2 = **88.3** "slice (of meat)" (cf. Arab. qaṣṣ "slice; breast"; cf. H. q-ṣ-ṣ, Arab. qaṣṣa "to cut")

*qṣ*ᶜ*t* 1.17:V:28 = **88.62** "bow" (cf. Ethiop. qaṣᶜa "to curve"?; cf. Arab. qaṣaᶜa "to crush"?)

qṣr "short" 1.16:VI:47 = **85.1** (H. constr. qəṣar, pl. constr. qiṣrē, Postbibl. H. qāṣēr, Arab. qaṣīr)

qṣrt 1.103:39 = **86.744** "shortness"

qr 1.16:I:27 = **88.73** "well" (cf. H. māqōr)

qr 1.14:III:16 = **88.71**, probably also 1.12:II:60 = **88.4** "noise" (cf. Postbibl. H. qirqēr, Jew.-Aram. qarqar, Arab. qarqara "to make noise (of domestic animals)")

qr 1.12:II:60 = **88.4** "dweller"(?); "dwelling"(?) (cf. Arab. qarra "to dwell"?) or "noise"?, see above *qr*

qr 1.114:8 = **88.3** see *qr*ᶜ

/q-r-ʾ/: *iqrakm*, *iqran*, *tqru*, part. fem. *qrit* /qāriʾt-/ "to call" (H. qārāʾ, yiqrāʾ, Arab. qaraʾa, yaqraʾu, Akkad. qerū)

/q-r-b/: *yqrb* 1.17:I:16 = **88.61** "to approach" (H. qārab, yiqrab, Arab. qariba, yaqrabu, Akkad. qerēbu)

qrb /qarb-/ "midst": 1.4.IV:22 = **85.2** "to the midst (of)"; *bqrb* 1.17:I:25 = **87.1** "in the midst (of)" (cf. H. (bə-)qǽræb)

qrd pl. *qrdm* 1.3:III:14 = **87.8** "hero"; 1.119:26 = **86.75** "warrior" (cf. Akkad. qarrādu "warrior, hero," used also as a divine epithet, qar-rad qar-ra-di "hero among heroes," qar-rad lā šanān "unequalled hero")

qrwn 4.277:3 = **86.52** PN; cf. 1.127:11 (cf. the more correct(?) form, *krwn* 4.85:3; *kur-wa-nu* U:V:83:3)

/q-r-y/: *nqryk* 1.17:VI:43 = **88.63** "to meet"; *qryy* imper. sing. fem. 1.3:III:14 = **87.8** "to offer" (cf. Eth. ʾaqāraya "to provide a guest with hot meal")

qrn /qarn-/: du. abs. *qrnm* 1.114:20 = **88.3**; du. constr. *qrn* 1.10:II:21, 22 = **88.56** "horn" (H., Aram. qǽræn, Arab. qarn, Akkad. qarnu)

*qr*ᶜ 1.114:8 = **88.3** "rod" (cf. Arab. miqraᶜat) or /q-r-ᶜ/ inf. abs.(?) (cf. Arab. qaraᶜa "to beat," H. qāraᶜ, yiqraᶜ "to tear")

qrš 1.4:IV:24 = **85.2** "precinct, domain" (or "pavilion"?) (cf. H. qǽræš "board," Akkad. qeršu "stripe," qarāšu "to cut up"; cf. Gr. temenos "a piece of land cut off and assigned as an offical domain")

qrt 2.61:7 = **86.44**, cf. *qa-ri-tu*[m] U:V:130:III:18′, with suff. *qrth*, *qrtn* "city"; *ynt.qr*[t] 1.109:6 = **86.71** (cf. 1.46:12) "a city pigeon"; cf. also *qryt* 1.14:II:28 (cf. Phoen. qrt, Qar-ti-, H. qǽræt, qiryā, Aram. qiryā, Syr. qrītā; Arab. qaryat)

qrt.ablm 1.19:IV:1 = **87.4** GN ("City of Water-streams"?, cf. H. ʾābēl in GN; "City of Mourners"?, cf. H. ʾābēl "mourning"(?))

qš 1.3:V:33 = **88.52** "chalice"(?) (cf. H. pl. qəśāwōt "jug")

qšt 1.17:V:27 = **88.62**, 1.17:VI:39 = **88.63** "bow" (H. qǽšæt, Syr. qeštā, Akkad. qaštu; cf. Arab. qaws)

/-q-ṯ-/: *yqṯ* 1.2:IV:27 = **88.51** "to draw out"(?) (cf. Arab. qaṯṯa, yaquṯṯu "to tear out"; cf. H. q-š-š Q. and Polel "to gather(?)/tear out(?) (straw, pieces of wood)"?)

/q-ṯ-q-ṯ/: *yqṯqṯ* 1.114:5 = **88.3** "to tear out"(?), "to drag"(?), cf. /-q-ṯ-/

r

rum pl. *rumm* "wild ox, buffalo" (H. rəʾēm, Akkad. rīmu)

/r-ʾ-š/: G/D(?) *yraš* 1.71:23 = **86.62** "to do (an action involving the head)"

riš /raʾš-/: *rišh*, *rišk*, pl. *rašm* /raʾaš-/ "head" (H. rō(ʾ)š, Arab. raʾs, Aram. rē(ʾ)š, Akkad. rēšu)

rb /rabb-/ 3.1:26 = **86.31**, f. *rbt* 1.100:63 = **86.73**, 1.14:III:30 = **88.71** "great"; *rb* 6.6 = **81.1**, 3.9:12 = **84.2**, 2.38:16 = **86.41** "chief" (cf. H., Aram. rab(b-), "great," "chief"; Phoen. rb, Arab. rabb "chief")

*rb*ᶜ 4.279:4 = **86.24**, 1.14:III:11 = **88.71** "fourth" (cf. Arab. rābiᶜ)

rbt /rabbat-/ 1.4:IV:31 = **85.2** "lady" (Phoen. rbt), see also *rb*

rbt 1.24:20 = **88.1** "10,000" (H., Aram. ribbō; H. rəbābā)

/r-g-m/: *rgmt*, *yrgm*, *argmk*, imp. *rgm* 2.16:3 = **84.1**, 2.38:2 = **86.41**, 1.3:III:11 = **87.8** "to say"; *yrgm* 1.4:V:12 = **88.53**, 1.16:I:20 = **88.73** Gp(?)

"to be said"(?) (cf. Akkad. ragāmu, irgumu "to call")

rgm "word" (Akkad. rigmu "sound, voice")

rḥ-: rḥm du. 1.6:II:34 = **88.55** "mill-stones; hand-mill" (H. rēḥáyim, Syr. raḥyā)

rḥ /rūḥ-/ 1.18:IV:25 = **88.64** "wind, spirit" (H., Aram. rū(a)ḥ, Arab. rūḥ)

rḥbn 4.143:1 = **81.5**, cf. *ra-aḫ-ba-na* gen. P:III:16.131:16, 21 (p. 139), GN

/r-ḥ-l/: ***trḥln*** 2.16:12 = **84.1** G(?)/D(?) "to make uncomfortable(?)" or "to frighten"(?) (cf. Arab. d-ḥ-l Pa.?)

rḥm 1.6:II:34 = **88.55** see *rḥ-*

rḥm 1.6:II:27 = **88.55** "girl" (cf. H. ráḥam Judges 5:30, cf. pl. rḥmt Mēšaᶜ of Moab [KAI 181]:17 "female slave")

/r-ḥ-ṣ/: ***rḥṣ*** "to wash"; Gt "to wash oneself" (H. rūḥaṣ, yirḥaṣ, Arab. raḥaḍa; cf. Akkad. raḫāṣu "to rinse")

/r-ḥ-q/: ***rḥq*** 1.14:III:28 = **88.71** imper. "to distrust; to withdraw oneself" (H. rāḥaq, yirḥaq, Akkad. rēqu)

rḥq(t)(?): form with *-m* or du.(?) *rḥqtm* 2.64:15 = **82.1** "distance," *mr-* /mir-r-/ "from (two?) (different)?) distances"(?), cf. *m-* /min-/ (cf. H. mē-rāḥōq Exod 2:4)

/r-ḫ-p/: D *arḫp, trḫpn* "to soar" (H. r-ḥ-p Pi.)

/r-k-b/: ***rkb*** part. 1.2:IV:8 = **88.51**, 1.10:III:37 = **88.57** "to mount" (H. r-k-b: rōkēb Ps 68:5; Arab. rakiba, Akkad. rakābu)

rmy 4.623:2 = **86.11**, cf. *ri-mi-ya* RS, Syria 28, 49: rev. 4, PN (cf. *re-mi-ya* U:V:88:11′ PN fem.?)

rmš(?) 1.109:7 = **86.71** DN(?) (cf. H. rǽmæś "crawling/small animals"?; cf. Old Akkad. Rimuś, name of a king?)

rᶜ: rᶜh, rᶜy "friend" (H. rē(a)ᶜ and rēᶜǣ, Imper. Aram. rᶜ, Akkad. rāʾu)

/r-ǵ-n/: ***rǵbt, rǵb*** inf. abs. "to be hungry" (H. rāᶜēb, yirᶜab; cf. Arab. raǵiba "to desire")

rǵbn "hunger" (H. rəᶜābōn)

/r-ǵ-n/: ***trǵnw*** 1.100:61 = **86.73** (*-w* may be the result of dittography) "to incline"(?) (cf. Arab. raǵana?)

/r-ǵ-ṯ/ "to suck" (cf. Arab. raǵaṯa?): D part. *mrǵṯm* 1.4:VI:56 = **87.7** "sucklings"(?) or "waiters"(?)

rpu /rapiʾ-/(?), *rpi* gen. 1.17:I:17 = **88.61** DN (God of Netherworld?) (cf. PN *am-mu-ra-pi*, see *ᶜm*), pl. gen.-acc. *rpim* 1.22:II:3 = **87.6** (cf. also 1.22:II:8) "netherworld gods; ghosts"

r[qḪ] 4.31:2 = **86.53** (cf. standard *rqḥ* 1.148:21) "perfumer" (H. rōqē(a)ḥ, raqqāḥ-)

/r-q-ṣ/: Gt *yrtqṣ, trtqṣ* "to swoop" (cf. Arab. raqaṣa I and VI "to dance")

ršp 1.109:22 = **86.71**, 1.78:4 = **86.743** DN (cf. PN abdi-[r]*a-ši-ip* U:V:98:8; *nu-ma-re-ša-ip* U:V:98:2; cf. H. rǽšæp "flame; pestilence")

rṯ 1.17:I:33 = **87.1** "mud" (cf. Arab. raṯṯa "to be shabby"?)

š and Š

š /šū/, /šī/, /šā/(?): *šh* "sheep" (H. śǣ; cf. Arab. coll. šāʾ; cf. Akkad. šuʾu "ram")

/š-ʾ-b/: part. f. pl. *šibt* "to draw (water)" (H. š-ʾ-b: tišʾab; cf. Akkad. sābu)

šiy 1.18:IV:23 = **88.64** "executioner"(?)

šin 2.15:4 = **86.45** "gift"(?) (< "soothing"?), (cf. H. šaʾănan "at ease"?)

šir 1.6:II:35, 37 = **88.55** "flesh," cf. *ši-i*(?)[-r]*u* U:V:130:II:3′ (H. šəʾēr, Akkad. šīru)

/š-b-ᶜ/: ***šbᶜ*** perf. 1.17:I:31 = **87.1** "to be satiated (with wine), drunk" (cf. H. śābaᶜ, tiśbaᶜ, Syr. sbaᶜ, nesbaᶜ, Arab. šabiᶜa, Akkad. šebū)

šbᶜ 1.114:3, 16 = **88.3** "satiety" (H. śóbaᶜ, cf. lā-śóbaᶜ Exod 16:3)

šbᶜ: šbᶜt 1.5:I:3 = **88.54** "7" (H. šǽbaᶜ, Arab. sabᶜ(at))

šbᶜ 1.14:III:15 = **88.71**, 1.17:I:15 = **88.61** "seventh" (cf. Arab. sābiᶜ)

šbᶜd 2.64:14 = **82.1** (cf. *šbᶜid* 2.12:9) "seven times"

šd /šadū/: *šdh, šdm*, cf. *:ša-du-ú* U:V:137: II:35′, "field" (H. śādǣ, ESA śdw; cf. Akkad. šadū "mountain")

/š-d-d/: ***yšdd*** 1.103:37 = **86.744** "to devastate" (H. š-d-d)

/š-d-p/ see *mšdpt*

/š-ḥ-y/ see /ḥ-w-y/

šḥlmmt 1.6:II:20 = **88.55** "plain of *mmt*"(?) GN(?) (cf. Arab. sāḥil "coastal plain"); "plain of the dead"(?) or cf. Akkad. DN Mametu(?)

šḥr "dawn," 3.5:15 = **86.33** "tomorrow"(?) (cf. *ᶜlmt*) (H. šáḥar), 1.23:52 = **88.2** DN (cf. Ps 139:9?) (cf. *šlm*)

šḥt 1.100:65 = **86.73** "shrub" (cf. H. śī(a)ḥ,

Arab. šīḥ)

šḫṭ 1.18:IV:24 = **88.64** "slaughterer, butcher" (cf. H. šōḥeṭ)

/š-y-r/: *yšr*, *ašr* "to sing," cf. *ši-i-ru* U:V:137: III:7 "song" (H. š-y-r)

/š-y-t/: *št*, *ašt*, *tštnn*, *yšt*, cf. inf. *ši-tu* U:V:130: III:10′ "to put, set"; Gp *št* 4.338:3 = **82.4** "to be put" (H. š-y-t, Phoen. št)

/š-k-ḥ/: N part. *nškḥ* 2.38:15 = **86.41** ("which was found" >) "which happened" (cf. Aram. š-k-ḥ Ha.(?) "to find," Hitpa. "to be found," also Imper. Aram., cf. Cowley 27:2; 34:4; cf. Syr. ʾeškaḥ and meškḥā "that which can happen")

/š-k-n/: D(?) *škn* 2.33:23 = **86.42** "to set"(?) (cf. Akkad. šakānu?)

škr 1.114:4 = **88.3** "drunkenness" (Arab. sukr; cf. Arab. sakira, H., Syr. š-k-r, Akkad. šakāru "to be drunk")

škrn 1.17:I:30 = **87.1** "drunkenness" (cf. H. šikkārōn)

/-š-l-/, /š-l-l/ (?): *šl* 2.61:6 = **86.44** inf. abs.(?) "to plunder"(?); *šl.hw* (cf. H. š-l-l, Akkad. šalālu) (see also /š-l-w/)

/š-l-w/: *ašlw* 1.14:III:45 = **88.71** "to repose" (H. š-l-y, cf. šālēw "quiet"; cf. Arab. salā(w), Syr. šlī)

/š-l-ḥ/: *išlḥ* 1.24:21 = **88.1** "to send"; D *ašlḥk* 1.17:VI:28 = **88.63** "to send" (H. šālaḥ, yišlaḥ, also Pi. (of God); Aram. šəlaḥ, yišlaḥ)

šlyṭ 1.5:I:3 = **88.54** "powerful; tyrant" (H. šallīṭ, cf. H., Aram. š-l-ṭ, Akkad. šalāṭu "to exert power")

/š-l-m/: *yšlm* 2.16:4 = **84.1**; 2.38:4 = **86.41** "to be intact/healthy, in order, at peace"; D?/C? *tšlmk* 2.16:6 = **84.1** "to give peace/well-being"; *yšlm* C 1.103:54 = **86.744** "to accord peace" (H. š-l-m, tišlam, cf. Job 5:23, Aram. šəlim; Akkad. šalāmu; Arab. salima, yaslamu)

šlm /šalām-/ "peace, well-being" (H. šālōm, Aram. šəlām, Arab. salām, Akkad. šalāmu)

šlm: pl. *šlmm* 1.14:III:26, 27 = **88.71** "gifts for obtaining peace"

šlm sing. 1.3:III:16 = **87.8**, pl. *šlmm* 1.115:9 = **82.5**, 1.109:10 = **86.71**, "peace-offering(s)"(?) (cf. H. pl. šəlāmīm, Phoen. šlm)

šlm /šalim-/ 1.23:52 = **88.2**, 1.109:8 = **86.71**, cf. *sa-li-mu* U:V:18:33, DN (cf. *šḥr*)

šm /šum-/: *šmk*, pl. *šmthm* "name" (cf. PN *šu-um-a-na-ti* P:III:15.139:9 (p. 167)) (Aram. šum, Akkad. šumu; cf. H. šēm, Arab. ism)

šmal: šma<.>l 1.103:37 = **86.744** "left" (H. śəm(ʾ)ōl)

/š-m-ḫ/: *tšmḫ*, *yšmḫ*, *nšmḫ* "to rejoice" (H. śamē(a)ḥ, yiśmaḥ)

šmk 1.10:II:12 = **88.56** GN

šmm /šamūma/, gen.-acc. /šamīma/, cf. *ša-mu-ma* U:V:137:III:13′, "heaven" (cf. H. šāmáyim, Aram. det. šəmayyā; cf. Arab. samāʾ, Akkad. šamū pl.)

šmmn 3.9:3 = **84.2**, cf. *ša-mu-ma-nu* P:III:16. 178:3 (p. 148), PN

Šmn 4.31:2, 11 = **86.53** "oil, fat" (H. šǽmæn, cf. Arab. samn, Akkad. šamnu)

šmn 2.15:6 = **86.45** PN(?) or "oil, fat"(?) or "to make butter"(?) or "there"(?) (cf. *ṯmn*?)

/š-m-ᶜ/: *šmᶜt*, *tšmᶜ*, *šmᶜ* "to hear"; Gt: *ištmᶜ* 1.16:VI:41 = **85.1** "to listen" (H. šāmē(a)ᶜ, yišmaᶜ, Aram. šəmaᶜ, yišmaᶜ, Arab. samiᶜa, yasmaᶜu, Akkad. šamū)

šmrr 1.100:4 = **86.73** see /m-r-r/

šmt 1.19:III:33 = **88.65** "(a piece of) fat" (see *šmn*)

/š-n-w/: *šnwt* 1.96:1 = **82.6** "to shine"(?) (cf. Arab. sanā, yasnū) or "to draw (water)"(?); but cf. /n-w-y/

šnm 1.114:19 = **88.3** DN; probably also in 1.4:IV:24 = **85.2**; or pl. of *šnt* "year"?

/š-n-n/: D *yšnn* "to gnash teeth" (cf. H. šēn, šinn-, Aram. šinn-, Arab. sinn, Akkad. šinnu "tooth"; cf. H. š-n-n Pi., Arab. s-n-n "to sharpen")

šnt /šanat-/ (cf. 1.22:I:13), pl. *šnt* /šanāt-/ 1.17:VI:29 = **88.63** "year" (on *šnth* 1.16:VI:58 = **85.1**(?), see *šnt* /šanīt-/; on *šnm* pl.(?) 1.4:IV:24 = **85.2** see *šnm*) (H. šānā, pl. šānīm, šənōt, Phoen. št (< *-nt-), pl. šnt, Aram. šənā, Arab. sanat, cf. Akkad. šattu)

šnt /šanīt-/ 1.16:VI:58 = **85.1** "loftiness"(?) (cf. Arab. sanīy "lofty"; cf. H. šntk Prov 5:9?, parallel to hōdǽkā; šnyt Isa 11:11?)

šnt /šinat-/: *šnth* 1.19:III:45 = **88.65** "sleep" (/y-š-n/) (H. šēnā, Aram. šint-, Arab. sinat, Akkad. šittu)

šᶜr 1.19:II:6 = **87.5** "barley" (H. śəᶜōrā, Syr. sᶜārtā, Arab. šaᶜīr) or "hair"(?) (see *šᶜrt*)

šᶜrt 4.630:7 = **82.2** "wool" (cf. Akkad. šārtu, H. śēᶜār, Arab. šaᶜ(a)r "hair")

špḥ 1.16:I:21, 23 = **88.73**, 1.14:III:40 = **88.71** "progeny, descendant" (cf. Phoen. špḥ, H. mišpāḥā "family, clan")

/š-p-k/: *špk* imper. 1.18:IV:23 = **88.64** "to spill" (H. šāpak, yišpok, Akkad. šapāku, Arab. safaka)

špš /šapš-/, cf. *ša-ap-šu* U:V:138:3′, "sun," *špšm* 1.14:III:14 = **88.71** "at sun(set)"; "Sun" (title of the Hittite king) 3.1:25 = **86.31**, 2.16:8 = **84.1**; "Sun" DN fem., cf. *ša-ap-šu* U:V:137: IVa:18, 1.100:2 = **86.73**, also 6.24:2 = **81.2** (cf. H. šǽmæš < *šamš-, Aram. šimš-, Arab. šams, Akkad. šamšu, and cf. Greek LXX Sampsōn, Nabat.-Aram. PN Sampsigeramos)

špt /šapat-/: du. *špthm* 1.23:49, 50 = **88.2** "lip" (H. śāpā, Syr. sep̱tā, Arab. šapat, Akkad. šaptu)

/š-q-y/: *yšqynh* 1.17:VI:31 = **88.63** G(?) or D(?) "to serve drinks"; Š: *tššqy* 1.17:V:29 = **88.62** "to give to drink" (cf. H. š-q-y Hi.; cf. Arab. saqā(y) I and IV "to give to drink"; cf. Akkad. šaqū)

/š-r-g/: *tšrgn* "to lie to" (cf. Arab. saraġa; cf. Syr. šragreg "to seem to do; to exhibit (for show only)")

šrg "lie"

šry 1.142:2 = **86.742** PN (cf. PN *šrn*) (cf. H. Śāray?)

/š-r-p/: *tšrpnn* 1.6:II:33 = **88.55** "to burn" (H. śārap, tiśrōp, Akkad. šarāpu)

šrp 1.109:10 = **86.71** "burnt (offering)"

šrš /šurš-/ "root, scion" (H. šóræš, Syr. šeršā, Akkad. šuršu)

ŠŠ 4.31:2 = **86.53** see *ṯṯ* "6"

št 4.338:3 = **82.4** see /š-y-t/

/-š-t-/, /š-t-t/ (?): *yšt* 1.2:IV:27 = **88.51** "to dismember"(?) (cf. Arab. šatta, yašittu "to disperse"?)

štḥwy see /ḥ-w-y/ Š

/š-t-y/: *ištn*, *tštn*, *tšty*, *yšt*, inf. abs. *šty(m)* "to drink" (H. šātā, yištǽ, Aram. perf. ʾištīw, Akkad. šatū)

šty 4.356:1 = **86.13** PN (cf. *ša-te-ya* RS 8.213:33, Syria 18, 253)

/š-t-k/: *štk* 1.12:II:58–60 = **88.4** "to desist" Gt: *išttk* 1.12:II:(56), 57 = **88.4** "to desist"(?) (cf. H. š-t-q "to become calm"?)

štql see /q-w-l/ Š

t

tant 1.3:III:24 = **87.8** "conversation; murmuring"(?) (cf. H. taʾănīyā, "mourning"(?))

tinṯt 1.17:VI:40 = **88.63** "womankind" (see *aṯt*)

/t-b-ᶜ/: *tbᶜ*, *ytbᶜ* "to depart" (Akkad. tebū)

tbṣr 6.24:1 = **81.2** PN fem.

tbq 4.31:1(?) = **86.53** GN

thmt 1.3:III:25 = **87.8**, du. *thmtm* "(primeval) Ocean, Deep" (cf. DN f. *ta-a-ma-tum* U:V: 137:III:34″; cf. Akkad. Tiʾāmat) (cf. H. təhōm(ōt), Akkad. t(iʾ)āmtu; cf. Arab. GN Tihāmat)

tḥm "message," "decree"

tḥt 1.114:5, 8 = **88.3** "under" (H. táḥat, Aram. təḥōt, Arab. taḥta)

tk /tōk-/ "midst, (toward) the midst (of)" 1.10:II:12 = **88.56**, 1.100:63 = **86.73**; *btk* "in the midst (of)" 1.12:II:55 = **88.4** (cf. H. tā́wæk, constr. tōk)

/t-k-n/ (?): tD(?) *ttkn* 1.12:II:57 = **88.4** "to fix"(?) (cf. H. t-k-n Pi.?)

tliyt 1.3:III:31 = **87.8** "victory"(?)

tlmyn 2.16:1 = **84.1** cf. *tal-mi-ya-na* gen. P:III: 16.145:5 (p. 169), PN (cf. Hurrian talmu "great")

tmn-: *tmnh* 1.2:IV:26 = **88.51** "countenance"(?) (cf. H. təmūnā "form"?)

tmtt "dying" (/m-w-t/); *rb.tmtt* 2.38:16 = **86.41** "officer (in charge) of dying (disabled ships)" (cf. H. təmūtā)

tsm 1.14:III:42 = **88.71** "beauty" (/y-s-m/) (cf. *ysmt*)

tᶜḏr 1.109:21 = **86.71** "help" (/ᶜ-ḏ-r/); cf. *i-zi-ir* U:V:131:7; *il.tᶜḏr.š* | *bᶜl.š* 1.109:21–22 = **86.71**, for *š* at the end of line 21 cf. *il.tᶜḏr.bᶜl* 1.148:8 and ilānu (M) til-la-at (d)adad U:V:18:25 "the god of the help of Baal/(H)adad" (cf. H. ᶜ-z-r, Syr. ᶜ-d-r)

tᶜrt 1.18:IV:18 = **88.64** "scabbard" (/ᶜ-r-y/) (cf. H. táᶜar "sheath")

tġt(?) 1.4:IV:33 = **85.2** "to journey afar"(?) (/t-ġ-y/) (cf. H., Jew.-Aram. t-ᶜ-y "to go astray"?) or read m!*ġt*(?) (/m-ġ-y/ ?)

tp(?) 1.96:2 = **82.6** "beauty" (/y-p-y/)

tr 1.10:II:11 = **88.56** see /y-r-w/

trbṣ 1.14:III:25 = **88.71**, *trbṣt* 1.14:III:37 = **88.71** (variant?/pl.?) "stable"(?) (cf. H. r-b-ṣ, Syr. r-b-ᶜ, Arab. r-b-ḍ, Akkad. rabāṣu "to lie down"; Akkad. tarbāṣu, Syr. tarbāṣā "stable, courtyard")

/t-r-ḫ/: *ytrḫ* 1.24:18, 33 = **88.1** "to marry (a woman by paying the bride-price)" (Akkad. tarāḫu; cf. Akkad. tirḫatu "bride-price")

/t-r-p/ (?): *ttrp* 1.5:I:4 = **88.54** "to become weak"(?) (or tD /r-p-y/ (?), cf. H., Syr. r-p-y "to be drooping"?)

trǵds 2.10:5 = **86.43** PN (Anatolian, cf. GN tar-ḫu-da-aš-ši P:IV:17.42:1,3 (p. 171))

trṯ 1.114:4 = **88.3** "wine" (cf. H. tīrōš; cf. Hieroglyphic Hittite tuwarsa)

tšᶜm "90" (H. tišᶜīm, Arab. tisᶜūna)

tṯṯb 2.16:19 = **84.1** see /ṯ-w-b/

ṯ

ṯigt 1.14:III:16 = **88.71** (cf. *ṯiqt* 1.14:V:8) "neighing, bellowing" (cf. H. šəʾāgā "roaring," cf. Arab. ṯaʾağa "to low")

ṯiṭ 1.17:I:33 = **87.1** "mud" (cf. Arab. ṯaʾṭat)

ṯat 1.6:II:29 = **88.55** "ewe"; pl. *ṯut* /ṯaʾōt-/ 1.80:3 = **86.51** (Anc.-Aram. šʾt, tʾtʾ; cf. Akkad. šuʾu "sheep"; cf. H. šwʾ Isa 5:18?)

/ṯ-b-r/: *ṯbr*, *yṯbr* "to break" (H. šābar, yišbōr, Aram. t-b-r, Akkad. šabāru; cf. Arab. ṯabara, yaṯburu "to destroy")

ṯbrn 1.6:II:23 = **88.55**; 1.4:VIII:19 "breach, opening" (/ṯ-b-r/), see also *qn*

ṯd 1.4:VI:56 = **87.7** "breast" (H. šáḏ, Syr. tḏā; cf. Arab. ṯady)

ṯdṯ 1.14:III:12 = **88.71** "sixth" (cf. *ṯṯ*) (cf. Arab. sādis)

ṯh 2.33:25, 29, 37 = **86.42** "really"(?) or "there"(?) "difficulty, jeopardy"(?) or GN(?)

/ṯ-w-b/: *ṯb*, *(w)ṯb* 3.4:19 = **86.32** consecutive perf.(?) "to come back"; Š: *ṯṯb* "to give back, return" (cf. H. š-w-b, Aram. t-w-b, Arab. ṯāba, yaṯūbu); *ṯṯṯb.rgm* 2.16:19 = **84.1** "to return a word, answer" (cf. H. hēšīb dābār)

/ṯ-w-y/: *ṯṯwy* 1.16:VI:44 = **85.1** "to govern"(?) (cf. H. šāwē Gen 14:17) or "to dwell"(?) (cf. Arab. ṯawā(y) 'to dwell"; passive "to be buried"); cf. also *ṯṯ* 2.38:24 = **86.41**, perf. 3. sing. fem.(?)

/ṯ-k-ḥ/: *ṯṯkḥ* 1.5:I:4 = **88.54** "to wilt"(?)

/ṯ-k-l/: G(?)/D(?) *ṯṯkl* 1.100:61 = **86.73** "to deprive (of virility)" (cf. *ṯkl* 1.23:8 "bereavement") (cf. H. š-k-l Pi. and Arab. ṯ-k-l IV "to bereave (of children)"; cf. Arab. ṯakila, yaṯkalu "to lose a child")

/ṯ-k-m/: *ṯkmt* part. fem. 1.19:II:6 = **87.5** "to (carry on the) shoulder" (Eth. sakama; cf. H. šəkæm "shoulder")

ṯkmn 1.114:18 = **88.3** DN, *ṯkmn wšnm* (cf. the two Kassite DN Šuqamuna and Šumaliya)

/ṯ-k-p/: *nṯkp* 2.10:14 = **86.43** "to press on"(?)

ṯlḥn, pl. *ṯlḥnt* "table" (H. šulḥān(ōt))

/ṯ-l-ṯ/: D(?) *yṯlṯ* 1.5:VI:20 = **87.3** "to plow"

ṯlṯ, *ṯlṯt* "3" (H. šālōš, Aram. təlāt, Arab. ṯalāṯ)

ṯlṯ 4.279:3 = **86.24**, 1.14:III:11 = **88.71**, "third" (cf. Arab. ṯāliṯ)

ṯlṯ: with suffix *ṯlṯh* 1.14:IV:43 = **88.72** "threefold her (weight)"

ṯlṯ 1.100:71 = **86.73** "bronze" (or another alloy?)

ṯlṯid 1.18:IV:23 = **88.64** "three times"

ṯm 1.14:IV:36 = **88.72** "there" (H. šām(mā), Aram. támmā, Arab. ṯamma)

ṯmn /tamman/ (?) 2.41:21 = **83.3** "there"

ṯmn /ṯamānī/ (?) 4.145:1 = **82.3** "8" (cf. H. šəmōnǣ, Arab. ṯamānin); cf. *ṯ*(m)*nt* 4.146:8 = **86.25**(?)

ṯmny 2.38:7 = **86.41** "there"; cf. *ṯm*

ṯmt 2.10:18 = **86.43** "there"; cf. *ṯm*

ṯn constr. gen. m. /ṯinē/ 4.146:3 = **86.25**, 4.360:4 = **86.12** "2" (cf. H. šnē, Arab. iṯnay); *ṯnt* fem.: *ṯnt.ᶜšrt* 4.146:8 = **86.25** "12" or *ṯ*(m)*nt*(?), see *ṯmn* /ṯamānī/

ṯn /ṯānī/ (?) 1.14:III:10 = **88.71** "second" (Arab. ṯānī; cf. H. šēnī)

ṯn: *ṯnh* 1.14:IV:42 = **88.72** "twofold her (weight)"

ṯnid 2.64:14 = **82.1** "twice"

/ṯ-n-y/: *ṯnt*, *aṯnyk*, *ṯny* "to repeat" (H. šānā, ʾæšnǣ, Syr. tnā, Akkad. šanū)

ṯnm 1.18:IV:22 = **88.64** "twice"

ṯnn 1.103:17 = **86.744**, *ša-na-ni* P:III:11.839:5 (p. 194), RA 38, 7 "soldier, charioteer, archer"

ṯnt 4.146:8 = **86.25** see *ṯn*

ṯnt: *ṯnth* 1.114:21 = **88.3** "urine" (cf. H. šē(y)n-, Syr. tīnṯā, Akkad. pl. šinātu)

ṯᶜ 1.16:VI:42 = **85.1**, 1.15:II:15 = **87.2**, epithet of king *krt*, "munificent"(?) or "offerer"(?) (cf. ESA mṯᶜy "offering") or "of (the tribe) *ṯᶜ*" (cf. *ṯᶜy*)

/ṯ-ᶜ-y/ (?): *ṯᶜy* 1.16:VI:59 = **85.1** perf. "he dedicated"(?) or *ṯᶜy*, a tribal name(?), cf. *ṯᶜ*

/ṯ-ᶜ-r/: *yṯᶜr* 1.24:35 = **88.1** "to arrange"(?)

ṯǵr 1.119:26 = **86.75** "gate" (H. šáᶜar)

ṯǵr 1.114:11 = **88.3**, 1.78:3 = **86.743** "gatekeeper" (H. šoᶜēr, cf. Aram. tārāᶜ-(!))

/ṯ-p-d/: *yṯpd* "to put, set" (cf. H. š-p-t, tišpōt, Akkad. šapātu)

/ṯ-p-ṭ/: *ṯṯpṭ* "to judge, adjudicate" (H. šāpaṭ, yišpōṭ, cf. Akkad. šapāṭu)

ṯpṭ /ṯāpiṭ-/ 1.2:IV:22 = **88.51**, 1.3:V:32 = **88.52** "judge, ruler" (H. šōpēṭ, Phoen, špṭ, suffet(es))

ṯpṭ /ṯapṭ-/ 1.16:VI:47 = **85.1** "suit, case" (cf. H. pl. šəpāṭīm)

ṯprt 4.146:4 = **86.25** a kind of garment (cf. Arab. ṯafar "a strap of saddle"?)

ṯql /ṯiql-/ (?) 3.9:16, 17 = **84.2** "shekel" (Akkad. šiqlu, H. šǽqæl, šiql-, Aram. təqel, tiqlā, cf. Gr. siklos; cf. Arab. ṯiql "weight")

ṯr /ṯōr-/ "bull" (H. šōr, Aram. tōr-, Arab. ṯawr, Akkad. šūru)

ṯryl 6.13:2 = **86.72**, 2.16:2 = **84.1**, cf. *šar-el-li* U:V:159:9–10, 12, PN f.(?) or title(?), of a queen (cf. Akkad. > Hurrian šarri "king," and Hurrian elli "sister")

/ṯ-r-m/: *ṯrm* inf. 1.18:IV:19 = **88.64** "to dine" (cf. Iraqi-Arab. ṯarama "to cut to pieces (food)"; cf. Akkad. šarāmu "to cut up/off")

ṯrml 1.14:III:44 = **88.71** a semi-precious stone, "alabaster"(?) (cf. PN fem. *šar-mi-la* gen. P:III:16.250:5 (p. 256))

ṯrmn 1.127:6 = **86.741** DN(?) (cf. 1.102:6); GN(?) (cf. 4.296:10?) or a kind of offering (cf. /ṯ-r-m/ ?); cf. also pl. *ṯrmnm* 4.182:3, 11, 13, 15 a kind of officer

ṯrr: f. *ṯrrt* 1.100:64 = **88.73**, 1.14:III:30 = **88.71** "well watered" (cf. Arab. ṯarr "rich on water," ṯarārāt "overflowing wells") or "small"(?) (cf. Akkad. šerru)

ṯš-(?): pl. *ṯšm* 1.16:VI:48 = **85.1** "plunder"(?) (part. pl. /ṯ-w-š/ (?) or /ṯ-š-y/ (?)) (cf. H. š-s-y: yišsǽ, šōsē- and š-s-s: šass-, yāšṓssū "to spoil, plunder," cf. Egypt. šꜣś.w "(plundering) nomads"?)

ṯt 2.38:24 = **86.41**, perf. 3. sing. fem. of /ṯ-w-y/ "to dwell"(?)

ṯtmnt 1.16:I:29 = **88.73** PN fem. (cf. *ṯmn* "8"; cf. Latin Octavia)

ṯṯ 4.630:6 = **82.2**, 1.78:1 = **86.743**, cf. *ŠŠ* 4.31:2 = **86.53**, *ṯṯt* 4.146:5 = **86.25** "6" (cf. *ṯdṯ* "sixth") (cf. H. šēš, Aram. šít, Akkad. šiššu)

ṯṯb 2.38:9, 23 = **86.41**, 1.14:III:32 = **88.71** see /ṯ-w-b/ Š

Part 10

Paradigms and Surveys

Paradigms and Surveys

101. *Paradigms of pronouns, nouns and verbs*

101.1. Personal pronouns

		independent	suffixed to sing. /kaspu/ "silver"
sing.	1.	/ʾanāku/	nom. /kasp-ī/ "my silver"
		/ʾanā/ (?)	gen. /kaspi-ya/
			acc. /kaspa-ya/
	2. m.	/ʾatta/	/kaspu-ka/
	2. f.	/ʾatti/ (?)	/kaspu-ki/ (?)
	3. m.	/huwa/	/kaspu-hu/
	3. f.	/hiya/	/kaspu-ha/
du.	1.		/kaspu-nayā/ (??)
	2.		/kaspu-kumā/
	3.	/humā/	/kaspu-humā/
pl.	1.		/kaspu-na/ (?), /-nū/ (?)
	2. m.	/ʾattum(u)/ (?)	/kaspu-kum(u)/ (?)
	2. f.		/kaspu-ki(n)na/ (?)
	3. m.	/hum(u)/ (?)	/kaspu-hum(u)/ (?)
	3. f.	/hi(n)na/ (?)	/kaspu-hi(n)na/ (?)

101.2. Nouns

		masc. /malku/ "king"		fem. /malkatu/ "queen"	
sing.		abs. and constr.		abs. and constr.	
	nom.	/malku/		/malkatu/	
	gen.	/malki/		/malkati/	
	acc.	/malka/		/malkata/	
du.		abs.	constr.	abs.	constr.
	nom.	/malkāmi/	/malkā/	/malkatāmi/	/malkatā/
	gen.-acc.	/malkēmi/	/malkē/	/malkatēmi/	/malkatē/
pl.		abs.	constr.	abs. and constr.	
	nom.	/malakūma/	/malakū/	/malkātu/	
	gen.-acc.	/malakīma/	/malakī/	/malkāti/	

101.3. Verbs: simple active pattern (G)

/l-ᵓ-k/ "to send"

		perfect	imperfect	jussive	imperative
sing.	1.	/laᵓiktu/ (?) /-tī/ (?)	/ᵓilᵓaku/	/ᵓilᵓak/	
	2. m.	/laᵓikta/	/tilᵓaku/	/tilᵓak/	/laᵓak(a)/
	2. f.	/laᵓikti/	/tilᵓakīna/	/tilᵓakī/	/laᵓakī/
	3. m.	/laᵓika/	/yilᵓaku/	/yilᵓak/	
	3. f.	/laᵓikat/	/tilᵓaku/	/tilᵓak/	
du.	1.	/laᵓiknayā/ (??)	/nilᵓakā/ (?)		
	2.	/laᵓiktumā/	/tilᵓakā(ni)/	/tilᵓakā/	/laᵓakā/
	3. m.	/laᵓikā/ (?)	/yilᵓakā(ni)/		
	3. f.	/laᵓikatā/ (?)	/tilᵓakā(ni)/		
pl.	1.	/laᵓiknū/ (?)	/nilᵓaku/	/nilᵓak/	
	2. m.	/laᵓiktum(u)/ (?)	/tilᵓakū(na)/	/tilᵓakū/	/laᵓakū/
	2. f.	/laᵓikti(n)na/ (?)	/tilᵓakna/ (?)		/laᵓakā/ (?)
	3. m.	/laᵓikū/	/tilᵓakū(na)/	/yilᵓakū/	
	3. f.	/laᵓikā/ (?)	/tilᵓakna/ (?)		

Infinitives: abs. /laᵓāku(m)/, constr. /laᵓk-/ (?)
Participles: act. /lāᵓiku/, pass. /laᵓīku/

101.4. Verbs: derived patterns

	perfect	imperfect
simple passive (Gp)	/nuṣiba/ (?)	/tulᵓakāni/
simple reflexive (Gt)		/ᵓimtaḫiṣu/
simple reciprocal (N)	/nal(a)qaḥat/ (?)	/tannatikna/ (?)
factitive active (D)	/malliᵓa/	/yabarriku/
factitive passive (Dp)		/tubaššar/
factitive reflexive (Dt)	/takammasa/	
causative active (Š)	/šaᶜlaya/	/ᵓašaᶜribu/
causative passive (Šp)		/yuṯaṯibu/ (?)
causative reflexive (Št)		/yaštaḥwiyu/

/n-ṣ-b/ "to stand," Gp "to be erected"; /m-ḫ-ṣ/ "to strike," Gt "to fight"; /l-q-ḥ/ "to take," N "to be taken"; /n-t-k/ "to pour"; /m-l-ᵓ/ "to be full," D "to fill"; /b-r-k/ D "to bless"; /b-š-r/ D "to bring (good) tidings"; /k-m-s/ tD "to be prostrate"; /ᶜ-l-y/ "to go up," Š "to bring up"; /ᶜ-r-b/ "to enter," Š "to let enter"; /y-ṯ-b/ "to sit," Šp "to be seated"; /ḥ-w-y/ "to live," Št "to ask for life," "to greet (by prostration)"

102. *Survey of nominal and verbal forms and markers*

102.1. Sequence of markers in verbal patterns and forms

prefix		infix		afformative	suffixed pronoun
personal	manner of action	voice			
/ʾ-/	/(-)š(a)-/	/(-)t-/	/-t-/	/-u/, /-a/, /-∅/	/-ī/
/y-/		/(-)n-/		/-at(ā)/	/-ya/
/n-/				/-na(yā)/ (?)	/-na(yā)/ (?)
/t-/				/-tum(u)/ (?)	/-ka/
participles:				/tin(na)/ (?)	/-ki/
/m-/				/-ī(na)/	/-hu/
				/-ū(na)/	/-ha/
				/-ā(ni)/	/-kum(ā)/ (?)
				energic:	/-kin(na)/ (?)
				/-an(na)/	/-hum(ā)/ (?)
				/-n(n)-/	/-hin(na)/ (?)

102.2. Homographic nominal and verbal forms

This survey shows various possibilities of reading and interpreting forms written in the same manner in non-vocalized alphabetic writing. It can serve also as an aid in identifying forms appearing in the texts.

The root /m-l-k/ is used, as a verb "to rule" and in the nouns, masculine /malk-/ "king" and feminine /malkat-/ "queen."

Nominal and verbal forms

nominal form		written form	verbal form	
category	reconstructed		reconstructed	category
sing. abs. & constr.		*mlk*	/malaka/	perf. sing. 3. m.
nom.	/malku/		/malakā/	du. 3. m.
gen.	/malki/		/malakū/	plur. 3. m.
acc.	/malka/		/malakā/ (?)	plur. 3. f.
du. constr.			/m(u)luk/	imper. sing. m.
nom.	/malkā/		/m(u)lukī/	sing. f.
gen.-acc.	/malkē/		/m(u)lukā/ (?)	du.
pl. constr.			/m(u)lukū/	plur. m.
nom.	/malkū/		/m(u)lukā/ (?)	plur. f.
gen.-acc.	/malkī/		/malāku/	infin. abs.
			/m(u)l(u)k/	constr.
			/mālik-/	partic. (sing. m.)
du. abs.		*mlkm*	/mālikāmi/	partic. (du. m.)
nom.	/malkāmi/		/mālikūma/	(plur. m.)
gen.-acc.	/malkēmi/			
pl. abs.				
nom.	/malakūma/			
gen.-acc.	/malakīma			
w. suff. 1. pl.	/malku-na/ (?)	*mlkn	/malaknū/ (?)	perf. plur. 1.
w. suff. 1. du.	/malku-nayā/ (??)	*mlkny	/malaknayā/ (??)	perf. du. 1.
f. sing. abs. & constr.		*mlkt*	/malaktu/ (?)	perf. sing. 1.
nom.	/malkatu/		/malaktā/	sing. 2. m.
gen.	/malkati/		/malakti/	sing. 2. f.
acc.	/malkata/		/malakat/	sing. 3. f.
f. du. constr.			/malakatā/	du. 3. f.
nom.	/malkatā/		/mālikat-/	partic. (sing. f.)
gen.-acc.	/malkatē/		/mālikāt-/	(pl. f.)
f. pl. abs. & constr.				
nom.	/malkātu/			
gen.-acc.	/malkāti/			
f. du. abs.		*mlktm	/malaktumā/	perf. du. 2.
nom.	/malkatāmi/		/malaktum(u)/	plur. 2. m.
gen.-acc.	/malkatēmi/		/mālikatāmi/	partic. (du. f.)
w. suff. 1. pl.	/malkatu-na/(?)	*mlktn	/malaktin(a)/ (?)	perf. plur. 2. f.

Verbal forms with prefixes

		imperf.	jussive
amlk	sing. 1.	/amluku/	/ʾamluk/
ilak		/ʾilʾaku/	/ʾilʾak/
ymlk	sing. 3. m.	/yamluku/	/yamluk/
	du. 3. m.		/yamlukā/
	plur. 3. m.		/yamlukū/
nmlk	plur. 1	/namluku/	/namluk/
*tmlk	sing. 2. m.	/tamluku/	/tamluk/
	2. f.		/tamlukī/
	3. f.	/tamluku/	/tamluk/
	du. 2.		/tamlukā/
	3. f.		/tamlukā/
	plur. 3. m.		/tamlukū/
	tD perf.	/tamallaka/	
*šmlk	Š perf.	/šamlaka/	
*mmlk	derived patterns	part.	

Verbal forms with prefixes and afformatives

		imperf. (and energic)
amlkn	sing. 1.	/ʾamlukan(na)/
*ymlkn	du. 3. m.	/yamlukāni/
	plur. 3. m.	/yamlukūni/
*tmlkn	sing. 2. f.	/tamlukīna/
	du. 2.	/tamlukāni/
	3. f.	/tamlukāni/
	plur. 2. m.	/tamlukūna/
	2. f.	/tamlukna/ (?)
	3. m.	/tamlukūna/
	3. f.	/tamlukna/ (?)